JAPAN IN THE WORLD ECONOMY

BELA BALASSA AND
MARCUS NOLAND

Japan in the
World Economy

INSTITUTE FOR INTERNATIONAL ECONOMICS
Washington, DC 1988

Bela Balassa, a Visiting Fellow at the Institute, is a Consultant to the World Bank and has written numerous books and articles on international trade and development.

Marcus Noland, a Research Associate at the Institute, is also a Visiting Assistant Professor in the Graduate School of Policy Sciences, Saitama University. He is the author of a number of articles on international economics and the Japanese economy.

The authors acknowledge the comments of participants in two study group meetings in Washington and two meetings of the US–Japan Consultative Group on Monetary Affairs where draft chapters of this book were discussed. They thank C. Fred Bergsten, Richard N. Cooper, Takatoshi Ito, Kazuo Sato, Hidetoshi Ukawa, Masaru Yoshitomi, and Kozo Yamamura who read and commented on the entire manuscript, and many other individuals who read and commented on parts of it. James Kiefer and Peter Uimonen provided tireless research assistance, and Cynthia Meredith and Cindy Ware prompt and accurate preparation of the manuscript.

B.B. *and* M.N.

INSTITUTE FOR INTERNATIONAL
ECONOMICS
11 Dupont Circle, NW
Washington, DC 20036
(202) 328-9000 Telex: 261271 IIEUR
FAX: (202) 328-5432

C. Fred Bergsten, *Director*

The Institute for International Economics was created by, and receives substantial support from, the German Marshall Fund of the United States.

Printed in the United States of America
92 91   5 4 3

Library of Congress Cataloging-in-Publication Data

Japan in the world economy
Balassa, Bela A.

Includes index.
1. Japan—Foreign economic relations. 2. Saving and investment—Japan. 3. Economic assistance, Japanese. 4. Japan—Economic policy—1945– . I. Noland, Marcus. II. Institute for International Economics (U.S.) III. Title.
HF1601.B35   1988 337.52   88-23067
ISBN 0-88132-041-2

Contents

vi

FIGURES

x

Preface

The dramatic growth of Japan's role in the world economy is one of the central events of the second half of this century. This book seeks to analyze how this transformation occurred, what it means for the world economy and the United States, and what future policy changes are needed—primarily in Japan itself—to foster stability and harmony between Japan and its economic partners.

This study is the latest product of the Institute's continuing research on Japan and its participation in the world economy. The book's focus on Japan's global role provides a complement to the bilateral theme of *The United States–Japan Economic Problem*, by William R. Cline and myself, which was originally released by the Institute in October 1985 and in revised form in January 1987. This new volume provides an in-depth analysis of several of the key structural features of the Japanese economy that were cited in the Bergsten-Cline study but could not be adequately addressed there. It also discusses elements of Japan's international position (such as defense spending and foreign assistance) that were not considered in the earlier study, and updates the macroeconomic dimensions of the Japan issue into the period of *endaka* (high yen) and the subsequent Japanese reorientation toward a reliance on the expansion of domestic demand, rather than exports, as the major source of economic growth.

This study is unusual in that it represents an attempt by non-Japanese authors to assess, and offer recommendations on, highly sensitive elements of the internal Japanese economy and society such as agriculture, education, and saving behavior. It does so because developments in these areas have a substantial impact on Japan's external economic position and its relations with the rest of the world, and thus need to be considered in an international as well as domestic context. The need for such analysis, despite the inherent sensitivities of the subject matter, is yet another manifestation of interdependence among national economies and Japan's increasingly vital role in the world economy.

The authors of the study, which was conducted over a period of more than two years, were assisted by a study group of American and Japanese experts who met to review drafts of manuscript chapters in March 1987 and January 1988. In addition, their work was informed by several discussions in the United States–Japan Consultative Group on International Monetary Affairs, a small group of American and Japanese economists that is chaired by the Institute. As is the Institute's standard practice, the final manuscript was rigorously reviewed by readers from both countries before a publication decision was reached.

The Institute for International Economics is a private nonprofit institution for the study and discussion of international economic policy. Its purpose is to analyze important issues in that area, and to develop and communicate practical new approaches for dealing with them. The Institute is completely nonpartisan.

The Institute was created by a generous commitment of funds from the German Marshall Fund of the United States in 1981 and now receives about twenty percent of its support from that source. In addition, major institutional grants are now being received from the Ford Foundation, the William and Flora Hewlett Foundation, and the Alfred P. Sloan Foundation. A number of other foundations and private corporations are contributing to the increasing diversification of the Institute's resources. The AT&T Foundation and the US–Japan Foundation helped to finance this particular study.

The Board of Directors bears overall responsibility for the Institute and gives general guidance and approval to its research program—including identification of topics that are likely to become important to international economic policymakers over the medium run (generally, one to three years), and which thus should be addressed by the Institute. The Director, working closely with the staff and outside Advisory Committee, is responsible for the development of particular projects and makes the final decision to publish an individual study.

The Institute hopes that its studies and other activities will contribute to building a stronger foundation for international economic policy around the world. We invite readers of these publications to let us know how they think we can best accomplish this objective.

C. FRED BERGSTEN
Director
August 1988

Introduction

This study examines a fundamental policy dilemma in Japan's external relationships today. Although Japan continues to run large current account surpluses, incurring the wrath of its trade partners, its net exports are declining in volume terms, which means that the impact of trade on Japan's gross domestic product has turned negative. Japan thus needs to maintain its recent emphasis on increasing domestic demand in order to exploit its growth potential while reducing its current account surplus. The expansion of domestic demand should be oriented towards improving the quality of life in Japan, in keeping with its new status as the country with the highest per capita income, at existing exchange rates, among the major industrial countries. Japan should also undertake the international obligations that go with such a status.

The study identifies a variety of macro- and microeconomic policies that may help solve Japan's policy dilemma. These policies involve the further liberalization of trade, the continued elimination of distortions that favor savings, and increases in investment rates. Among the relevant policy instruments, trade and tax measures are emphasized along with monetary and fiscal policies.

The first chapter reviews the pattern of Japanese growth in a comparative perspective. It is noted that the contribution of net exports to economic growth has become negative in the high-yen (*endaka*) period, necessitating a sustained shift from externally oriented to domestically oriented growth. Such a shift would improve living standards, housing in particular. The chapter also considers other possibilities for enhancing the quality of life and addresses the fears of "deindustrialization" and "hollowing out" in Japan.

Chapter 2 analyzes the shifts in Japan's comparative advantage from unskilled labor- and physical capital-intensive industries to skilled-labor and research-intensive industries. This chapter also looks at the role of industrial policy in the transformation of the Japanese export and industrial structures, and examines the conditions for Japan's continued progress in high-technology exports.

Chapter 3 focuses on trade policy. It reviews the protectionist measures applied in Japanese agriculture and industry and makes recommendations for their removal. It also reviews evidence suggesting that the level of Japan's imports is not commensurate with its population size, its per capita income, and its other economic attributes.

The export–import balance is the mirror image of the savings–investment balance. Chapter 4 examines the determinants of personal, business, and government saving in Japan. The analysis focuses on incentives for personal saving—giving the high price of housing a central place—and makes recommendations for removing distortions in these incentives.

Chapter 5 looks at investment behavior. It considers the long-run determinants of the level of investment and investigates the cyclical behavior of investment activity. Policy recommendations are formulated, aimed both at smoothing business cycle fluctuations and increasing the rates of private and public investment.

Chapter 6 examines the interrelationships among the savings–investment balance, the current account balance, and the exchange rate. It develops a set of proposals, concentrating on fiscal policy, which address both immediate concerns and the longer-run evolution of the Japanese economy.

Chapter 7 examines Japan's responsibilities, as an ascendant world economic power, in the provision of international public goods. It focuses on defense policy and on assistance to developing countries.

Finally, Chapter 8 summarizes the recommendations for resolving the fundamental policy dilemma in Japan's external relationships: the continued accumulation of current account surpluses while the contribution of net exports to economic growth has become negative. It notes the need to continue with domestically oriented growth in order both to offset the adverse economic effects of the desirable reduction in Japan's current account surplus and to improve its quality of life. Attention is also given to Japan's potential contributions to the international economy.

The book's policy proposals emphasize changes in taxation and land-use policies aimed at promoting more and better housing; the adoption of a medium-term expansionary fiscal package; an accommodating monetary policy; trade liberalization and a leadership role in the Uruguay Round; a larger role in the provision of collective international security; and increased financial assistance to developing countries.

1

The Japanese Economy: Past and Future

This chapter will review Japan's past economic performance in a comparative perspective and examine the factors that may have contributed to higher rates of economic growth in Japan than in the other major industrial countries. The chapter will also consider the future prospects of the Japanese economy, devoting some attention to the alleged threats of "hollowing out" and "de-industrialization," and indicate the need for, and the possible modalities of, domestically based expansion.

Japan's Pre-1986 Economic Performance in Comparative Perspective

The devastation of World War II left Japan's per capita income in 1950 at less than three-fourths its prewar level. With rapid economic growth, per capita income attained the prewar level in the mid-1950s and doubled this level by 1963, as Japan largely surmounted the foreign exchange shortages of previous years.[1] By 1963, Japan surpassed Italy, which had a higher per capita income before the war, and entered the ranks of the industrial countries.

Japan maintained its growth momentum after 1963, steadily catching up with the other major industrial countries in terms of per capita income. Per capita income in Japan, measured in terms of purchasing power parities, reached 81 percent of the US level and 94 percent of the German level in 1985, surpassing France's income by 2 percent, the United Kingdom's by 28 percent, and Italy's by 47 percent (table 1.1).[2]

---

1. Data for 1937 and 1950, in 1955 prices and exchange rates, are provided in Maizels (1963); data from 1950 onward, in 1975 purchasing power parities, are from Summers and Heston (1984).

2. The advantages of purchasing power parity calculations are discussed below.

Table 1.1 Per capita GDP in the principal industrial countries, selected years

	At 1975 purchasing power parities[a]						At exchange rates[b]
	1963	1973	1980	1985	1986	1987	1987
Japan	2206	5025	5996	7026	7124	7302	23,022
France	3616	5777	6678	6919	7030	7107	17,657
Germany	3999	5914	6967	7481	7668	7783	21,022
Italy	2749	3971	4661	4792	4912	5037	14,903
United Kingdom	3589	4709	4990	5459	5623	5817	13,395
United States	5589	7480	8121	8721	8854	9009	18,163

a. 1963–80, 1975 prices and purchasing power parities derived from R. Summers and A. Heston, "Improved International Comparisons of Real Product and its Composition," *Review of Income and Wealth* 2 (June 1984): 207–60. 1985–87, 1975 prices and purchasing power parities using updated 1980 estimates from OECD, *Economic Outlook,* various issues, and the July 1986 estimates of the US Department of Commerce.
b. Estimated at 31 December 1987 exchange rate.

Japan outperformed the other major industrial countries in terms of total factor productivity growth (the combined productivity of labor and capital inputs) during the 1966–73 period, the earliest for which comparative data are available. It fell behind France and Germany in total factor productivity growth during the 1973–85 period, but remained well ahead of the United States (table 1.2). Japan maintained its lead, however, in capital formation. Between 1973 and 1985 the rate of growth of its capital stock was about double that of the other major industrial countries, with the disparity being the smallest vis-à-vis France and the largest vis-à-vis the United States.

Despite declining over time, the share of investment in the gross domestic product (GDP) thus remained substantially higher in Japan than in the other major industrial countries (table 1.3). During the same period, the rate of domestic savings decreased much less than that of domestic investment in Japan, leading to an outflow of savings equal to 3.4 percent of GDP in 1985. Among the major industrial countries, the outflow of savings reached the Japanese ratio only in Germany. In contrast, the inflow of savings amounted to 3.0 percent of the gross domestic product in the United States in 1985.

The mirror image of the savings–investment balance is the balance between exports and imports. Data on the share of imports of goods and services in GDP (or import shares, for short) show that Japan was able to offset increases in oil prices through reductions in the volume of its oil and non-oil imports.

The rise in Japan's import share, from less than 11 percent in 1973 to more than 15 percent in 1974, in the wake of the quadrupling of oil prices, was more than undone by 1978. An increase in import shares occurred again after 1978, when oil prices tripled; this was in large part reversed after 1980 (table 1.3).[3]

Increases in the share of exports of goods and services in Japan's GDP (export shares) can also be seen as a response to the rise of oil prices, because Japan needed foreign exchange to pay its higher oil bill. These increases were not undone in subsequent years, however. In 1985 exports surpassed 16 percent of Japan's GDP, compared with less than 11 percent in 1973, while import shares were 13 percent in 1985, as against 11 percent in 1973, leading to a large trade surplus.

Export shares rose substantially in Germany as well. Although these increases were offset by the rise in import shares prior to 1980, import shares declined in subsequent years while export shares continued to rise. In contrast, imports increased more rapidly than exports in the first part of the period in France and Italy but reversed after 1980; the opposite occurred in the United Kingdom. Export and import shares rose in parallel fashion in the United States during the first part of the period, growing from less than 7 percent in 1973 to more than 10 percent in 1980. Import shares changed little in subsequent years, but export shares declined to 7 percent by 1985.

It is clear that the largest shifts in current account balances occurred in the 1980–85 period, when the dollar was strong. These shifts represented significant changes in net foreign savings. On the one hand, net inflows of savings, equal to 0.9 percent of GDP in Japan and 0.6 percent in Germany in 1980, turned into net outflows of 3.4 percent and 3.6 percent, respectively, by 1985. On the other hand, in the United States a net inflow of savings equal to 0.6 percent of GDP in 1980 increased to 3.0 percent of GDP in 1985. Generally smaller changes took place in the other three major industrial countries; the current account balances of France and Italy improved and the United Kingdom's deteriorated.

The data in table 1.3 on the exports and imports of goods and services have been expressed in terms of current domestic prices.[4] The contributions of exports and imports to economic growth are measured in terms of constant domestic prices, however. These are shown in table 1.4, which also indicates the contribution of domestic expenditures (consumption, fixed investment,

---

3. On changes in export and import prices, see table 2.4.

4. This explains the large decline in export and import shares in 1986 in countries other than the United States. Dollar prices were translated into domestic currency prices at appreciating exchange rates.

Table 1.2   Growth rates of GDP/GNP, factor supplies, and factor productivity, selected periods

	1966–73	1973–80	1980–85	1973–85	1966–85	1986	1987
Japan							
GNP	10.1	4.3	3.8	4.1	6.3	2.4	4.2
Employment (manhours)	0.6	0.4	0.9	0.6	0.6	0.8	0.8
Capital Services	14.3	7.7	5.1	6.6	9.4	n.a.	n.a.
Output per Manhour	9.5	3.8	2.9	3.5	5.7	1.6	3.5
Capital per Manhour	13.7	7.3	4.1	6.0	8.8	n.a.	n.a.
Multifactor Productivity	4.5	1.7	1.8	1.8	2.8	n.a.	n.a.
France							
GDP	5.8	2.9	1.1	2.2	3.5	2.1	1.9
Employment (manhours)	0.2	−0.6	−1.3	−0.9	−0.6	−0.1	−0.3
Capital Services	8.6	4.8	2.2	3.8	5.5	n.a.	n.a.
Output per Manhour	5.5	3.5	2.4	3.2	4.1	2.2	2.2
Capital per Manhour	8.4	5.5	3.6	4.7	6.1	n.a.	n.a.
Multifactor Productivity	3.1	2.2	1.7	2.1	2.5	n.a.	n.a.
Germany							
GNP	4.3	2.6	1.4	2.1	2.8	2.5	1.7
Employment (manhours)	−0.4	−0.5	−0.8	−0.7	−0.6	1.0	0.5
Capital Services	6.1	3.6	2.3	3.0	4.1	n.a.	n.a.
Output per Manhour	4.7	3.1	2.2	2.8	3.5	1.5	1.2
Capital per Manhour	6.6	4.2	3.1	3.7	4.8	n.a.	n.a.
Multifactor Productivity	3.0	2.2	2.0	2.1	2.5	n.a.	n.a.
Italy							
GDP	5.1	3.5	1.8	2.5	3.3	2.9	3.1
Employment (manhours)	−0.3	0.7	0.7	0.6	0.3	0.8	0.5
Capital Services	6.0	3.9	3.3	3.6	4.4	n.a.	n.a.
Output per Manhour	5.4	2.8	0.9	1.8	2.9	2.1	2.6

and inventory accumulation) to economic growth. Increases in net exports (exports less imports) made a substantial contribution to GDP growth in Japan between 1973 and 1985; their contribution increased over time, reaching 42 percent of the annual increment of GDP in the 1980–1985 period, on the average.[5] This ratio was exceeded only in Germany, where

---

5. This macroeconomic measure should not be confused with export-led growth—a rise in exports in excess of that of GDP—which can be associated with zero net exports as long as there is a commensurate increase in imports.

Table 1.2—*Continued*

	1966–73	1973–80	1980–85	1973–85	1966–85	1986	1987
Capital per Manhour	6.3	3.2	2.2	2.8	4.0	n.a.	n.a.
Multifactor Productivity	3.3	1.8	0.4	1.1	1.7	n.a.	n.a.
United Kingdom							
GDP	3.0	1.7	1.3	1.8	2.0	3.3	4.5
Employment (manhours)	−0.5	−0.2	−0.7	−0.2	−0.5	0.5	1.5
Capital Services	6.1	3.4	2.3	3.0	4.0	n.a.	n.a.
Output per Manhour	3.5	1.8	2.0	2.0	2.5	2.8	3.0
Capital per Manhour	6.7	3.5	3.0	3.2	4.5	n.a.	n.a.
Multifactor Productivity	2.3	1.3	1.5	1.4	1.7	n.a.	n.a.
United States							
GNP	3.6	2.5	1.9	2.5	2.8	2.9	2.9
Employment (manhours)	1.7	1.8	1.0	1.6	1.6	2.3	2.8
Capital Services	5.5	3.2	2.0	2.9	3.7	n.a.	n.a.
Output per Manhour	1.9	0.7	0.9	0.8	1.2	0.6	0.1
Capital per Manhour	3.7	1.4	1.0	1.2	2.1	n.a.	n.a.
Multifactor Productivity	1.1	0.4	0.7	0.6	0.8	n.a.	n.a.

Sources: OECD, *Economic Outlook,* various issues. OECD, *Labor Force Statistics,* various issues. OECD, *National Accounts,* various issues. ILO, *Yearbook of Labor Force Statistics,* various issues. Summers, R. and Heston, A., "Improved International Comparisons of Real Product and Its Composition." *Review of Income and Wealth* (June 1984): 207–60.

Note: The capital services measure was derived by multiplying capital stock by the ratio of employment to the labor force. Employment expressed in manhours. Growth rates of labor productivity and employment for 1986 and 1987 are based on employed persons, not manhours.

it was 67 percent during 1980–85. The ratio was 24 percent in Italy, 21 percent in France, − 9 percent in the United Kingdom, and − 19 percent in the United States.

Developments in 1986–87

The situation changed after 1985. As a result of the depreciation of the US dollar, the contribution of net exports to economic growth turned negative

Table 1.3 Investment, saving, exports, and imports, 1973–1986
(percentage of GDP)

	1973	1974	1975	1976	1977	1978
Japan						
Domestic Investment	38.1	37.3	32.8	31.8	30.8	30.9
Domestic Saving	38.1	36.6	32.8	32.6	32.5	32.6
Foreign Saving	0.0	0.7	0.0	−0.8	−1.6	−1.7
Exports	10.8	14.5	13.7	14.3	13.8	11.8
Imports	10.7	15.4	13.7	13.6	12.2	10.0
France						
Domestic Investment	26.2	26.7	23.0	24.5	24.4	23.2
Domestic Saving	26.8	25.2	23.7	23.3	24.6	24.5
Foreign Saving	−0.6	1.5	−0.7	1.1	−0.1	−1.3
Exports	17.2	20.5	18.5	19.1	20.5	20.4
Imports	16.6	22.0	17.8	20.3	20.4	19.1
Germany						
Domestic Investment	25.3	22.1	19.9	21.6	21.0	21.2
Domestic Saving	28.2	26.5	22.6	23.8	23.4	23.6
Foreign Saving	−3.0	−4.4	−2.7	−2.2	−2.3	−2.4
Exports	23.7	28.3	26.4	27.6	27.2	26.8
Imports	20.5	23.9	23.5	25.0	24.8	23.9
Italy						
Domestic Investment	24.2	26.6	20.3	23.7	21.4	20.0
Domestic Saving	21.0	21.0	19.1	21.1	20.9	20.7
Foreign Saving	3.2	5.6	1.2	2.5	0.5	−0.7
Exports	17.0	20.7	21.0	22.9	24.0	24.3
Imports	20.2	26.2	22.2	25.4	24.5	23.6
United Kingdom						
Domestic Investment	22.1	22.1	18.6	20.1	19.8	19.6
Domestic Saving	19.7	17.0	16.9	18.8	20.3	20.7
Foreign Saving	2.4	5.1	1.7	1.3	−0.5	−1.2
Exports	23.3	27.5	25.6	27.8	29.8	28.3
Imports	25.7	32.6	27.3	29.2	29.3	27.1
United States						
Domestic Investment	20.4	19.5	17.0	18.5	20.1	21.3
Domestic Saving	20.4	19.3	17.8	18.4	18.9	20.2
Foreign Saving	0.0	0.2	−0.8	0.1	1.2	1.2
Exports	6.8	8.4	8.5	8.3	7.9	8.2
Imports	6.7	8.6	7.6	8.4	9.1	9.4

Source: IMF, *International Financial Statistics.*
Note: Foreign saving is derived from the difference between gross domestic investment
and gross domestic saving; it also equals the difference between exports and imports
of goods and services, adjusted for net factor incomes from abroad.

Table 1.3—Continued

1979	1980	1981	1982	1983	1984	1985	1986
32.5	32.2	31.2	30.1	28.3	28.3	28.5	28.1
31.6	31.3	32.0	30.9	30.1	31.1	31.9	32.5
0.9	0.9	− 0.8	− 0.8	− 1.8	− 2.8	− 3.4	− 4.4
12.6	14.9	16.2	16.5	15.5	16.8	16.5	13.1
13.4	15.8	15.7	15.7	13.6	13.9	12.7	8.7
26.7	24.2	21.9	21.9	19.9	19.1	18.8	19.1
24.3	23.0	20.9	20.0	19.7	19.8	19.4	20.1
2.4	1.2	1.0	1.9	0.2	− 0.7	− 0.6	− 1.0
21.2	21.5	22.6	21.8	22.5	24.1	24.0	21.5
20.6	22.7	23.5	23.7	22.6	23.5	23.4	20.5
23.5	23.7	21.0	19.7	20.4	20.5	19.9	19.5
24.0	23.0	21.7	22.1	22.4	22.9	23.5	24.7
− 0.5	0.6	− 0.7	− 2.4	− 1.9	− 2.4	− 3.6	− 5.2
27.1	28.6	31.3	32.4	31.3	33.5	35.2	32.7
26.3	28.8	30.3	30.0	29.1	30.7	31.2	27.2
21.3	26.8	24.8	23.5	22.9	22.8	22.5	21.2
20.6	22.6	21.6	20.9	20.9	21.0	20.7	21.7
0.7	4.2	3.2	2.6	2.1	1.8	1.9	− 0.5
25.3	19.8	21.4	20.9	20.1	20.9	21.0	18.7
26.0	24.0	24.5	23.6	21.0	22.7	22.9	18.1
19.9	16.9	15.3	15.7	16.4	17.2	17.3	17.4
20.1	19.2	18.1	17.5	17.4	17.0	18.3	16.6
− 0.2	− 2.3	− 2.8	− 1.8	− 0.9	0.2	− 1.1	0.8
28.0	27.4	26.7	26.5	26.7	28.7	29.1	26.2
27.8	25.1	23.9	24.7	25.8	28.9	28.0	27.0
20.9	18.9	19.6	16.8	16.9	19.8	19.2	18.8
19.9	18.4	19.0	16.0	15.2	16.9	16.1	15.4
1.0	0.6	0.6	0.8	1.7	2.9	3.0	3.4
9.1	10.2	9.7	8.7	7.9	7.6	7.0	6.8
10.1	10.7	10.3	9.5	9.5	10.4	10.1	10.2

Table 1.4 Contributions to changes in real GDP/GNP, 1979–1987
(as a percentage of real GDP/GNP in the previous period)

	1979	1980	1981	1982
Japan				
Domestic Expenditures	6.9	1.0	0.7	1.8
Exports	1.2	4.0	2.9	1.0
Imports	−2.1	−0.3	−0.8	−1.0
Net Exports	−0.9	3.8	2.1	0.0
GNP Growth	5.9	5.0	2.9	2.0
France				
Domestic Expenditures	3.9	2.3	−0.9	2.5
Exports	1.5	0.5	1.0	0.5
Imports	−2.1	−1.3	0.3	−1.0
Net Exports	−0.6	−0.8	1.3	−0.5
GDP Growth	3.3	1.8	0.3	2.3
Germany				
Domestic Expenditures	5.9	1.3	−2.4	−1.5
Exports	1.6	1.8	2.7	2.8
Imports	−2.9	−1.5	−0.6	−0.8
Net Exports	−1.3	0.3	2.1	2.0
GNP Growth	4.5	1.8	−0.3	1.0
Italy				
Domestic Expenditures	5.2	4.5	−2.6	0.3
Exports	2.4	0.3	1.2	1.5
Imports	−2.7	−1.3	1.1	−0.5
Net Exports	−0.3	−1.0	2.3	1.0
GDP Growth	5.0	3.8	−0.2	1.5
United Kingdom				
Domestic Expenditures	3.9	−3.5	−2.1	2.0
Exports	0.8	0.3	−0.4	0.5
Imports	−3.1	1.0	0.2	−1.8
Net Exports	−2.3	1.3	−0.2	−1.3
GDP Growth	1.5	−2.3	−2.2	1.3
United States				
Domestic Expenditures	1.9	−1.5	2.5	−0.8
Exports	0.8	0.5	0.0	−0.8
Imports	−0.3	0.3	−0.4	0.3
Net Exports	0.5	0.8	−0.4	−0.5
GNP Growth	2.3	−0.8	2.0	−1.5

Sources: OECD, *Economic Outlook,* various issues. Data for Japan, Germany, and the United States in 1987 drawn from official figures published in March 1988.

Table 1.4—Continued

1983	1984	1985	1986	1987	Average 1980–85	Average 1986–87
1.7	3.7	3.8	3.9	5.0	2.1	4.5
0.7	2.9	1.0	− 1.0	0.6	2.1	− 0.2
0.8	− 1.6	0.0	− 0.4	− 1.3	− 0.5	− 0.9
1.5	1.3	1.0	− 1.4	− 0.7	1.6	− 1.1
3.2	5.1	4.7	2.4	4.2	3.8	3.3
− 0.5	0.7	2.1	3.8	3.2	1.0	3.5
1.0	1.7	0.5	− 0.2	0.3	0.9	0.0
0.2	− 0.9	− 1.0	− 1.5	− 1.5	− 0.6	− 1.5
1.2	0.8	− 0.5	− 1.7	− 1.2	0.3	− 1.5
0.7	1.5	1.7	2.1	1.9	1.4	2.0
2.3	1.8	0.9	3.6	2.7	0.4	3.2
− 0.2	2.7	2.4	− 0.1	0.3	2.0	0.1
− 0.2	− 1.5	− 1.4	− 1.1	− 1.4	− 1.0	− 1.3
− 0.4	1.2	1.0	− 1.2	− 1.1	1.0	− 1.2
1.8	3.0	2.0	2.5	1.7	1.5	2.1
− 1.1	3.2	3.1	3.2	4.8	1.2	4.0
0.8	1.6	0.9	0.8	0.8	1.0	0.8
0.1	− 1.9	− 1.3	− 1.1	− 2.4	− 0.6	− 1.8
0.9	− 0.3	− 0.4	− 0.3	− 1.6	0.4	− 1.0
− 0.2	2.8	2.7	2.9	3.1	1.7	3.0
4.3	3.5	2.8	4.1	5.1	1.2	4.6
0.6	1.9	1.6	0.9	1.6	0.7	1.3
− 1.4	− 2.4	− 0.8	− 1.8	− 2.2	− 0.9	− 2.0
− 0.8	− 0.5	0.8	− 0.9	− 0.6	− 0.1	− 0.8
3.4	3.0	3.6	3.3	4.5	1.1	3.9
5.0	8.5	3.6	4.0	2.7	2.9	3.4
− 0.4	0.7	− 0.2	0.3	1.3	0.0	0.8
1.0	− 2.6	− 0.5	− 1.4	− 1.0	− 0.3	− 1.2
0.6	− 1.9	− 0.7	− 1.1	0.3	− 0.4	− 0.4
3.6	6.4	3.0	2.9	2.9	2.1	2.9

in Japan and Germany and slightly positive in the United States. In Japan, and to a lesser extent in Germany, the adverse shift in net exports was cushioned by a rise in domestic expenditures. Conversely, the growth of domestic expenditures slowed in the United States.

As a result of these changes, GDP increased substantially more in Japan than in Germany between 1985 and 1987; the difference between the Japanese and US growth rates was smaller. Japan's growth performance was also superior to that of France and Italy, but was surpassed by the United Kingdom.

As a consequence of changes in the terms of trade following exchange rate movements, the observed shifts in net exports have not been translated into equivalent changes in current account balances. In fact, the US current account deficit increased in absolute terms in 1986 and 1987. While declining in terms of domestic currency, the current account surpluses of Japan and Germany increased slightly in 1987 in dollar terms, though decreasing in the course of the year.

Changes in exchange rates have also modified per capita income rankings. Measured at the exchange rates in effect on 31 December 1987, and in current prices, Japan leads the major industrial countries in 1987 with a per capita income of $23,022, followed by Germany ($21,022), the United States ($18,163), France ($17,657), Italy ($14,905), and the United Kingdom ($13,395) (table 1.1). These figures contrast with the purchasing power parity calculations reported in table 1.1, which show the United States to be substantially ahead of the other countries, with a 1987 per capita income of $9009 at 1975 purchasing power parities and prices. The United States is followed by Germany ($7783), Japan ($7302), France ($7107), the United Kingdom ($5817), and Italy ($5037).

Of the two sets of calculations, the purchasing power parity figures provide a better welfare measure because they account for international differences in the prices of nontraded goods and services, which affect the living standards of the population. This is of particular importance in Japan, where government policies and institutional factors tend to keep the prices of these goods and services high (especially food and housing), thereby reducing the domestic purchasing power of the currency.

Prospects for the Future

Japan successfully adjusted to the oil crisis and maintained GDP growth rates higher than the other major industrial countries until 1985. During this period, Japan's rising export surplus provided an important stimulus to its economic growth. The rate of economic growth declined in 1986, when the large appreciation of the yen caused a shift from a positive to a negative contribution of net exports to GDP, while the contribution of domestic demand to economic growth hardly changed (table 1.4). Growth rates increased again in 1987, when domestic expenditures rose substantially. The negative contribution of net exports declined in response to the slowing of the rate of appreciation of the yen under the Louvre agreement (until the sharp depreciation in December of that year).

It is appropriate to ask how Japan's rapid growth rates can be maintained when the decline in its trade surplus, necessary to lessen the existing balance of payments disequilibrium, will adversely affect the country's economy. A further question concerns whether the "hollowing out" of the Japanese corporation, through the production of inputs abroad, and "deindustrialization," through a shift to services, are serious dangers for Japan. In this connection, recent changes in Japanese exports and imports will be considered.

Until 1985 net exports increased in Japan, with export growth surpassing that of imports. According to national accounts data, the ratio of exports of goods and services to GDP increased from 10 percent in 1973 to 19 percent in 1985. In that year, the Ministry of International Trade and Industry (MITI) reported, exports provided markets for 30 percent of the domestic production of iron and steel, for 42 percent of electronic communications equipment and electrical machinery production, 48 percent of automobile production, and 54 percent of precision machinery production (MITI 1986, 65). Among Japan's principal export products, the volume of steel exports fell by 23 percent and that of automobiles by 9 percent between 1985 and 1987. Decreases were even larger for television sets (60 percent) and radios (41 percent). The decline in total exports, 4 percent, was smaller mainly because Japan dominates the world markets for several electronics products, such as video cassette recorders and compact disc players.[6]

Decreases in the volume of exports have been limited by the lack of a full price adjustment in foreign currency terms following the appreciation of the yen. In 1986 the average pass-through ratio for Japanese exports was 55 percent;[7] it was 64 percent in 1987.[8] These overall averages encompass considerable interindustry variation in the pass-through ratio. Ratios have

---

6. Bank of Japan, *Economic Statistics Monthly*, various issues. The same source has been used for calculating the pass-through ratios below.

7. The pass-through ratio indicates the extent to which an appreciation of the yen is translated into higher dollar prices for Japanese exports. The higher the ratio for a given product, the greater will be the increase in that product's dollar price following an appreciation of the yen.

8. The less than proportional adjustment in the dollar prices of Japanese exports following the yen's appreciation led to charges of dumping on the part of the United States. Dumping charges were leveled against roller bearings, color television picture

been high for differentiated products, in which Japan has a strong market position, and low for standardized products in which Japan competes with other countries, particularly East Asian newly industrializing countries (NICs). In 1987 the pass-through ratio averaged 80 percent for transport equipment (including cars), 66 percent for general machinery and precision equipment, 64 percent for chemicals, 62 percent for metals and related products, 59 percent for textiles, and 47 percent for electrical machinery, in which competition from the East Asian NICs is especially strong.

While these low pass-through ratios can be partly explained by the fall of material prices during this period (especially for oil, which is priced in US dollars), an additional factor was the decline in profits derived from exporting. According to the Organisation for Economic Cooperation and Development (OECD), between 1979 and 1984 export-oriented industries (iron and steel, industrial machinery, electrical machinery, shipbuilding, motor vehicles, and precision machinery) earned on the average between 5 and 5.5 percent on sales, which compared favorably with the overall industrial average of 2–2.5 percent, but their profits declined to the overall average in 1986 (OECD 1986a, 20). Exporting firms responded to declines in profit margins by reducing costs in their domestic operations and by locating abroad and increasing overseas sourcing. The latter developments have led to fears about the "hollowing out" of the Japanese corporation and the "deindustrialization" of the economy. These fears are much exaggerated.

Despite increases in recent years, Japanese foreign direct investment amounted to only $33.4 billion in 1987.[9] Within this total, the share of Japanese investment in Asia, where much foreign sourcing occurs, declined from 34 percent in 1975 to 15 percent in 1987. Increases were concentrated in the United States and Canada (from 28 to 46 percent) and in Europe (from 10 to 20 percent). However, there have also been considerable increases in Japanese foreign direct investment in the East Asian NICs in recent years.

As discussed in Chapter 5, manufacturing investments accounted for a relatively small proportion of Japanese foreign direct investment—23.5 percent in 1987 (table 5.2). Investment in manufacturing in the United States and Europe is aimed at selling in the local market rather than at producing parts and components for factories in Japan. Furthermore, 70 percent of the parts, components, and other inputs used by Japanese ventures abroad are imported from Japan—"reverse sourcing" (Ozawa 1986, 158).

---

tubes, and forklift trucks in the course of 1987 (*Washington Post*, 20 November 1987). There have also been an increasing number of cases in which goods exported to the United States are reimported to Japan (*Business Week*, 16 March 1988).

9. These data refer to the Japanese fiscal year, which begins in March.

The ratio of Japanese parts exports to total exports rose from 10 percent in 1980 to 14 percent in 1986 (MITI 1987, 17). These ratios, and increases thereof, were especially large in Asian markets (16 percent in 1981 and 22 percent in 1986), where Japanese parts and components are incorporated into final products for export by domestic manufacturers.

In addition, the level of foreign sourcing of Japanese corporations for their home market is well below that of US and European companies. According to the Industrial Bank of Japan, the ratio of domestically sold overseas production to total domestic manufacturing output is only 3.2 percent, compared with 20 percent in the United States. While the Japanese ratio is expected to reach 8.7 percent in 1990, it would still remain far below the US ratio.[10]

Foreign sourcing is a precondition for maintaining the competitiveness of Japanese corporations in domestic and world markets. As Michael Porter notes, "hollowing represents a natural evolution of international strategy and has been characteristic of the development of every advanced industrial nation" (1987, 26). It yields benefits through cost savings and market access without necessarily leading to losses in domestic employment. This has been shown by the experience of Swedish and Swiss firms (1987, 27–28).

For similar reasons, one should not speak about deindustrialization in Japan, although the composition of manufacturing industry will change, as discussed later. There will also be an increase in the share of services in the Japanese economy, but this is a natural concomitant of rising incomes. By international standards, the share of manufacturing in Japan's gross domestic product is high, and that of services low, suggesting the possibility of shifts in sectoral composition. In 1985 the share of manufacturing in the gross domestic product was 30 percent in Japan, compared with 31 percent in Germany, 25 percent in France, 22 percent in the United Kingdom, and 20 percent in the United States (World Bank 1987, 207). Japan lags behind all other major industrial countries in terms of the share of services in GDP. Between 1970 and 1980 it also experienced a smaller increase in the share of services in total employment than did the large European countries. The United States was already ahead of these countries in terms of services employment in 1970 (Tachi 1985, 68).

The share of services is bound to increase with the continued decline in Japan's reliance on exports as a source of economic growth. The latter had previously contributed to the high manufacturing share and the low services share in Japan's (as well as Germany's) economy. A greater reliance on domestic demand will also raise the services share, given the high income

---

10. *Business Week*, 13 July 1987.

elasticity of demand for services. This leads to the question of the prospective role of domestic demand in promoting Japanese economic growth.

Domestic Demand–Based Growth

Between 1984 and 1986, Japan experienced a steady increase in the contribution of domestic expenditures to economic growth. This contribution accelerated in 1987. Domestic expenditures equalled 3.7 percent of GDP in 1984, 3.8 percent in 1985, 3.9 percent in 1986, and 5.0 percent in 1987. In the latter year, the increase of 1.1 percentage points was complemented by a decline in the negative contribution of net exports from 1.4 to 0.8 percent of GDP. The rate of economic growth consequently rose from 2.4 percent in 1986 to 4.2 percent in 1987.

A rise in government spending contributed to the increase in domestic expenditures in 1987. Following the introduction of a supplementary budget, the general account expenditure of the central government is estimated to have risen by 8.5 percent from FY 1986 to FY 1987. Within this total, spending on public works increased by 8.7 percent and grants-in-aid to local governments by 13.6 percent.[11]

The FY 1988 budget projects a 2.6 percent decline in central government general account expenditures.[12] The government also forecasts a further reduction in the size of the negative contribution of net exports to GDP, together with a decrease in the positive contribution of domestic expenditures, thereby providing offsetting influences. Substantially reducing Japan's current account surplus, however, would require the contribution of net exports to GDP growth to become more rather than less negative. This would in turn necessitate stepping up domestic expansion and thus increases rather than decreases in government spending. Revenues from the privatization of Nippon Telephone and Telegraph (NTT) and Japan Air Lines (JAL) can provide some of the financing for these increased expenditures.

The shift from export-based to domestically based growth should not be looked upon as a short-term expedient. Japan needs further declines in net exports over time in order to reduce its large current account surplus.[13] At

---

11. Because of the rise in land prices, these figures overestimate the increase in public works in volume terms. Land purchases now account for about 95 percent of the cost of public works projects in Tokyo (*Economist,* 5 December 1987).

12. In his annual policy speech to the Diet on 25 January 1988, Prime Minister Takeshita spoke of "clamping down harshly on general expenditures" in drawing up the fiscal 1988 budget bill (1988, 13).

13. In fact, the official Japanese projection for 1992 forecasts that domestic demand will make an important positive contribution and net exports a negative contribution to economic growth.

the same time, domestic expansion will allow improvements in the quality of life, which has not been commensurate with Japan's rising per capita income. In fact, the second of the two influential Maekawa Reports called for a "revolutionary improvement in the quality of life" (*Policy Recommendations of the Economic Council* 1987, 4).[14] A day in the life of a typical city dweller was described as follows by a high-level group of experts in *Japan in the Global Community*: ". . . he leaves his cramped quarters every morning, is jostled about during a long commute on a crowded train, reports for duty in an attractive office building and works on until late at night" (Murakami and Kosai 1986, 113).[15] A scholarly analysis of living standards in Japan noted that "Japan, especially urban Japan, has serious quality-of-life problems centering on housing, commuting time, and inadequate public facilities" (Bronfenbrenner and Yasuba 1987, 93).

The need for an improvement in the quality of life is also stressed in a Japanese book with the evocative title, *The "Hollowing" of Japanese Life*. The author speaks of "an astounding contrast in Japan between the place where people live and where they do not live":

In defiance of common sense, the pattern is for the wealth and amenities to be concentrated where no one lives. Japan's riches are to be seen not in people's homes but in the luxurious office buildings at the hub of its economy, in the glittering row of fashionable shops, the spanking new factories, the latest fully-computerized "intelligent buildings," elegant hotels and sprawling airports, the auditoriums with their painstakingly calculated acoustics, or the facilities of the recent Tsukuba Science Expo before they were demolished. Such grandiose capital investment takes first priority in Japan, while responses to the less spectacular needs of the people are postponed. Only 34 per cent of all private residences have sewer connections, for example, and no more than 51 percent of the country's roads are paved. Compare this to figures of 95 per cent and more for England, with its declining economy, and 85 percent for the United States, with its vast stretches of territory. There are plenty of paved roads in Japan, too—where no one lives—and their infrastructure is almost futuristic in its perfection. But amenities at home have all but been forgotten (cited in Inoguchi 1987, 62).

The same author notes the limited availability of amenities in the social infrastructure of Japan. For example, per capita municipal park space in

---

14. The two Maekawa Reports were prepared by the Advisory Group on Economic Structural Adjustment for International Harmony, which was appointed by then Prime Minister Nakasone and chaired by the former Governor of the Bank of Japan, Haruo Maekawa.

15. Compared to the United States, however, the space allocations of Japanese office buildings cannot be regarded as luxurious.

Tokyo is one-fifth that of Paris, one-fifteenth that of London, and one-twentieth that of Washington (OECD 1986b, 81).

The existence of poor housing conditions in Japan is well-known.[16] The main cause is the high price of housing. From 1950 to 1983, the housing price/income ratio rose from 1.0 to 7.9 in metropolitan areas and from 1.1 to 6.7 in the country as a whole (OECD 1986a, 113). While regional trends were rather similar until 1983, increases in land prices since that year have raised housing costs in Tokyo much more than elsewhere in Japan. After increasing by 3.2 percent in 1984, and 3.9 percent in 1985, residential land prices in Tokyo rose by 10.0 percent in 1986 and 76.8 percent in 1987. The corresponding increases were 3.0 percent, 2.2 percent, 2.2 percent, and 7.6 percent in the whole of Japan.[17] At the same time, one of every four Japanese today lives within 30 miles of the Imperial Palace in Tokyo.[18]

In 1986 the average price of a house or apartment in a middle-class district of Tokyo was between seven and ten times the annual pretax earnings of its owner; in most American and European cities this multiple was only four or five for homes that were at least twice the size.[19] Japanese home prices increased further in 1987, bringing the cost of a small apartment 90 minutes by train from central Tokyo to nearly one-half million dollars at the 1987 year-end exchange rate.[20] While there has been a decline in land prices since September 1987, it has mainly affected commercial property districts.[21]

The quantitative importance of housing in the Japanese economy is indicated by the fact that residential structures and land account for 65.0 percent of the portfolios of Japanese households; the corresponding figure is 30.5 percent in the United States (Noland 1988a, 136). Furthermore, the share of households in the flow of net savings is 90 percent in Japan.

Improving housing conditions would require measures to increase the

---

16. According to the Ministry of Construction, 51 percent of all families live in homes less than 80 square meters in total area, and 11 percent in homes less than 50 square meters in size (*Le Monde*, 14 November 1986). A comparative study reports that if the United States is assigned an index number of 100, the quantity index for Japan is 50 and the quality index 75; the combined index for housing is 37.5 (Kravis, Heston, and Summers 1982, 58). Housing in Japan is poor even in comparison with that of less affluent countries in East Asia—the average Japanese worker lives in a house half the size than that of the average Korean worker (*Economist*, 3 October 1987).

17. *Economist*, 3 October 1987.

18. *New York Times*, 10 March 1988.

19. *Economist*, 2 May 1987.

20. *Economist*, 3 October 1987.

21. *Financial Times*, 31 January 1988.

availability, and lower the cost, of housing. On the demand side, increasing the ratio of mortgage loans to downpayments would reduce the immediate expense of housing purchases. Supply could be increased by eliminating the preferential tax treatment of agricultural land in urban areas;[22] increasing incentives to sell land that is poorly utilized;[23] augmenting the size of the land area available for housing;[24] and modifying zoning regulations, as proposed in the second Maekawa Report.[25] In addition, construction costs could be reduced by taking strong action against price fixing by contractors, a practice (known as the *dangoh*), which flourishes despite legal prohibitions, and whose proceeds are in part used to support political candidates.[26]

The construction of larger and more numerous houses and apartments would in turn create greater demand for household appliances, furniture, and other consumer durables. New multi-level dwellings would include garages, thereby increasing Japanese ownership of automobiles, which is considerably lower than in other major industrial countries (236 per thousand population in 1986, compared with 561 in the United States, 446 in Germany, 386 in Italy, 381 in France, and 336 in the United Kingdom).[27] Increased infrastructural investment would be needed to upgrade sewage facilities and to improve roads. There would also be a need for investment in social infrastructure, ranging from parks to libraries.

Furthermore, as noted in the two Maekawa Reports, increased physical and social infrastructural investment would be necessary to support the changing composition of domestic output. For example, a growing demand for leisure activities would require the construction of vacation resorts and the expansion of the leisure industry in general. While private industry can

---

22. Six percent of Tokyo's land area is classified as farmland. Taxes on this land are one-eighth of those for residential land. (*Economist*, 23 May 1987; *Policy Recommendations of the Economic Council* 1987, 9).

23. Taxation is based on the actual rather than the potential uses of land. Capital gains taxes are 90 percent for property held fewer than 10 years and 50 percent for property held more than 10 years.

24. According to the second Maekawa Report, this may involve landfilling public waters and establishing transportation links to outlying areas, as well as promoting the efficient use of government-owned sites and transferring public facilities outside the cities. There have also been proposals for transferring the capital outside of Tokyo (*New York Times*, 10 March 1988).

25. Existing regulations restrict the height of buildings and limit construction through so-called sunshine rights. Buildings over three stories high must be approved by neighbors. For additional recommendations in the area of housing policy, see Chapter 4.

26. For a discussion of the *dangoh* system, see Woronoff (1985, Chapter 3).

27. Data provided by the US Motor Vehicle Manufacturers' Association.

be relied upon to respond to such demand, reductions in working hours would facilitate a shift toward leisure activities.

In 1984, Japanese employees worked 2,180 hours per year, compared with 1,934 hours in the United States, 1,944 in the United Kingdom, 1,649 in France, and 1,654 in Germany (Planning Subcommittee 1986, 23). In the cases of the United States and the United Kingdom, these differences principally represent variations in the length of the workweek; with respect to France and Germany, they represent differences in the workweek as well as in the length of vacations.

The second Maekawa Report recommends a target of 2,000 annual working hours by 1990 and suggests further reductions to about 1800 hours by the end of the century. These reductions could be achieved with a five-day workweek and 20 paid vacation days each year and by giving workers longer vacations over the "golden week" holidays in late April to early May, during the summer, and over the New Year holidays (*Policy Recommendations of the Economic Council* 1987, 11).

Reductions in working hours could have a significant effect on leisure-type activities. Reducing the workweek to five days would increase demand for weekend vacations, which are not practicable with the present six-day workweek, while longer vacations would generate demand for resorts outside of residential areas. Increased leisure time would also add to demand for luxuries and semi-luxuries, which would be used during vacations or at home. The financing of these goods and services would require changes in Japan's banking laws, which do not permit banks to offer revolving credit.[28]

Recent legislation adopted the 40-hour workweek as a target but only reduced current working hours from 48 to 46 hours per week for 1988. Companies with fewer than 300 workers, which employ 65 percent of the labor force, were given a three-year grace period to comply with the new law. Provisions were also introduced for flexible work hours, which would enable companies to cut their overtime bills. These provisions have led some labor unions to charge that the law actually lowers labor costs.[29] Whatever the validity of these charges, we agree with the second Maekawa Report that it would be desirable to accelerate the shift to a 40-hour workweek. The public sector could take the lead in this regard and adopt the 40-hour workweek at an early date.

The "greying" of the Japanese population will also provide a new source

---

28. *Business Week*, 25 May 1987. Reducing working hours is likely to reduce total GDP, however, because the rise in hourly productivity is not expected to compensate fully for decreases in hours.

29. *Business Week*, 28 September 1987.

of domestic demand. While in 1980 only 11 percent of Japanese population was over 65 years old (compared with 14–15 percent in France, Germany, and the United Kingdom), it is estimated that this ratio will reach 15 percent in 1990 and 21 percent in 2000, surpassing those of the major European countries (OECD 1986a, 77). This growing aged population will demand an increasing variety of goods and services, including travel and personal services, adult education, health care and medical equipment, and retirement homes. The need for retirement homes will increase further as a result of the decline in the custom of living with one's children. In fact, the Ministry of Health and Welfare estimates that by the year 2000 the number of people living in retirement homes will triple.[30]

Taking appropriate measures to augment physical and social infrastructure, to promote housing, and to reduce working hours will improve the quality of life in Japan. Measures have already been taken in these areas, but additional steps will be needed to further the objectives enunciated in the first Maekawa Report. As stated in the economic policy speech of Eiichi Nakao, Minister of State for Economic Planning, to the 112th Session of the Diet, such measures will permit Japan "to realize a standard of living that will allow the people to feel their own affluence by reaping the fruits of Japan's economic development" (1988, 6).

The measures described in this chapter, together with the growing needs of the aged, would contribute to the shift from export-based to domestic demand-based growth in Japan. Domestic demand may be satisfied both by service and by manufacturing industries. This will in turn necessitate shifts in domestic production, because the composition of domestic demand is different from that of export demand. Further shifts will accompany changes in Japan's comparative advantage. These changes will be considered in Chapter 2.

---

30. *Business Week,* 15 June 1987.

2

The Changing Pattern of International Specialization and Industrial Policy

Chapter 1 examined Japan's past economic performance and future prospects in a macroeconomic context. This chapter will review changes in Japan's trade balance and in the composition of its exports and imports. It will consider changes in both the geographical and commodity composition of Japanese trade and provide estimates on shifts in Japan's comparative advantage, giving special attention to high-technology products. The chapter will also discuss the potential contribution of government policies to observed trends in international specialization and will analyze prospective changes in Japan's future specialization.

Changes in Japanese Trade Patterns

In Chapter 1, we compared the contribution of net exports to GDP growth in Japan, measured in terms of constant domestic prices, with that of the other major industrial countries. In discussions on the changing position of Japan in world trade, however, attention has focused on the trade balance in terms of US dollars. Table 2.1 shows Japan's merchandise trade balance with 12 countries and country groupings for the years 1973, 1980, 1985, and 1986.[1]

Japan's balance of trade showed a small overall deficit in 1973. The deficit reached $10 billion in 1980, following repeated increases in oil prices. By 1985, however, Japan had a surplus of nearly $50 billion. This surplus grew to $90 billion in 1986 and declined only slightly in 1987. A counterpart of the rising Japanese trade surplus was the growing US trade deficit vis-à-vis Japan. From a position of balance in 1973, US bilateral trade with Japan

---

1. The data exclude trade in services, which was included with merchandise trade, in tables 1.3 and 1.4.

**Table 2.1 The geographical distribution of Japan's trade balance,
selected years** (exports in f.o.b. prices; imports in c.i.f. prices)

	1973	1980	1985	1986
	Billion dollars			
United States	0.3	7.2	40.2	54.7
European Common Market	1.7	9.5	11.7	17.3
Other Western Europe	0.8	2.3	2.8	5.1
Canada, Australia, New Zealand	− 3.5	− 6.0	− 1.9	− 0.4
East Asian NICs	2.9	11.8	12.7	17.5
East Asian LDCs	− 1.2	− 10.6	− 8.4	− 6.3
China	0.1	0.8	6.0	4.2
South Asia	− 0.6	− 2.3	− 0.4	1.0
Middle East and North Africa	− 3.2	− 30.2	− 17.5	− 8.7
Latin America and Caribbean	0.7	2.7	1.2	2.4
Sub-Saharan Africa and Others	1.0	2.7	0.9	0.8
Socialist Countries	− 0.5	1.8	2.1	2.2
World	− 1.4	− 10.3	48.3	89.7
	As a percentage of Japanese imports			
United States	0	29	155	206
European Common Market	53	124	138	144
Other Western Europe	98	102	112	158
Canada, Australia, New Zealand	− 58	− 48	− 15	− 4
East Asian NICs	111	160	130	140
East Asian LDCs	− 35	− 54	− 56	− 46
China	7	17	92	74
South Asia	− 44	− 44	− 9	28
Middle East and North Africa	− 64	− 67	− 58	− 47
Latin America and Caribbean	41	50	20	40
Sub-saharan Africa and Others	41	74	34	25
Socialist Countries	− 31	74	111	92
World	− 4	− 7	38	75

Source: GATT tapes.

posted deficits of $7 billion in 1980, $40 billion in 1985, and $55 billion in
1986. The trade deficits of the European Community and the East Asian
NICs with Japan also increased. Conversely, Japan's trade deficit with the
oil-producing countries among the East Asian less developed countries
(LDCs) and in the Middle East and North Africa grew substantially between

1973 and 1980, but declined afterwards. Expressed as a percentage of merchandise imports, the Japanese overall trade balance shifted from a deficit of 4 percent in 1973 to a surplus of 75 percent in 1986 (table 2.1). In 1986, the ratio was 206 percent for trade with the United States, 144 percent for trade with the European Community, 158 percent with other countries in Western Europe, and 140 percent with the East Asian NICs.

The United States has become an increasingly important market for Japan, taking 26 percent of its exports in 1973 and 39 percent in 1986 (table 2.2). China's share of Japanese exports also rose. There were declines in the export shares of non-oil primary product-exporting countries, whose foreign exchange earnings were adversely affected by the fall in their own export prices and their debt burdens. The United States and non-oil primary producers lost export market shares in Japan during the 1973–1986 period, while the East Asian NICs were the chief gainers. As oil prices declined, oil-exporting countries lost some of the substantial gains they had made following earlier increases in oil prices.

Manufactured products continue to dominate Japan's exports, accounting for 95 percent of the total in 1973 and 98 percent in 1986 (table 2.3). The difference between the two figures is explained by the decline in the share of Japan's small primary product exports. Changes in oil prices have substantially affected the commodity composition of Japan's imports. The mineral fuel share of imports rose from 22 percent in 1973 to 50 percent in 1980, but declined again to 44 percent in 1985 and 31 percent in 1986 (table 2.3). The share of non-fuel primary products in Japan's imports fell from 52 percent in 1973 to 34 percent in 1986, while that of manufactured goods increased from 26 to 35 percent, rising further in 1987.[2]

Japan's terms of trade have been affected by the composition of its exports and imports.[3] During the period of rising oil prices, the terms of trade deteriorated more in Japan than in other industrial countries, which had lower shares of oil in their total imports. The opposite occurred in the period of falling prices for oil and other primary products. Between 1973 and 1985, Japan's terms of trade declined by 36 percent, compared with declines of 24 percent in Italy, 19 percent in Germany, 17 percent in the United States, and 10 percent in France. In the same period, the terms of trade improved by 9 percent in the United Kingdom, which benefited from increases in oil prices. Between 1985 and 1986, however, the terms of trade improved by

---

2. "Manufactured goods" here excludes nonferrous metals (category 68 in the UN Standard International Trade Classification system), which are considered primary commodities.

3. The following terms of trade data are drawn from the International Monetary Fund, *International Financial Statistics*, various issues.

Table 2.2   The changing geographical composition of Japan's trade, selected years (percentage)

	Exports				Imports			
	1973	1980	1985	1986	1973	1980	1985	1986
United States	25.9	24.4	37.6	38.9	24.2	17.5	20.3	22.2
European Common Market	13.2	13.2	11.4	14.0	8.3	5.5	6.6	10.1
Other Western Europe	4.6	3.5	3.0	3.9	2.3	1.6	2.0	2.7
Canada, Australia, New Zealand	6.7	5.0	6.2	5.7	15.5	9.0	10.1	10.3
East Asian NICs	14.8	14.8	12.8	14.3	6.8	5.3	7.7	10.5
East Asian LDCs	6.1	7.0	4.2	3.6	9.0	14.1	13.1	11.5
China	2.8	3.9	7.1	4.7	2.5	3.1	5.1	4.7
South Asia	2.1	2.2	2.1	2.1	3.6	3.7	3.2	2.9
Middle East and North Africa	4.7	11.4	7.1	4.8	12.8	32.1	23.6	15.6
Latin America and Caribbean	6.7	6.3	4.1	3.9	4.6	3.9	4.7	4.9
Sub-Sahara Africa and other	9.7	4.9	2.1	1.9	6.6	2.6	2.1	2.6
Socialist Countries	2.8	3.3	2.3	2.2	3.9	1.8	1.5	1.9
World	100.0	100.0	100.0	100.0	100.0	100.0	100.0	100.0

Source: GATT tapes.

39 percent in Japan, 16 percent in Italy, 15 percent in Germany, 4 percent in the United States, and 3 percent in the United Kingdom; data for France are not available (table 2.4). For the entire 1973–86 period, the terms of trade changes were as follows: the United Kingdom, 12 percent; Germany, −7 percent; Italy and Japan, −12 percent; and the United States, −14 percent.

The deterioration of Japan's terms of trade between 1973 and 1985 was more than offset by the growth of its export volume relative to the volume of its imports. Among the major industrial countries, Japan had by far the highest annual export growth rate (8.4 percent) and the lowest import growth rate (1.5 percent) during this period. Italy came next with an export growth rate of 5.3 percent. The other European countries were in the 3.7 to 4.5 percent range, with the United States (1.9 percent) far behind. Over the same period, the United States led in terms of annual import growth rates

Table 2.3 The changing commodity composition of Japan's trade, selected years (percentage)

	1973	1980	1985	1986
Exports				
Mineral fuels	0.3	0.4	0.3	0.3
Nonfuel primary products	5.1	3.9	2.4	2.2
Manufactured goods	94.7	95.7	97.3	97.5
Total Exports	100.0	100.0	100.0	100.0
Imports				
Mineral Fuels	21.8	50.0	43.8	30.9
Nonfuel primary products	52.0	30.7	29.5	33.8
Manufactured goods	26.2	19.3	26.7	35.3
Total Imports	100.0	100.0	100.0	100.0

Source: GATT tapes.

(4.7 percent), with the European countries ranging from 3.7 percent (France) to 2.1 percent (Italy).

Japan's export volume declined in 1986, as did that of the United States, while Italy and Germany experienced practically no change. At the same time, import volumes increased substantially in all the major industrial countries. The results for 1986 hardly change the outcome for the entire 1973–86 period, however. The ratio of the volume of exports to that of imports increased 1.9 times in Japan during this period; the corresponding ratios were 1.4 for Italy, 1.1 for the United Kingdom, France, and Germany, and 0.6 for the United States.

Shifts in Japan's Comparative Advantage

Changes in Japan's overall trade position were accompanied by shifts in its comparative advantage. This is demonstrated by indices of "revealed" comparative advantage, which can be used to gauge changes in international specialization (Balassa 1965). The export index of "revealed" comparative advantage is defined as the ratio of a country's share in the exports of a particular commodity category to the country's share in total merchandise exports. A value greater than (less than) one for a particular industry is interpreted as reflecting comparative advantage (disadvantage) in that industry. In the following, the export index of comparative advantage will be used in preference to the net export (exports less imports) index—which is defined as the ratio of net exports to the sum of exports and imports—

Table 2.4 Export and import values, unit values, and volumes, selected periods (ratios of end-of-period values to beginning-of-period values, expressed in percentage terms)

	1973–80	1980–85	1973–85	1985–86	1973–86
Japan					
Export Value	352.4	135.8	478.6	119.0	569.4
Export Unit Value	188.3	95.7	180.2	120.2	216.6
Export Volume	186.6	141.3	263.6	99.4	262.1
Import Value	368.1	92.4	339.9	97.8	332.3
Import Unit Value	333.3	84.9	203.0	86.7	245.3
Import Volume	109.8	108.9	119.5	113.1	135.2
France					
Export Value	316.7	87.6	277.5	122.9	341.1
Export Unit Value	215.1	78.2	168.2	n.a.	n.a.
Export Volume	145.6	111.7	162.6	n.a.	n.a.
Import Value	357.8	80.3	287.1	119.5	343.2
Import Unit Value	247.5	75.7	187.4	n.a.	n.a.
Import Volume	147.3	104.6	154.1	n.a.	n.a.
Germany					
Export Value	285.5	95.4	272.2	132.3	360.1
Export Unit Value	216.5	74.6	161.5	131.1	211.7
Export Volume	133.7	126.9	169.7	101.3	169.7
Import Value	342.5	84.3	288.7	120.6	348.1
Import Unit Value	260.4	76.5	199.2	113.9	226.8
Import Volume	132.5	109.7	145.3	106.1	154.2

because the net export index is affected by changes in a country's overall trade balance, making intertemporal comparisons difficult. For econometric investigations of comparative advantage in individual years, however, this problem does not arise, and we chose to use the net export index, which conforms better to international trade theory.[4]

We may begin our story in 1967. At that time, Japan's comparative advantage lay in unskilled labor-intensive commodities, such as textiles, apparel, rubber and plastic products, leather and leather products, stone,

---

4. Appendix A describes the methodology we employ.

Table 2.4—*Continued*

	1973–80	1980–85	1973–85	1985–86	1973–86
Italy					
Export Value	349.5	101.7	355.6	123.8	440.2
Export Unit Value	237.0	80.5	190.8	122.1	232.9
Export Volume	147.7	125.7	185.7	101.8	189.1
Import Value	358.5	91.4	327.5	109.8	359.5
Import Unit Value	290.7	86.4	251.2	105.4	264.8
Import Volume	121.5	105.2	116.4	104.6	133.7
United Kingdom					
Export Value	371.7	91.9	341.6	10.6	361.0
Export Unit Value	290.7	79.2	230.2	117.0	269.5
Export Volume	130.4	119.2	155.4	104.0	161.7
Import Value	299.9	94.3	282.8	115.8	327.5
Import Unit Value	266.7	79.0	210.7	114.2	240.5
Import Volume	110.6	124.3	137.5	107.0	147.1
United States					
Export Value	309.2	96.5	298.5	98.1	304.3
Export Unit Value	211.0	112.2	236.7	100.3	237.3
Export Volume	147.1	85.0	125.0	99.1	123.8
Import Value	346.0	140.7	486.8	107.0	521.1
Import Unit Value	290.7	98.8	287.2	96.6	277.3
Import Volume	120.0	144.8	173.8	110.6	192.2

Source: IMF, *International Financial Statistics.*

clay, and glass products, and miscellaneous manufactured products.[5] This is shown in figure 2.1, as well as in appendix table A.1.[6] Japan also had, to varying degrees, a comparative advantage in certain skill- or human capital-intensive products, such as nonelectrical machinery, electrical machinery, transportation equipment, and instruments and related products.

---

5. The relative unskilled-labor, skilled-labor, and physical-capital intensity of individual industries is shown in appendix table A.3.

6. Figures 2.1–2.4 apply a technique employed in Scott (1985). Appendix table A.2 shows the results obtained with the net export index of comparative advantage, which give a similar overall picture. In all cases, the data exclude fuels.

Figure 2.1 Revealed comparative advantages for exports, Japan, 1967–1983

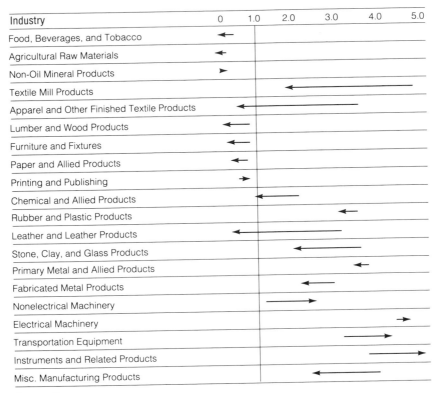

Source: See text.
Note: Values greater than (less than) one reflect the comparative advantage (disadvantage) in a given industry. The direction and length of each arrow indicate the direction and size of the shift in comparative advantage during the 1967–1983 period.

Physical capital intensive products, such as paper and paper products, chemicals, and primary metals, were a mixed category in 1967, with Japanese steel exports benefiting from the use of the sea route to import coking coal and iron ore and to export steel.

As a consequence of its poor natural resource endowment, Japan had a comparative disadvantage in 1967 in food, beverages, and tobacco, agricultural raw materials, and non-oil mineral products. This was also the case, to a lesser extent, for lumber and wood products and for furniture, in which the labor-intensive character of the production process partly compensated for the limited availability of natural resources.

Japan's pattern of international specialization was significantly transformed during the 1967–83 period. It shifted from a position of comparative advantage to one of comparative disadvantage in apparel and leather and leather products, the most unskilled labor-intensive categories. Japan's comparative advantage declined in the other unskilled labor-intensive categories as well, although in these cases the extent of the shift was smaller. Japan's initial comparative disadvantage increased further in natural resource-intensive commodities, whether in a primary form (food, beverages, and tobacco; agricultural raw materials) or in a transformed state (lumber and wood products; furniture). Little change occurred in the non-oil mineral industry, however. Furthermore, Japan reduced somewhat its specialization in physical capital-intensive products. At the same time, it greatly strengthened its comparative advantage in skill-intensive products, with the largest change occurring in non-electrical machinery.

The data for Japan may be contrasted with those for the United States. In 1967, US comparative advantage lay in three categories: primary products, physical capital-intensive products, and human capital-intensive products. It had a comparative disadvantage in most unskilled labor-intensive commodities. Transformed natural resource-intensive products were an intermediate category (figure 2.2 and appendix table A.2). Between 1967 and 1983, the United States generally increased its comparative advantage in natural resource-intensive products, at the expense of manufactured goods, but it gained market shares in human capital-intensive commodities, such as non-electrical machinery and miscellaneous manufacturing products.

In the regression analysis of comparative advantage in manufactured goods, consideration has also been given to the research intensity of the production process. The regression results confirm the shift in Japan's comparative advantage from unskilled labor- to skilled labor-intensive products. They also show Japan gaining comparative advantage in research-intensive products, while little change occurred in the physical-capital intensity of its exports (appendix tables A.4 and A.5). The regression analysis further indicates that between 1967 and 1983 the United States increased its comparative advantage in research-intensive products and maintained the strength of its comparative advantage in human capital-intensive products. The US comparative advantage in physical capital-intensive products, and its comparative disadvantage in unskilled labor-intensive products, experienced little change during this period (appendix tables A.6 and A.7).

The pattern of comparative advantage in high-technology products—defined as those for which research and development expenditures accounted for at least 3.5 percent of the value of a given product's output in the United States in the mid-1970s—is of particular interest. An indicator of the relative importance of these products is their average ranking on the comparative

Figure 2.2 Revealed comparative advantages for exports, United States, 1967–1983 Industry

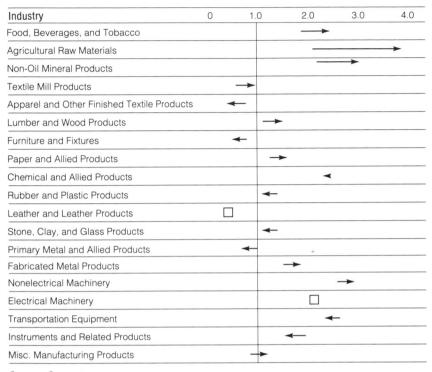

Industry	0	1.0	2.0	3.0	4.0
Food, Beverages, and Tobacco			→		
Agricultural Raw Materials			——→		
Non-Oil Mineral Products			——→		
Textile Mill Products		→			
Apparel and Other Finished Textile Products		←			
Lumber and Wood Products		→			
Furniture and Fixtures		←			
Paper and Allied Products		→			
Chemical and Allied Products			◄		
Rubber and Plastic Products		←			
Leather and Leather Products	□				
Stone, Clay, and Glass Products		←			
Primary Metal and Allied Products		←			
Fabricated Metal Products		→			
Nonelectrical Machinery			→		
Electrical Machinery		□			
Transportation Equipment			←		
Instruments and Related Products		←			
Misc. Manufacturing Products		→			

Source: See text.
Note: Values greater than (less than) one reflect the comparative advantage (disadvantage) in a given industry. The direction and length of each arrow indicate the direction and size of the shift in comparative advantage during the 1967–1983 period.

advantage scale of each nation. In Japan, the figure was 89 in 1967 and rose to 60 in 1983; it was 54 in 1967 and 32 in 1983 in the United States. High-technology products are thus a more important component of US than of Japanese exports. In fact, the average ranking of these products was higher in the United States at the beginning of the period than it was in Japan at the end.

It further appears that, with a few exceptions, the United States increased its comparative advantage in high-technology products over time (figure 2.3 and appendix table A.8).[7] By 1983 such products occupied the first four

---

7. Results obtained with the net export index are shown in appendix table 2.9.

places on the revealed comparative advantage scale of the United States (aircraft, aircraft engines, office machinery, steam engines and turbines); this had been the case for only one product group (aircraft) in 1967. The exceptions were photographic equipment and supplies, scientific instruments, calculating and accounting machines, platework and boilers, and medical instruments. In each of these product categories, the United States lost and Japan gained comparative advantage. Japan increased its comparative advantage in twelve out of nineteen high-technology product categories (figure 2.4 and appendix table A.8). The exceptions were aircraft, optical instruments, agricultural chemicals, synthetic fibers, cellulose fibers, and steam engines, and turbines. The declines in these product categories were the mirror image of the increases observed in the United States.[8]

The results show a complementary pattern of specialization in the high-technology area, with Japan having a comparative advantage in products in which the United States has a disadvantage and vice versa. Apart from the obvious implication that the two countries dominate the world exports of a number of high-technology products, several largely complementary explanations are consistent with these data. One explanation is that the pattern of specialization reflects the strategic interactions of firms in internationally oligopolistic markets. The revealed comparative advantage of the United States grew in categories in which product development and production is characterized by large sunk costs (aircraft, mainframe computers), while Japan made advances in industries with lower entry costs. Given the earlier specialization of the United States in high-technology products, this pattern would be consistent with strategic trade-theoretic models in which existing firms use investment to precommit production that acts as a deterrent to potential entrants. The efficacy of this strategy depends in part on the size of the sunk costs of production: the greater the sunk costs, the greater the deterrent effect.

A complementary explanation of this pattern of specialization is derived from an analysis of the types of R&D activities pursued in different industries. The notion here is that different industries are characterized by different kinds of R&D activities, and that the United States and Japan have specialized in different industries according to their relative comparative advantages in various R&D activities. Specifically, the United States tends to specialize in science-based industries such as chemicals, which are dominated by large firms capable of financing the basic research necessary for innovation. Conversely, Japan fares better in industries in which research is more product-specific and the management of research activities is more important (Kodama 1986).

---

8. Appendix A describes the results in greater detail.

Figure 2.3 Revealed comparative advantages for high-technology exports, United States,1967–1983

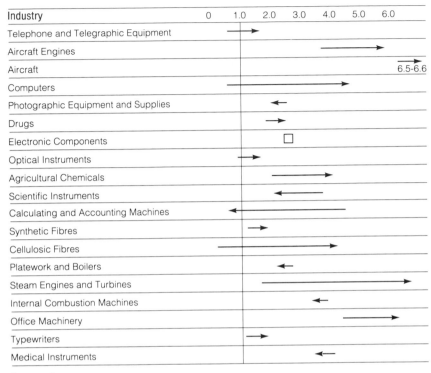

Industry	0	1.0	2.0	3.0	4.0	5.0	6.0
Telephone and Telegraphic Equipment		→					
Aircraft Engines				→			
Aircraft							→ 6.5-6.6
Computers			→				
Photographic Equipment and Supplies		←					
Drugs		→					
Electronic Components		□					
Optical Instruments		→					
Agricultural Chemicals			→				
Scientific Instruments		←					
Calculating and Accounting Machines	←						
Synthetic Fibres		→					
Cellulosic Fibres			→				
Platework and Boilers		←					
Steam Engines and Turbines					→		
Internal Combustion Machines		←					
Office Machinery				→			
Typewriters		→					
Medical Instruments		←					

Source: See text.
Note: Values greater than (less than) one reflect the comparative advantage (disadvantage) in a given industry. The direction and length of each arrow indicate the direction and size of the shift in comparative advantage during the 1967–1983 period.

In addition, the use of heterogeneous product categories obscures the tendency of Japanese industry to perform particularly well in the large-batch or mass manufacturing of high-technology products, while US firms appear better able to customize products. One example is the semiconductor industry, in which Japanese firms dominate in the mass production of standardized chips and US firms excel in the production of more sophisticated or specialized chips. More generally, as we discuss below, Japanese firms tend to do well in industries that depend on applied research dealing with known parameters and relatively predictable technological outcomes.

Figure 2.4 Revealed comparative advantage for high-technology exports,
Japan,1967–1983

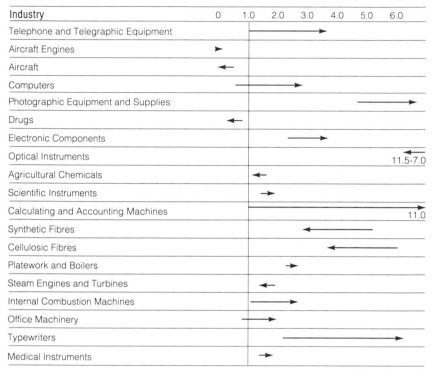

Industry	0	1.0	2.0	3.0	4.0	5.0	6.0
Telephone and Telegraphic Equipment							
Aircraft Engines							
Aircraft							
Computers							
Photographic Equipment and Supplies							
Drugs							
Electronic Components							
Optical Instruments							11.5-7.0
Agricultural Chemicals							
Scientific Instruments							
Calculating and Accounting Machines							11.0
Synthetic Fibres							
Cellulosic Fibres							
Platework and Boilers							
Steam Engines and Turbines							
Internal Combustion Machines							
Office Machinery							
Typewriters							
Medical Instruments							

Source: See text.
Note: Values greater than (less than) one reflect the comparative advantage (disadvantage) in a given industry. The direction and length of each arrow indicate the direction and size of the shift in comparative advantage during the 1967–1983 period.

Industrial Policy in Japan

The analysis shows that Japan's comparative advantage shifted from unskilled labor-intensive products to skilled labor-intensive and high-technology products. At the same time, the United States increased its comparative advantage in high-technology products.

It is important to ask to what extent changes in comparative advantage in Japan were promoted by industrial policies of MITI. Opinions are divided on this issue. The negative view was clearly expressed by Charles Schultze:

Those who attribute Japan's economic success principally to MITI's industrial policy seem to be suggesting that without MITI the huge 30 to 35 percent of GNP that the Japanese invested in the past several decades would have gone mainly into such industries as textiles, shoes, plastic souvenirs, and fisheries. This is sheer nonsense. Given the quality of Japanese business executives, those massive investment funds probably would have wound up roughly where they actually did. And to the extent that there would have been differences, there is no reason to believe that MITI's influence, on balance, improved the choices in any major way.

Schultze added, though, that "all of this is not to suggest that MITI had no influence on the direction of Japanese investment" (1983, 7).

According to Chalmers Johnson, the "government's industrial policy made the difference in the rate of investment in certain economically strategic industries" (1982, 9). MITI's role in this has been emphasized by Ozaki and several Japanese authors, Shinohara and Morishima in particular. Ozaki writes:

MITI's functions are comprehensive and far-reaching. It is responsible for shaping the structure of industry and making necessary adjustments for industrial dislocations as they occur, properly guiding the development of specific industries and the production and distribution of their products, managing Japanese foreign trade and commercial relations with other nations, ensuring an adequate supply of energy and raw materials to industry and managing particular areas such as small business policy, patents, and regional development. To achieve these diverse goals, MITI plays many roles ranging from that of broad policy architect to ad hoc working-level problem-solver, and from formal regulator to regional policy arbiter or informal administrative guide. In some areas MITI holds strong statutory authority; elsewhere it has only a broad and weak influence (1984, 54).

Shinohara (1982) considered the case of two industries, steel and automobiles, which played an important role in Japanese industrial development. His data show that the ratio of Japanese to US steel production increased from 9 percent in 1955 to 25 percent in 1960 and, subsequently, from 35 percent in 1965 to 78 percent in 1970. The latter period coincided with a spurt in Japanese automobile production as well, from 8 to 49 percent of US output.

In his effort to explain these developments, Morishima emphasized the role of moral suasion on the part of MITI. In his view, "even though a government communication might be no more than a suggestion, a request or a notification, and with no binding force, in as far as it came from MITI at all any enterprise feared a cold reception should they fail to comply and therefore had no choice but to do so" (1982, 189). Shinohara noted that "MITI used administrative guidance, import restriction, coordination of investment in plant and equipment, merger and other methods of production consolidation, approval of cartels, postponing of liberalization of direct investment from outside, tax incentives for leading industries, low interest loans, and other measures" (1982, 48).

In the case of steel, according to one observer, the measures applied included "(1) encouraging investment in the industry through the strategic supply of funds and tax reductions, (2) promoting technical changes and exports through tax reduction provisions, (3) importing strategic technologies, and (4) protecting the industry from foreign competition" (Yamawaki 1988, 286). For automobiles, the guidelines developed by MITI included, in the words of Hiromichi Mutoh, the following: "(1) Domestic manufacturers would be protected from direct investment by foreign firms and from import of foreign vehicles. (2) Domestic manufacturers would be permitted to import foreign technology under favorable terms. (3) The government would provide financial assistance" (Mutoh 1988, 312–13). He describes the measures applied in the case of automobiles in greater detail. "First, protectionist policies were composed of four elements, (1) protective tariffs, (2) a commodity tax system favorable to domestic autos, (3) the restriction of imports using the allocation of foreign exchange, and (4) foreign exchange controls on foreign direct investment in Japan" (Mutoh 1988, 313). "Corresponding to these protectionist policies were promotion policies, including (1) supplying low-interest rate loans through government financial institutions, (2) granting subsidies, (3) providing special depreciation allowances, (4) exempting necessary equipment from import tariffs, and (5) approving essential foreign technology" (Mutoh 1988, 314).

"Because of these measures," Shinohara claims, "the steel and automobile industries . . . have now acquired a leading world position . . ." (Shinohara 1982, 48). The most rapid expansion of these two industries occurred when MITI was concentrating on their development—steel, under the "Five Year Plan for Economic Self-Reliance" and the "New Long Term Economic Plan" in the second half of the 1950s, and automobiles, under the "National Income Doubling Plan" during the second half of the 1960s. The rapid expansion of automobile production also contributed to the second spurt of steel production by increasing the demand for steel.

Among the measures cited above, import protection was of particular importance. According to Morishima, "initial measures to provide protection from competition from foreign enterprises included the limitation of imports by imposing quotas on foreign currency, directly limiting the amount of imports by such measures as the introduction of an import licensing system, and indirectly regulating imports by such means as imposing a high protective tariff on imports and introducing a preferential commodity tax for domestically produced goods" (Morishima 1982, 188–89). At the same time, limitations on foreign direct investment under the Foreign Capital Law of 1950 ensured that the protected domestic market was supplied by national firms. MITI's approval was also required for all technology licenses purchased abroad. This not only avoided competitive bidding for foreign licenses by Japanese firms, but permitted the exploitation of monopsony positions vis-à-vis foreign firms that did not have the options of exporting to, and locating in, Japan.

One might ask how the Japanese steel and automobile industries could become internationally competitive in the context of protection from imports and from foreign investment, when in developing countries protective measures have generally led to the establishment of high-cost industries. The answer to this question may lie in the fact that MITI promoted the simultaneous development of several firms, fostering competition among them.[9] Competition was possible in Japan's domestic market, which was much larger than that of individual developing countries. In addition, exports were promoted from an early stage and subsequently became a means of competition among Japanese firms seeking to reduce costs through the use of large-scale production methods. As a result, while in the early postwar period Japanese exports were dominated by textiles, steel exports assumed considerable importance around 1960 and automobile exports around 1970.

Following the development of steel production and automobile manufacturing (the latter of which was part of the promotion of machinery industries), MITI's attention shifted to high-technology industries. In November 1971 MITI issued a report entitled "The Basic Direction of Trade and Industry in the 1970s," which proposed the development of a "knowledge-intensive" industrial structure. This would include the promotion of R&D-intensive industries (such as computers, industrial robots, and integrated circuits), high-speed processing industries (such as office communication equipment and numerically controlled machine tools), and knowledge industries (such as information-supplying services, computer software, and systems engineering). In 1981 MITI launched its ten-year Next-Generation Industries Basic Technologies Project. This project encompasses biotechnology, new materials (such as fine ceramics and electrical conductors), as well as further research on electronics in the framework of 12 projects. Other areas supported by the government include space technology, aircraft, telecommunications, computer software, and medical equipment.

The Next-Generation Industries Basic Technologies Project and an earlier scheme, the Very Large-Scale Integration (VLSI) project of 1976, have attracted the most attention. While Saxonhouse (1983b) suggests that the funds devoted to these projects have been relatively small, MITI should be

---

9. However, as noted below, MITI unsuccessfully opposed the entry of new automobile manufacturing firms.

viewed as having provided "seed money," which is linked to spending on R&D by private firms. Furthermore, the projects have contributed to the diffusion and development of technology and have reduced risks for industrial firms, as discussed further in Chapter 3. According to Yamamura and Vandenberg, "the argument that the financial contribution made by the Japanese government is not a huge sum provides us with little comfort because of the profound impact the organization of research projects could have on the timing of innovation, on patterns of interfirm competition and cooperation, and on industrial structure" (1986, 269).

Among individual industries, Saxonhouse (1983b) singles out machine tools. He claims that the "$44 million MITI-sponsored cooperation project on laser-using complex manufacturing systems . . . in spite of involving the cooperative effort of twenty Japanese firms, could not really be a centerpiece for the intimate coordination of collusive activities by members of the Japanese machine tool industry [that] has experienced extremely rapid growth. . . ." But MITI's support for the Japanese machine tool industry is not of recent origin.[10] It was designated as one of the major recipients of government aid in the early 1950s, and the June 1956 "Extraordinary Measures Law for the Promotion of the Machinery Industry" instituted a program of financial support for the machine tool industry. Imports were also controlled through foreign exchange allocation and tariffs. In the early 1970s MITI encouraged the specialization of firms in the industry and set as a production target a 50 percent share of the domestic market for numerically controlled (NC) machine tools by the end of the decade. At the same time, it provided a 10–15 percent R&D subsidy to the industry, while high tariffs were maintained by classifying machine tools as computers. Although foreign companies were allowed to establish joint ventures in Japan, they had to license NC technology to their Japanese partners. Finally, the $44 million MITI-financed research project, which essentially provided seed money for R&D activities in the machine tool industry, was complemented by the provision of low-interest loans.

Saxonhouse also discusses the computer industry, arguing that the special financing provided by the government could not have been considered "critical" (1983b, 260). In the 1966–72 period, however, MITI provided a substantial part of the financing for the "1966 Super High-Performance Computer Project," and sextupled its contribution to the subsequent five-year "New Series" project. In addition, MITI supplied two-fifths of the financing for the VLSI project, which lasted from 1976 to 1979, and fully funded the Next-Generation Industries Basic Technologies project, extending over the 1981–90 period.

---

10. The following discussion derives from Collis 1987.

A recent review of government policies applied in the computer industry stated that "the policy goal during the course of MITI promotion of the computer industry was to protect the domestic market from domination by the foreign manufacturers headed by IBM by fostering domestic mainframe manufacturers who would compete against them" (Shinjo 1988, 354). According to this analysis, "The greatest contribution was the protection given to domestic manufacturers from imports and the regulation of technical licensing and foreign investment in the 1950s and 1960s, where there was a conspicuous technical gap between the domestic and the foreign manufacturers" (Shinjo 1988, 356). In later years, "a distinctive feature of the policies promoting the computer industry in Japan was the use of the joint government–private R&D projects" (Shinjo 1988, 358). And while IBM Japan was established the year before the 1950 Foreign Capital Law limiting foreign direct investment, its share was set at 3.5 percent of public procurement (Eads and Yamamura 1987, 456). In 1986 only 1.4 percent of the sales of IBM–Japan was to government agencies and educational institutions.[11] More generally, it has been argued that "the government to reserve a certain proportion of demand for domestic firms and to provide assistance in sales financing and R&D activities had a positive effect in permitting firms to maintain an aggressive management strategy by reducing the risk borne by firms in a situation in which the future development of the industry was uncertain" (Shinjo 1988, 355–56).

MITI continues to play an important role in the Japanese computer industry. An official US report on recent negotiations on supercomputers went so far as to claim that, "the exchange of views furnished persuasive evidence that the Japanese authorities and industry are engaged in the early stages of a comprehensive programme of industrial and technological targeting aimed towards dominance of the computer industry."[12]

The development of the computer industry was linked to that of semiconductors, where the VLSI project was complemented by domestic protection and licensing regulations. "Since MITI controlled access to the Japanese market and its approval was required for the implementation of licensing deals," noted one analysis, "it was in the powerful monopsonist's position of being able to dictate the terms of exchange [and] in line with the characteristic emphasis on export strategy, MITI often linked the import of particular technologies to the acquiring firm's ability to develop export products using that technology" (Borrus, Millstein, and Zysman 1983, 202–03).

---

11. *Fortune,* 28 March 1988.

12. Cited in the *Washington Post,* 28 April 1987.

These cases conform to the pattern described earlier, in which domestic production is pursued under high protection, to the full or partial exclusion of foreign firms, while the government regulates the importation of foreign technology.[13] The development of a given industry is further assisted until it becomes internationally competitive. These measures are taken selectively, with different industries favored at different stages in Japan's industrial development.

It has been suggested that "Japanese government involvement tends to be heaviest in "sunrise" and "sunset" industries—during periods when market forces, left alone, threaten to produce outcomes (such as foreign domination of strategic industries or corporate bankruptcies) that are deemed unacceptable" (Okimoto 1987, 99). But, as shown in Chapter 3, protection has been sustained over time in some industries in which Japan has never been able to compete internationally.

According to Eads and Yamamura, "the touchstone for [Japanese industrial] policies was competitiveness in international markets" (1987, 434). While this statement may apply to sunrise industries, it does not explain renewed protection for sunset industries or the continued protection of industries in which Japan is at a comparative disadvantage.

If industrial policy is regarded as an application of the infant industry argument, it makes sense to ask whether it has benefited the national economy. Paul Krugman claims that the industries favored by the government have not been particularly profitable: steel-producing firms, for example, have less than average profitability and semi-conductors have been unprofitable (1984, 104).[14] However, inasmuch as they have become internationally competitive, both industries meet the Eads–Yamamura test. Furthermore, the steel industry has provided low-cost inputs for industries producing machinery and transport equipment, and the Japanese semiconductor industry has practically established a worldwide monopoly in 64K RAM chips, which makes possible future profits while supplying low-cost inputs for computers and other industries. Several other promoted industries, such as automobiles and machine tools, have been highly profitable.

---

13. Henry Rosovsky calls this pattern the "denial of the profits of innovation." He argues that it has long been practiced by Japan to the detriment of American innovation and that maximum pressure for its removal is warranted. See his commentary, "Trade, Japan, and the Year 2000," *New York Times,* 6 September 1985, cited in Press 1987.

14. In a subsequent paper, Baldwin and Krugman (1986) find that Japan experienced social losses (with losses to consumers exceeding gains to producers) in the case of 16K random access memories (RAMs) for which US costs were said to be lower than Japanese costs. This conclusion does not hold for 64K RAMs, however, for which Japan has become the dominant producer. The domestic production of 16K RAMs may be considered part of the learning process for building more powerful chips.

This is not to say that MITI succeeded in every industry. Aluminum and commercial aircraft in an earlier period, chemicals and pharmaceuticals subsequently, and computer software more recently can be classified as failures or near-failures. In addition, one successful industry, automobile manufacturing, developed differently than projected by MITI, with a larger number of companies coming into existence. Finally, questions have arisen concerning the measures used to defend depressed industries (see Chapter 3 and Eads and Yamamura 1987).

Apart from microeconomic efficiency and interindustry relationships, however, one also needs to consider the beneficial macroeconomic effects of the government's promotion of key industries. During the early postwar period government policies brought foreign exchange savings and, subsequently, foreign exchange earnings, which eased the foreign exchange constraint under which Japan labored at the time.

The preceding discussion should not be interpreted as implying that MITI's power has remained undiminished during the postwar period. While in the early part of the period it could rely on import quotas and credit facilities to influence corporate activity, MITI no longer has these instruments at its disposal and now assumes a largely organizational role, emphasizing consensus-building. Yet according to a well-informed observer, "in shaping the direction of basic research, MITI officials are playing a much more visible and important role today than in the 1950s and 1960s in promoting the technological capabilities of major industries" (Yamamura 1983, 28). Furthermore, procurement regulations and administrative guidance are used to limit imports, as discussed in Chapter 3.

It should also be emphasized that MITI's actions took place in a favorable macroeconomic environment, characterized by abundant domestic savings, favorable conditions for technological change, and widespread education. This environment enhanced the effectiveness of MITI's actions.

Prospective Changes in International Specialization

The next question concerns the effects of *endaka* (the high yen) on the Japanese industrial landscape. Comparisons with the impact of the oil shocks are not quite valid here, since these shocks affected all industrial economies to some extent while *endaka* strongly favors the United States and countries that generally follow the dollar, including the NICs and Canada.[15] Japan will increasingly be at a disadvantage in natural resource-

---

15. In the US case, this represents a reversal of the earlier situation, when the dollar was greatly overvalued.

intensive industries vis-à-vis the United States and Canada, and in unskilled labor-intensive industries vis-à-vis developing countries. It will also lose ground to the NICs in industries such as steel, automobiles, and consumer electronics, where production technology is standardized and is easily copied. These industries require skilled labor that is becoming increasingly available at low cost in the NICs and/or physical capital that is becoming increasingly mobile internationally. Finally, the competitive strength of the United States will improve in high-technology products.

Some improvement in the US competitive position vis-à-vis Japan is evident from table 2.5. The table provides data on unit labor costs in the manufacturing sector, defined as the ratio of total hourly labor costs, inclusive of social charges, to labor productivity (output per hour). Although these data are subject to considerable error, they are indicative of overall orders of magnitude. The data suggest that while the higher cost of US labor was largely offset by higher US productivity in 1980, the overvaluation of the dollar and gains in Japanese productivity caused unit labor costs in the United States to exceed those of Japan by 19 percent in 1984. The situation was reversed in the next two years as the yen appreciated and labor productivity grew slightly more in the United States than in Japan. As a result, estimated unit labor costs in 1986 were 22 percent higher in Japan than in the United States. However, Japan increased its labor-cost advantage vis-à-vis Germany, whose currency appreciated in similar proportions but whose labor productivity declined. Japan also continued to have lower unit labor costs than Italy and the United Kingdom, but not France.

Table 2.5 provides labor cost estimates for 1987, derived from the projections of the EC Commission and adjusted for actual changes in effective (trade-weighted) exchange rates. According to the projections, unit labor costs were expected to decline by 11.8 percent in the United States, 3.2 percent in France, and 1.8 percent in the United Kingdom in 1987; they were expected to increase 6.4 percent in Japan, 6.5 percent in Germany, and 2.5 percent in Italy. These projected changes in large part reflect exchange rate movements, with France being the principal exception. In 1987 the effective (trade-weighted) exchange rate, as measured by the International Monetary Fund, depreciated by 11.8 percent in the United States and 0.4 percent in the United Kingdom, while increasing 8.2 percent in Japan, 7.6 percent in Germany, 1.9 percent in Italy, and 2.4 percent in France. In terms of national currencies, the range of estimated 1987 increases in unit labor costs is between 0.5 percent (Japan) and 2.8 percent (Italy). The Japanese figures may be on the high side, since firms have reportedly reduced their work forces in response to the appreciation of the yen, but it appears that the Japanese competitive position vis-à-vis the United States deteriorated again in 1987.

Table 2.5 Unit labor costs in manufacturing, selected years (index numbers)[a]

	Total Hourly Labor Costs			Labor Productivity (output per hour)			Unit Labor Costs			
	1980	1984	1986	1980	1984	1986	1980	1984	1986	1987
Japan	80	109	129	196	177	176	41	62	73	83
France	121	114	122	193	179	184	63	64	66	72
Germany	165	153	173	255	232	178	65	66	97	113
Italy	108	117	127	173	156	155	62	75	82	93
United States	126	194	161	273	262	267	46	74	60	60

Sources: G. F. Ray, "Labor Costs in Manufacturing," *National Institute Economic Review*, May 1987. Percentage changes in unit labor costs for 1987 from EC Commission, *European Economy*, April 1987.

a. Figures are index numbers, with United Kingdom = 100. Unit labor cost figures for 1987 derived by multiplying the 1986 figure by the ratio of the country's 1987 percentage change in unit labor costs to the percentage change in unit labor costs for the United Kingdom in 1987.

If real exchange rate movements are not reversed, Japan has to be prepared for substantial changes in its export composition. In particular, Japan would need increasingly to export high-technology products. This would in turn require greater emphasis on basic research, certain reforms in the educational system, and changes at the firm level.

Japan trails the United States in terms of the amount of funds devoted to basic research. On a per capita basis, expenditures on basic research by governmental institutions in the United States are twice those of Japan; Germany's are four times as high and France's 2.4 times. Per capita university expenditures on basic research in the United States, Germany and France are 1.3 times higher than in Japan (Fukukawa 1987, 4). Furthermore, with some exceptions, such as optoelectronics and superceramics, Japanese firms "have had difficulty dealing with technologies that are highly complex, not very predictable, and heavily dependent on basic research," such as lasers, computer software, and the development of computer-aided design and manufacturing systems (Okimoto 1986, 555).[16] According to a high technology survey in the *Economist*, "Japan's success in high-technology products

---

16. According to *Fortune*, "The High Tech Race: Who is Ahead" (12 October 1985), on a 1 to 10 scale measuring relative technological capabilities, the United States earns 9.9 points for computers, compared to 7.3 points for Japan; the corresponding figures were 8.9 and 5.7 for biotechnology, 7.7 and 6.3 for new materials, and 7.8 and 9.5 for optoelectronics.

has been almost exclusively with developments that were predictable—like packing more and more circuits into dynamic RAM chips, or making video recorders smarter and smaller."[17]

The movement toward the technological frontier would require greater emphasis on the basic sciences and on fundamental innovation. According to one observer, "Japan may have to embark on a crash program to expand and upgrade its infrastructure in science and technology so that it can innovate. It can no longer exploit the advantages of latecomer status. It may not be able to follow a low-cost, low-risk strategy of second-to-market by capitalizing on low production costs" (Okimoto 1986, 566). Japan's past performance in the basic sciences was not particularly strong. It won four Nobel Prizes in science, compared with 158 in the United States, and a much smaller number of seminal breakthroughs have been made in Japan than in the United States.[18] Japan actually has won fewer Nobel Prizes in the sciences than have several smaller countries, such as Sweden, Switzerland, and the Netherlands.[19]

However, Japan will be building from a strong base in the sciences. It has increased its overall research effort in recent years, and it ranks second in the world in the number of scientific and technical journals published. Furthermore, private R&D spending by corporations is high, amounting to 2.1 percent of GNP in 1986, compared to 1.4 percent in the United States (Office of Technology Assessment 1988, 5).

Nonetheless, the level of research at Japanese universities remains lower than that of the United States. The excessively bureaucratic character of the university system, the limited availability of research funds, and the lack of peer reviews are all said to retard research at Japanese universities.[20] The number of doctoral degrees awarded by Japanese universities in the natural sciences was only one-sixth that of US universities in 1981 (Okimoto and Saxonhouse 1987, 412), although thousands of Japanese students receive graduate training in the United States.

The government is beginning to address these problems. Its commitment

---

17. *Economist*, 23 August 1986.

18. *Economist*, 23 August 1986.

19. Dreyfuss describes the views of Susumu Tonegawa, a Japanese-born MIT researcher who won the 1987 Nobel Prize in Medicine, as follows: "Japanese culture remains a major block to true creativity. Scientific thinking, he argues, is a product of individualism, and 'in Japan, individualism has never been of personal value.' The Japanese excel at applied science, says Tonegawa, because teamwork is important to success" (1987, 84).

20. The amounts available for research and engineering are about one-tenth of the sum available at American universities (*US Department of Education* 1987, 53).

to promoting basic research is demonstrated by the initiation of the Exploratory Research for Advanced Technology (ERATO) and Japan Key Technology Center (or Japan Key-Tech) programs[21] and by its encouragement of the importing of foreign scientific know-how.[22] Parallel efforts have been proposed for the universities.

Recommendations have also been made for education below the university level. Education is justly credited for significantly contributing to Japan's economic success during the postwar period. In recent years, however, questions have been raised in Japan about the appropriateness of the educational system for the future requirements of industries on the frontier of new technology. In this connection, a statement by a member of the Council on Education Reform, which was appointed by former Prime Minister Nakasone, is of interest: "During the stage when Japan was still catching up, companies welcomed the mass produced supply of workers equipped with a uniform, homogenous education. The resounding success of total quality control is closely tied to the uniform educational background and ability of Japanese workers." He added "the big question now is whether what has succeeded in the twentieth century will also lead to success in the twenty-first century" (Pyle 1987, 20).

According to the first report of the Council, while "catching up" required intense work, uniformity, unquestioning adherence to a set curriculum, and a stress on rote memory work, "respect for individuality, freedom, autonomy, self-responsibility, and human values . . . tended to be ignored" (Pyle 1987, 24). The report proposes measures to ensure greater diversity and hetero-geneity in Japanese schools, with a view to fostering individuality and creativity. The second report of the Council declares that the rigidity and uniformity of the Japanese educational system have created problems:

The Council asserts that the rigid, uniform school programs, exercise controls on students, and other factors prevent sound character formation, increase pressures on children, and create frustration. The Council fears

---

21. For a description of these programs, see the *Financial Times* survey of Japanese industry (15 December 1986). Increased spending on basic research by Japan is said to be not only in the Japanese interest but also in the general interest because of the external economies it would generate worldwide (Press 1987, 40).

22. As far as the importation of foreign scientific know-how is concerned, there is said to be "a new development in the sense that the government itself now shows interest in becoming a partner for foreign multinationals and scientists so that Japan can gain access to their research capacities (their core ownership advantage). In this way the government is going beyond its past effort to gain access to existing technologies" (Ozawa 1986, 156–57).

that an excessive emphasis on memorization has produced many conform-ist people who are unable to think independently and creatively (US Department of Education 1987, 65).

It proposes remedying this situation through educational reforms aimed at "coping with the changes of the times." Prime Minister Takeshita indicated his intention to carry out the recommendations of the Council in his annual policy speech to the 112th session of the Diet on 25 January 1988 (1988, 20).

Movement toward the technological frontier also has implications for the firm. The group approach, the lifetime employment system, and the rigid seniority system all contributed to Japan's industrial successes in the past by facilitating intra-firm training and fostering workers' commitment to the objectives of the firm. Innovation at the high-technology frontier, however, would require greater flexibility and promotion by merit, as well as the establishment of technologically advanced, small firms.[23]

Finally, shifts in Japan's comparative advantage will necessitate eschewing the protection of high-cost, inefficient sectors. Yet one finds some hardening of Japanese attitudes toward trade liberalization. US trade officials reported that, "Japan is showing new resistance to demands that it lift restrictions on sales of foreign goods because of the battering its industries have taken in their export sales by the year-long rise in the value of the yen."[24] Similar views were expressed seven months later following a week of negotiations on several key trade issues.[25] And on his visit to Washington in January 1988, Prime Minister Takeshita brought with him a list of trade liberalization measures undertaken in 1987 that was shorter than expected.[26]

Domestic political obstacles were invoked by Japanese government offi-cials to justify their limited response to the findings of a GATT panel investigating protectionist and discriminatory measures applied by Japan to imported liquor. And, while Japan accepted eight out of the ten recommendations of the GATT panel for removing quotas on some minor foodstuffs, it is reportedly contemplating imposing tariffs on these products.[27]

Such an attitude is contrary to Japan's well-conceived interests. Import limitations are bound to contribute to the balance of payments surplus,

---

23. At the same time, greater interfirm mobility of technical labor would discourage intrafirm training and necessitate the upgrading of university education.

24. *Washington Post*, 15 February 1987.

25. *Washington Post*, 22 August 1987.

26. *Wall Street Journal*, 14 March 1988.

27. *Washington Post*, 2 February 1988.

causing a further appreciation of the yen. This will harm industries in which Japan has an actual or potential comparative advantage. Japan should instead follow up the recent agreement with the United States liberalizing imports of beef and oranges with comparable initiatives in other sectors.[28]

Import liberalization is thus a necessity from the Japanese point of view, just as it is a bonus for countries exporting to Japan. The status of Japanese protection will be discussed in Chapter 3.

---

28. *Wall Street Journal*, 20 June 1988.

Trade Policy

3

This chapter will examine trade policy in Japan and its effects on international trade flows. First, we will review formal barriers to trade, including tariffs and nontariff barriers. We will then discuss informal barriers to trade. In the case of formal barriers to trade, we will compare Japan with the United States and the European Community (EC). In the case of informal barriers to trade, however, the discussion will be limited to Japan. This raises the question of whether Japan is a special case among industrial countries. In attempting to answer this question, we will draw on international comparisons of import shares for manufactured products and utilize the results of econometric investigations of the extent of different countries' participation in the international division of labor.

While the results show that Japan is an outlier among the industrial countries, this does not mean that its present current account surplus was caused by import protection. The Japanese surplus increased to a considerable extent in the space of a few years, without any major changes in trade barriers.

Formal Barriers to Imports

Tariffs

Japan lowered its tariffs to a considerable extent during the 1960s and the 1970s. This process continued in the first half of the 1980s. In 1985 import duties were eliminated on about 1800 narrowly defined product categories (tariff lines), for which tariffs were generally below 5 percent. Duties were reduced by one-fifth on selected products with tariffs above 5 percent.

On the whole, tariff rates on non-agricultural products in Japan approximate those of the European Community and the United States. Before the latest reductions, Japanese tariffs averaged 0.5 percent on raw materials,

49

4.6 percent on semi-manufactures, and 6.0 percent on finished manufactures, compared with 0.2, 3.0, and 5.7 percent, respectively, in the United States and 0.2, 4.2, and 6.9 percent in the European Community (Balassa and Michalopoulos 1986, table 1).[1] At the same time, however, Japanese tariffs tend to be higher than average for raw and processed agricultural commodities (including fishery and forestry products). This is particularly the case for fresh and preserved fruits, alcoholic beverages, and wood products.

Even after the recent reductions, tariffs remain relatively high on fresh and preserved fruits in Japan. Following the Tokyo round of multilateral trade negotiations, duties on fresh fruits averaged 26.0 percent in Japan, 1.5 percent in the United States, and 14.8 percent in the European Community. The corresponding figures were 24.7, 11.6, and 20.1 percent for preserved fruits (UN Conference on Trade and Development 1982, table 1).

Alcoholic beverages bear the highest tariffs in Japan, and these tariffs are supplemented by progressive excise taxes. According to a study prepared for the EC Commission, duties were 5.5 to 9.3 times higher for bottled wine than for bulk wine imported under preferential rates in Japan in 1985, and this difference increased slightly following subsequent reductions in tariffs (EC Commission 1985a, 1:33, 46–48). Effective 1 April 1988, tariffs on bottled wine were set at 30 percent, averaging 55 cents a liter; duties are 12 to 14 cents a liter in the European Community and 10 cents in the United States (Joint Economic Committee 1987, 48–49).

The EC study also reported that duties on bottled whiskey in 1985 were 6.5 to 7.2 times higher in Japan than in the European Community and that specific taxes on imported special-grade whiskey were seven times those for second-grade (domestically produced) whiskey (EC Commission 1985a, 1:33, 46–48). Japanese government proposals to tax special- and first-grade imported whiskey at equal rates, while maintaining the same ratio of specific taxes for low-grade domestic spirits and eliminating ad valorem taxes, were not accepted by the EC Commission, which submitted the matter to a panel of the General Agreement on Tariffs and Trade (GATT). The GATT panel endorsed the EC position, concluded that Japanese taxes on alcohol are discriminatory and protectionist, and called for the elimination of the grading system in setting specific taxes.[2]

Among wood products, duties of 15 percent are levied on veneer, compared with zero in the United States and 4 percent in the European Community.

---

1. These data are unweighted averages. The overall weighted tariff average is now lower in Japan than in the United States and the European Community, but Japan's average is considerably biased downwards because of its large imports of duty-free raw materials.

2. *Le Monde,* 5 October 1987; *Financial Times,* 12 November 1987.

The corresponding rates are 10–15, 8, and 10 percent for plywood, and 8, 4, and 10 percent for particle board. With no tariffs on logs, and a relatively low value-added, Japan's effective rate of protection (the protection of value-added) of these panel products is high. This may explain why even though log imports supply two-thirds of Japan's needs, the average import share of panel products is less than six percent.

Nontariff Barriers

For the purposes of the following discussion, nontariff barriers are defined to include all transparent border measures that directly or indirectly limit imports. Among these measures, quantitative import restrictions and so-called voluntary export restraints limit imports directly. In turn, variable import levies, minimum price requirements for imports, voluntary export price agreements, and tariff quotas involving the imposition of higher duties above a predetermined quantity have indirect effects on imports.

A substantial proportion of Japanese and EC agricultural imports are protected by nontariff measures, thereby raising domestic producer prices above world market prices. The price differentials are especially large in Japan. The ratio of Japanese domestic producer prices to the world market prices of the seven principal agricultural products averaged 2.44 in 1980–82. The average was 1.54 in the European Community and 1.16 in the United States (table 3.1). The price ratio in Japan was the highest for coarse grains (4.3), followed by beef and lamb (4.0), wheat (3.8), rice (3.3), and sugar (3.0).[3]

It is estimated that, in the event of the elimination of agricultural protection, Japanese imports would increase twelvefold in the case of beef and lamb,[4] elevenfold for dairy products, tenfold for pork and chicken,[5] and fourfold for rice. In turn, with the decline in livestock raising, imports of coarse grains would fall by one-fourth and there would be a one-twelfth decrease in wheat imports. Imports of sugar would rise by one-fourth, however (Anderson and Tyers 1987, 138).

Beef has attracted considerable attention in US–Japanese negotiations. Japan strictly limits beef imports, and annual consumption levels (6 kg. per

---

3. These ratios increased further following the appreciation of the Japanese yen in 1985–87. (The average yen–dollar exchange rate in the years 1980–82 was 232).

4. Eighty-five percent of the total is beef, which is subject to quotas; tariffs apply to lamb.

5. Four-fifths of the total is pork, which is subject to variable duties that act like quotas; informal barriers apply to chicken.

3.1 Ratios of domestic to world market prices in the major industrial countries, 1980–82

	Japan		EC		US	
	producer price	consumer price	producer price	consumer price	producer price	consumer price
Wheat	3.80	1.25	1.25	1.30	1.15	1.00
Coarse Grains	4.30	1.30	1.40	1.40	1.00	1.00
Rice	3.30	2.90	1.40	1.40	1.30	1.00
Beef and Lamb	4.00	4.00	1.90	1.90	1.00	1.00
Pork and Poultry	1.50	1.50	1.25	1.25	1.00	1.00
Dairy Products	2.90	2.90	1.75	1.80	2.00	2.00
Sugar	3.00	2.60	1.50	1.70	1.40	1.40
Weighted average	2.44	2.08	1.54	1.56	1.16	1.17

Source: World Bank, *World Development Report 1986,* Table 6.1.

capita) are much lower than in the European Community (27 kg.) and the United States (44 kg.). These differences are partly explained by variations in diet, since fish is much more important in Japan than in the United States (although the Japanese diet has been changing rapidly, with the per capita consumption of beef increasing fourfold between 1960 and 1986). Another factor is the high price of beef to consumers. According to the study cited above, with the elimination of protection, the per capita consumption of beef would reach 21 kg. in Japan and 35 kg. in the European Community.[6]

Imports of beef to Japan are limited by quotas. Under the June 1988 agreement between Japan and the United States, the US quotas would nearly double between 1987 and 1990 and would eventually be eliminated. Tariffs would rise substantially, however, and additional duties may be imposed in the event of rapid increases in imports.[7] In addition, the 1988 budget provides nearly $1 billion in subsidies for beef producers.[8]

Quotas on oranges would also be phased out over a three-year period, with tariffs maintained at present levels, and a nearly $1 billion subsidy. In 1986 the per capita consumption of oranges was only 4 kg. in Japan, compared with 26 kg. in the United States and 16 kg. in the European

---

6. These results are confirmed by estimates made on the basis of data on production, consumption, and their responsiveness to price changes provided in another study (Zietz and Valdes 1985, Appendix Table). According to these estimates, following the elimination of protection, the per capita consumption of beef would attain 26 kg. in Japan and 33 kg. in the European Community.

7. *Wall Street Journal,* 20 June 1988.

8. *Japan Economic Journal,* 2 July 1988.

Community. In the same year, the per capita consumption of domestically produced tangerines, which are protected by quotas, was 18 kg. per capita in Japan, compared with 2 kg. per capita in both the United States and the European Community.[9] The elimination of protection would increase the share of oranges relative to tangerines in Japanese consumption, with the total consumption of citrus fruit rising in response to lower prices.

Altogether, Japan has 22 quotas on agricultural and fishery products, compared with 1 in the United States, 2 in Belgium, 19 in France, 3 in Germany, 3 in Italy, and 1 in the United Kingdom. The Japanese number does not include tobacco, although the state trading company is obligated by law to buy the entire tobacco crop in Japan at about three times the world market price.

In concentrating on beef and oranges, US–Japan negotiations side-stepped the issue of rice.[10] Yet at the existing exchange rate, Japan's rice farmers receive seven times the world market price.[11] Rice farming is done inefficiently on average plots of 0.8 hectares, although cultivation machinery can be used efficiently on only 10–20 hectares (Hillman and Rothenberg 1985, 51). From the end of the Korean war until 1960, rice prices remained relatively stable, only slightly exceeding world market prices. By the late 1970s, however, producer prices were three to four times higher than world market prices. Price increases have not been limited to rice. Between 1960 and 1980, agricultural prices expressed in US dollars rose eightfold in Japan while tripling in the major EC countries and increasing by 150 percent in the United States (OECD 1985, 62).

As a result of these increases, Japan's average nominal rate of protection, defined as the percentage of excess of domestic over world market prices, for 13 major agricultural products (wheat, rye, barley, oats, maize, rice, beef,

---

9. These data are from the OECD.

10. The US Rice Millers Association filed a complaint with the US Trade Representative (USTR), requesting that action be taken against Japanese import restraints for rice. According to the Association, the opening of the Japanese market would permit US rice exports to Japan to rise by 2.5 million tons (*Financial Times,* 12 September 1986); this compares with the increase of 4.2 million tons from all sources estimated by Anderson and Tyers (1987, Table III). The USTR declined to challenge directly Japan's rice policies (*Journal of Commerce,* 24 October 1986) and the US Secretary of Agriculture, who subsequently raised the issue, was rebuffed by his counterpart in Japan (*Washington Post,* 21 April 1987).

11. In August 1986, the Japanese government proposed a reduction in the price of rice but, in response to protests from ruling party politicians who depend on rural rice-growing areas for support, Prime Minister Nakasone intervened personally to block the reduction (*Financial Times,* 12 August 1986). There was a 6 percent reduction in May 1987, reportedly in response to lower fertilizer and other production costs (*Economist,* 23 May 1987), and a 4.6 percent reduction in July 1988 (*JEI Report* 288, 22 July 1988).

pork, chicken, eggs, milk, sugar beet, and potatoes) rose from 41.1 percent in 1960 to 83.5 percent in 1980. During the same period, the average nominal rate of protection increased from 32.8 to 35.7 percent in the European Community and declined slightly, from 0.9 to −0.1 percent, in the United States (Honma and Hayami 1986).[12] More recent data show a near-doubling of the protection of grains and a near-tripling of the protection of livestock products between 1980 and 1986 in Japan (Vincent 1988, table 1). High levels of protection burden the taxpayer and the consumer. The OECD estimated the taxpayer burden, expressed in terms of producer-subsidy equivalents, to have averaged 55.4 percent in Japan in 1979–81, and to have risen to 63.3 percent in 1985, for ten agricultural products (1987).

Partly as a consequence of the profitability of agriculture, farmland prices rose 9.3 times between 1960 and 1982 in Japan. By 1982 agricultural land sold for an average $56,000 per hectare in Japan, about 3.4 times the price in Germany, 8.5 times that in the United Kingdom, and 16 times that in France (Reich, Endo, and Timmer 1986, 165). An acre of rice paddy costs $30,000 in Japan, compared with $1,600 in California.[13]

Nontariff barriers also apply to raw silk and twisted silk yarn. Between 1979 and 1986, raw silk imports from developing countries declined from 8801 to 6026 metric tons, while imports from Korea, where Japanese restrictions are most severe, fell from 910 to 18 metric tons. Declines also occurred during the same period in imports of silk yarn, from 3261 to 2418 metric tons from all developing countries and from 777 to 713 metric tons from Korea. A request by the Korean government for the repeal of the quotas was rejected by Japan on the grounds that "the circumstances surrounding the raw silk industry are extremely unfavorable." The official reply of the Japanese government further stated that "the import of twisted silk yarn has never been sanctioned by law. . . . In fact, the import authorization system was introduced for the purpose of preventing the import of twisted silk yarn."[14]

---

12. Even larger increases are seen if one goes back to 1955, when average nominal protection rates were 17.5 percent in Japan, 30.7 percent in the European Community, and 2.4 percent in the United States. The results for Japan are explained by the fact that the prices of agricultural products other than rice rose to a considerable extent between 1955 and 1960.

13. *Economist,* 2 May 1987.

14. All references to Korean observations on Japanese protection, and the official replies of the Japanese government, originate from the English translation of the official report (in Korean) of the First Investment Office, Overseas Cooperation Council of the Republic of Korea, entitled "Korean Demand for Removal of Nontariff Barriers and Official Japanese Response," September 1984. See Balassa 1986b for a more detailed discussion.

Bilateral restraint agreements apply to silk fabrics imported from China, Korea, and Taiwan, while imports from other developing countries require prior approval by MITI. This so-called prior confirmation system in effect acts like a quota. In response to an official Korean request for the deregulation of imports, the Japanese government claimed that "given the structurally depressed demand for silk in Japan," the measures currently applied could not be modified. In the seven years following the introduction of these measures in 1979, Japanese imports of silk fabrics from developing countries declined by one-fifth in volume, while imports originating from Korea fell by one-fourth.

Since May 1980 MITI has subjected Korean and Taiwanese silk products, such as apparel and accessories, to the prior confirmation system. While the Japanese government claims that "the prior confirmation system was introduced for no other purpose than to monitor the trends in these silk product imports," the absence of separate data for imports of silk products makes it difficult to establish trends for silk imports.

Japan has traditionally applied quantitative restrictions to leather and leather shoes. In response to the adverse findings of a GATT panel, these restrictions were transformed in April 1986 into a tariff-quota system, in which tariffs of 60 percent or more apply above the quotas. Imports up to the quota limits are dutiable at 15 to 20 percent for leather and 27 percent for leather shoes, but they account for only 3 percent and 1 percent, respectively, of Japanese consumption (USTR 1987, 173). Imports of leather and leather shoes have remained relatively small since the changes in protective measures. In 1986 per capita imports of leather and leather shoes, respectively, amounted to only $0.7 and $2.5 in Japan, compared with $1.8 and $20.9 in the United States, and $8.6 and $20.5 in the European Community. In the same year Japanese shoe imports from the developing countries were less than one-fifteenth of US imports from those countries.

A prior confirmation system applies to tuna imports into Japan from all sources of supply. The Japanese government declared that this "is vital for correctly monitoring the trend in tuna imports. The system, therefore, is not amenable to elimination." It added that "it is necessary to maintain the current quantitative level from the point of view of maintaining tuna prices in Japan." The Japanese government has expressed its unwillingness to eliminate quotas for other kinds of fish and seafood on the grounds that these "account for the principal fish types harvested by Japan's inshore and nearshore fishing entities which are generally poorly financed. For this reason, these commodities are still under the import quota allocation system and this condition is not conducive to its early removal."

Apart from the cases cited, Japanese import quotas apply to a number of foodstuffs that are of interest to developing countries. There is also a variable duty on pork and pork products which acts like a quota; tariff-quotas apply to corn and sorghum; and imports of wheat and barley are controlled by an agency of the Ministry of Agriculture, Fisheries, and Forestry (MAFF), which annually determines the amount imported.

According to official submissions to the GATT, information on the amounts allocated for several items under quotas is not made available by the Japanese government. The US government contends:

> In addition to the quotas themselves, the lack of transparency in their establishment and maintenance adversely affect U.S. exports. Problems include arbitrary changes in quota size and late announcement levels. The involvement of domestic competition in administering quotas severely restricts even the limited access to the Japanese market granted under the quotas (USTR 1982, 9).

This view was supported in a document prepared by the EC Commission (1985b, 16).

In 1987 the United States lodged a complaint at the GATT concerning Japanese import restrictions on twelve relatively minor agricultural commodities. The GATT panel concluded that Japan has no grounds to continue applying such restrictions to ten of the twelve commodities (lactose, processed cheese, dairy preparations, processed beef, sugared fruit preparations, tomato ketchup, tomato juice, starch, and powdered skim milk). Except for the last two items, Japan accepted the recommendations of the panel, and a schedule for liberalization was announced in July 1988.[15]

Informal Barriers to Imports

We have thus far considered formal barriers to trade in Japan. Tariffs are high on selected products while nontariff measures apply to a variety of agricultural and fishery products and to some manufactured goods. In the case of manufactured goods, informal barriers are much more important than formal barriers. Informal barriers take a variety of forms, including administrative guidance; customs procedures; standards, testing, and certification requirements; public procurement practices; the defense of depressed industries; the promotion of high-technology industries; regulations on intellectual property; and distribution channels. We will review each of these in turn.[16]

---

15. *Wall Street Journal,* 6 January 1988; *Japan Economic Journal,* 13 February 1988; *New York Times,* 22 July 1988.

16. See Appendix B for a more detailed discussion of these barriers.

Administrative Guidance

According to one definition, "administrative guidance is a process that consists of a government ministry's giving suggestions or advice to private business or public organizations over which the ministry has regulatory jurisdiction" (USTR 1982, 58–59). Administrative guidance does not carry a legal sanction. Its effectiveness derives from the supervisory role of the ministry.

There are several products for which administrative guidance is used to limit imports into Japan. These include petroleum products (from all suppliers), steel (from Korea), and cotton yarn and cotton cloth (from developing countries). Administrative guidance also plays a role in high-technology industries.

Customs Procedures

The restrictive interpretation of rules and regulations by Japanese customs authorities has been considered a nontariff barrier. In recent years, there have been improvements in import procedures for foodstuffs, pharmaceuticals, and cosmetics. Nevertheless, there continue to be complaints, especially from developing-country exporters, concerning the difficulty of clearing individual shipments through customs in Japan.

Furthermore, import permits are given to Japanese importers rather than to foreign exporters, which creates problems in the event that an exporter wishes to change importers. Products subject to import barriers receive permits for periods of 3 to 7 years and application procedures must start again following a permit's expiration.

Standards, Testing, and Certification Requirements

Nearly a decade ago, it was said that "the applicable project approval standards, the methods by which such standards are promulgated and the procedures established to test and certify imported products for compliance with these standards all provide significant impediments to the importation into Japan of many U.S. goods" (Weil and Glick 1979, 865–86). While certain improvements were made subsequently, standards, testing, and certification requirements continue to be regarded as an informal nontariff barrier in Japan.

Complaints about the standard-setting process have concerned the exclusion of foreign firms. In response to these complaints, the Japanese government declared in July 1985 that foreigners would be provided with opportunities to convey their opinions of proposed standards. Nevertheless, US officials have noted, "it is still difficult for foreigners to have meaningful input into the Japanese standards-drafting process [as the] program is neither sufficiently transparent nor does it permit effective foreign participation" (USTR 1986, 149–51).

With regard to product testing and certification, imported products have not been able to use the factory-negotiation and model approach, which allows for the self-certification of Japanese producers, but are instead subject to time-consuming and costly lot-testing at the time of importation. And while the private US Underwriting Laboratories has been authorized to carry out factory inspection and product testing in the United States for exporting to Japan, few US factories have been approved to date.

The Ministry of Post and Telecommunications, however, has begun to accept manufacturer-generated data to meet standards aimed at ensuring that foreign equipment does not harm the Japanese telecommunications network. MITI also reduced the number of products subject to the standard-setting process. Finally, the Ministry of Health and Welfare declared its willingness to accept foreign clinical test data for a number of pharmaceuticals and has approved four new food additives. The number of approved food additives nevertheless remains small and, under regulations effective since 1 March 1988, synthetic (but not natural) additives used extensively in foreign products must be labelled. A number of industrial products are also simultaneously subject to several laws, each of which sets up different requirements.

Public Procurement Practices

Complaints about government procurement in Japan have focused traditionally on high-technology products and on military equipment. More recently, bidding on construction projects has generated considerable controversy. Foreign firms could not participate in the large first construction phase of the $8 billion Kansai International Airport, which involved building a 1,265 acre artificial island in Osaka Bay and a bridge to the mainland. Although Japanese officials, in response to President Reagan's intervention, subsequently agreed to permit foreign firms to bid on the later phases of the project, the contracts awarded to foreign firms amounted to only $17.7 million. Originally, the exclusion of foreign contractors from the Kansai airport project was defended on the grounds that it was built by a private corporation. In November 1987, however, the Japanese government effectively excluded foreign contractors from the lucrative public construction market. In response to US pressure, the government agreed in March 1988 to open fourteen public projects to American construction firms.

Japanese government procurement has been criticized for its reliance on single tenders, its short bid times, its complex qualifications procedures, and its lack of transparency. The July 1985 Action Program of the Japanese government promised improvements in these areas, but it is still too early to evaluate the results.

The Defense of Depressed Industries

In 1978 fourteen sectors were designated "structurally depressed industries" under the Law on Temporary Measures for the Stabilization of Specified Industries. The law established a "Basic Stabilization Plan" for such industries, which included reducing existing capacity, creating a special guarantee fund, and empowering supervisory ministries to set up cartels. In March 1983 the Temporary Measures Law for Structural Improvement of Specific Industries replaced the earlier law, which had expired. The new law, adopted over the opposition of the Japanese Fair Trade Commission (JFTC), covers 22 sectors. It aims at retrenchment as well as revival in these industries, with capacity reductions accompanied by mergers, joint production, and specialization agreements, which can involve the establishment of cartels. In fact, legal cartels are in operation in seven sectors.

Capacity reductions in depressed industries were more than offset by higher operating rates. Production increases were achieved as import-penetration rates changed little in Japan while rising to a considerable extent in the other major industrial countries. The exception to this rule was aluminum, where import-penetration rates rose to a considerable extent. This may be explained by the fact that aluminum is the principal input for the aluminum fabricating industry, which competes in foreign markets. In other sectors increases in import penetration were avoided through informal measures. In this connection, two industries, urea and soda ash, in which the United States has a considerable natural advantage, deserve mention.

Despite the large cost advantages of US firms, imported urea provided less than 3 percent of domestic consumption in 1983. According to one explanation, "there is apparently a consensus among Japanese government officials, urea manufacturers, and distributors to keep price-competitive imports out of Japan, and several US firms have received suggestions that they not attempt to export more to Japan" (Rapp 1986, 30).

Imported soda ash supplied only 5 percent of the Japanese market in 1981, with five US exporters each assigned an unofficial quota of 12,000 tons. Following a ruling by the JFTC that imports were unreasonably restrained, US soda ash exports to Japan quadrupled by 1984. In September 1984, however, the US–Japan Trade Study Group noted that "Japanese [soda ash] producers are now reportedly trying to check [the US] import surge by pressuring users and distributors to limit purchases from US suppliers" (1984, 65). By 1985, Japanese producers apparently had succeeded in blocking further increases in soda ash imports from the United States.

Various arrangements are used to limit imports in depressed industries. These measures were summarized as follows:

"Some (including fabricated aluminum, paper, plywood, and lumber) are protected from a large increase in imports by high tariffs. Others such as chemical fertilizers, however, seem import resistant due to various legal arrangements, while apparent industry collusion safeguards soda ash, synthetic rubber, and caustic soda firms. The total Japanese market for such products exceeds $80 billion, yet with the exception of aluminum-ingot and electronic furnace products, import penetration is surprisingly low, usually less than 6 or 7 percent" (Rapp 1986, 23–24).

The Promotion of High-Technology Industries

In 1981 MITI launched the ten-year Next Generation Industries Basic Technologies Project. While the funds made available for this project are relatively limited, MITI plays an important organizing role, selecting a relatively small number of firms to participate in joint research projects. It also plays a major role in the development of research agendas for the projects. Japanese firms are eager to participate in the projects because they expect to derive important benefits. According to the OECD:

"The advantages of such cooperation are evident: every firm can learn from the other's mistakes, and the costs of research are much lower. The emergence of consensus between the major companies about future strategy is also important, and uncertainty is thus reduced. [Furthermore], discriminatory public purchasing policy (for example, the procurement policies of NTT) and administrative guidance about imports also helped firms to reap economies of scale and to move down the learning curve before facing international competition (1985, 75).

Information on market shares provides evidence of import limitations in the case of semiconductors, and the US International Trade Commission established the existence of dumping of 64K DRAM chips. Anti-dumping duties were not imposed, however, under a US–Japanese agreement that committed Japanese firms to sell at "fair market prices" and called for opening the domestic market to US exports of semiconductors. The US government subsequently charged that Japan violated the agreement and it imposed retaliatory tariffs on Japanese electronics products in April 1987. These tariffs were partially removed in November 1987, with full removal conditioned upon improvements in the access of the US semiconductor industry to the Japanese market.

Telecommunications services are also important. In the cases of pocket pagers and cellular telephones, the market share of Motorola, the world leader, is limited in Japan. The Ministry of Post and Telecommunications also tried to limit the role of foreign companies in the provision of international telephone services. Following repeated interventions by Prime Minister Thatcher and President Reagan, however, a satisfactory solution was reached.

Foreign telecommunications firms remain excluded from the domestic common carrier market in Japan. While competition between domestic and foreign firms in enhanced communication services like value-added networks is permitted, entry is subject to approval by the Ministry of Post and Telecommunications.

Regulations Concerning Intellectual Property

The Japanese patent system is the object of considerable criticism. It takes about six years for the Japanese patent office to register patents, compared with two years in the United States. Once patent applications have been filed and published in Japan, applicants are said to be vulnerable to unauthorized copying of their inventions by competing firms.

Registering trademarks is also a slow process, requiring about four years, compared with one year in the United States. Furthermore, while in the United States the rights to a trademark belong to the firm that first used it commercially, in Japan foreign trademarks may be registered by domestic firms to preempt their subsequent introduction by foreign firms that have used them at home or abroad. The protection of trademarks does not extend to service marks, the equivalent of trademarks for service companies. Finally, Japan is the only major industrial country without effective protection of trade secrets. Yet such protection is considered vital to the US information-processing and pharmaceutical industries, in particular.

Distribution Channels

It has been argued that distribution channels in Japan are excessively complicated and discriminate against foreign-made goods. When importers and distributors belong to the same business group, they often favor within-group sales to imports. It also appears that imports are disadvantaged in cases where there is a choice between buying from a domestic group or from abroad. In textiles, for example, representatives of trading companies reportedly stated that they would accept foreign orders only if it did not adversely affect domestic industry. These actions were said to have been taken in response to demands by MITI for limits on imports which could cause market disruption.

The domestic sale of imported goods is also hindered by a 1974 law and by informal administrative directives, renewed in 1984, limiting the establishment of supermarkets and department stores. Furthermore, the so-called Fair Competition Codes of the JFTC limit the opportunities for foreign firms to introduce new marketing techniques to Japan. Finally, a government survey has found that distribution margins for a variety of imports are more than twice as high as for competing domestic products.

Japan's International Trade Position

Import Penetration in Manufacturing

How have Japan's protective measures affected its place in international trade? In attempting to answer this question, we use data on import-penetration ratios for manufactured goods, defined as the ratio of imports to apparent consumption (production plus imports, less exports). These ratios were estimated by the OECD, applying the International Standard Industrial Classification, which includes processed foods, beverages, tobacco products, petroleum products, and nonferrous metals among manufactured goods (Brodin and Blades 1986). The results are reported in table 3.2 for the years 1975 and 1985, in order to abstract from the impact of the quadrupling of petroleum prices in 1973 on imports of manufactured goods. The estimates have been updated to 1986 utilizing data for the gross national product in place of data for the consumption of manufactured goods, which are not available. Manufactured imports have been defined according to the UN Standard International Trade classification (with the exclusion of non-ferrous metals).

The estimates show contrasting trends in import-penetration ratios in Japan and the other major industrial countries. Between 1975 and 1986, the average import-penetration ratio for manufactured goods from all countries rose from 7.0 to 13.8 percent in the United States, from 17.9 to 26.7 percent in France, from 24.3 to 37.2 percent in Germany, from 21.9 to 28.8 percent in Italy, and from 22.0 to 31.2 percent in the United Kingdom.

Table 3.2 Import penetration ratios in manufacturing, 1975, 1985, and 1986
(Imports as a percentage of apparent consumption)[a]

	United States	France	Germany	Italy	United Kingdom	Japan
World						
1975	7.0	17.9	24.3	21.9	22.0	4.9
1985	12.9	27.6	39.5	31.2	31.4	5.4
1986	13.8	26.7	37.2	28.8	31.2	4.4
OECD						
1975	4.9	15.9	20.5	18.7	17.6	2.9
1985	8.8	23.4	32.5	24.7	26.2	3.2
1986	9.3	22.6	30.6	23.1	26.1	2.6
Developing Countries						
1975	2.1	1.5	2.6	2.2	3.0	1.8
1985	3.9	2.9	4.5	4.9	3.3	2.0
1986	4.2	2.8	4.4	4.0	3.3	1.8
Japan						
1975	1.2	0.5	0.8	0.4	0.9	—
1985	3.1	1.0	2.3	0.7	1.8	—
1986	3.5	1.1	2.5	0.7	2.0	—

Sources: Brodin and Blades (1986), and special communication.
a. Apparent consumption equals domestic production plus imports, minus exports. Because of the lack of information for the 1985–86 period, data on changes in the gross domestic product were used instead of manufacturing production data.

The ratio declined from 4.9 to 4.4 percent in Japan during this period. For the same years, the ratios for imports from the OECD countries were 4.9 and 9.3 percent for the United States, 15.9 and 22.6 percent for France, 20.5 and 30.6 percent for Germany, 18.7 and 23.1 percent for Italy, and 17.6 and 26.1 percent for the United Kingdom, compared with 2.9 and 2.6 percent for Japan.

The data in table 3.2 also show declines in Japan's import-penetration ratios from 1985 to 1986. This may appear surprising, given the considerable attention paid to rapid increases in Japanese imports of manufactured goods during that period. According to official Japanese statistics, these imports grew by 24.8 percent between 1985 and 1986 in dollar terms, but decreased by 11.8 percent in terms of yen, owing to its appreciation from 238.5 to 168.5 yen per dollar. With the nominal value of Japanese GDP rising by 4.3 percent during this period, the import-penetration ratio for imports from all sources fell from 5.4 to 4.4. This decline was only partly offset in 1987, when the 24.8 percent rise in imports in dollar terms corresponded to a 7.1 percent increase in terms of yen, and the average exchange rate was 144.6 yen per dollar. With a 3.2 percent rise in the nominal value of GDP, the import-penetration ratio was 4.6 in Japan in 1987.[17]

The higher import-penetration ratios in European countries are partly explained by their participation in integration schemes. This does not explain the rise in their ratios, however, since tariffs on intra-European trade in manufactured goods were eliminated long before 1975. In addition, Japanese import penetration in Western Europe increased much more rapidly than did the ratios of import penetration among European countries themselves. This increased Japanese import penetration in the major European countries was not accompanied by increased European import penetration in Japan.

Also during the 1975–1986 period, the share of developing countries in the consumption of manufactured goods remained at 1.8 percent in Japan, while it rose to a considerable extent in the other major industrial countries. The relevant ratios, for 1975 and 1986, were 2.1 and 4.2 percent for the United States, 1.5 and 2.8 percent for France, 2.6 and 4.4 percent in Germany, 2.2 and 4.0 percent in Italy, and 3.0 and 3.3 percent in the United Kingdom. However, rapid increases in imports from the NICs were only partly offset by the further appreciation of the yen in 1987.

It has been suggested that Japan's limited endowment of natural resources tends to lower its import-penetration ratios in manufacturing by requiring it to import large quantities of natural resource products. This argument does not hold for changes in import-penetration ratios over time, however. As for its overall relevance, readers are referred to the discussion below of the openness of national economies.

Intraindustry Specialization

A related question concerns the level of intraindustry specialization in Japan, as compared with the other major industrial countries. This question has been examined by Scott, who compared national patterns of exports and imports in individual product categories for the year 1985 (1987). Figures 3.1–3.4 reproduce his Exhibits 23, 24, 25 and 26 for France, Germany, the United States, and Japan.

France, Germany, and the United States exhibit a high degree of intraindustry specialization. Import points are located at small distances to the left

---

17. Export shares declined more rapidly than import shares in 1986–87, causing foreign trade to make a negative contribution to economic growth.

Figure 3.1 Manufactured exports and imports as a percentage of total exports, 1985: France

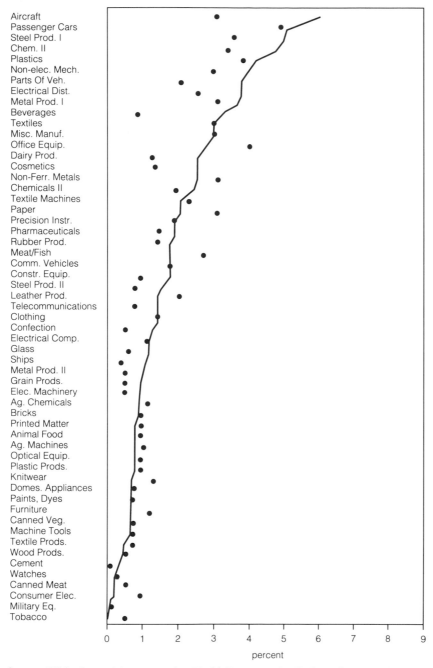

Source: "U.S. Competitiveness in the World Economy: An Update" by Bruce Scott, a paper presented at the Workshop on Competitiveness, Harvard Business School, July 12–18, 1987. Copyright © 1987 by the President and Fellows of Harvard College. Reprinted by permission of the Harvard Business School.
Note: imports = ●; exports = ———— .

Figure 3.2 Manufactured exports and imports as a percentage of total exports, 1985: Germany

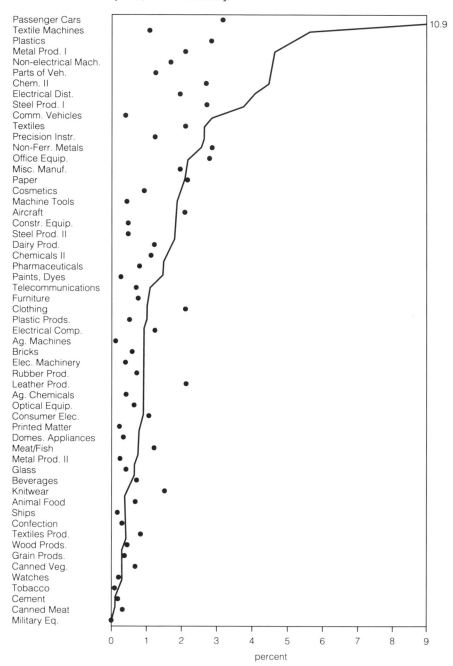

Source: "U.S. Competitiveness in the World Economy: An Update" by Bruce Scott, a paper presented at the Workshop on Competitiveness, Harvard Business School, July 12–18, 1987. Copyright © 1987 by the President and Fellows of Harvard College. Reprinted by permission of the Harvard Business School.
Note: imports = ●; exports = ——— .

Figure 3.3 Manufactured exports and imports as a percentage of total exports, 1985: United States

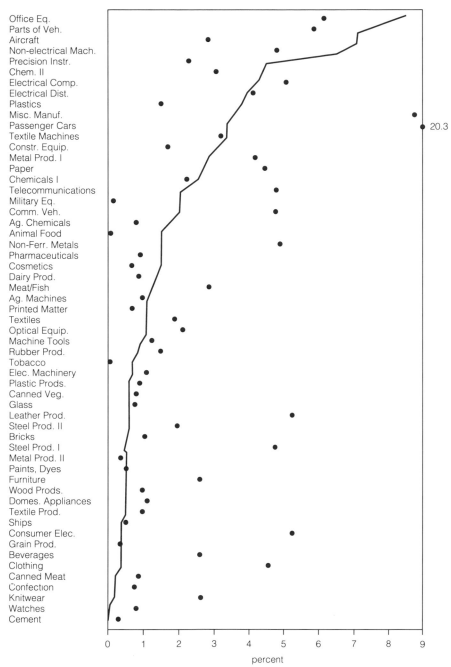

percent

Source: "U.S. Competitiveness in the World Economy: An Update" by Bruce Scott, a paper presented at the Workshop on Competitiveness, Harvard Business School, July 12–18, 1987. Copyright © 1987 by the President and Fellows of Harvard College. Reprinted by permission of the Harvard Business School.
Note: imports = ●; exports = ——— .

Figure 3.4 Manufactured exports and imports as a percentage of total exports, 1985: Japan

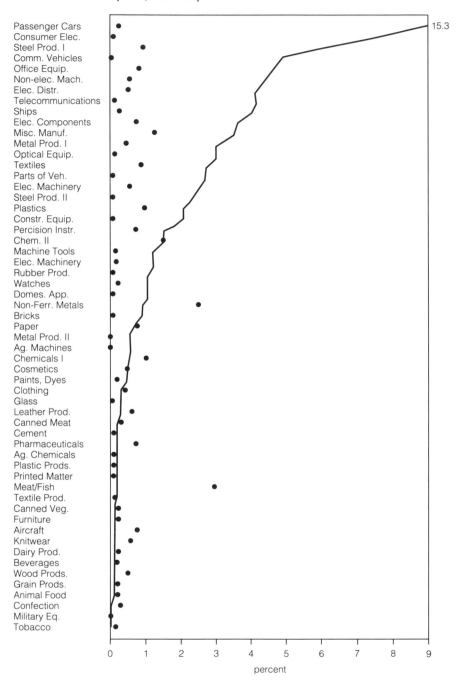

Source: "U.S. Competitiveness in the World Economy: An Update" by Bruce Scott, a paper presented at the Workshop on Competitiveness, Harvard Business School, July 12–18, 1987. Copyright © 1987 by the President and Fellows of Harvard College. Reprinted by permission of the Harvard Business School.
Note: imports = ●; exports = ———.

and the right of the export points in France, and even in Germany, which has a considerable manufacturing trade surplus. The distances are larger, but the overall pattern is similar in the United States. By contrast, in Japan there is no evidence of intraindustry specialization in a large number of industries. In the three cases in which a substantial import surplus exists (petroleum derivatives, meat and fish, and nonferrous metals), Japan has limited natural resources.

It would appear, then, that the extent of intraindustry specialization is much smaller in Japan than in other major industrial countries. Recent estimates indicate that the extent of intraindustry trade in Japan is one-third to four-tenths that of the other major industrial countries (Lawrence 1987, table 2). While Bergsten and Cline (1987, 83) reached different results, they failed to consider the fact that the estimates they cite (Balassa 1986a) were adjusted for the degree of openness of national economies, a subject to which we now turn.

The Relative Openness of the Major Industrial Economies

Appendix C describes the methodology and presents the results of Balassa's empirical investigation into the relative openness of the national economies of the major industrial countries, and compares these with the results obtained by other researchers.[18] The estimates pertain to the 1973–83 period and are derived from data for each of the countries for each year of the period.[19] The model attempts to explain international differences in the ratio of imports to the gross domestic product in terms of several national economic attributes, including the level of economic development (measured by per capita income), the size of the domestic market (measured by population size), the availability of natural resources (measured, alternatively, by the share of primary commodities in total imports and by the domestic availability of natural resources), and transportation costs (based on comparisons of the c.i.f. and f.o.b. values of a country's imports). In addition, dummy variables have been introduced for participation in the European Community and the European Free Trade Association and for each of the industrial countries.

---

18. Earlier results were presented in Balassa 1986c.

19. The inclusion of developing countries as importers would not have been appropriate. For one thing, the lower level of economic development of these countries might affect their participation in the international division of labor beyond the impact of measurable variables, such as per capita income. For another thing, protection levels in the developing countries are much higher than in the industrial countries. In view of its level of economic development, Japan should be compared with the industrial rather than the developing countries.

Limiting attention to the latter, the results show Japan alone to be an "outlier" in the negative direction: It imports considerably less than would be expected given its attributes. The disparities range from 25 to 45 percent of the imports of all commodities from all sources of supply.[20] In contrast, Saxonhouse (1984; 1986) and Bergsten and Cline (1987) have not found Japan to be an outlier. Similarly, Noland (1987a) found Japanese imports to be only 4 percent less than would be expected.[21] Lawrence's more recent analysis, however, shows Japan to be an outlier: ". . . in 1980 . . . as the equations in this study indicate, unusual barriers and preferences reduced Japanese manufactured goods imports about 40 percent" (1987, 546). Comparable results have been reached for 1970 and 1983.[22]

An indirect indication of the effects of Japanese protection is provided by a study of the impact of US and Japanese protection on productive factors (Staiger, Deardorff, and Stern 1987). This study shows a much larger distortionary impact on domestic factor markets in Japan than in the United States. The differential impact on the biggest relative gainer and loser among factors of production was 14.5 percentage points in Japan and 0.9 percentage points in the United States.[23] Furthermore, while the differential impact of Japanese protection on US productive factors was found to be 1.9 percentage points, the impact of US protection on Japanese factors was only 0.3 percentage points. The authors concluded that "Japanese commercial policy introduces a greater degree of distortion into American factor markets than does American commercial policy itself" (1987, 10).

As Leamer (1987) suggested, it would be desirable to try to calculate the effects of observed barriers on imports. This has been done in the case of agriculture, for which estimates are available in the Anderson and Tyers study cited earlier in the chapter. According to that study, the combined imports of rice, wheat, coarse grains, beef and lamb, pork and chicken,

---

20. Calculations have also been done for primary imports and for manufactured imports, as well as for imports from the industrial countries and from developing countries.

21. The results of a study by Leamer are not comparable to those reported here. Leamer suggests that "in the absence of direct measures of barriers it will be impossible to determine the degree of openness for most countries with much subjective confidence" (1987, 41).

22. Saxonhouse and Stern (1988) reestimated Lawrence's equation using a different specification and did not find Japan to be an outlier. Their results are vitiated, however, by the fact that they expanded the 13 industrial country sample to a sample of 55 countries dominated by developing countries with very different economic structures and high protection.

23. Gainers and losers are defined in terms of net factor exports (exports minus imports), expressed as a percentage of the factor endowment.

dairy products, and sugar into Japan from its five major suppliers (the United States, Australia, Canada, New Zealand and Thailand) would rise by $6.5 billion, in terms of 1985 prices, in the event of the elimination of trade barriers. The largest increases, $4.6 billion, would occur in imports from the United States (Anderson and Tyers 1987, table V).

These estimates may be compared to the 1986 Japanese imports of $3.8 billion of these agricultural staples from the five countries above; $2.2 billion of this originated in the United States. Total Japanese imports of these products in 1986 were $5.7 billion. The estimates understate prospective increases in imports, however, since the appreciation of the yen has greatly increased the protective impact of agricultural quotas. Eliminating trade barriers would also increase imports of fish, fruits and vegetables, beverages, and tobacco, which have import volumes slightly exceeding those of the main agricultural staples in Japan.

From available information it further appears that there would be considerable increases in the importation of products of the so-called depressed industries—including petrochemicals, fertilizers, chemical fibers, textiles, steel, and ships—if informal barriers were removed. For example, aluminum imports rose from 37 percent of domestic production in 1979 to 83 percent in 1982, following the application of liberalization measures.

There are also possibilities for increasing imports of high-technology products. Although estimates for these products have not been made, we can indicate the implications for the level of total manufactured imports of prospective increases in import-penetration ratios. As noted above, the 1986 import-penetration ratio in Japan was 4.4 percent. The corresponding import value for the same year was $40.4 billion.[24] It follows that each one percentage point increase in Japan's import-penetration ratio would add nearly $10 billion to its manufactured imports.

The results cited above indicate the potential for considerable increases in Japanese imports following a liberalization of trade. The ultimate impact of trade liberalization on the trade balance will depend on saving and investment behavior. A variety of outcomes are possible, depending on the propensities to save and invest in various affected sectors (Corden 1987). In the case of Japan, saving might be expected to decline as increased foreign competition reduced rents, profits, and bonus wages in the deprotected industries. Investment would also fall in these mainly labor-intensive industries, but this would be offset by additional investment, stimulated by the exchange rate depreciation, in other traded-goods industries.

---

24. As noted earlier, manufactured imports have been defined according to the UN Standard International Trade Classification, with the exclusion of nonferrous metals.

Conclusion

This chapter has reviewed Japanese policies that appear to have limited imports, thereby contributing to Japan's status as an "outlier" among industrial countries as far as participation in international trade is concerned. It has not covered factors, whose contribution to the import shortfall is more difficult to gauge, such as differences in national attitudes.

These findings lead us to the question of the measures Japan could take to open its economy. An appropriate point of departure is the first of the two Maekawa Reports, published in April 1986. With regard to agriculture, the report suggests that, "with the exception of basic farm products, efforts should be made toward a steady increase in imports of products (including agricultural processed products) whose domestic prices and the international market differ markedly. These price differences should be reduced, while agriculture should be rationalized and made more efficient" (*Report of the Advisory Group on Economic Structural Adjustment* 1986, 9). This is an admirable statement, but it should be applied to basic farm products as well, for this would reverse the tendency of the last 25 years for Japanese agricultural prices increasingly to exceed not only world market prices, but also those of the European Community, whose protectionist agricultural policies have long been criticized.

It has been claimed that reducing agricultural protection would be politically suicidal for the ruling Liberal Democratic Party (LDP). The share of farmers among LDP voters has declined to a considerable extent in recent years, however, while the protection of agriculture has substantially increased. Whereas farmers comprised 43 percent of all LDP voters in 1960, their proportion declined below 18 percent in 1980, when 45 percent of the LDP vote originated in urban and metropolitan constituencies. Further shifts have occurred since then.[25] These trends suggest that the long-term interests of the LDP lie increasingly with urban consumers, who are disadvantaged by the protection of agriculture. This conclusion is strengthened if we consider that off-farm earnings have come to represent an increasing proportion of farm household income, rising from 56 percent in 1965 to 85 percent in 1985 (Fitchett 1988, table 5).[26] In fact, six-sevenths of farm

---

25. Nevertheless, rural voters continue to dominate in a number of electoral districts, including those that elected several LDP leaders.

26. In this connection, note that manufactured exports provide an increasing part of the livelihood of farmer families. It has been reported that

Kyushu, home of much of Japan's beef and orange production, is now known as Silicon Island and produces 40 percent of Japan's integrated circuits in semi-rural surroundings. The rural Tohoku region in the northeast produces another 20 percent. Nagano Prefecture, long one of Japan's major fruit-growing areas, is now one

households are part-time farmers who have been the main beneficiaries of the protection of agriculture (in particular, of rice).[27] The livelihood of full-time farmers could be assured at a lower cost to the Japanese economy, and to other countries, with income-maintenance schemes rather than through high protection.

Food security also should not be confused with self-sufficiency. The estimates reported earlier indicate that Japanese agriculture would survive even under free trade, with varying decreases in output. It is estimated that domestic production would decline by one-fifth in the case of rice, one-fourth for pork and poultry, three-tenths for wheat and coarse grains, and four-tenths for sugar. Even in Japan's high-cost livestock industry, production would continue at one-half of its present level (Anderson and Tyers 1987). Two American economists, writing about adjustment in Japanese agriculture, have suggested that "if Japan justifies its access to the US auto market by arguing that 'structural adjustments' are necessary for American workers to compete with Japanese industrial products, then the same argument holds in reverse for Japanese farmers and American agricultural products" (Timmer and Reich 1983, 19). We would add that, apart from automobiles, adjustment has occurred also in US agriculture. This adjustment has been described in a recent study which contrasts it with the lack of adjustment in Japanese agriculture, where prices have maintained high levels:

The price of agricultural land in the United States rose sharply in the 1970s, not because of governmental intervention in price policy, but because of the boom prices generated during the 'world food crisis' of 1972 to 1974. Those prices were capitalized into land values, as in Japan. The higher land values, reflected in the financial carrying costs of mortgages incurred as farmers expanded their operations, significantly raised the costs of production, especially when interest rates were de-regulated.

Unlike Japanese farmers, however, most American farmers do not have the strong guarantee of a high and stable output price. As real interest rates rose sharply as the exchange rate of the dollar rose, and as world market prices declined, American farmers faced in the mid-1980s their lowest relative real incomes since the Great Depression, plus a very significant erosion of their assets (Reich, Endo, and Timmer 1986, 172).[28]

---

of the largest manufacturers of video tape recorder components in Japan (Calder 1982, 91).

27. Rice supplies 53 percent of the agricultural income of part-time farmers that rely mainly on non-farm income, compared with 17 percent for full-time farmers (Fitchett 1988, 8).

28. It should be added that US farmland prices declined by one-third between 1981 and 1987 (*Economist,* 26 September 1987).

The statements in the first Maekawa Report concerning policies to encourage imports of manufactured goods also deserve full quotation:

Further active efforts should be made to encourage imports of manufactured goods, together with steady implementation of various structural measures, including overseas investment which will contribute to the international division of labor, such as local production and expanded imports of semi-finished and finished products. Together with promoting the streamlining of distribution mechanisms and conducting review of the various restrictions pertaining to distribution and sales, efforts should also be made to ensure the strict enforcement of the Antimonopoly Law for the prevention of unfair business transactions and to strengthen domestic arrangements to eliminate illegal acts with regard to foreign trade marks and counterfeit products (*Report of the Advisory Group on Economic Structural Adjustment* 1986, 10).

Notwithstanding the references at the end of this excerpt, the report provides few specifics but rather is couched in general terms.[29] Furthermore, the guidelines subsequently issued by the government emphasized domestic measures and omitted several major recommendations concerning trade policies in the Maekawa Report. Among those omitted were proposals for increasing agricultural imports, reducing differences between domestic and international prices for agricultural products, reviewing restrictions on distribution and sales, and strengthening domestic arrangements to eliminate illegal uses of foreign trademarks and counterfeit products (Government of Japan 1986).

The second Maekawa Report, published in May 1987, concentrated on domestic measures and offered only the following, rather general, recommendations for import liberalization:

3.4   Stepped-up Imports of Manufactured Goods;
3.4.1. Promoting the abolition of tariffs on manufactured products in the
       GATT Uruguay Round;
3.4.2. Improving the government procurement system and promoting
       governmental imports of manufactured goods;

3.5   Agriculture;
3.5.1. Raising productivity and promoting appropriate import policies
       aiming at reducing the differential between Japanese and overseas
       foodstuff prices (*Policy Recommendations of the Economic Council*
       1987, 24).

There remains a need for specific market measures, since past agreements on market-opening have had only limited effects and the same issues have

---

29. According to an informed observer, "this is a document any bureaucrat would be proud to authorize (the goals listed are clearly desirable in principle, and thus cannot be faulted, and the means to implement these goals are described in general terms to offend the fewest people possible)" (Yamamura 1987, 36).

been raised repeatedly over the years.[30] Nobumitsu Kasami, one of the directors of Nomura Securities, is reported to have said that, "notwithstanding all its promises, the Japanese government . . . has really done nothing to open markets."[31] In a recent book, *Beyond National Borders,* Kenichi Ohmae, head of the Tokyo Office of McKinsey & Co., speaks of a national hypocrisy in Japan with respect to import liberalization: "We open our markets slowly, but smugly preach free trade to the rest of the world."[32]

The member countries of the Association of Southeast Asian Nations (ASEAN), in particular, have complained about Japanese protection. It has been suggested that "the low import penetration of ASEAN manufactured products in the Japanese market reflects how closed the Japanese market is—a complaint expressed by ASEAN countries" (Sanchez 1987, 4). The author adds that "Japan has taken measures to open its doors to foreign products but the impact of these moves on ASEAN–Japan trade expansion has not been satisfactory. The test of Japan's sincerity to improve trade relations with ASEAN countries rests, in part, on the elimination of those non-tariff barriers affecting exports from ASEAN" (1987, 7). It was also reported that at the Fifth ASEAN Roundtable Conference, "ASEAN representatives had underscored several times over their accusation that Japan is still a closed market despite Tokyo's pledge to open up the country to more foreign manufactured products."[33] Finally, ASEAN leaders pressed Prime Minister Takeshita to liberalize imports during the 1987 Manila summit.[34]

Japanese imports of manufacturing goods from developing countries did rise to a considerable extent in 1986 and 1987 in terms of US dollars. The increases extended from inputs to consumer goods and originated largely

---

30. In retrospect, it is interesting to read Saxonhouse's statement on the Japanese market-opening measures proposed several years ago. He expressed the view that "if Japanese commitments to fully and fairly implement these steps, backed by an explicit statement by Prime Minister Suzuki, can be taken at face value, then a substantial part of the objectives of more than ten years of strenuous criticism of the character of the application of Japanese standards, health and safety legislation and even of Japanese government procurement will have been achieved" (1983a, 263).

31. *Le Monde,* 1 April 1987. Furthermore, US observers have suggested that "accumulating case studies document the disparity between agreements made by the Japanese government to open markets and the impediments that remain and prevent access to those markets" (Timmer and Reich 1983, 20), and that "despite all the threats of trade sanctions in the West, there is still mostly talk of opening Japan to foreign imports" (Drucker 1987, 935). Another observer refers to "a gap between Japanese promises and implementation," suggesting that "the bilateral negotiating process allowed the Japanese to pursue an essentially mercantilist self-centered trade strategy at minimal costs" (Cohen 1985, 116, 120).

32. Cited in the *Washington Post,* 1 July 1987.

33. *Journal of Commerce,* 4 November 1987.

34. *Washington Post,* 16 December 1987.

in the East Asian NICs. Import-penetration ratios remain relatively low, however.

It must be emphasized that opening its economy would be in Japan's own interest. While it has been argued that opening the economy could lead to short-term losses,[35] in the medium to long run economic growth is bound to accelerate as economic resources are allocated more efficiently. This will require the drawing of resources and, in particular, new investment funds away from both agriculture, which is highly inefficient in Japan, and from labor-intensive branches of industry, where developing countries would be the main beneficiaries.[36] Even the short-run effects appear likely to be favorable when one takes account of the interdependence of exchange rates and import protection. Thus, as suggested in Chapter 1, failure to liberalize imports would lead to a further appreciation of the yen, with unfavorable effects for Japan's efficient industries.

Finally, steps toward trade liberalization would ease protectionist pressures in other countries against Japanese exports. This is especially the case since Japan's large export surplus invites protectionist reactions. At the same time, Japan's increasing weight in the world economy bestows upon it a responsibility for strengthening the trade system. Japan should play an important role in the Uruguay Round of multilateral trade negotiations.

In the framework of the Uruguay Round, trade liberalization measures would be taken by all participants. But if Japan were to liberalize its own trade, protection against its goods would be reduced at an early date. Some foreign protective measures have been taken in retaliation for Japanese protection, others have been in response to the Japanese current account surplus, and again others are long-standing barriers (for example, Italy's limits on car imports from Japan to 1 percent of domestic sales). Japan would thus derive further benefits from trade liberalization through resource allocation according to comparative advantage.

---

35. Atsushi Miyauchi of the Institute for Monetary and Economic Studies of the Bank of Japan suggested that Japanese economic growth would fall because of the damage to import-competing industries caused by the opening of the economy. On the controversy concerning the possible effects of market-opening measures in Japan, see the *Wall Street Journal,* 2 August and 22 August 1986.

36. In fact, the relative inefficiency of Japanese agriculture has increased over time. The ratio of labor productivity in agriculture to average GDP per worker in Japan fell from 23 percent in 1955 to 18 percent in 1980, while increasing from 52 to 129 percent in the United States and from 37–42 to 56–84 percent in the three largest EC nations (France, Germany, and the United Kingdom). Another index of comparative advantage, the ratio of average agricultural land area per farm worker to average GDP per capita (the so-called factor ratio) declined from 3.0 to 1.4 in Japan during the same period, while increasing from 6.9 to 11.0 in the United States and remaining in the 11–25 range in the three EC countries (Honma and Hayami 1986, table 2). Note finally that the cost of agricultural protection has been estimated at 1 percent of GNP in Japan (Anderson and Tyers 1987, 139).

4

Saving Behavior

An outstanding feature of the postwar Japanese economy has been the high rate of national saving. As shown in table 1.3, Japan has maintained a saving rate of more than 30 percent of GDP every year since 1973, while none of the other major industrial countries achieved that rate in any single year during the period. This high rate of saving has contributed to (and may in part have been a response to) high rates of economic growth, thereby facilitating the process of structural change outlined in Chapter 2.

At the same time, the decline in the rate of Japanese investment after the second oil shock, and the reduction in Japanese government budget deficits, has led to large outflows of domestic savings, contributing to current account surpluses of 4.4 percent of GDP in 1986, and 3.6 percent of GDP in 1987. The result has been that while Japan has upgraded its *pattern* of export specialization and Japanese firms have become increasingly important in high value-added and high-technology products, macroeconomic forces have pushed the *aggregate* trade surplus higher, exacerbating trade frictions with other industrial countries.

In this chapter we examine Japanese saving behavior in an attempt to understand why Japan's saving rate is so high. In the following chapter we analyze why the rate of investment has fallen in Japan, and in Chapter 6 we investigate the interactions between domestic and international macroeconomic forces and their implications for Japan and the world economy.

Japanese Saving in Comparative Perspective

Three issues must be addressed in any comparative analysis of saving behavior. First, saving must be defined. The simplest definition, in theoretical terms, is deferred consumption. This definition encompasses purchases of both real and financial assets and implies that the correct way to value these assets is in terms of their future consumption equivalent. That is, the value of current saving is the present discounted value of future consumption.

While this general definition of saving offers a useful starting point, other definitions of saving and different means of valuation will be appropriate for different analytical purposes. For example, the *ex post* national accounts definition of gross saving at current prices is the relevant definition when examining the savings–investment balance and trade balance from a national accounting standpoint. For longer-run questions of growth, a net saving definition, which recognizes the existence of a depreciable stock of assets, or a vintage capital model, which incorporates technological change, would be the most appropriate choice. Finally, since the present discounted value of the current stock of assets will affect the choice between present and future consumption, the revaluation of assets accumulated in the past to reflect current prices would be relevant in analyzing agents' prospective asset accumulation decisions. The most appropriate definition of saving thus depends on the specific issue under consideration. Consequently, a variety of definitions will be considered below.

The second issue is the appropriate level of aggregation. For many macroeconomic issues the national rate of saving is relevant. Much of the research into the determinants of saving has focused on behavior at the household level, however. While this is a defensible strategy, since the household sector typically accounts for much of the savings accumulated in an economy, it is not an entirely adequate approach. In the case of Japan, this approach may be particularly misleading, because there are good reasons to believe that there are interactions between household saving and saving in other sectors of the economy. In a practical sense, movements in the household saving rate and the national saving rate have exhibited divergent tendencies.

Finally, there are significant differences among national accounts systems. For example, the US national income and product accounts (NIPA) system correctly measures depreciation at replacement costs, but treats all government expenditure as consumption and thus understates true saving by ignoring tangible assets accumulated by the government. The Japanese system of accounts includes government capital but measures depreciation according to historical, rather than replacement, costs. Obviously a consistent set of accounting practices must be adopted to insure meaningful international comparisons.

The strategy adopted here is to start with a set of gross national saving estimates derived from a consistent set of accounting practices. These estimates are then amended to reflect some theoretically justifiable reclassifications of expenditure. Depreciation is considered next, and net saving rates are reported. Finally, we take up the issue of the proper valuation of accumulated assets, and a set of saving rates reflecting the revaluation of accumulated assets is presented.

The starting point is the set of gross national saving rates for the United States, Japan, Germany, France, and the United Kingdom reported on the first line of table 4.1. These figures are calculated according to the System of National Accounts (SNA) used by the United Nations and the OECD. The major difference between the SNA figures and those derived from the US national accounting system is that the SNA treats government accumulation of tangible assets as saving and the US system does not. As a result, during the 1970–1980 period US saving rates averaged about two percentage points higher under the international accounting system than under the US national accounts system (Blades and Sturm 1982, 2–6). Even with this adjustment, however, the United States has the lowest saving rate reported (18.6 percent), 5.8 percentage points below the mean of 24.4. Japan, with a saving rate of 35.0 percent, has the highest figure, 10.6 percent above the mean.

The SNA definition of saving can be criticized for failing to classify all expenditures in the most appropriate way. Among the needed adjustments, the most important quantitatively is the reclassification of expenditures on

Table 4.1   National gross saving rates, 1970–1980
(annual average percentages)

	US	Japan	Germany	France	UK
SNA basis	18.6	35.0	25.1	24.1	19.0
Including expenditure on consumer durables	24.3	37.0	n.a.	28.9	23.4
Including private expenditure on research and development	19.5	36.1	25.9	24.6	19.3
Adjustment for direct & indirect taxes	19.6	36.7	27.7	27.6	20.9
Combined adjustments including adjustment for direct and indirect taxes	26.1	38.9	n.a.	33.5	25.1

Source: Blades (1983, Tables 11–14).
Note: Saving rates are expressed as a percentage of gross national disposable income. The total adjustment is not the sum of the individual adjustments, because two of the adjustments are to saving (the numerator of the ratio), while the other affects income (the denominator).

consumer durables from consumption to saving, since these expenditures represent households' investment in real assets. This has been done by Blades (1983), whose results for the 1970–1980 period appear on the second line of table 4.1. The adjustments narrow the dispersion of national saving rates, with the US saving rate increasing by nearly six percentage points, while the Japanese rate increases by only two. According to this measure, the United Kingdom has the lowest national saving rate, 23.4 percent.

Blades makes some further adjustments. He reclassifies private research and development expenditures as investment (hence saving) and he standardizes the denominator (gross national disposable income) for international differences in the relative importance of direct and indirect taxes.[1] The effects of these adjustments are relatively minor, as shown by lines 3 and 4 of table 4.1.

These three adjustments—the reclassifications of expenditures on consumer durables and privately funded research and development, and the standardization of taxes—are combined in the last line of table 4.1. The overall effect is to compress the dispersion of saving rates, as the lowest savers (the United States and the United Kingdom) register the largest increases (7.5 and 6.1 percentage points, respectively) and the highest saver, Japan, showed the smallest gain (3.9 percentage points). Nonetheless, Japan's saving rate (38.9 percent) is still about 50 percent higher than that of the United Kingdom (25.1 percent) or the United States (26.1 percent).

While gross saving is important insofar as technological change is embodied in the capital stock, net saving is also of considerable interest because it represents net additions to the capital stock, and hence changes in the capital–labor ratio. The major issue here is how to measure depreciation properly. Depreciation is calculated using either historical or replacement costs. During periods of prolonged inflation the use of historical costs will result in a considerable underestimate of depreciation and a commensurate overestimate of net saving. In the case of Japan, Hayashi (1986, 162) found that the use of historical costs led to a greater than six percentage point overestimate of the rate of net national saving in 1984.

As in the case of gross national saving rates, when net national saving rates are adjusted to include the reclassification of expenditures on consumer durables and government assets as saving, and depreciation is calculated at replacement costs, the saving gap between Japan and the United States narrows.[2] Two studies found that these adjustments raise the net US saving rate between two and four percentage points, to about 7.0 percent, while

---

1. Blades defines the denominator, gross national disposable income, as the sum of savings and consumption expenditures, which includes indirect, but not direct, taxes.

2. Comparable figures for other countries are not available.

Japan's rate is lowered by two to seven points, to about 15.4 percent (Hamada and Iwata 1985, 14; Hayashi 1986, 201–210). While accounting adjustments thus reduce the saving gap, a large difference remains, with Japanese rates of net national saving around twice as high on the average as those for the United States.

Finally, it is useful to examine saving data with accumulated assets revalued to reflect current prices. This would then represent current wealth, which could be relevant for future saving plans. This revaluation could be quite important in periods of prolonged inflation such as the 1970s. It is especially important for Japan, where a substantial share of total assets consist of land holdings on which large capital gains were made. Hayashi's revaluation of US and Japanese data for the 1970–1984 period is reported in figure 4.1. While the adjustment again reduces the differential between Japanese and US rates, it gives rise to considerable variation over time, and the Japanese rates remain quite high, averaging 31 percent, or more than two and one-half times the US average (12 percent), for the period.[3]

The conclusion is inescapable. Under a variety of definitions and criteria, applying a common set of accounting conventions, Japan has consistently exhibited a substantially higher rate of saving than the United States and other industrial countries.

These high rates of Japanese saving are a relatively recent phenomenon, however. As shown in table 4.2, prewar Japanese gross saving rates were unremarkable. In fact, they were consistently lower than US rates (see Kuznets 1952). In only one five-year period (1915–1919) did the Japanese net national saving rate exceed 10 percent, and at no other time before the Second World War did personal saving reach that level. Postwar gross saving rates of more than 20 percent are unprecedented in Japan, and, as shown in table 4.2, the ratio of postwar to prewar saving is higher for Japan than any of the other nine countries in the sample.

Certainly much postwar saving was motivated by a desire to rebuild the capital stock destroyed in the war. High rates of saving continued long after the prewar capital stock had been rebuilt, however. At the same time, these high rates of saving have been confined to the household sector, and have been declining since the mid–1970s, as table 4.3 shows. In contrast to the household sector, saving in the corporate and government sectors since 1974 has been effectively nonexistent. Consequently, the rate of net national saving has declined since 1973, falling to less than half its earlier level.

A final issue is the secular decline in the rate of saving. The saving rates of the household, corporate, and government sectors have all declined from

---

3. The volatility in the revalued Japanese data is largely due to huge capital gains and losses on land (Hayashi 1986, 160).

Figure 4.1 Ratio of net saving to NNP, unadjusted and revalued:
Japan and the United States, 1970–1984

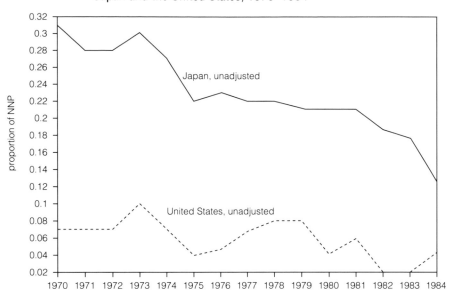

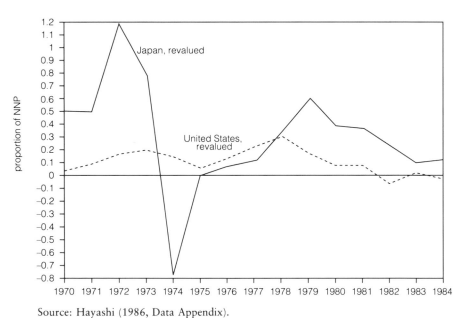

Source: Hayashi (1986, Data Appendix).

Table 4.2   Historical gross saving rates, ten countries

		Percentage of GNP			Ratio to pre-WWII	
		Pre-WWII	1950–59	1960–84	1950–59	1960–84
United States	18.7	(1869–1938)	18.4	18.0	0.99	0.96
Australia	12.4	(1861–1938)	26.2	22.7	2.12	1.84
Canada	14.0	(1870–1930)	22.4	21.2	1.61	1.52
Japan	11.7	(1887–1936)	30.2	32.5	2.59	2.79
Denmark	10.1	(1870–1930)	18.9	19.6	1.87	1.94
Germany	20.0	(1851–1928)	26.8	23.7	1.34	1.19
Italy	12.0	(1861–1930)	19.8	21.0	1.65	1.75
Norway	11.5	(1865–1934)	27.5	27.1	2.40	2.36
Sweden	12.2	(1861–1940)	21.4	21.4	1.75	1.75
United Kingdom	12.3	(1860–1929)	16.2	18.1	1.32	1.47

Sources: Lipsey and Kravis (1987, Table 1); Kuznets (1966, Table 5.3); OECD, *Historical Statistics,* 1960–84.
Note: Average of the figures for the periods weighted by lengths of periods.

their peaks in the early 1970s (table 4.3). In all of these sectors, saving declines can be partly attributed to the slowdown in growth since that time. In the case of the government sector, the fall in the saving rate was mainly a product of the large fiscal deficits following the first oil shock. As a result of slow growth in revenues, the deficits persisted and governmental saving remained depressed. In the corporate sector, the reduction in high profits associated with appropriating existing technologies from abroad was aggravated by the slowdown in aggregate demand. (This issue is discussed in detail in the following chapter.)

In the household sector the fall in the rate of saving is related to changing demographics and the slowdown in economic growth. Demographic changes have increased the proportion of low-saving older people in the population. The fall in the rate of growth has affected saving behavior through several channels. Lower growth has contributed to a reduction in unanticipated household income and a slowing of the rate of income-elastic housing-related saving. Disposable income grew even more slowly than GNP, as increases in income and social security taxes absorbed increases in pretax incomes.

Table 4.3 Japanese sectoral saving rates, 1970–1984
(ratio of adjusted net saving to NNP)

	Household	Corporate	Private	Government	Total
1970	.12	.11	.23	.06	.29
1971	.12	.08	.20	.06	.26
1972	.13	.09	.22	.05	.26
1973	.14	.07	.21	.06	.27
1974	.17	−.02	.15	.05	.20
1975	.18	−.03	.15	.00	.15
1976	.19	−.02	.17	−.01	.16
1977	.17	−.01	.16	−.01	.15
1978	.16	.01	.18	−.02	.16
1979	.13	.02	.15	−.01	.14
1980	.13	.01	.13	−.01	.12
1981	.13	.00	.13	−.01	.12
1982	.12	.01	.12	−.01	.11
1983	.12	.00	.12	−.02	.10
1984	.11	.01	.12	−.00	.12
Average	.14	.02	.16	.01	.17

Source: Hayashi (1986, Tables A-1, A-2).

The Japanese rate of saving has nonetheless remained higher than that of other industrial countries, although it has exhibited substantial variation. It is important to understand the extent to which the high saving rate in Japan has been a response to government policies. The recent historic character of the high saving rate suggests there is more to the story than simple thrift. It is to these possible explanations that we now turn.

Personal Saving Behavior

Analysts have identified three broad explanations for the pattern of Japanese saving. One explanation emphasizes the impact of the bonus wage system (a large semi-annual bonus paid to workers in addition to their regular wage). Another focuses on what motivates individual Japanese to save. Finally, some analysts have pointed to provisions in the tax system that encourage saving.

Bonus Payment System

Japanese workers' wages have two distinct components. The first is the regular wage. The second is the semi-annual bonus based on company performance. The two forms of payment have different legal status and would be expected to have different economic effects, because the periodicity and variance of the payment streams differ, with the bonus payments being more lumpy and more uncertain. Some time-series data on wages and bonuses are presented in figure 4.2.

Ishikawa and Ueda suggested that Japanese households consume according to the "habit-buffer income hypothesis," which holds that saving and consumption decisions are conditioned by slowly changing conventions, habits, rules of thumb, etc. They submit that bonus income is a source of

Figure 4.2 Bonus payments as a proportion of income in Japan, 1958–78

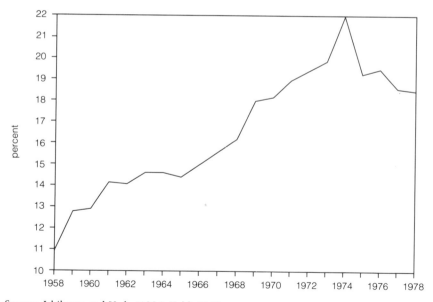

Source: Ishikawa and Ueda (1984, Table V-1).

buffer income used for saving in the form of financial assets and consumer durables. On the basis of several simulations, Ishikawa and Ueda concluded that "the bonus payment system has exerted a statistically significant affect on Japanese personal savings. . . . However, the quantitative magnitude of its contribution to the aggregate weight of personal savings is rather small, at most three percentage points (on average) for the period of 1958–78, when the aggregate rate of personal savings averaged 20 percent" (1984, 174).

In a dissent, Shibuya has argued that the bonus payment system does not explain Japanese personal saving behavior. While in theory bonuses could play the role Ishikawa and Ueda describe, Shibuya believes that "in fact . . . bonuses have become an integral and anticipated component of worker compensation" (1988, 10). Moreover, in the regression model of saving that he estimates, the coefficient for bonus income is insignificant.

Life Cycle and "Target" Savings Explanations

A second family of approaches to understanding saving behavior involves analyzing saving decisions in terms of agents' attempts to allocate consumption optimally over time. This class of models includes the life-cycle hypothesis (LCH) and various target-motive explanations, in which agents save to meet some particular future consumption goal. Japan's high personal saving rates are thought to be a consequence of the desire to provide for education, housing, and bequests.

The LCH predicts that households will exhibit a "humped" pattern of saving over their lifetimes. That is, households' saving rates will rise during the peak earning period of middle age, then decline as savings are disbursed during retirement. It can be shown that in the aggregate under LCH, the household saving rate will be higher, the higher "(1) the ratio of the retirement span to lifespan, (2) the rate of population growth, and (3) the rate of productivity growth" (Horioka 1984, 31). Analyzing data on these indicators for OECD countries, Horioka found that Japan ranked high on all three criteria. He concluded that, "on balance, the life cycle hypothesis predicts that Japan should have displayed an aggregate household saving rate that is well above the average for the OECD countries, and this prediction is consistent with the high household saving rate actually observed in Japan during the postwar period" (1984, 40).

Researchers working with actual Japanese household data, however, have had difficulty establishing the empirical validity of the LCH. Two econometric studies (Horioka 1984; Ando and Kennickell 1985) found only limited support for the LCH, though there is reason to believe that deficiencies in survey data may have distorted the results.[4] In fact, annual surveys by the Central Council on Savings Promotion reveal the prevalence of savings planning and targeting among Japanese households. Nearly half the respondents indicated that they had a saving plan, and 86.8 percent had a saving target. The average time frame of the plans was seven to eight years, and the desired wealth/income ratio was between six and seven (Sato 1987).

Survey results reported by Horioka indicate that the relative importance of motives for saving changed little between the survey years of 1966, 1978, and 1983. Saving "for illness and other unexpected emergencies" was cited in 1983 by 36.1 percent of the respondents as their single most important motive for saving. Other motives, and the percentage of respondents ranking them as most important in 1983, included "for life during retirement" (15.4 percent), "housing related expenses" (14.3 percent), and "children's educational and marriage expenses" (10.7 percent).[5]

Japanese housing has a reputation for low quality and high prices. In 1983, the most recent year for which data are available, the ratio of housing price to annual income was 6.7 nationwide, and 7.9 in metropolitan areas—substantially higher than comparable ratios in other developed countries (OECD 1986b, 67). If differences in floorspace are taken into account, housing prices are 2.5 to 2.7 times higher than in the United States (Horioka 1988, 5). This has led a number of researchers to investigate the possible influence of high housing prices on saving behavior, either estimating the

---

4. One statistical difficulty encountered by both Horioka and Ando and Kennickell was that the prevalence of multigenerational households gave rise to errors in the classification of households by age. In addition, the inclusion of the majority of elderly persons into younger households obscured their behavior in the survey data.

Confronted with these problems, both Horioka and Ando and Kennickell concluded that their results might be due to deficiencies in the data sets. In particular, Ando and Kennickell argue that there are good reasons to believe that the minority of the elderly who maintained independent households displayed saving behavior quite different from those who lived with their children.

One investigation which does claim to find support for the LCH is the aggregate time-series study by Shibuya (1988). His resuscitation of the LCH appears to turn on a semantic point, however: "Even if the primary motive for saving in Japan is ostensibly bequests, it really amounts to provision for retirement, which is achieved through the implicit annuity contract between the elderly and their children" (4). The issue of bequests is taken up below.

5. Horioka has investigated the impact of education and marriage expenses on saving behavior. He concluded that "though the aggregate amount of net financial saving for education has been positive...it has constituted only a small proportion of total household saving, and moreover, it can explain movements over time in the overall household saving rate to only a limited extent" (Horioka 1985a, 71). Likewise, in the case of marriage expenses, "the aggregate amount of marriage-related saving is negligible..." (Horioka 1987, 47).

effects econometrically, or quantifying them through the use of simulation modeling.[6]

As a result of differences in methodology and assumptions, estimates of the housing-related saving share of total household saving range from 46.8 percent (Horioka 1988) to nearly two-thirds (Hayashi, Ito, and Slemrod 1988).[7] Down payment requirements were found to have a discernible but not very large effect on the saving rate. Larger down payment requirements meant that prospective buyers had to accumulate larger pre-purchase stocks of financial assets, but this was partially offset by a tendency to purchase smaller houses to reduce the down payment burden. Furthermore, housing-related saving and the housing tenure pattern were shown to be sensitive to individuals' desire to leave bequests in the Hayashi, Ito, and Slemrod study. We take up the issue of bequests next.

Retirement, Pensions, and Bequests

The final target saving motive that has been examined is the provision of income during retirement. In the simple formulation of the LCH, this is the sole purpose of saving and generates the "humped" lifetime savings profile.

---

6. In a stationary, steady-state economy, the net amount of housing-related saving would be zero, since the financial saving would equal the value of the real asset adjusted for depreciation. However, in a non-stationary economy, housing-related saving could be positive or negative. To paraphrase Horioka, if the aggregate amount of purchases (investment) is increasing, then housing-related saving will be positive, since pre-purchase saving will be larger than post-purchase saving through mortgage payments and depreciation. Common reasons why aggregate purchases (investment) will increase over time include: population growth; a decline in average household size (due to an increasing prevalence of independent households and nuclear families); income increases (assuming housing is a superior good, i.e., its income elasticity is greater than one); an increase in demand for new housing due to relocation (urbanization, for instance); an increase in housing or land prices combined with price-inelastic demand.

In the national accounts, purchases of housing are treated as investment. However, the net amount of housing-related saving could be larger or smaller than this figure for the reasons cited above.

7. The Horioka figure refers to housing-related saving as a share of gross household saving, which is the relevant saving concept from the balance of payments point of view. However, he concludes that due to the imputed depreciation of the housing stock, the contribution of housing-related saving to net household saving has been negative.

However, the simple LCH story is complicated by the existence of pensions and, in the case of Japan, intergenerational transfers, an additional source of income. As it turns out, the interaction of intergenerational resource transfers and the high cost of housing may have a strong impact on Japanese household saving rates.

A number of studies (mostly for the United States) have attempted to estimate the impact of public and private pensions on the personal saving rate. The fundamental notion is that households regard pensions as a substitute for private saving; as pension benefits are increased, private saving will go down. While this argument may be plausible, it has not been supported by the preponderance of econometric evidence. The jury is still out on this issue.

It has been suggested that Japan's high personal saving rates were due, at least in part, to an underdeveloped social security system, and that the decline in the saving rate may have been associated with the considerable improvements in benefits in the 1970s. As with the United States, however, a review of the empirical literature led one analyst to conclude that "the development of social security has had a relatively minor effect on the personal savings rate if any" (Sato 1985, 17). Extensive research on the United States and Japan by Ando and Kennickell suggests that expectations concerning future benefit streams and needs are so uncertain that marginal changes in future benefits have little influence on current (pre-retirement) behavior. Once retirement is reached, agents simply consume whatever income streams are realized at that time.

In contrast, the role of intergenerational transfers and bequests appears to be crucial in understanding Japanese saving behavior. As table 4.4 illustrates, far more Japanese expect to have their children finance their retirements than in other industrial countries. Likewise, table 4.5 shows that a majority of the Japanese elderly live with their children.

The Japanese elderly fall into two basic groups. A small minority of Japanese workers reaching retirement age are invited to become senior officers of corporations, where their salaries are frequently three to five times higher than those they had previously earned. They maintain independent households and apparently engage in saving as their consumption pattern changes little. This conclusion applies more generally to people maintaining independent households after the usual retirement age of 55–60, including entrepreneurs and professionals. As Ando and Kennickell concluded, "for this group, it is clear that the conventional life cycle theory does not apply" (1985, 49).

However, a majority of Japanese retirees experience a significant reduction in earned income (even if they remain employed in some capacity) and

Table 4.4   An international comparison of attitudes toward the financing of living expenses during retirement

	Japan	Thailand	US	UK	France
View 1. One should prepare for retirement during one's working years and not depend on one's family or on others.	55.0	24.7	60.7	44.2	27.5
View 2. One's family members should meet one's living expenses during retirement.	18.8	61.4	0.6	0.2	2.2
View 3. One's living expenses during retirement should be financed by social security.	21.8	10.6	29.1	47.1	66.1
Other	2.5	0.8	6.0	6.4	2.9
No Answer	1.9	2.5	3.6	2.1	1.3
Total	100.0	100.0	100.0	100.0	100.0

Source: Horioka (1984, Table 11).
Note: The figures represent the percentage of respondents indicating that their own view corresponds most closely to each view.

merge with younger households. Ando and Kennickell found that for this group "there is some dissaving by older persons or reduced saving activities by younger households after older persons join them. . . . Net worth does decline moderately after retirement, but even at very advanced age, older individuals are still carrying a fairly substantial amount of net worth, say roughly one half of the net worth possessed at the time of their retirement" (1985, 54). At the same time, "preliminary calculations indicate that the saving by independent older households outweighs dissaving of older persons living in younger households in the aggregate" (1985, 54).

The maintenance of assets by older people contradicts conventionally held notions about life cycle behavior. Survey data indicate that over three-quarters of Japanese respondents feel that their estates should be distributed to their heirs according to how much financial and other assistance they received from them (Horioka 1984, 54). This "strategic bequest motive"

**Table 4.5 An international comparison of the living arrangements
of the elderly** (percentage of respondents who currently live
with each category of family member)

	Japan	Thailand	US	UK	France
Your spouse	65.4	51.1	47.0	49.1	55.8
Your married child (male)	41.0	25.3	0.9	0.5	3.5
Your married child (female)	9.2	37.8	2.5	1.9	5.6
Your child's spouse	34.0	49.2	1.6	0.7	3.5
Your unmarried child	18.7	33.0	9.0	5.1	10.6
Your grandchild	41.0	62.6	3.8	1.1	5.8
Other relatives	2.9	8.2	4.1	4.2	5.3
Non-relatives	0.7	3.4	2.3	1.2	1.0
Living alone	5.7	4.7	41.3	41.6	30.0
No answer	0.3	0.0	0.3	0.0	0.4
Totals	219.0	275.3	112.8	105.3	121.7

Source: Horioka (1984, Table 12).

implies a different pattern of post-retirement behavior among the elderly:
Rather than simply dissaving, the elderly maintain the value of their assets
partly in order to purchase more or better services from their heirs.

Several explanations for this behavior have been proposed, including risk
aversion on the part of the elderly and a strong cultural emphasis on familial
obligations. One explanation is particularly compelling: the high price of
land. Mainly because of the high price of land, housing makes up fully 65
percent of Japanese personal portfolios. (The comparable figure for the
United States is 31 percent.) As a consequence, many Japanese face relatively
long retirements with most of their portfolio tied up in a relatively illiquid
asset yielding no financial return. This difficulty is exacerbated by the fact
that, due to relatively early retirements and long life expectancies, the period
of retirement can be quite long, on the order of 20 years. Since many
Japanese wives are significantly younger than their husbands, and have
longer life expectancies, the effective retirement period for the dependent
spouse can be 30 years.

High taxes on the appreciation of land at the time of sale and low appraisals for property tax purposes significantly add to the illiquidity problem.[8] It is not surprising, then, that when households merge, the parents usually invite the eldest son to move in with them, rather than the aged parents moving into the child's home, as frequently occurs in the United States.[9]

The intergenerational merging of households acts, in effect, as a pension program. Why do the Japanese enter into these non-market arrangements when presumably they could simply purchase annuities? The consensus is that the extraordinarily high price of land—largely a product of extremely inefficient land-use policies and high taxes on capital gains—absorbs such a large part of savings that it is impossible for the elderly to purchase sufficient annuities. Even generous public social welfare programs cannot effectively address this problem. As Ando and Kennickell conclude, "The price of residence is so high that anything like social security benefits, however generous, cannot be adequate to provide private living quarters for older persons" (1985, 60).

To summarize, we have seen that the LCH does not do a very good job of explaining Japanese saving behavior. Nor do public and private pensions appear to have a particularly significant impact on saving behavior. Rather, imperfections in capital markets lead to a "lumpy" pattern of financial saving, in which Japanese save for specific purposes: education, marriage, and, most importantly, housing.

The price of housing is high because of the natural scarcity of land and building materials and extremely inefficient land-use policies.[10] The high

8. Noguchi (1983, 64) argues that although the nominal rate of property tax is 1.4 percent, the effective rate is as low as 0.1 percent because of undervaluation.

9. On the other hand, it has been suggested that households might engage in dissaving if they accumulate housing-related savings and then receive a house as a gift or bequest. There is some evidence that this occurs. The rate of saving for households that purchased houses was 14.1 percent, compared to 11.5 percent for those households that were given their homes (Horioka 1985, table 4).

In fact, Ando and Kennickell estimated that the presence of each retired person in a "young" household increased that household's marginal propensity to consume out of expected labor income by 5 percent (1985, 48). But this dissaving does not outweigh the *ex ante* saving by the young, nor the tendency of the elderly to maintain their assets. The net effect of the system is to raise household savings.

10. The inefficient use of land is not discouraged by property taxes. Noguchi reports that, due to the underassessment of land values, the effective rate of property tax is 0.1 percent, and in the case of farmland, 0.001 percent. As a result, as much as 10 percent of the Tokyo metropolitan area designated as "city zone" remains under cultivation. Similarly, building height restrictions further discourage rational land use. For example, as much as 10 percent of Tokyo is designated as area where buildings cannot exceed 10 meters in height. The average height of residential buildings is thus just over two stories (Noguchi 1983, 62–63), although the November 1987 revision of the Construction Standards Law permits the construction of three-story wooden houses in much of Tokyo.

price of housing (and mortgage loan markets that may be underdeveloped) forces younger couples to accumulate large amounts of savings to purchase homes. Conversely, older households face retirement with much of their savings in a relatively illiquid asset with no monetary return. This reduces both the interest income available to finance retirement and the ability to smooth dissaving. The problem is exacerbated by the regulation of Japanese financial markets, which has depressed the rate of return on personal saving instruments (for example, postal savings accounts and time deposits) relative to the rate of return on tangible assets. As a result, there is widespread intergenerational household merging and a maintenance of savings by elderly Japanese according to the strategic bequest motive.

The combination of high housing costs and the strategic bequest motive thus provides a principal explanation for the high Japanese saving rate. With the elderly saving, on balance, the dissaving predicted by the LCH does not occur. Changes in the saving rate are then primarily produced by changes in the housing market (which strongly affects saving behavior) and shifting demographics (which affects the proportions of high- and low-savers in the population).

Personal Taxes and Saving

Two things must be established in order to determine the tax system's effect on saving. The first is the effective marginal tax on income from saving. The second is the after-tax interest elasticity of saving.

Under the *maruyu* ("tax free") system, interest income from principal of up to 9 million yen per person, and 5.5 million yen per household, was tax-exempt.[11] In addition, certain bonds were taxed at a rate of 16 percent. In the case of equities, capital gains were not taxed if they were below a certain amount or the annual number of stock transactions was less than 50.

These provisions were apparently subject to widespread abuse. People established several tax-free accounts in different names, or transferred funds to family members' accounts without paying the gift tax, or traded with a number of brokers to escape capital gains taxation. Because of legal exemptions and illegal evasion, it is estimated that 58–70 percent of Japanese personal financial saving was not taxed (Sato 1985, N9; Hayashi, Ito, and Slemrod 1988, 1; Shoven 1985, 10).

As a result, marginal tax rates on interest income and income from equities are low. Shoven and Tachibanaki (1985) estimated these rates to be 9.6

---

11. The recently enacted tax reform restricts the *maruyu* system to those aged 65 and older, the handicapped, and to women supporting families on their own. A special "asset-building" scheme has been retained under which up to 5 million yen of savings per person is taxed at a preferential rate of 5 percent.

percent and 18.1 percent, respectively. This contrasts with marginal rates on earned income, which are as high as 80 percent (Hayashi 1986, 195). Furthermore, unlike the US tax system, interest payments on debt are not deductible from taxable income. All in all, the Japanese tax system is biased toward saving because income from capital is taxed at a substantially lower rate than earned income and there are no deductions for interest paid.

Having established that the rate of taxation on income from capital is low, the next step is to analyze the responsiveness of saving to the after-tax rate of return. Presumably, current consumption (saving) would be negatively (positively) related to the intertemporal terms of trade. In other words, saving should be positively related to expected after-tax rates of return.[12] Two researchers attempted to estimate econometrically the responsiveness of saving to the rate of return in Japan (Makin 1985; Hayashi 1986). Neither found any significant effect, leading one to conclude that "on the whole there is no strong evidence for a high interest elasticity of saving or for the effectiveness of the tax incentives for savings" (Hayashi 1986, 197).

Another study took a different approach, analyzing the effect of tax policy on the saving rate through the housing market. Based on a simulation of the housing market, the researchers found that "abolition of the 'maruyu' accounts in Japan would cause a drop in the steady-state saving rate by 3 to 4 percentage points. The housing tenure pattern would also change, so that the Japanese would rent 10 or more years before purchasing a house" (Hayashi, Ito, and Slemrod 1988, 26). Our evaluation of the evidence suggests that the bequest motive is important, so we would tend to favor a smaller estimate of the impact on saving. The authors concluded that the adoption of the US tax system's treatment of interest income and interest payments (including the deductibility of mortgage interest payments) would result in an additional 3.5 percentage point decline in net national saving.

Complementarity Between Saving and Work

An additional explanation for Japan's high personal saving rate is the long Japanese work day. The central notion is that there is a complementarity between leisure and consumption. Saving is a byproduct of the fact that the Japanese spend so much time working and commuting that they have little time to shop or consume. In particular, the tradition of working a half-day on Saturday limits the feasibility of weekend vacations and associated

---

12. This might not be the case, however, if individuals save for some target income in the future. In this case, an increase in the real rate of return might reduce current saving, since the same future income stream could be attained through lower current saving.

consumer goods purchases—boats, for example. This constraint is reinforced by the limited business hours of banks. (Automatic teller machines are also open only during limited hours.)

Conclusions

Japanese personal saving rates remain quite high, though they have fallen from their 1974 peak. Three groups of explanations (bonus system, life cycle/target savings, and tax incentives) have been examined here.

It has been argued that the bonus system raises the personal saving rate, but the evidence is not particularly convincing. The econometric evidence reviewed does not support the simple life cycle hypothesis of a "humped" savings pattern, nor does it point to a major impact of public and private pensions on personal saving rates. The modified LCH explanations of saving instead indicate that Japanese personal saving behavior is intimately tied to the high price of housing.

The high price of housing affects saving in two ways. The first is through the incentive to accumulate savings as a down payment on a future purchase (the target savings effect). Second, once housing is purchased the residence comprises a large component of the household's asset portfolio. A house, however, is not a good asset for retirees—it yields no income and is relatively illiquid. This fact, combined with the high prices faced by young households entering the market, encourages house owners to use their residences as vehicles for intergenerational transfers. This strategic bequest motive, in contrast to life cycle motives, encourages the elderly to maintain their savings (including their houses) in order to effectively purchase an annuity from their heirs. The high price of housing thus raises the aggregate level of personal saving through both of these channels.

Shibuya (1988) makes the important point, however, that rising prices may generate an offsetting wealth effect: As housing prices rise, the wealth of owner households increases, and they may reduce current saving to counterbalance their growing wealth. Shibuya estimates that this offsetting wealth effect is nearly as large as the initial target saving effect, and, taken together, he concludes that increases in housing prices may not have contributed significantly to Japanese saving in the aggregate. Although the specific estimate he obtains has yet to be confirmed by other researchers, his general point about wealth effects partially offsetting the increases in target saving is well taken.

Although the relative price of housing in Japan may be high because of the natural scarcity of land and building materials, government policies have exacerbated the problem. Capital market imperfections and tax regulations have retarded the conversion of farmland to other uses, and building code and zoning restrictions on high-rises have led to inefficient land-use patterns. In addition, low taxes on land, the high taxation of capital gains, and low rates of return on regulated savings accounts discourage the sale of land for building purposes.

Japanese tax legislation is generous in its treatment of income from capital, but does not exempt interest payments on consumer debt from taxation. Over all, the tax system could be said to be saving-biased with respect to saving and consumption decisions and relatively neutral with respect to the allocation of savings between different assets. Econometric studies have uncovered little evidence that the tax system has had a major impact on personal saving behavior, however.

Business Saving Behavior

There is a two-way causality between saving and investment, on one hand, and economic growth, on the other. High rates of growth encourage saving and investment in part because the marginal saving propensity tends to exceed the average propensity and in part by increasing opportunities for profitable investment. Conversely, increases in productive capacity raise the level of potential output and the long-run growth trajectory of an economy.

As noted earlier, the Japanese business sector is a net debtor, absorbing excess personal saving through the intermediation of private and government financial institutions. In terms of saving rates, two things stand out in the figures reported in table 4.3. First, corporate saving has been relatively low, and second, the rate of corporate saving has been declining since at least the early 1970s. As with personal saving behavior, several hypotheses attempt to explain these results. The interpretations focus on the bonus wage payments system, the rate of return on capital, and the tax system.

It has been argued that the system of bonus wage payments is effectively a mechanism for circumventing the tax system. Since tax rates are lower on personal income than on retained corporate profits, and corporate debt payments (unlike household debt payments) are tax deductible, the real corporate tax burden is reduced by disbursing profits as bonus payments and borrowing the funds back through the banking system. Significantly, over the 1974–1984 period nearly 85 percent of corporate funds were raised by borrowing. Less than 10 percent were raised through the issuance of stock. It could also be argued, though, that the bonus payments are not profit transfers, but variable labor costs. The driving force behind the net debtor position of the business sector is the high rate of personal saving, which facilitates high levels of borrowing for investment purposes.

A large pool of loanable funds, combined with international capital controls (which historically had been the norm), would result in a low cost of capital, as saving was effectively contained in the domestic economy. Investment would appear to be high since a larger number of potential projects are profitable at the going interest rate. In essence, investment would accommodate the large supply of investible funds. One would thus expect to observe low rates of return on capital. Alternatively, if domestic producers faced favorable investment opportunities (for example, through adopting product or process innovations already developed abroad), the rate of investment would appear high even though the cost of capital was not low by international standards. As it turns out, both of these explanations contain some truth. A more detailed treatment of the cost of capital issue appears in Chapter 5.

With regard to the tax system, several studies found that capital is taxed more heavily in Japan than in the United States (Ando and Auerbach 1985; Hayashi 1985; Sato 1985; and Shoven 1985). Ogura and Yoshino (1988) calculated that the total financial benefits of Japanese subsidized loan programs and special depreciation allowances amounted to 2.0 percent of investment in manufacturing over the 1961–1973 period, and 2.1 percent from 1974–1980. Although these magnitudes are not large, they are not entirely inconsequential either, and probably understate the true subsidy to capital since the industrial consumption of electricity was also subsidized.

One possible source of reduced tax incidence is the interest deductibility of corporate debt. However, according to the calculations of Ando and Auerbach, the upper bound estimates of the impact of this provision are "negligible." They conclude that even with the interest deductibility of debt, "Japanese real investments appear to be more, rather than less, heavily taxed than those in the U.S." (1987, 37).

In an interesting dissent, Shoven argued that simply comparing rates of corporate taxation fundamentally misses the point. While in an accounting sense different rates of corporate taxation will affect the rate of return on capital and the *corporate* saving rate, what is relevant to *national* saving and investment incentives is the rate of return realized by the individual investor. The effective tax rate (the tax wedge) is the difference between the return the investment actually earns and the return received by the investor, and is thus a function of both corporate and personal tax rates. In the case of Japan, it is possible that the effective tax on capital is low even though corporate tax rates are high by international standards, since income from capital is taxed lightly at the personal level.

Shoven has calculated effective tax rates in the United States and Japan for three types of assets (machinery, buildings, and inventories), three financial instruments (debt, retained earnings, and new equity issues), three industries (manufacturing, commerce, and "other"), and three classes of investors (households, tax-exempt institutions, and insurance companies). All told, there are 81 different combinations, each associated with a different effective rate of taxation. The calculated results indicate a high degree of dispersion of effective tax rates in both countries, creating inefficiencies by distorting savings and investment incentives. The most striking results, however, are the economy-wide differences in the effective tax rates on different financial instruments in Japan. Shoven calculated that in 1980 the effective tax rate on debt, new share issues, and retained earnings in Japan were − 60.6, 80.8, and 64.3 percent, respectively. (The corresponding figures for the United States were − 16.3 for debt, 91.2 for new share issues, and 62.4 for retained earnings.) These figures indicate that Japanese equity capital is highly taxed and debt capital is effectively subsidized. The reason is that equity capital is taxed at the corporate level, while interest payments on corporate debt are deductible.[13] In this context, the continued reliance of Japanese corporations on debt financing is patently clear.

For the overall economy, Shoven calculated that the effective rate of taxation on capital was higher in the United States than in Japan. A summary of his results is presented in table 4.6. These figures indicate that the overall tax wedge between actual economic rates of return and the rate that an investor would receive is smaller in Japan than in the United States. If projects had equal rates of return in both countries, Japanese investors would thus receive a greater after-tax rate of return on their investment. Presumably this would represent a greater incentive to save.

Government Saving Behavior

In examining government saving behavior it is important to distinguish between tangible and financial assets. One typically thinks of government net saving as identical to the current budget surplus. This is the case for financial saving and is the relevant concept for some purposes (such as determining the effect of international capital flows on exchange rate determination). However, government net saving also includes saving in the form of tangible assets (mostly infrastructural investments) that are

---

13. The figures were calculated based on an average rate of inflation of 9 percent for the 1970–1980 period. Since inflation will tend to favor debt finance (because the real value of the debt is eroded, while nominal interest payment deductions increase), these figures may overstate the difference between debt and equity finance in lower inflation periods. Calculations performed under the assumption of zero inflation found the effective tax rates on Japanese debt, equity, and retained earnings were 2.9, 57.6, and 51.9 percent, respectively.

Table 4.6 Effective tax rates on investment in the United States and Japan, 1980 and 1985 (percentage)

	1980	1985	Administration proposal for tax reform
United States	37.0	31	34
Japan	7.4	22	22
Difference between effective tax rates in the US and Japan	400	41	55

Source: Shoven (1985, Table 5).

important for long-run growth. It may thus be possible for total government net saving to be positive even if the current budget is in deficit.

Japanese government saving is depicted in figure 4.3. As was seen earlier, Japanese government net saving fell during the 1970s from around 6 percent to roughly zero in the 1980s, because of a dramatic rise in central government deficits. Financial dissaving has declined as government deficits have fallen

Figure 4.3 Japanese government saving, 1965–1983

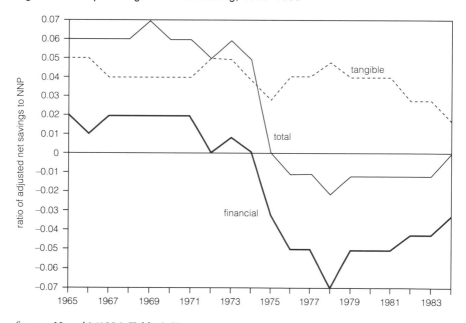

Source: Hayashi (1986, Table A-2).

through the 1980s, but this has been somewhat offset by a fall in the net accumulation of tangible assets.

As a result of high levels of investment in infrastructural projects, the rate of government saving in tangible assets remained constant at four to five percent through the 1960s and 1970s. It has been suggested, though, that this was in large part due to a once-and-for-all build-up in infrastructure, and that saving tangible assets would decline gradually in the future, as it has during the 1980s (Boskin and Roberts 1986). But in light of recent proposals for large public works investment programs (for example, the Maekawa Reports and the 1987 supplementary budget), the future course of Japanese government capital investment is by no means clear. This is examined in greater detail in Chapter 6.

Policy Recommendations

The purpose of saving is to reallocate the intertemporal opportunities for consumption, and in so doing to maximize the utility associated with a stream of consumption. Saving decisions are thus conditional on expectations concerning future income streams and future consumption needs, on the one hand, and opportunities for intertemporal transfers of income, on the other. As we have seen, much of Japanese saving behavior appears to be motivated by the desires to obtain satisfactory housing and finance retirement. In the case of housing, a combination of government policies and market failures have contributed to its high cost.[14] The high cost of housing, and incomplete markets for the provision of retirement income, in turn, strongly affect how Japanese finance their retirements. Finally, government intervention through the tax system has a variety of effects on the level and composition of Japanese saving. The existence of market distortions and failures indicates the potential for welfare improvements through new policy initiatives. Moreover, the high saving rate contributes to the trade surplus which has led to tensions abroad. Policy action thus holds the promise of doubly improving the Japanese situation—by improving welfare at home and reducing foreign tensions.

Land-Use Policies

The rate of saving is intimately tied to the high price of land and housing. While the relative scarcity of land implies that housing might be costly

---

14. This is not to say that government policies were adopted with the intention of creating microeconomic distortions, but rather that policies adopted for a variety of reasons in the past have had significant distortionary effects in the present, as discussed below.

under any regime, the situation is exacerbated by the concentration of the population in a few urban areas and by extremely inefficient land-use policies. These problems could be resolved with a combination of policies that brought more land effectively into use by encouraging population dispersion and making more efficient use of land already under development.

There is virtually no effective property tax on agricultural land in Japan. This fact, combined with special inheritance tax provisions and high taxes at the time of sale, retards the conversion of farmland to other uses and encourages part-time farming and speculative holding. Landowners' incomes are maintained by a combination of restrictive agricultural policies and generous subsidies that keep the domestic producer price of rice around seven times the world market price. As a result, the urban areas of Japan are dotted with small agricultural plots tended by part-time farmers. In Tokyo, for instance, there are 125,000 "farmers" who farm 130 square kilometers, or about 6 percent of the city's total area. If this land were converted into housing, it would increase Tokyo's residential area by nearly 20 percent.[15] These part-time farmers are not poor. Their incomes exceed the blue-collar average by 30 percent (Fitchett 1988). These policies amount to a systematic income transfer from the mass of the urban population to a relatively well-off class of landowners.

What is clearly needed is a set of reforms to encourage the more rational use of land. This would include a reduction in agricultural protection and subsidization, an equalization of property taxes across land under different uses, and a reduction of taxes at the time of sale.[16] The goal here would be to move to a system in which public policy would be neutral with respect to alternative land uses, thus encouraging land to be allocated to its socially most productive uses. Specifically, this would entail an increase in the effective rate of taxation on urban farmland.

The main political obstacle to such reform is that farmers, both full- and part-time, make up an important constituency within the ruling LDP, and the parliamentary districting system grossly overrepresents rural interests. One solution might be to draft legislation that, for purposes of taxation,

---

15. The basic administrative and planning unit is the city planning area, which is divided into Urbanization Promotion Areas (where development is allowed) and Urbanization Controls Areas (where further development is effectively prohibited). Agricultural land makes up 20 percent of the Tokyo metropolitan Urban Promotion Area (OECD 1986a, 63).

16. The government appears to be moving in this direction. In a recent speech to the Diet, Prime Minister Takeshita announced that "The Administration has put together the outline of the Emergency Land Measures in line with the recommendations of the Special Advisory Council on the enforcement of administrative reform and is now working steadfastly to promote these measures to normalize land dealings" (1988, 16). The proposed measures include a variety of tax changes affecting the sale of land.

differentiated between rural and urban farmland, with much higher rates of taxation assessed on the urban farmland. That would reduce the commonality of interests between actual full-time farmers, and owners of urban farmland, and increase the likelihood that the reform would be enacted.

In addition to the prevalence of urban farms, the availability of housing is further restricted by archaic zoning laws which limit the height of buildings.[17] (The development of earthquake-proof construction technologies has eliminated the safety justification for the height restrictions.) "Sunshine laws," ostensibly enacted to insure access to sunlight for homeowners, effectively prohibit the construction of high-rise apartment buildings. Consequently, the average height of residential buildings in Tokyo is just over two stories. The result is metropolitan sprawl and lengthy commutes for urban workers.

One obstacle to eliminating the sunshine regulations is that each current individual homeowner could be expected to oppose repealing the law for his neighborhood (roughly the level of jurisdiction at which these ordinances are administered), since the construction of a large high-rise would reduce the value of surrounding homes, because of increased congestion, reduced sunlight, etc.[18] If current homeowners are able to prevent new construction though legal obstacles, however, a less than socially optimal quantity of housing will be built. This is what has happened in Japan. Yet, if developers are not required to compensate current homeowners, too much housing will be built because losses to existing homeowners will not be taken into account. There is thus a need to devise a system of incentives that would yield the socially optimal amount of housing.[19]

Two standard ways of coping with situations of this kind are internalization and compensation. An internalized solution to the housing problem might work as follows. First, the municipal government would pass legislation overriding current sunshine regulations citywide.[20] At the same time,

---

17. As mentioned earlier, one of these has been recently changed to permit the building of three-story wooden houses in most of the Tokyo area. Previously only two-story wooden homes were permitted because of fire prevention concerns.

18. In economic terminology, the construction of the high-rise imposes a negative externality on the homeowners. An externality occurs when the welfare of one economic agent is dependent on the activities of another and private costs do not reflect this dependency.

19. In addition to changes in the incentive system, a streamlining of the development regulatory system would be desirable. Under the current system, any significant development must be approved by several layers of government (local, prefectural, central) and a variety of government ministries. The result is an increase in project uncertainty and time delays.

20. In areas where development could conceivably involve several municipalities, development coordination could be handled by the prefectural Governor's office through his administration of the Urban Promotion Areas.

a law modeled after those existing in other countries could be enacted requiring developers to purchase additional surrounding tracts on a per housing-unit basis, and convert a specified percentage of the land into underdeveloped public spaces—i.e., parks and playgrounds. (Japan ranks last among OECD countries in per capita park space.) Instead of buying a single plot and building a single high-rise amid residential homes, developers would be required to purchase additional plots and develop a residential complex, thereby internalizing the true social cost of development.

Alternatively, one could repeal the sunshine laws and permit single lot high-rise construction, but require developers to compensate those adversely affected by the high-rise. A simple rule would require developers to compensate homeowners in the affected neighborhood for the value of their structures, but not their land. Land and structures are contracted for separately in Japan, and it would be relatively easy to assess the value of the structure. Current homeowners would then be free to remain, and suffer the discomfort, or would be free to sell their land and relocate elsewhere.

Without some means of compensating those adversely affected by development, the status quo situation of a gross underprovision of housing will persist. With nearly two-thirds of their wealth tied up in housing, current homeowners have every incentive to resist strongly any initiative that could potentially lower the value of their major asset, and the existing zoning laws provide them the mechanism with which to do so. The exercise of each individual's rational self-interest would lead to collective disaster.

Whatever approach is adopted, the compensation formula and enforcement provisions must be clearly defined. This could be done most effectively with a central government-initiated reform package aimed at rationalizing the development process by reducing governmental administrative overlap. Compensation is a serious issue, because any significant change in the relative price of housing would in effect cause a significant redistribution of wealth.[21] The choice, though, is not between a static wealth distribution and a redistribution under reform; it is among alternative redistributional paths. The status quo carries with it its own distributional implications, as rising land prices generate rents which have contributed to widening wealth inequalities.

Similarly, banks which have invested heavily in property could be financially squeezed if relative land prices fell precipitously. Again, compensatory deals could be arranged, and the Bank of Japan would have to be willing to deal with unexpected contingencies. In all likelihood such

---

21. Some have gone so far as to argue that a reduction in the relative price of land would reduce total household wealth and lead to an increase in saving aimed at regaining household target wealth levels.

fears are overstated, "as the latest view within the banking industry is that average Tokyo land prices would have to fall by at least 40 percent from their peak before even the weakest of financial institutions felt a whisker of discomfort." [22]

In addition to rationalizing land use, there is scope for increasing the amount of land development. While some of this could be accomplished through actual land reclamation projects, such as the Kobe Port Island, population decentralization probably has a greater potential impact. The initiative for population dispersion would have to come from the Prime Minister's Office, through its responsibility for the National Land Agency and its coordination of other central government ministries, most notably the Ministry of Construction. The Prime Minister's Office also has strong influence at the prefectural (state) level, since the Prefectural Governors must rely on central government finance for many development undertakings (for example, water management and major infrastructural investment).

The central government could encourage decentralization in at least three ways. One is to expand the development of new towns, along the lines of the Tsukuba Academic City Act, which established a high technology-oriented model city north of Tokyo. Another would be to increase the quality of transport and other infrastructure in outlying regions. As outlying areas become more accessible, firms would have incentives to relocate production to these areas to take advantage of lower costs. The development of the "high-tech" corridor along Route 128 in Massachusetts could become a model for Japanese policy. Finally, the central government could begin moving some of its offices out of Tokyo. At present, virtually all central government bureaus are located in Tokyo. There is no reason why offices handling many government functions could not be dispersed around the country.[23]

Assuming that tax, zoning, and development policies were reformed to increase the availability of housing, what would be the effect on Japanese living standards and the saving rate? One study concluded that if the price of Japanese housing relative to per capita income were reduced to levels comparable to the United States, "housing related saving would be far lower than it is now (up to 25 percent lower) and the household saving would also be lower (by about two percentage points)" (Horioka 1985b, 24). Subsequent research casts doubt on the accuracy of some of the parameter estimates underlying these results, however (Horioka 1986; Noland 1988a).

---

22. *Economist,* 9 January 1988.

23. Again, the government appears to be moving in this direction. Prime Minister Takeshita has endorsed a plan to have each government ministry or agency move one function to a non-Tokyo locale.

In particular, the demand for housing appears to be more income-elastic than previously thought. Econometric estimates indicate that the price elasticity of housing is around -0.8, and the income elasticity is around 1.4 (Horioka 1986).

Much of the rise in housing-related savings can be attributed to the rapid rise of Japanese income. As income growth continues to slow, the growth in the demand for housing (and housing-related saving) will thus continue to fall rapidly. A recent United Nations–World Bank study found that, in an international comparison, both the quality and quantity of Japanese housing were quite low relative to real income. With the United States equal to 100, the housing quantity index for Japan was 49.9, and the quality index was 75.0 (Kravis, Heston, and Summers 1982, 58). There is consequently a great deal of room for quality upgrading driven by the high price and income elasticities of housing.

Hence a major impact of an increased availability of housing in Japan would be an upgrading of the quality of the housing stock. Rather than the current norm of poor, cramped quarters and long commutes, the Japanese could look forward to a future of larger and better houses with greater capacity for the use of consumer durables and greater access to recreational park areas. With increased housing investments, then, the savings–investment balance will be affected.

A decrease in the relative price of Japanese housing to a level similar to that of the United States would probably reduce household saving by around 1 percent as a proportion of GNP.[24] Furthermore, a fall in the price of housing could change the present pattern of strategic bequest saving if the elderly reallocated their portfolios toward financial assets, and reduced their reliance on their heirs for post-retirement income.

A final reform of the housing market which could have a significant impact on the saving rate would be the widespread introduction of housing equity conversion programs for retirees. These would include sale lease-back arrangements and reverse mortgages. Under a sale lease-back, the owner sells the house, receiving financial compensation, then leases back the house from the new owner. The financial proceeds from the sale can then be invested to generate an income stream. Under a reverse mortgage, an agent (frequently a quasi-governmental organization) pays the homeowner a stream of rents, then receives possession of the home at the time of the owner's death. What is common to the two schemes is that the homeowner exchanges control over the ultimate disposition of the property

---

24. It should be remembered that at any given time only about 20 percent of all households are engaging in pre-purchase anticipatory housing-related saving, and there may be significant offsets due to wealth effects.

for a stream of income. The income stream would presumably reduce precautionary saving to finance retirement. By providing retirees with a non-contingent source of income, home equity conversion arrangements would presumably also encourage dissaving during retirement by reducing the need to maintain the accumulated asset stock for either precautionary or strategic bequest motives. The result would be to reduce oversaving caused by an inadequate market for annuities, and thus facilitate the intertemporal allocation of consumption by Japanese citizens.

A reverse mortgage scheme was introduced on an experimental basis for roughly one dozen houses in the Tokyo suburb of Musashino in the late 1970s. Housing equities were collateralized in exchange for home nursing care and hospitalization. The program encountered some practical difficulties, however, and in the end, all the heirs exercised their buy-back options. This contrasts with the United States, where earlier problems have been ironed out and home equity conversion plans are rapidly gaining popularity. That suggests that the Japanese government may in the future want to reevaluate this option on the basis of the American experience, especially as fewer young families rely on their extended families for housing.

Tax Reform

The goal of public finance should be to design a tax system which embodies saving–consumption neutrality—that is, a system which does not distort the terms of trade between present and future consumption. As discussed earlier, the current Japanese tax system can be regarded as saving-biased, as incomes from capital (dividends, interest, and capital gains) are taxed at a lower rate than incomes from labor (wages). Hence, as with property taxes, tax reform should aim at equalizing the rate of taxation on different sources of income.

A comprehensive tax reform proposal which included the abolition of the *maruyu* system, the introduction of a value-added tax, and a new system of taxing businesses proved to be politically unpopular, and the government was forced to withdraw the measure. A revised version of the plan was then submitted. The second proposal included reductions in and restructuring of the number of personal income tax brackets, and the abolition of the *maruyu* system, but dropped the proposal to introduce a value-added tax.[25] This bill became law in April 1988.

---

25. Under the new law the *maruyu* exemptions are still available to those over 65, the handicapped, and to women supporting families on their own. In addition, an "asset-building" provision has been retained under which up to 5 million yen of saving per person is taxed at a preferential rate of 5 percent.

The quantitative effect of these changes on aggregate saving behavior is uncertain. The econometric evidence suggests that the after-tax interest elasticity of saving is quite small, so one would not expect an increase in the tax rate on income from capital to have a major impact on aggregate saving. Yet there is reason to believe that these estimates understate the true interest elasticity of saving. The reason is that the bequest motive may be so strong that it swamps the variation in saving due to changes in the rate of return. In a simulation model discussed earlier, Hayashi, Ito, and Slemrod (1988) estimated that abolishing the *maruyu* system would reduce the saving rate by three to four percentage points depending on how strong the bequest motive was. That highlights the fact that changes in the tax system and changes in the housing and annuity markets may interact strongly in determining aggregate saving behavior. The more important the bequest motive, the less impact changes in the tax code will have. However, if the desire for bequests is motivated by strategic considerations, the provision of higher levels of non-contingent post-retirement income streams (through either social security, private pensions, or reverse mortgages) would strongly reduce this motive to accumulate saving. In this case, tax reforms might have a big impact on savings. The point is that the effect of tax code changes on saving behavior is highly dependent on other policies. Tax reform alone, without changes in these other markets, may have little effect on saving. But a reform of the tax code, along with the removal of housing market imperfections and the introduction of home equity conversions, could have a major impact on saving behavior.

Demographics and Social Security

One final issue of policy relevance is the rapid aging of the Japanese population and its implications for the social security system. Over the next fifteen years the percentage of the Japanese population over age 65 is expected to grow at a rate of three to four percent annually, reaching 21 percent of the population in 2000. As a result, employee contributions to private and government pension funds are expected to rise steeply to support the large number of retirees. It is thus frequently argued that the current high rate of saving is necessitated by the need to accumulate assets to finance future retirement needs. Alternatively, it is argued that the high rate of saving is a response to the expected future insolvency of the publicly funded social security system. While individuals should certainly engage in precautionary saving consistent with their expectations of the future and their degree of risk aversion, concern about the social security system is misplaced.

First, part of the high cost of retirement is due to policy measures and market failures, as previously noted. Housing policy reforms could reduce the cost of retirement, and hence the necessary level of social security benefits. Second, as noted in Chapter 1, Japan has consistently exhibited one of the highest rates of growth in labor productivity and total factor productivity among the major industrialized countries. There is no reason to believe that Japan will not continue to upgrade its pattern of production and that per capita incomes will not continue to rise, given appropriate policies. As a result, the effective burden of pension contributions will be far less onerous than would at first appear. Third, the age of retirement will increase. As a smaller number of workers enter the workforce, firms increasingly will retain older workers who otherwise might retire. Firms are already raising retirement ages. While 55 years was previously the norm, over half of Japanese firms have raised this to 60, a trend that should continue. The increasing employment opportunities for older workers will encourage them to postpone retirement, reducing the number of actual public pensioners and increasing the pool of contributors. Conversely, longer working lives will mean shorter (and hence less costly) retirements. The bottom line is that the concern over future social security insolvency is overstated.

Conclusion

By any standard, the Japanese saving rate is higher than the international norm. That presumably reflects welfare-maximizing behavior on the part of the Japanese. The question, then, is why this behavior involves a rate of saving higher than those observed elsewhere. In part, the answer is that, because of a confluence of microeconomic distortions and market failures, the Japanese people face a set of incentives that encourage them to accumulate and maintain large stocks of savings. The focus of policy action should be the distortions and incomplete markets, not the level of saving itself. The goal is to formulate a set of policy interventions that remove the distortions and enhance economic welfare.

The major reason for the high national saving rate is the high rate of personal saving in Japan. The rates of corporate and government saving are not unusual by international standards. In focusing on household saving behavior, a variety of explanations, including the bonus wage payment system, life cycle hypothesis, bequest motives, and the tax system have been examined. It is striking how all these elements interact to encourage high rates of personal saving.

Central to this story is the high price of housing. The price of housing is kept high by a variety of extremely inefficient land-use policies. As a consequence, large amounts of savings must be accumulated to purchase housing. This behavior is facilitated by the bonus payments system and the tax system, which taxes saving at preferential rates.

Having secured housing, many Japanese face retirement with most of their savings tied up in a relatively illiquid asset with no monetary return. Unable to acquire sufficient annuities, they engage in an intergenerational merging of households involving a contingent contract: the elderly exchange their accumulated assets (including the house) for a share of their working children's current income streams. The effect of this strategic bequest motive is to encourage the accumulation and maintenance of a large stock of assets by the elderly in order to enter into the intergenerational contract.

While this system is functional, few would argue that it would be preferable to a system of improved housing and consumption possibilities, more security in old age, and fewer implicit intergenerational contracts. Moreover, the generation of excess domestic saving has contributed to international tensions by underwriting the maintenance of the large trade surplus. Three reforms should be considered. First, land-use policies should be reformed to reduce the cost of land. The major impact of this initiative would be to increase the availability of high quality affordable housing. A decline in housing costs would also reduce both the stock of assets needed to finance housing acquisition and the share of real assets in the household portfolio.

Second, the government might want to reevaluate home equity conversion plans, in light of their potential benefits and their successful introduction in the United States. The increased availability of reverse mortgages, together with a higher share of financial assets in the household portfolio, would augment income from other sources (pensions, social security) during retirement. Higher income streams during retirement would increase the independence of the elderly and discourage excessive intergenerational merging and post-retirement saving for strategic bequest reasons. This is not to say that the Japanese would stop leaving bequests. They would likely leave smaller bequests for altruistic reasons, rather than large bequests motivated by strategic considerations.

Finally, in conjunction with the other reforms, it would be desirable to move the tax system toward greater saving–consumption neutrality. As it now stands, the Japanese tax system distorts the intertemporal terms of trade by taxing income from capital at a lower rate than income from wages.

Taken together, these actions would greatly enhance Japanese welfare. They would also affect saving behavior. At the same time, the prominence of housing in bequests increases the impact on saving of changes in housing regulations. These changes might reduce Japanese saving, as a proportion of GNP, by as much as 1 to 2 percent. Since much of this reduction would come from developments in housing tenure and financing patterns, the change would not occur quickly, but rather would materialize gradually over a period of years, if not decades. It is important for policymakers to recognize that these policy changes would have substantial, though not rapidly apparent, results.

Some commentators have urged Japan to maintain a high rate of saving to compensate for low saving rates elsewhere. This position implies that policy should attempt to manipulate aggregate national saving (which largely involves private decisions) to achieve international targets. We disagree. The proper role of policy in this area is to support freely chosen intertemporal allocation decisions by removing policy distortions and compensating for market failures.

In practice, our proposals would probably encourage a small reduction in Japan's saving rate. Given the high rate of national saving, such a decline should not be cause for alarm. On the contrary, it would contribute to a reduction in the savings–investment imbalance, and in so doing ease trade tensions with other countries.

5

Investment Behavior

The rate of investment in Japan fell from 32.3 percent of GDP in 1980 to 27.5 percent in 1987, adding to the generation of excess domestic savings and the rise in the current account surplus. These large surpluses have contributed significantly to trade frictions with Japan's major trading partners.

The rate of private investment is fundamentally determined by the profitability of marginal additions to the capital stock. The rate of profit is in turn affected by the level of aggregate demand, the cost of capital, technological innovation, and the need for replacement capital. Some of these determinants influence the long-run rate of investment, while others tend to have more pronounced short-run or cyclical impacts on investment activity. Furthermore, the composition of investment can be a leading indicator of structural change in the economy. Foreign direct investment is particularly important from an international standpoint. Both will play important roles in the upgrading of the Japanese industrial structure, promoting higher productivity at home and providing a means to reduce trade tensions abroad.

First we examine the long-run determinants of the level of investment. We then investigate the cyclical behavior of investment activity, focusing on the impact of government policies. We also analyze the changing composition of investment, with particular emphasis on emerging patterns of foreign direct investment. We then formulate a set of policy recommendations aimed both at smoothing business cycle fluctuations and furthering the ongoing transformation of the economy, paying special attention to the ways housing policy can be used to address these needs.

Determinants of the Level of Investment

Aggregate Demand

The rate of investment is strongly influenced by growth in foreign and domestic demand. Empirical results from a small macroeconometric model bear this out.[1] The estimates show that a 100 yen increase in real output in the current period will increase gross private fixed investment by 30 yen in the next period. In addition, because the Japanese economy is heavily dependent on exports, a rise in the incomes of Japan's trading partners also has an impact on investment. Growth in foreign demand increases the demand for investment goods used in the production of exports, and, indirectly, the demand for other investment goods. This is confirmed by the econometric estimates.

Much of the decline in investment can thus be attributed to the slowing of domestic and foreign growth. Japanese GDP growth fell from 6.1 percent during the 1973–1980 period to 4.0 percent over the 1980–1987 period. This was mirrored by a slowdown in OECD growth from 4.6 percent to 3.4 during the same periods. As a result, the growth rate of Japanese investment fell from 2.9 percent to 2.3 percent.

The Cost of Capital

The econometric estimates indicate that the rate of investment is also influenced by the cost of capital. Specifically, the model results show that for a 1 percent rise in the real interest rate, private fixed investment declines by 41 billion yen.

---

1. The econometric results for the investment equation are as follows:

$$IFIX_t = -153276.7 + .304GNP_{t-1} - 41.26DRREAL_t + 241.02GWP_{t-2}$$
$$ (-.45) \qquad (3.29) \qquad (-1.81) \qquad (1.72)$$

$R^{-2} = .960$　SER $= 6882.00$　DW $= 2.05$　rho $= 0.99$

where IFIX = gross domestic private fixed investment
GNP　　　= real GNP
DRREAL　= the change in the real rate of interest (the rate on long-term government
　　　　　　bonds, less the rate of inflation)
GWP　　　= partner-country economic activity.

This investment function was estimated in the context of a five-equation (consumption, investment, money, current account, exchange rate) macroeconomic model using a two-stage least squares technique with a correction for first-order serial correlation. The numbers in parentheses are t-statistics. The adjusted coefficient of determination (R^{-2}), the standard error of the regression (SER), and the Durbin–Watson statistic are also given.

Q-theory, originated by Nobel Prize-winner James Tobin, links investment demand with the valuation of stock prices. The rate of investment is a function of *q*, defined as the ratio of the market value of new investment goods to their replacement cost. As it turns out, this theory is equivalent to the standard economic theory of investment, in which firms are thought to choose their capital stocks to maximize the discounted stream of expected future profits. That is, firms attempt to maximize their current discounted value, and stock prices indicate the appropriate rate of investment. Takenaka (1986) applied this approach to Japan and found that the elasticity of Japanese capital investment with respect to the marginal *q* was 1.42, indicating that Japanese investment is indeed sensitive to the cost of capital.

The negative effects of higher capital costs on investment are consistent with the results of Ando and Auerbach (1987), who, using a sample of nearly 2,000 firms on the Tokyo Stock Exchange, found that both the before- and after-tax costs of capital in Japan have risen steadily since 1974 (Ando and Auerbach 1987, table 3). The most likely explanation for the increase in the cost of capital is that for much of the period under investigation (1967–1984), international capital flows were imperfectly mobile.[2] As a result, the cost of capital was to a large extent determined by the rate of domestic saving. We noted earlier that the rate of domestic saving was quite high in Japan, implying a relatively low cost of capital. As saving declined after 1973, and capital flows were liberalized in the 1980s, savings that had theretofore been bottled up in the domestic economy began to flow abroad, raising the domestic cost of capital. This was exacerbated by the worldwide increase in real interest rates in the early 1980s.

In addition to the interest rate effects analyzed in our model, Ando and Auerbach examined a variety of tax measures. They concluded that tax provisions had a quantitatively minor impact on the cost of capital and investment. Similarly, Takenaka investigated Japan's investment tax credit provisions, finding that the tax credit rate was low (7 percent) and that the program covered only about 4 percent of capital investment. He concluded that, "from the standpoint of having a stimulating effect on investment in a macroeconomic sense, [the impact] of investment tax credit in Japan is rather negligible" (Takenaka 1986, 8).

Changes over time in the rate of corporate saving and investment also do

---

2. An alternative explanation is that Japanese firms have become riskier investments, or, alternatively, investors in Japanese firms have become more risk-averse. In either case, the risk premium associated with any expected rate of return would increase. The problem with this explanation is that it is essentially unfalsifiable. Intuitively, however, it seems difficult to rationalize the steady, monotonic increase in risk-aversion, spread over more than a decade, which would be needed to generate the observed pattern.

not appear to be highly correlated with changes in tax provisions. The tax-adjusted q, as the name implies, takes into account the impact of investment tax provisions on future earnings streams. For Japan, changes in the value of the tax-adjusted q have been found to be dominated by changes in stock prices, not changes in taxes, indicating that the profitability of capital, not tax changes, has been the driving force behind investment in postwar Japan (Hayashi 1985, 24).

Finally, the cost of capital could be reduced by governmental subsidies, and a decline in subsidies could increase the cost of capital and thus reduce investment. As previously mentioned, the Japanese government has used a variety of programs to subsidize investment in targeted sectors. It is much less clear, however, that these subsidies had any impact on the aggregate rate of investment.[3] The subsidies should instead be regarded as having shifted the sectoral composition of investment, not its aggregate level.

Technological Catch-up

A major determinant of the long-run rate of investment is the rate of technological innovation. The invention of new products and processes will create opportunities for profitable investment. Innovation is costly, however. Once developed, innovative production technologies and marketing techniques must be standardized. The counterpart to the costs of being on the cutting edge of technology is what Gerschenkron (1952) called "the advantages of relative backwardness." Technological followers have the advantage of adopting standardized technologies and products and avoiding the costs of research, development, and technological failure.

Japan is the quintessential example of the Gerschenkron model. With a large and highly educated population, the Japanese rapidly appropriated, imitated, and adapted technology produced in the West. As a result, over the 1870–1979 period Japanese productivity and per capita incomes converged toward the levels attained by more advanced industrialized countries (Baumol 1986). This long-run evidence is confirmed by more recent microeconomic results obtained by Horiye. He found that the adoption of new technologies contributed strongly to the capture of scale economies and the reduction of costs by Japanese firms (1987, 63–68). This in turn encouraged further investment and expansion of capacity.

---

3. As noted earlier, Ogura and Yoshino (1988) calculated that the total financial benefits of Japanese subsidized loan programs and special depreciation allowances amounted to about 2.0 percent of total investment in manufacturing between 1961 and 1980.

As we noted in Chapter 2, however, as the Japanese economy approaches the technological cutting edge, the stock of appropriable innovations developed elsewhere shrinks commensurately. As a result, Japanese firms must increasingly develop their own innovations. The increased costs associated with technical advance slow the rate of investment. The Japanese experience in the 1970s and 1980s is consistent with this broad perspective.

Replacement Capital

Over time, the economic value of the capital stock depreciates because of physical wear and tear. Product innovation and technological progress hasten depreciation. Older vintage capital equipment, best suited for the production of older-style products, or embodying inefficient production techniques, becomes less valuable relative to capital equipment of more recent vintage. As a consequence, the absolute value of investment must increase every period to maintain the value of the capital stock. If the labor force is growing, additional investment is needed to maintain a given capital–labor ratio.

This point can be illustrated by a simple counterfactual experiment. Figure 5.1 shows the amount of investment that would have been required to maintain the 1973 capital–labor ratio, given employment growth and

Figure 5.1 Replacement investment required to maintain 1973 capital–labor ratio

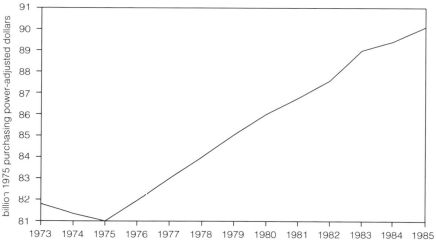

Note: Figures are for capital–employment ratio assuming 6 percent depreciation rate.

depreciation. As the figure demonstrates, increasing amounts of investment are needed just to maintain the same capital–labor ratio. This does not imply, however, that the rate of replacement investment must necessarily increase.

The share of replacement investment will rise, though, if capital-deepening occurs (that is, if the capital–labor ratio increases), or if the effective rate of depreciation rises due to an acceleration of technological change. Takenaka did these calculations for the Japanese economy, finding that "the percentage of replacement investment increased sharply from early to latter part of the 1970s" (1986, 5). In the 1980s, however, the rate of increase slowed and the share of replacement investment has stabilized at around 40–50 percent, approaching the US share of 50–70 percent. This is consistent with the technological backlog hypothesis advanced earlier.

The picture that emerges is one in which Japanese companies faced extraordinary opportunities for investment in the 1960s and 1970s, possibly associated with the free rider advantages of technological catch-up, the emergence of dynamic comparative advantage in more advanced industrial sectors, and high rates of domestic and global economic growth. As a result, Japanese companies exhibited high rates of investment, financed largely through bank borrowing facilitated by the high rate of domestic saving. However, as growth rates fell after the oil shocks, so did revenues, investment, and corporate saving. The worsening investment situation was further exacerbated by the rise in the cost of capital and the need to develop new technologies.

The Changing Composition of Japanese Output

Amid this background of slowing domestic and foreign growth, increases in the cost of capital and the need to generate technological innovations, changes in the composition of Japanese output had a significant impact on the level and composition of investment. Specifically, the so-called "softization" of the Japanese economy led to a shift in output away from traditional heavy industries such as iron and steel, toward less capital-intensive industries and services. As a result, the composition of investment has shifted dramatically away from "big ticket" items for heavy industry, and toward factory and office automation systems, in particular, flexible manufacturing systems (FMS). In fact, the amount of fixed investment by the automation industry now exceeds that of steel and autos combined (Tachi et al. 1985, 91).

A substantial part of this investment has been in the form of computerized numerically controlled machine tools (CNCs). Investment in CNCs is so great that 40 percent of the world's "make-anything" machines are now in Japan (Jaikumar 1986, 70). Aside from their large numbers, the utilization rates of these machines are quite high. A recent study found that the utilization rate of the CNCs was 84 percent in Japan, compared to 52 percent in the United States. In fact, 18 of the 60 Japanese FMS installations surveyed were running unattended all night (Jaikumar 1986, 72). Japan also has the most robots of any country in the world, with 36 robots for every 10,000 workers, roughly six times the ratio in Europe. The rate of robot usage in the United States is even lower.[4]

The development of these new technologies has had a significant impact on Japan's industrial market structure and labor markets. Two out of three CNCs are in small- to medium-sized firms, and small- and medium-sized non-manufacturing firms now account for over 40 percent of total private fixed investment. These are primarily engineering and consulting firms that lease automation equipment and provide technical assistance to the manufacturing sector and, to a lesser extent, the service sector. In fact, medium-sized non-manufacturing firms are the only sector that has exhibited consistently positive investment growth in the 1980s (Tachi et al. 1985, 91). As a consequence, corporate investment is now much more widely spread among a number of firms than in previous years. And since investment in the high-technology sector has been relatively stable, there is some indication that cyclical instability in the rate of investment will moderate, a conclusion supported by recent econometric work at the Bank of Japan (Horiye et al. 1987).

The new technologies require complementary human capital-intensive inputs, and this is changing the character of Japanese labor markets. The introduction of FMS typically results in a reduction in engineering staff, but this is accompanied by an even greater reduction in less skilled production positions. As a result, the ratio of engineers to production workers generally rises from around 1:2 to 3:1 (Jaikumar 1986, 73). Remaining production workers are then used much more intensively, with individual workers responsible for multiple machines.

This has profound implications for labor markets. The most rapid increases in employment have been in white collar technical positions. Wage rate increases in these occupations have consistently outpaced those attained by production workers (Tachi et al. 1985, table 9). The differential would have probably widened further if Japan did not graduate so many engineers (twice the per capita rate of France or the United Kingdom, half again as many as the United States). An upgrading of production techniques has

---

4. *Economist*, 30 May 1987.

thus accompanied the upgrading of Japan's international specialization and its emergence as a skill-abundant economy.

A recent industry-level study suggests that the adoption of these new technologies has been an important element in the cost competitiveness and international strength of Japanese industries (Horiye 1986). In the case of automobiles, research for the MIT project on the car industry indicates that the introduction of innovative production technologies and factory management techniques has led to the dominance of Japanese-owned factories over North American and European rivals in terms of quality and cost (Kraftcik 1986).

The picture here is of an economy undergoing major changes in the composition of its output, changes that are reflected by shifts in the types of inputs demanded by firms in the investment goods and labor markets. An important implication of these trends is that by installing more flexible manufacturing systems and upgrading their work forces, Japanese firms have increased their ability to change rapidly the configurations of their products in response to changes in consumer tastes, foreign protection, and the need to switch between production of goods for export and domestic consumption. In particular, these changes enhance Japanese companies' ability to shift toward a more domestic demand-oriented pattern of growth.

Foreign Direct Investment

Instead of investing at home, firms have the option of investing in new facilities abroad. As noted in Chapter 1, Japanese production abroad is still relatively small: Only about 3.2 percent of the production of Japanese firms is done offshore, compared with 20 percent for US firms. Nevertheless, Japanese FDI has grown rapidly, reaching $33.4 billion in FY 1987 (table 5.1). The ratio of overseas to domestic production is expected to rise to 8.7 percent by 1990. MITI has estimated that this will "cost" the Japanese balance of payments $53 billion by 2001.

Cumulative net FDI, shown in figure 5.2, has also risen steadily, reaching nearly 3 percent of GNP in 1985. This trend is expected to accelerate in the future in response to the appreciation of the yen. As a result, one Japanese research institute estimates that the outstanding balance of direct investment by manufacturing firms will more than quadruple by 1995 (Okumura 1987, 1).

As table 5.1 shows, the geographical pattern of FDI has been shifting as well, reflecting changing motivations. Through the 1960s and 1970s, the largest share of FDI went to the developing countries of Asia. More recently, however, Japanese FDI has shifted toward developed countries, with the United States now accounting for the single largest share (44 percent).

Table 5.1   Japanese foreign direct investment, 1975 and 1987

	FY 1975		FY 1987	
	Million dollars	Percentage share	Million dollars	Percentage share
North America	905	27.6	15,357	46.0
Latin America	372	11.3	4,816	14.4
Europe	333	10.2	6,576	19.7
Asia	1,100	33.5	4,868	14.6
Oceania	182	5.5	1,413	4.2
Africa	192	5.9	272	0.8
Middle East	196	6.0	62	0.2
Total	3,280		33,364	

Source: Japan Economic Institute, *JEI Report,* 17 June 1988.

Figure 5.2   Cumulative foreign direct investment position of Japan,1962–87

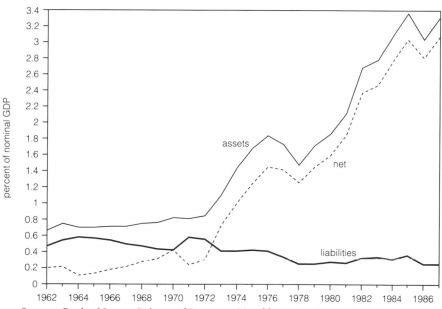

Sources: Bank of Japan, *Balance of Payments Monthly*, various issues; IMF, *International Financial Statistics*, various issues.

Table 5.2   Sectoral composition of Japan's foreign direct investment, 1987

	Amount (million dollars)	Percentage share
Manufacturing	7,832	23.5
Food Products	328	1.0
Textiles	206	0.6
Wood Products	317	1.0
Chemicals	910	2.7
Metals	786	2.4
Nonelectric Machinery	687	2.1
Electric Machinery	2,421	7.3
Transport Equipment	1,473	4.4
Other	703	2.1
Nonmanufacturing	25,088	75.2
Agriculture/Forestry	97	0.3
Fisheries	44	0.1
Mining	511	1.5
Construction	87	0.3
Trade/Sales	2,269	6.8
Banking/Finance/Insurance	10,673	32.0
Services	2,780	8.3
Transportation	2,145	6.4
Real Estate	5,428	16.3
Other	1,047	3.1
Branch Offices	452	1.3
Total	33,364	100.0

Source: Japan Economic Institute, *JEI Report,* 17 June 1988.

The sectoral distribution of Japanese FDI in 1986 is reported in table 5.2. The largest single industry total was registered by the financial sector, which accounted for 32.0 percent of FDI. This was followed by real estate (16.3 percent) and transportation services (8.3 percent). Investment in manufacturing accounted for a 23.5 percent share, with the largest sub-shares found in electric machinery (7.3 percent) and transport equipment (4.4 percent).

These aggregate figures disguise, however, differences in Japanese FDI in developing and in developed countries. In the developing countries, Japanese FDI has traditionally gone into trade-related operations, natural resource-extractive industries (mining, petroleum, and timber), or manufacturing (Kojima 1985). Investment in extractive industries was generally undertaken with an eye toward supplying the Japanese home market, frequently with government support. The Japanese government underwrote the financial risks of overseas natural resource development projects and encouraged the creation of consortia, for example, in oil and bauxite extraction projects (Pangetsu 1980). Government promotion of such projects was viewed as necessary in light of the large capital costs and relatively small size of the Japanese firms involved. As a consequence of governmental bureaucratic delays, however, more companies are opting to enter into joint projects with foreign firms rather than into government consortia (Pangetsu 1980).

In the case of manufacturing, most Japanese FDI initially went into labor-intensive sectors such as textiles, where Japanese comparative advantage was eroding because of rising labor costs. Japanese FDI in the developing countries continues to be concentrated in sectors characterized by declining Japanese comparative advantage. As a result, FDI has begun to occur even in more capital-intensive industries such as basic metals and machinery. Some FDI in automobiles and parts also occurred in developing countries, to exploit labor-cost advantages.

Furthermore, Japanese manufacturing FDI in the developing countries has displayed some distinctive national characteristics. The initial foray into overseas production of labor-intensive manufactures was facilitated by large Japanese trading companies with international business acumen and an extensive knowledge of local markets (Pangetsu 1980). The trading firms encouraged Japanese domestic firms with production and marketing expertise to relocate overseas in order to exploit abundant cheap labor. Once established, Japanese firms tended to both sell a greater share of output in the local market and to export a greater share back to the home market, in comparison with non-Japanese foreign firms (Hill and Johns 1985). That is, Japanese firms used their knowledge of products and marketing techniques appropriate to a certain level of economic development to sell in the local market. They also used their knowledge of, and access to, the Japanese market to export from host countries back to Japan. Japanese firms exported less to third country markets than did other foreign firms.

More recently, there has been a surge of Japanese FDI into the East Asian NICs. Japanese FDI in Korea, Taiwan, and Hong Kong more than sextupled, from $379 million in FY 1985 to $2.58 billion in FY 1987, with further increases anticipated. As in the past, significant exports back to Japan are expected, and, in fact, the growth of exports from these countries to Japan accelerated strongly in 1987.

Investment in developed countries has an entirely different character. Japanese FDI in the developed countries has largely taken the form of investment in the financial sector, portfolio investments in real estate, or investment in manufacturing motivated by a desire to jump over trade barriers against Japanese exports.[5] A case in point is the United States. In 1986 only 13.6 percent of Japanese FDI in the United States was in manufacturing. The majority (61 percent) was either by trading firms in their US subsidiaries or in real estate. In contrast, 46.9 percent of US FDI in Japan was in manufacturing, and another 23.0 percent was in petroleum. United States manufacturing FDI in Japan exceeded Japanese manufacturing FDI in the United States by $2.3 billion in 1986.[6]

The largest share of Japanese FDI in the United States in 1986 went into electronics, followed by the transport industry.[7] Analysts predict that Japanese firms will produce 2.1–2.2 million cars in the United States by 1990, or roughly the amount they currently export to the US market (Kiuchi 1987).[8] This expansion of capacity, combined with an expected reduction of exports from Japan, means that by 1990 Japanese firms will produce more cars in the United States than they export there.[9] In fact, Japanese firms plan to export from the United States. Honda, for instance, recently announced plans to export 70,000 cars from US plants to Japan and Europe by 1991.[10] Similarly, NEC expects eventually to export semiconductors to Europe and Japan from expanded US facilities, and Sanyo has announced that it will export to Japan 5,000–6,000 luxury television sets from a plant in Arkansas.[11]

Existing Japanese majority-owned production facilities in the United States employ about 113,000 workers (Japan Economic Institute 1987, 3). Including employment at minority-owned firms and plants begun but not yet onstream, the total employment associated with Japanese FDI in the United States will soon exceed 150,000.

Direct investment in new production facilities is not the only form that Japanese FDI in the developed countries takes. Japanese firms have also entered into joint ventures or tie-ins with existing local firms, though these approaches appear to be declining in popularity, at least in the United States (Japan Economic Institute 1987, 2).

A final avenue of Japanese FDI has been mergers and acquisitions of existing firms. The pace of acquisitions of foreign companies by Japanese

---

5. In this regard, Japanese investment in the Mexican *maquiladoras* represents an interesting case, since it combines the motivation behind FDI in LDCs (cheap labor) with the desire to circumvent export barriers in the United States.

6. US Department of Commerce, *Survey of Current Business*, various issues.

7. *JEI Report*, 2 July 1987.

8. Also see *Wall Street Journal*, 27 February 1987.

9. *Economist*, 2 May 1987.

10. *Washington Post*, 18 September 1987.

11. *Washington Post*, 6 February 1988; 9 January 1988.

firms has accelerated in response to the yen appreciation, which has at once raised production costs in Japan and made foreign assets relatively cheap. In the US electronics industry alone, Japanese firms made around 400 acquisitions in 1986.[12] The biggest single acquisition so far has been Bridgestone's purchase of Firestone Tire and Rubber for $2.6 billion. The most celebrated Japanese acquisition, however, was one that was never consummated—the proposed Fujitsu purchase of Fairchild Industries, which was opposed by the US government on national security grounds. The Fairchild case was expected by some analysts to put a short-run damper on Japanese acquisitions of US firms, though the long-run impact will probably not be great.[13]

The Fairchild case points to a possible area of future contention between Japan and other industrial countries. As long as mergers and acquisitions are relatively rare in Japan, the great preponderance of takeovers will involve Japanese firms acquiring foreign firms, rather than foreign firms buying Japanese firms. If merger and acquisition activity runs in one direction it could provoke political opposition in OECD host countries. The absence of host country firms with a matching stake in Japanese firms eliminates one potential source of host country domestic political resistance to future schemes to restrict Japanese investment. Just as it is sometimes argued that intraindustry trade in goods encourages political opposition to protection, corporate interpenetration could act as a political counterweight to restrictions on international investment.

The rapid growth of Japanese FDI has led to fears of the "hollowing out" of the home islands and the deindustrialization of Japan. As noted in Chapter 1, these fears are exaggerated. Apart from the factors mentioned there, the absorptive capacities of the NICs are too small to accommodate a mass exodus of manufacturing from Japan: The combined GNPs of Korea and Taiwan are only 7 percent of Japan's (Kiuchi 1987). Furthermore, the growth in FDI is not incompatible with the growth of employment opportunities at home. Indeed, by advancing the international division of labor, offshore production will facilitate the upgrading of domestic jobs, shifting workers into higher productivity, higher wage jobs, and raising the domestic standard of living.

Portfolio Investment

Though large and growing, foreign direct investment is dwarfed by financial investment, which increased from a net $8.4 billion in 1980 to $117.6 billion

---

12. *Business Week*, 17 November 1986.

13. *New York Times*, 7 July 1987.

in 1986 (Kawai and Okumura 1987, table 4). Investment in foreign securities took a lion's share of this increase, shifting from a net inflow of $9.4 billion in 1980 to a net outflow of $116.0 in 1987 (Kawai and Okumura 1987, table 5). The largest share of this outflow has gone to the United States (48 percent), followed by EC countries (40 percent) and other OECD countries (7 percent) (Kawai and Okumura 1987, table 4). As these figures show, the vast majority of Japanese portfolio investment is in other developed countries.

Econometric models of Japanese portfolio investment that emphasize the role of interest rate differentials, exchange risk, etc., have not been particularly successful in explaining the rapid growth of capital outflows (Kawai 1987; Ueda 1987). Instead, attention has focused on several institutional changes that occurred over the period and contributed to the outflow. The most important of these was probably the dramatic liberalization of capital controls, which began with the Foreign Exchange Law of December 1980.[14] While this law abolished the system of prior approval for foreign securities investment, an extensive system of monitoring and administrative guidance remained in place, complete with ceilings for purchases of foreign securities. In effect, with the liberalization of capital controls, Japanese investors were permitted to undertake a portfolio reallocation toward foreign securities, albeit slowed by the ceilings for foreign security purchases.

This movement was reinforced by a portfolio shift within Japan, from depository-type savings institutions with a low securities orientation, such as postal saving, toward more securities-oriented contractual-type savings institutions, such as insurance companies and investment trusts (Okumura 1987, 3–5). As a result, the trend toward foreign securities holding was reinforced by the greater overall prominence of securities in Japanese portfolios. The movement toward larger and more experienced institutions in the foreign investment arena may have also contributed to a reduction in transactions costs and the degree of risk aversion (Ueda 1987, 21–22).

An important implication of this analysis is that much of the recent increase in Japanese portfolio investment may represent a once-and-for-all shift in portfolio allocation toward foreign securities. Recent growth trends thus may not continue indefinitely into the future. Furthermore, once an equilibrium portfolio allocation has been attained, interest rate differentials, exchange risk, and exchange rate volatility may play a much greater role in determining investment decisions at the margin. As a consequence, the exchange rate may exhibit a greater elasticity with respect to interest rate differentials in the future, possibly indicating a more important role for monetary and fiscal policies in determining the exchange rate.

---

14. See Frankel (1984) for an analysis of this process.

Cyclical Variation in Investment Activity

The analysis so far has been concerned with the long-run determinants of investment behavior. Investment, like all macroeconomic aggregates, also exhibits significant cyclical variation.[15] From both a domestic and a global standpoint, it is useful to understand this cyclical behavior and attempt to design policies to reduce the amplitude of swings in investment cycles.

As we saw earlier, long-run trends in investment will be significantly affected by the level of domestic and foreign economic activity. In the short run, however, sudden or unexpected changes in the economy—shocks—will cause investment to fluctuate significantly around the longer-run trend. Monetarists would identify unexpected changes in the money supply as the principal source of shocks. Other economists would argue that real shocks play a more important role. Keynesians would identify sudden changes in real demand as the most likely source of real shocks in the economy, while "real business cycle" economists would assign that role to supply-side shocks (from technological change, for example).

Yoshikawa and Ohtake (1987) used data for both aggregate and individual industry output to examine this question. They found that a purely monetary explanation of Japanese postwar business cycles could be decisively rejected. Of the two competing real shock theories, they found that the data appeared to support more strongly the Keynesian demand-side approach. Two such shocks are unexpected changes in foreign and domestic demand. The estimated responses of Japanese net investment to negative shocks in domestic and foreign demand are illustrated in figure 5.3.[16] Downward shocks in both domestic and foreign demand lead to a decline in net investment. The decline in investment in response to a downturn in domestic growth is felt quickly, reaching maximum impact after three quarters, while the world growth slowdown filters through the system more slowly, peaking in the sixth quarter. As might be expected, the impact of an external shock

---

15. The most cyclical component of investment is inventories. Inventory investment will not be treated separately, because, as Horiye et al. (1987) note, in the Japanese case "its influence on GNP is relatively small because the contribution ratio to GNP is decreasing" (51). Furthermore, "the impact of inventory cycles has become much smaller, because the importance of inventory investment in GNP has declined markedly due to changes in economic structure" (74).

16. These figures are impulse responses derived from a vector autoregression (VAR) model of Japanese net investment. The endogenous variables were net investment, GNP, partner-country GDP, and the exchange rate. The interest rate was included as a deterministic variable. All variables were expressed in real terms. The model was estimated using deseasonalized quarterly data from 1970:1–1984:4. For further details see Appendix D. For an introduction to VAR methodology see Sims (1980). The responses mapped in figure 5.3 are for one standard deviation, hence, typical shocks.

Figure 5.3 Estimated responses of Japanese net investment to shocks in domestic and foreign demand

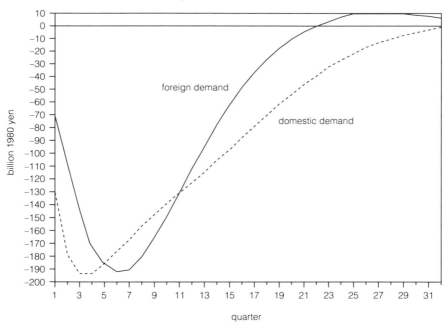

is more ephemeral, while shocks to the domestic economy are more persistent. Research by Horiye, though, suggests that the increasing reliance of the Japanese economy on export-led growth in the early 1980s has made domestic absorption and investment even more sensitive to foreign demand (1987, 43).

Shocks to investment can also come from the exchange rate, by affecting export performance and altering the profitability of trade and investment in traded goods industries.[17] An exchange rate depreciation will tend to make domestic tradable goods industries more internationally competitive and encourage exports. Such a change can lead to windfall profits among exporting firms, raising corporate saving and encouraging a further expan-

---

17. One avenue through which the exchange rate could affect saving and investment is through wealth effects. Changes in the exchange rate affect the real value of accumulated wealth, and could encourage compensating behavior among asset holders. So, for example, a depreciation would reduce the real value of wealth held in domestically denominated assets (in terms of a consumption basket containing both domestic and imported goods) and induce saving to restore the real balances.

Figure 5.4 Japanese MERM rate, 1971–1987

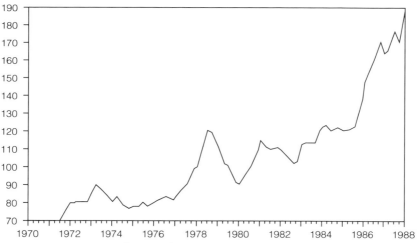

Source: IMF, *International Financial Statistics*, various issues.

sion of capacity. Conversely, an exchange rate appreciation stimulates imports, putting pressure on domestic import-competing industries and reducing profit margins on exports.

As shown in figure 5.4, the Japanese exchange rate has exhibited several periods of rapid appreciation or depreciation. The exchange rate rose rapidly in 1977–1978, then fell with equal swiftness in 1979, reaching a trough in the second quarter of 1980. From there it appreciated through the first quarter of 1981, depreciated for about a year and a half, then stabilized. In the fall of 1985, however, it began to appreciate rapidly, ushering in the period of *endaka* or high yen.

In the current Japanese context it is therefore more appropriate to speak of the effects of a sudden *appreciation* in the exchange rate. The effect of an upward shock to the exchange rate is to reduce gross savings and investment by squeezing the tradables sector.[18] The econometric results displayed in figure 5.5 are confirmed by a variety of sectoral evidence. MITI's sectoral indices of productive capacity show that during the low-yen period the electrical machinery sector exhibited by far the highest rate of capacity increase, more than doubling capacity between 1980 and 1986. The second

---

18. It should be noted, though, that it would have an opposite effect on the non-tradables sector. The result shown in figure 5.5 could be interpreted as indicating that the effect on the tradables sector is dominant under export-led growth. This issue is treated more fully in Chapter 6.

Figure 5.5 Estimated response of Japanese fixed investment to an exchange rate appreciation

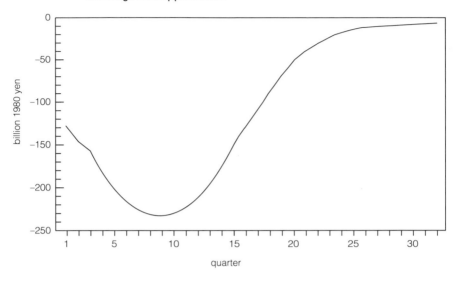

highest growth rate was in the precision instruments sector, identified in Chapter 2 as an area of dynamic comparative advantage. Industries oriented toward the domestic market (such as chemicals, oil refining, paper, and food) all showed slower than average growth in capacity. Conversely, exchange rate appreciation reduces the profitability of investment in the tradables sector.

The importance of the response of investment activity to external shocks is well illustrated by the severe supply-side shock caused by the tripling of oil prices in 1979. Japan was particularly hard hit, because oil makes up a large share of the Japanese import basket. Oil imports as a percentage of GDP more than doubled, from 3.05 percent in 1978 to 6.11 percent in 1980. This sudden shock to domestic absorption was accompanied by a slowdown in growth worldwide. The direct impact of these developments was exacerbated by the fact that changes in the rate of investment activity have feedback effects on overall economic growth.

The oil price increase in 1979 was a particularly hard shock for the world economy. It was felt throughout the world and involved significant changes in relative prices. Japanese firms needed to adopt new production technologies in the wake of major changes in the relative prices of productive inputs. Specifically, this necessitated investment in energy-conserving or non-oil-consuming technologies. However, the slowdown in growth reduced revenues at precisely the time that the oil shock had rendered much of the old capital stock obsolete.[19] As a result, the effective capital stock in Japan returned to its normal growth path slowly, and the Japanese economy exhibited a prolonged downward deviation from its normal growth trajectory.

Policy Recommendations

Our analysis of Japanese investment behavior suggests that policymakers face two sets of interrelated but conceptually distinct issues. One set of problems concerns the the cyclical variability of investment activity, and the sensitivity of the Japanese economy to external shocks in the form of sudden changes in foreign demand, commodity prices, and the exchange rate. A second set of issues pertains to the secular decline in Japanese investment, especially in light of the large current account surplus.

To address these issues in turn, there is a need to improve countercyclical policies in order to reduce fluctuations in investment. As noted earlier, some reduction in the amplitude of the cycles may have come naturally through the shift in investment composition away from "big ticket" items for heavy industry. This effect may be accentuated by the dispersion of investment across an increasing number of firms.

Policymakers have been reasonably adept in using off-budget items—especially the Fiscal Investment and Loan Program (FILP)—as a counter-cyclical investment tool. The May 1987 supplementary budget is a case in point. A strengthening of automatic stabilizers would be desirable, though. One possibility would be to introduce a system of countercyclical investment tax measures focusing on business investment and housing. With regard to business investment, the tax measures could take at least two forms.

One option would be a countercyclical system of investment tax credits (ITC). This could be accomplished with an ITC that automatically varied with a specified index of economic indicators (such as a moving average of the rate of change of GDP) or was automatically triggered by such an index. The problem with ITCs is that it is by no means obvious how successful they are at inducing additional investment at the margin. While firms will typically claim large amounts of tax writeoffs through ITCs, it is the incremental change in investment, not the total credit claimed, that is relevant here. In light of the difficulty in using the tax system to spur investment in the short run, a countercyclical corporate income tax might be preferable.

---

19. The exchange rate depreciation which accompanied the oil shock helped stabilize investment by increasing the profitability of export activities.

A countercyclical tax (again, either in the form of a varying tax rate or a countercyclical surcharge) would tend to smooth after-tax profits (the most volatile component in national income) across the business cycle. Presumably this would have some impact on smoothing investment. Since bonus wage payments vary with profits, it would also tend to smooth bonus wage payments across the business cycle and act as a countercyclical stabilizer for consumer, as well as investment, demand. Taking a longer-run perspective, the marginal propensity to consume out of bonus payments would tend to rise as the bonus payment stream became more smooth and predictable.

The other area in which government policy could exert a stabilizing force on investment demand is housing. On the supply side, the government has an important role in the provision of housing. Again, special measures could be taken to strengthen the countercyclical impact of government construction. One possibility would be to establish a special construction fund in the Japan Housing and Urban Development Corporation that would be triggered by a precipitous drop in housing starts or construction activity. On the demand side, policies could be implemented through the Housing Loan Public Corporation, the primary government mortgage institution. The potential impact of programs of this sort are large, since the government accounts for over 40 percent of total housing loans (Lincoln 1988, 279).

As in the case of the ITC, it is unclear what the actual impact of countercyclically easing mortgage requirements would be, because part of the effect would simply be to shift financing from private to government sources. The impact might be greater if these actions were coordinated with government countercyclical supply-side measures. One could imagine, for instance, a program in which recession-induced housing slumps would trigger the initiation of new construction projects from the Ministry of Construction's Special Fund, matched by the issuance of special mortgage contracts designated for these dwellings.

Two caveats should be noted, however. First, policymakers must be very careful when designing countercyclical policies. The emphasis on automaticity in the preceding recommendations is intended to reduce the uncertainty associated with government policy and to insure its prompt implementation. Failure to act promptly is highly undesirable. For one thing, a downturn would be needlessly intensified. Then, when action comes, there is a risk that it will be too late, leaning with, rather than against, the wind and opening up the real danger that policy intervention could intensify rather than moderate cyclical fluctuations in economic activity. In designing countercyclical policies, timing is everything.

The second caveat is that countercyclical measures cannot address the longer-run issue of the secular decline in investment in Japan. Specific policies are needed to address this. One place to start would be in the area of research and development. As noted in Chapter 2, the Japanese government's support for R&D activities is not particularly strong. The strengthening of current efforts and the introduction of reforms along the lines mentioned in Chapter 2 would enhance Japan's research capabilities. This would in turn spur technological advance, which would encourage investment and more broadly improve the quality of life.

Housing is another candidate for attention. When real private housing investment leveled off in 1986, this halted the nearly 20 percent decline that had taken place since 1978. At the same time, there was a major shortfall in the government's plans. The goal of the fourth Five-Year Housing Plan was to construct 7.7 million units over the 1981–1985 period. Only 5.9 million units were built, even though the Housing Loan Corporation eventually assumed a greater financing burden than originally had been planned.

Spurred by low interest rates and a fall in materials prices, the housing market went into a cyclical boom in 1986–1988. Nonetheless, the number of housing starts remained below the previous peak years of 1972–1973, and are expected to fall in 1988.[20] The depressed condition of the housing industry in prior years, the inability of the government to reach its housing goals, and the generally low quality of Japanese housing indicate that substantial scope remains for expanding and upgrading the Japanese housing stock.

Since the status of the Japanese housing market was discussed in detail in earlier chapters, it should suffice to reiterate that the causes of much of the housing problem lie in a combination of poor land policies and extensive regulation. Marginal countercyclical increases in public housing subsidies neither address these issues nor constitute a long-term solution to the problem. While fiscal stimulus to the housing industry (and infrastructural investment in general) may be part of the solution, to be really effective such stimulus needs to be part of a more comprehensive package that addresses a number of microeconomic distortions and market failures.

Such a program should contain a variety of elements. First, there is a clear need for land-use policy reform along the lines outlined in Chapter 4. As it now stands, much government expenditure on housing and infrastructure simply goes to the purchase of overpriced land. For example, land purchases account for around 95 percent of the cost of public works in the Tokyo area.[21] The reform of land-use policies should aim at rationalizing the use of land—specifically, discouraging speculation and eliminating urban farms.

---

20. *Nomura Quarterly Economic Review*, August 1988, 2–3.

21. *Economist*, 5 December 1987.

A reduction in agricultural protection could contribute to this goal, as would higher property taxes on urban farmland.

Second, there is a need for housing regulatory reform. One of the proposals outlined in Chapter 4 for addressing the sunshine regulation/high-rise conundrum should be adopted. That would pave the way for the replacement of smaller structures with high-rise apartments and condominiums surrounded by more open space, in the major urban areas. Third, population dispersal out of the three largest metropolitan areas should be encouraged. The relocation of government offices outside Tokyo would be a start; as mentioned earlier, the government is moving in this direction. This process could be further encouraged by increasing infrastructural investment in outlying areas, as discussed in previous chapters.

The result of all these reforms would be to lower greatly the land component cost of housing. Given the high income elasticity of housing, and provided that supply is forthcoming, this reduction would be offset by increased size and quality, which would constitute an important stimulus to domestic investment.

A sophisticated econometric analysis by Yoshikawa and Ohtake (1987) demonstrates that increases in construction demand have had powerful and pervasive effects throughout the Japanese economy because of the strong interindustry links among construction and other sectors. Larger houses would mean an increased capacity and demand for consumer durables.[22] Likewise, higher quality dwellings would mean improvements in plumbing and more room for furniture and other belongings. Furthermore, an increase in high-rise apartment buildings would reduce commuting time and facilitate leisure activities. A comprehensive expansion and upgrading of the housing stock would thus have strong indirect effects throughout the economy.

In particular, the widespread introduction of flexible manufacturing systems gives Japanese firms a strong capability to reorient production from the foreign to the domestic market as demand conditions change. This will facilitate the shift from reliance on export-led growth to a more domestic orientation. A comprehensive program of housing rebuilding and renewal would begin to address both the housing related problems detailed in the previous chapter and the quality of life issues raised in Chapter 1.

Conclusion

In our analysis of Japanese investment behavior, we have noted that the rate of gross investment (including housing) in Japan has declined sub-

---

22. In urban areas land use rationalization would also encourage the construction of multilevel parking garages and facilitate the ownership of automobiles.

stantially since the early 1970s. Saving remains relatively high and, as a result, the external surplus has grown to over 3 percent of GNP. This development has in turn contributed to increasing tensions with Japan's trading partners, and it poses major diplomatic problems for the Japanese.

Policies designed to moderate cyclical swings in investment, to sustain the overall rate of investment in the medium run, and to encourage a shift toward domestic demand-led growth in the long run, would be desirable. The necessity of building a more stable basis for economic growth is widely recognized, and the May 1987 supplementary budget represents a step in the right direction. What is now needed is a program to focus on longer-run issues, along the lines of the Maekawa Commission reports.

Our analysis has led to a number of recommendations for policy. One thing that stands out is the potentially significant contribution that housing policy can make to the government's economic program. Housing is a natural place to start since the government plays a major role on both the demand side (through its mortgage financing functions) and the supply side (as a producer), and since construction activity has a strong indirect impact throughout the economy. An innovative housing policy could help meet both the short- and medium-run goals of investment policy and contribute to a significant improvement in Japanese living standards.

6

The Interaction of Domestic and International Macroeconomic Forces

In previous chapters we have investigated the determinants of Japanese saving and investment. In this chapter we analyze the interrelationships between domestic and international macroeconomic forces. We then examine the role of macroeconomic policy in addressing immediate concerns and the longer-run evolution of the Japanese economy and its role in the global economic system.

The Interaction of Macroeconomic Aggregates

In an *ex post*, accounting sense, the excess of domestic savings over investment (S–I) is identically equal to the current account (the balance on merchandise trade in goods and services, plus remittances and unilateral transfers). There is nothing that requires that this relationship hold *ex ante*. Economic agents' plans may generate excess demands or supplies, which are then equilibrated by price changes (in international trade, by exchange rate changes) that lead to the accounting identity holding *ex post*.

Recently, however, there has been a revival of an old view that regards the current account as simply the balance between exogenously determined domestic saving and investment propensities. This position is controversial since it implies that neither exchange rates (Mundell 1987; McKinnon and Ohno 1986) nor trade policy (Saxonhouse 1985) have any effect on the current account. It has been criticized on the grounds that it substitutes an accounting identity for a behavioral model (Krugman and Baldwin 1987). While in an accounting sense it is true that the current account is the difference between domestic savings and investment, the levels of domestic savings and investment should properly be regarded as endogenously determined; in the short to medium run, they may exhibit significant variation due to changes in interest rates, exchange rates, trade policy, and economic activity.

This is because these variables are all interrelated. For example, changes in the exchange rate have substantial and persistent effects on the aggregate level of domestic investment, as well as on its sectoral composition, and on the real wage and the profitability of trade, as seen in Chapter 5. In turn, the adjustment of domestic saving and investment would presumably generate excess demand and supply in product and asset markets, which would induce equilibrating movements in prices and exchange rates and in the level of economic activity both at home and abroad. It would be desirable, then, to have some way of tracing these repercussions through the economy in order to understand the medium-run behavior of these aggregates and, possibly, the impact of policy changes.

Recent advances in statistical methodology have given researchers the tools to analyze the causal relationships among these variables.[1] Analyses of the causal relations among Japanese macroeconomic variables have been undertaken by Horiye et al. (1987) and Yoshikawa and Ohtake (1987). Horiye et al. analyzed the patterns of cyclical fluctuation in real activity in the postwar period. They concluded that the severity of Japanese business cycles had declined since the mid-1970s, though there was some evidence of greater instability since 1985. They ascribed the decline in the amplitude of the business cycle to two factors: first, more stable macroeconomic policies, and second, a reduction in investment cycles. The reduction in investment cycles, as noted in the previous chapter, is related to the increasing diffusion of investment demand across industries and firms that has been associated with the introduction of automation and the move toward service industries.

Yoshikawa and Ohtake obtained a result consistent with this interpretation. They found that in the period before the first oil shock, changes in investment caused changes in real GNP, but did not in the post-oil shock period. They attribute this to the heavily construction industry-oriented character of investment activity in the earlier period, which brought with it

---

1. The conceptual basis of this work was formulated by Granger (1969) and rests on two propositions. The first is that a variable X causes a variable Y if taking into account past observations of X contributes to improved predictions on Y. In other words, there is relevant information about Y contained in X that is not contained in Y itself. The second proposition is that the future cannot predict the past: causality can only run from the past to the present or future, it cannot run in the opposite direction.

Sims (1972) developed a way of implementing Granger's notion of causality using regressions involving past, current, and future values of X and Y. Later (1980), he extended this technique to multivariate cases using the technique of vector auto-regression (VAR). (A more detailed description of this technique, and the statistical results underlying the following discussion, are contained in Appendix D.)

large interindustry effects throughout the economy. In contrast, investment activities in the more recent period have had smaller indirect effects, and thus smaller impacts on the overall level of economic activity.

While these results indicate that macroeconomic policy and changes in investment patterns have contributed to a dampening of Japanese business cycles in the recent period, export behavior has had the opposite effect. Horiye et al. found that, in the period prior to the mid-1970s, exports responded to slackness in the domestic market—that is, they were "vent-for-surplus" or "recession-driven." However, in the subsequent period, Japanese growth was literally "export-led," as the direction of causality began to run the other way (Horiye 1987, 43). At the same time, the responsiveness of exports to changes in US demand conditions increased, and the business cycles of the two countries began to synchronize.

In this study, we analyze the causal relations among Japanese macroeconomic variables, including Japanese GNP, saving, investment, domestic absorption, current account, foreign income, the exchange rate, and the real interest rate. The results are reported in detail in Appendix D. These results indicate that there were strong feedback relationships among many of the variables. Domestic absorption, foreign income, and the exchange rate all were found to exert independent causal influence on the level of the current account. Conversely, changes in the current account, foreign income, and the exchange rate were shown to cause changes in domestic absorption. All the variables in the system affect the exchange rate, albeit only to a limited extent. The rate of interest was found to be exogenous.[2] These relationships are perhaps most usefully illustrated in table 6.1, which provides the results of a variance decomposition of the estimates.

The table reports the share of the forecast variance (the variance of the forecast error) accounted for by each variable at one, four, eight and twelve quarters. The model has been triangularized so that the forecast errors are due entirely to unexpected changes in the left-hand side variable itself in step one (i.e., its own share in step one is 100). This unanticipated change in the left-hand side variable (a shock), affects the other variables in the system. Changes in these other variables, then, feed back and affect the left-hand side variable further. Table 6.1 reports the percentage of the forecast error variance accounted for by each variable; together the shares in each row sum to 100.

A variable that was completely unaffected by changes in the other variables

---

2. Note that this does not mean that the real interest rate was *independent* of the other variables (or vice versa), merely that the other variables did not statistically cause variations in the real interest rate. This is consistent with a similar result obtained by Litterman and Weiss (1985) and Noland (1987b) for the United States.

Table 6.1   Decomposition of forecast variances for Japanese macroeconomic variables

Left-hand side variable: CA

STEP	SERR	CA	ABSORB	GWP	ER
1	184.02	100.00	0.00	0.00	0.00
4	270.01	65.67	12.74	8.26	13.33
8	398.60	48.15	7.92	15.74	28.19
12	502.05	43.31	6.84	11.73	38.12

Left-hand side variable: ABSORB

STEP	SERR	ABSORB	CA	GWP	ER
1	1383.43	100.00	0.00	0.00	0.00
4	1972.21	52.72	7.09	25.93	14.25
8	2569.25	33.98	31.46	16.37	18.19
12	2778.04	35.01	27.62	15.67	21.69

Left-hand side variable: GWP

STEP	SERR	GWP	ER	CA	ABSORB
1	0.31	100.00	0.00	0.00	0.00
4	0.50	83.72	3.96	5.15	7.16
8	1.11	21.04	53.27	23.54	2.15
12	1.62	11.03	57.18	30.16	1.62

Left-hand side variable: ER

STEP	SERR	ER	CA	ABSORB	GWP
1	1.78	100.00	0.00	0.00	0.00
4	3.00	68.64	22.17	2.04	7.15
8	6.16	77.90	7.24	1.94	12.92
12	7.28	71.60	6.72	1.46	20.22

Note: The data are as follows: (1) STEP is the quarter for which the forecast is made; (2) SERR is the standard error of forecast for the left-hand side variable; (3) the remaining data are the percentages of the forecast error variances of the left-hand side variable accounted for by innovations in the right-hand side variable. The variables are the Japanese current account (CA); Japanese domestic absorption (ABSORB); gross world product, excluding Japan (GWP); and the multilateral effective exchange rate (ER).

in the system (in statistical terminology, a strictly exogenous variable) would display 100 in its own column at each time horizon. Conversely, the lower the share of forecast error variance accounted for by unanticipated changes in the variable itself, the more its path is determined by other variables in the system; the magnitude of their shares indicates the strength of their influence.

The variance decomposition for the current account appears in the first panel of table 6.1. At four quarters, the variables relating to the level of economic activity—domestic absorption (ABSORB) and gross world product (GWP)—have a larger combined impact than the exchange rate (ER). The effects of changes in domestic absorption appear more quickly than those in foreign income, which, as in the case of investment in Chapter 5, take longer to be felt. However, while the exchange rate's initial impact is small, it builds steadily, and accounts for a larger share of forecast error variance than the two activity variables combined at eight and twelve quarters.

The variance decomposition of domestic absorption is presented in the next panel of table 6.1. The path of domestic absorption is strongly affected by the other variables, with each of the others accounting for a significant share of forecast variance at all time horizons.[3]

The variance decomposition for gross world product shows that, as might be expected in the short run, it is the least affected by unexpected changes in the other variables in the system, with its own changes accounting for 80 percent of its total change after four quarters. This share then plummets as the effects of exchange rate and current account shocks work their way through the system, and the rest of the world responds to changes in the Japanese economy.[4]

---

3. Some of these results are puzzling, though. The share accounted for by the exchange rate at four quarters is slightly larger in the absorption decomposition than the current account decomposition. One would presumably expect the opposite. Likewise, GWP accounts for a large share of forecast variance at four quarters. In other words, domestic absorption appears to be sensitive to changes in external conditions, and with regard to the exchange rate, more sensitive than the current account itself.

The sensitivity of domestic absorption is consistent with the results on export cycles presented by Horiye (1987) and Horiye et al. (1987). Furthermore, as shown in Appendix D, the exchange rate causes domestic saving according to the statistical criteria of Granger and Sims. Likewise, variations in GWP cause (in this statistical sense) changes in both saving and investment. Given the export orientation of the Japanese economy, this should not be surprising: Changes in the exchange rate and foreign demand generate shocks to corporate profits, and hence saving, and/or act as a signal to induce investment activity.

4. It should be stressed that the shares accounted for by individual right-hand side variables are affected by their position in the ordering of the decomposition. Thus, for example, if the positions of ABSORB and ER are reversed in the GWP decompositon, the forecast variance share of ER never reaches 50 percent, although it remains the predominant causal influence at 8 and 12 quarters. The reason for this

The exchange rate appears to be the next most exogenous variable, with its own share never falling below 70 percent in any reported forecast horizon. Current account changes affect the exchange rate almost immediately; unanticipated changes in foreign income are felt more slowly.

Overall, the results in table 6.1 tell a plausible and consistent story, in which changes in domestic economic variables affect the system quickly and changes in foreign variables are associated with longer lags. The current account is affected by shocks in real activity variables and by the exchange rate. Changes in domestic activity have the most immediate effects; the impact of changes in foreign activity is felt more slowly. Changes in the exchange rate have the most significant effects on the current account, but accumulate more slowly still. This pattern of responses is consistent with those obtained from the estimates of trade equations in the following section, and could explain so-called "J-curve" effects in the current account balance.

These results are of considerable policy interest. They indicate that while changes in the exchange rate will eventually have substantial effects on external balances, these effects will have considerable lags. Changes in activity, particularly domestic activity, will have a much more immediate impact on the current account. This suggests that policy initiatives aimed at domestic absorption, such as fiscal policy, may be more effective in the short run (i.e., within one year) than those aimed at the exchange rate. Experience indicates that sterilized intervention in the foreign exchange market (in which changes in the domestic money supply are offset by open-market operations) has only minor and temporary effects. Unsterilized intervention (which does change the domestic money supply) does affect the exchange rate, but even here the uncertainty surrounding the magnitudes of these effects warns against attempting to fine tune the exchange rate. It should be reiterated, however, that the exchange rate has significant medium-run importance. The difficulty from a political standpoint is that these effects may be associated with unacceptably long lags.

Our analysis of the responsiveness of the current account to temporary shocks in domestic absorption indicates that the effect is felt quickly, peaking and then declining after about one quarter. This suggests that countercyclical investment stabilization measures such as the ones discussed in the previous chapter could be effective in smoothing cycles for both real activity and the current account. The VAR results imply that longer-run sustained adjustment policies to increase domestic absorption, such as the

---

is that when right-hand side variables used in the decomposition move closely together (ER and ABSORB in this example), the variable that receives "credit" for influence on the series being decomposed (in this case GWP) depends upon which variable is considered first in the ordering.

land-use or tax reforms discussed in Chapters 4 and 5, would result in a gradual adjustment of the current account of a similar magnitude to the change in saving or investment.

The analysis of the impact of exchange rate changes on the trade balance and the current account is complicated by the long lags of these effects, as well as by the distinction between value and volume changes resulting from shifts in the terms of trade. It is to this topic that we now turn.

The Exchange Rate and the Japanese Trade Balance

The exchange rate affects the trade balance by changing the relative prices of imports and exports. In the short run, however, changes in the exchange rate have a perverse effect, because changes in actual flows of goods and services lag behind movements in the exchange rate. This gives rise to the familiar J-curve effect, in which the trade balance initially deteriorates in response to a depreciation of the currency.

In the case of the recent Japanese experience, one should examine the effects of a currency appreciation. The immediate impact of an appreciation is to improve the trade balance, as prices of traded goods incorporate the appreciation quickly while volumes take longer to adjust, leading to a divergence of the real and nominal trade balance. As a result of the appreciation, exporting activity becomes less profitable: competitors' goods become relatively cheaper in foreign markets and production at home for the domestic market becomes more attractive. The volume of exports begins to fall. Likewise, the higher-valued currency makes imports more attractive and the demand for imported goods increases. Eventually, the higher volume of imports and lower volume of exports bring the trade balance back to its original level. From this point on, the trade surplus continues to decline, stabilizing at a new, lower level.

Trade equations have been estimated for Japan, and the response of the Japanese trade balance to a yen appreciation is shown in figure 6.1.[5] Starting from a position of balanced trade, these estimates indicate that the contemporaneous elasticity of the trade balance (normalized by the value of imports) with respect to a yen appreciation is around 0.9. In other words, the immediate impact of a 10 percent exchange rate appreciation is to *increase* the trade balance by around 9 percent (of the value of imports). Seven to eight quarters after the initial change, the trade account returns to balance, and in the long run, for every 1.0 percent increase in the exchange rate, the trade balance declines 0.4 to 0.5 percent (of the initial value of imports).

---

5. Details of the econometric estimation procedure used to obtain the parameter estimates underlying this diagram are given in Noland (1988b).

Figure 6.1 *Endaka*—Estimated effects of a yen appreciation on the Japanese trade balance

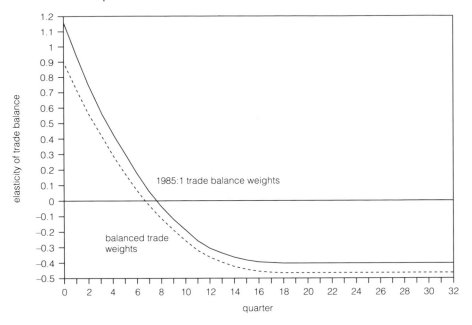

This is the case of balanced trade. Significantly, though, the magnitude of this effect is different if the country starts from a position of net surplus or deficit. In the case of Japan, exports exceeded imports by around 30 percent in the first quarter of 1985, the start of the most recent yen appreciation. Consequently, the initial improvement in the trade balance in response to the yen appreciation would be expected to be even larger than it otherwise might have been. This effect is illustrated in figure 6.1, where, along with the estimates for the balanced trade case, the impact on the trade balance of a currency appreciation using 1985:1 import and export values is also illustrated. In this case the initial increase in the trade balance is even larger (the contemporaneous elasticity is 1.18). The trade surplus then declines steadily, though the negative impact of the appreciation is not felt until nine quarters after the initial appreciation. In the long run, the elasticity of the trade balance with respect to an appreciation is −0.40; i.e., for every 1.0 percent increase in the exchange rate, the trade balance declines by 0.4 percent (of the initial value of imports).[6]

---

6. One caveat should be noted, however. These trade elasticities have been estimated in a partial equilibrium framework; that is, the analysis does not take into account

The point of this analysis is that, in value terms, the effects of the exchange rate on the trade balance take a long time to become apparent. This is particularly true for Japan, since it had a large trade surplus when the current depreciation began. As a result, Japan will continue to run a large surplus in value terms (incurring the wrath of its trade partners) while in volume terms its traded goods output declines (reducing production and employment at home). Eventually, though, the changes in volume will swamp the perverse J-curve valuation effect, and the trade balance will fall in value terms. As a baseline projection, we estimate that the appreciation of the yen that occurred through 1987 will ultimately reduce the Japanese trade surplus by 35 percent from its mid-1987 level, or by around 2 percent of GNP, by 1990.[7]

Beyond these normal adjustment lags, some commentators have argued that the current episode is historically atypical, in that the Japanese trade surplus is not declining (even in volume terms) as much as would be expected on the basis of past behavior. These arguments emphasize the allegedly slow pass-through of the yen's appreciation to export prices in foreign currency terms. (The pass-through ratio indicates the degree to which exchange rate changes are reflected in the foreign prices for exported goods. For example, if the yen appreciates 10 percent against the dollar, and the dollar price of Japanese exports to the United States rises 4 percent, the pass-through ratio would be 40 percent.) Several studies (summarized in Loopesko and Johnson 1987) have found that the pass-throughs exhibited over the 1985–1986 period have been generally smaller than those obtained for a comparable period of yen appreciation in 1977–1978. Loopesko and Johnson calculate a pass-through of 47.6 percent (for total exports) of the

---

the impact of changes in the exchange rate on the level of economic activity. From an econometric standpoint there is a trade-off between intensively modeling the pattern of lagged responses in a few equations and constructing a model with many equations. In Noland (1988b) the emphasis was on the former. Amano (1987) does the latter. He estimates a general equilibrium model of the Japanese trade balance, albeit with a very simple lag pattern. Amano found that, like the results reported here, the "perverse" movement of the J-curve lasts about two years. The ultimate impact of an exchange rate change on the trade balance is also similar to that reported here.

7. This would occur through a slowing of export growth (exports could continue to increase as a result of growth in world demand) and a rapid increase in imports (due both to price and income effects). There would be a relative contraction of the tradables sector and an expansion of the non-tradables sector, in particular, construction and services. Excess domestic saving would decline *ex post* as profits were reduced in the tradables sector and investment in non-tradables rose. The specific estimates are conditional on the path of the exchange rate. The baseline projection is for sustained yen appreciation. If this were to reverse, so would the adjustment of the trade balance.

41 percent yen/dollar appreciation from February 1985 to February 1987. In comparison, they calculate a 66 percent pass-through of the 37 percent appreciation between November 1976 and November 1978.

Several explanations have been proposed for this apparent change in behavior. One explanation points to the emergence of the East Asian NICs. As a result of increased competition from the NICs, Japanese producers are unable to raise the foreign currency export prices of their goods without a significant loss of markets. Industry data appear to support this explanation, as pass-throughs have been much lower in basic industries (chemicals and metals) than in more sophisticated differentiated product industries, such as precision instruments and transportation equipment.

Secondly, it has been pointed out that the current yen appreciation has coincided with a period of falling commodity prices, particularly for oil. Since Japanese exports have a large imported input content, this reduction in input prices has partially offset the appreciation of the yen. When this is taken into account, the current pass-through rates appear unexceptional. Loopesko and Johnson concluded that "the increase in international competition is a key factor in explaining slower pass-through in a few industries; but in most industries, the slower pass-through is more strongly related to the recent declines in raw materials input costs" (1987, 20).

A final set of explanations center on specific characteristics of Japanese industrial organization and production. One explanation is related to the notion of hysteresis, or the apparent failure of the trade balance to respond symmetrically to changes in the exchange rate. Extensive econometric analysis of production and cost functions for Japanese industry by Horiye (1987) indicates that the big expansion of exports in the 1970s and 1980s was accompanied by the introduction of new technologies, the capture of scale economies, and a reduction in costs for a wide range of Japanese manufacturing industries. Japanese firms emerged bigger, more efficient, and more competitive internationally. As a result, these firms are in better position to weather adverse exchange rate movements.

At the same time, the upgrading of the composition of Japanese exports has meant that the markets in which Japanese firms operate are increasingly oligopolistic, differentiated product markets. As research by Yamawaki (1986) has shown, the pricing behavior of Japanese firms in these markets is strongly influenced by the pricing decisions of the domestic firms in the export market. If, as in the case of the US auto industry, US firms raise domestic prices following a yen appreciation, it will reduce foreign firms' loss of market share in the United States and blunt the negative effect of the appreciation on foreign export volumes. Even in competitive industries, one can observe incomplete pass-through and a "hysteretic" pattern of trade if there are costs to firms' entry and exit and uncertainty concerning future levels of the exchange rate (Dixit 1987). In this case, pricing to market, within some bounds, is consistent with long-run profit-maximizing behavior. This may be particularly true for large Japanese corporations, whose commitment to the lifetime employment system may impose large implicit costs to market exit and labor shedding.

Loopesko and Johnson ascribe a possibly more predatory character to this behavior, however. Japanese firms exhibit asymmetrical responses to appreciation and depreciation of the yen. They argue that Japanese firms apply strategic pricing policies to maintain market share. Specifically, they attempt "to keep the dollar price of exports constant in the face of a yen appreciation (i.e., reduce export prices), but would allow some decline in dollar export prices with yen depreciations (i.e., not increase yen export prices)" (1987, 20). Nevertheless, while Japanese firms may forestall the yen appreciation, sustained large movements in the exchange rate will eventually force changes in trade patterns. As noted in Chapter 1, the pass-through rate has risen from 55 percent in 1986 to 64 percent in 1987, possibly indicating a weakening of Japanese firms' abilities to absorb the yen appreciation.

Medium-Run Targets for the Exchange Rate

As noted above, if the yen appreciation were sustained, the trade surplus would fall by approximately 2 percentage points by 1990 from its peak of over four percent of GNP. This is without trade liberalization, which would entail further expenditure-switching on the import side. The question then becomes what is the appropriate level for the exchange rate in the medium run? Are additional measures to target the exchange rate desirable? This question can be answered in one of two ways.

One approach is based on some form of relative purchasing power parity (PPP) calculation, in which the exchange rate moves to equilibrate differential rates of inflation. The precise estimate one obtains will vary depending on the base period and the price level indicator (consumer prices, wholesale prices, unit labor costs, etc.) selected. A number of such calculations are presented in McKinnon and Ohno (1987), who estimated that the PPP yen/dollar rate in 1986:1 was in the range 180–200. On this basis they concluded that, at the current exchange rate, the yen was substantially overvalued.

One problem with this sort of calculation is that if productivity increases are concentrated in the traded goods industries, then PPP calculations based on economywide price indices will be biased (Balassa 1964). Marston (1986) has shown that productivity increases in the Japanese traded goods sector have, in fact, far outstripped gains in the non-traded goods sector. Based on this evidence, Krugman (1986) performs a PPP calculation in which he adjusts for differential rates of productivity growth in the traded- and non-traded goods sectors, assuming that this differential remains constant. Due to the more rapid productivity growth in the traded goods sector, Krugman obtains a PPP yen/dollar rate of 140.

An alternative method of estimating medium-run exchange rate targets involves estimating "sustainable equilibria." The idea here is that the exchange rate should be set to induce a current account balance consistent with the underlying capital flows determined by the savings–investment balance. The equilibria are defined by national saving and investment propensities and by monetary and fiscal policies, which imply a set of underlying capital flows over the relevant horizon. The exchange rate target—in Williamson's terminology (1983), the fundamental equilibrium exchange rate (FEER)—is the exchange rate that would induce a set of matching commodity flows. Working in the Williamson framework, Bergsten and Cline (1987) estimated a yen/dollar FEER of 140–145 for 1987. However, policy reforms (in particular, deficit reduction in the United States) have not been forthcoming, and this estimate has been revised upward by Bergsten to 115 in subsequent remarks, based on analysis in Marris (1987).[8]

Somewhat different sustainability calculations were done by Krugman (1985, 1988). Krugman calculated the US debt to GNP ratio conditional on a variety of exchange rate paths. He concluded that the debt/GNP ratios implied by the contemporaneous exchange rates in 1985 and 1986 were unsustainably high and, as a result, it was likely that the dollar would depreciate substantially. Krugman later updated his evaluations, and concluded in the spring of 1987, when the yen/dollar rate was around 140, that, "while there may still be some need for a further decline in the dollar, the clear-cut case against sustainability is no longer there" (Krugman 1988, 94).

Krause (1986) asked what exchange rate would be consistent with a balanced US current account in 1990 or 1991. Working backward from this proposition, he concluded that a yen/dollar rate of 100 would be necessary for the United States to achieve such a current account position. Finally, Rudiger Dornbusch advocates even more yen appreciation to reduce the US trade deficit to a sustainable level. He estimates that this might require a further 40 percent rise in the yen against the dollar from its January 1988 level, or a rate of 70 to 80 yen per dollar.[9] Martin Feldstein has made similar pronouncements.

---

8. *Washington Post,* 17 September 1987.

9. *Economist,* 23 January 1988.

The appropriate yen/dollar exchange rate estimates identified by these studies thus vary enormously, with the purchasing power parity calculations centering around 140–180, and the sustainability calculations tending toward the 80–130 range. While a certain amount of divergence is to be expected, given the different analytical perspectives, one cannot help but conclude that the estimation of equilibrium exchange rates is a very inexact science.

In summary, the Japanese trade balance and current account are strongly influenced by macroeconomic conditions both at home and abroad. The exchange rate has a considerable impact on the trade balance, but its effects are associated with long and uncertain lags. Moreover, there is considerable disagreement as to what is the most appropriate medium-run target for the exchange rate. The level of foreign economic activity also has a significant impact on the trade balance, though once again these effects are associated with substantial lags. In any event, Japanese policymakers are largely unable to affect economic conditions abroad. In contrast, the effects of domestic economic activity on the trade balance are felt quickly, and macroeconomic policy is under the purview of domestic policymakers. If Japanese policymakers wish to reduce the current account surplus, macroeconomic policy will thus play a central role. We will now turn to this topic.

Recent Monetary and Fiscal Policy

One obvious way of responding to the bind of *endaka* and the need for domestic expansion would be through an easing of monetary policy. Increased monetary growth could be expected to contribute to a depreciation of the exchange rate, and, through its impact on interest rates, to act as a spur to domestic investment. Not surprisingly, the Bank of Japan cut the discount rate from 4.0 percent to 2.5 percent, its lowest level ever. Interest rates fell in parallel fashion and the money supply began growing rapidly, reaching double-digit levels in May 1987. Fueled by the easy money policy, domestic demand responded strongly, pulling the economy out of the *endaka*-induced recession of 1986 and early 1987.

In response to the October 1987 stock market crash, the Bank of Japan poured liquidity into the economy. The key broad money supply indicator rose 12.4 percent in November and 11.5 percent in December. Long-term interest rates drifted downward, dampening the appreciation of the yen, though they remained above their mid-1987 levels. The Bank of Japan's emphasis on the behavior of asset prices and the exchange rate suggests that the relatively easy monetary policy will continue, and the real money supply is expected to grow at a rate of 10–11 percent through 1988.[10] A

---

10. *Nomura Quarterly Review*, August 1988, table 9.

policy of accommodating increases in money demand while keeping a close eye on the spread between long- and short-term rates (as an indicator of inflationary expectations) would seem appropriate. In this connection, consumer prices have remained stable in 1988, giving little indication of inflationary pressures.

On the fiscal policy front, the central and local governments have traditionally run deficits, while the social security fund has run a substantial surplus. The losses of state enterprises have been large. As a result of a consolidated effort to reduce public borrowing, local government deficits have been largely eliminated and the central government has pursued an official medium-run goal of eliminating the issuance of deficit financing bonds by 1990. Most of this fiscal consolidation has been accomplished by greatly limiting spending: Real government expenditure grew at an annual rate of less than one percent over the 1980–1985 period, and the central government deficit fell from 5.5 percent of GNP in 1978 to 1.5 percent in 1986. Altogether, general public sector borrowing (including the social security fund) has fallen steadily from 7 percent of GNP in 1978 to 3 percent in 1986 (OECD 1986, 29).

In response to *endaka,* the government announced an emergency economic package designed to increase domestic demand by 6 trillion yen (between 1 and 2 percent of GNP). This stimulus, which will be spread over several years, is to be accomplished through a combination of tax cuts, new public works initiatives, and front-loading previously authorized projects. The plan includes 2,450 billion yen for public works, 1,000 billion yen in income tax cuts, 800 billion yen for local government projects, 700 billion yen for housing loans, 450 billion yen for disaster relief and reconstruction, 350 billion yen for public education and research facilities, and 250 billion yen for highway construction. In June 1987 the cabinet approved a 2.08 trillion yen supplementary budget for fiscal year 1987 to begin implementing the package. There may have been less here than immediately met the eye, however.[11]

---

11. For one thing, 1 trillion yen of the stimulus is in the form of income tax cuts, and it is by no means clear that this amount will actually be translated into increased consumer spending. A great deal of uncertainty surrounds this legislation; there have been negotiations for nearly one year over various tax reform proposals. If individuals regard the tax reduction as a temporary measure, most of the windfall will probably be saved.

The rest of the package is basically earmarked for increased public works spending and is to be financed through a combination of higher than anticipated tax revenues, construction bond issues, and proceeds from state enterprise privatization sales (including NTT and JAL). Stimulus to the housing market will come through an increase in the value of houses qualifying for loans from the Housing Loan Public Corporation, the primary mortgage institution. These loans could total about 0.7

Led by rapid growth in private demand, the economy rebounded strongly in late 1987 and early 1988, surprising both government and private forecasters. In the tradables sector, the decline in oil prices (denominated in dollars) and the appreciation of the yen reduced input costs, permitting domestic producers to maintain output in the face of declining yen export prices. In the non-tradables sector, there was a construction boom (with its characteristic large indirect effects throughout the economy) spurred by the Bank of Japan's low interest rate policy (facilitated by the exchange rate appreciation) and demand growth resulting from fiscal policy. As a consequence of strong growth, tax revenues rose sharply, and are now expected to exceed original projections, even with the tax cut. Proceeds from the privatization of NTT have also contributed to government revenues.

The government budget for FY 1988 further reduces the level of expenditures by 2.6 percent from the revised 1987 budget. As a result, the government deficit is projected to decline considerably, in accordance with the medium-run goal of eliminating the issuance of deficit financing bonds by 1990. However, some of the proceeds from the sale of NTT have been earmarked for expenditure on public works and for loans to private sector infrastructural renewal projects. Public works expenditures should thus remain at the level of the combined regular and supplementary budgets of FY 1987.

Macroeconomic Policy and the Current Account

In light of these developments, it makes sense to ask what should be the government's macroeconomic policy stance. Using an Economic Planning Agency (EPA) macromodel that treats world trade and the exchange rate as exogenous variables, Yoshitomi estimates that Japan has a natural high-employment current account surplus of 1.0 to 1.5 percent of GNP (1985, 8–9). A similar conclusion was reached by a group of 33 prominent international economists (including two Nobel Prize winners), who stated that "it may remain appropriate for Japan to run a modest current account surplus, on the order of 1.0 to 1.5 percent of GNP (about $25–35 billion at present), in

---

trillion yen. This is not, however, 0.7 trillion yen of additional stimulus—much of this will simply amount to a shift of finance from private to government sources. The actual net increase in housing finance created by this rule change is by no means clear. Other provisions include increases in foreign aid, including a package of untied loans to Africa, and an increase in government purchases of foreign products, including US-built supercomputers and aircraft.

light of its high (if declining) savings rate and somewhat lower potential for domestic investment" (*Resolving the Global Economic Crisis* 1987, 8). Yoshitomi concludes that "if macroeconomic policy is to be used to remove current account imbalances, it should not attempt to eliminate the whole imbalance but just the cyclical components" (1985, 21). According to this criterion, Japan's current account surplus is far above its high-employment level. And, with the prospect of contractionary policies in the United States over the medium run, it would appear, on the basis of Yoshitomi's criterion, that Japan should pursue expansionary macroeconomic policies. In this context it is desirable to examine the prospective impact of Japanese monetary and fiscal expansion.

A recent study by the BOJ suggests that the impact of changes in Japanese fiscal policy on the rest of the world would not be large. Using a simulation model, the BOJ concluded that a 3 trillion yen fiscal expansion (around $20 billion at contemporaneous exchange rates) would lower the Japanese trade balance by around 1.5 billion dollars after two years.[12] In yen terms, this implies that the elasticity of the trade balance with respect to fiscal stimulation would be less than -0.10 in absolute value. Assuming that the response is linear with respect to the magnitude of the stimulation, it suggests that in the long run the emergency measures announced in May 1987 could be expected to reduce the Japanese trade surplus by around $3.0 billion. The trade surplus stood at over $96 billion in 1987.

With regard to the United States, these policy changes would not have a major impact on either the global or the bilateral trade deficit. The BOJ study found that a Japanese 3 trillion yen fiscal expansion would reduce the US trade deficit by just over $500 million after two years. (It is currently running at over $140 billion annually. The US–Japan bilateral deficit is in excess of $50 billion.) Thus, even if all the improvement occurred in the bilateral account, the BOJ estimates imply that the current emergency program would only reduce the bilateral deficit by around 1 percent.[13]

An alternative set of calculations is provided by Loopesko and Johnson (1987). Using the Federal Reserve System's Multicountry Model (MCM), they estimate that 3 trillion yen of additional fiscal stimulus would lower the Japanese current account by $5.9 billion, and the bilateral surplus with the United States by $0.9 billion, after five years. Again, assuming a linear response, this implies that the current government stimulus package would

---

12. *Nihon Keizai Shimbun*, 12 June 1987.

13. This would be higher, of course, if the government simply purchased US-made products. The emergency import provision of the government's package effectively does just that.

reduce the Japanese current account surplus by nearly $12 billion, and the bilateral surplus with the United States by nearly $2 billion, after five years.

Our own econometric simulations of fiscal policy indicate that the ultimate impact of changes in fiscal policy would be greater than what the BOJ study, but less than what the Fed study, suggest. The VAR model outlined in Appendix D indicates that if the Japanese public sector deficit remained constant in real terms at around 3 percent of GNP, the current account surplus would hold steady in the range of 2.5–3.0 percent of GNP for the remainder of the decade. (It was 3.6 percent of GNP in 1987.) However, if the government abandons its recent moves toward fiscal expansion through supplementary expenditures, and pursues its medium-run objective of eliminating central government bond issues by the end of the decade, the current account surplus could climb to over 5 percent of GNP in 1990.[14]

Given the need to maintain the pace of economic expansion, additional fiscal stimulus measures may be advisable. For illustrative purposes, we have estimated the impact of a 9 trillion yen fiscal stimulus package (instead of the 6 trillion yen program initiated in 1987). Under such a program, the public sector deficit would rise from 3–4 percent of GNP to around 5 percent, with the privatization sales of NTT and JAL providing offsetting revenues. The current account surplus would fall by $13.8 billion to around 2 percent of GNP by the beginning of the 1990s. This would shrink the Japanese current account surplus and reduce bilateral trade frictions, while maintaining a sustainable outflow of saving to be invested abroad.

Such a fiscal policy, in conjunction with other policy reforms, would facilitate the reorientation of manufacturing firms to production for the domestic market in the medium run. In aggregate terms, the fiscal stimulus to domestic absorption would offset the drag caused by the reduction in net exports in the short run.

With respect to the bilateral balance with the United States, we also estimate that fiscal policy changes would have an impact larger than that forecast by the BOJ, but less than that forecast by the Fed. A fiscal stimulus package of 9 trillion yen introduced over 1987–1989 (instead of the 6 trillion yen 1987 supplementary budget and tax cut) would have brought the deficit down by $2 billion from the baseline scenario, compared to $1.5 billion obtained by extrapolating the Bank of Japan estimate and $2.7 billion derived from the Fed's figure.

Finally, since the Japanese fiscal expansion may occur in the context of a

---

14. Net government bond issues were 9.9 trillion yen in 1986.

US fiscal contraction, the impact of a US contraction is a relevant consideration. The Bank of Japan estimates that a US fiscal contraction of 1 percent of GNP (around $40 billion) would reduce the Japanese current account surplus by $22.3 billion in the second year. The US current account deficit would improve even more, decreasing by $64.8 billion and $120.6 billion in the first and second years, respectively. Far smaller results are obtained using the Fed model. Loopesko and Johnson estimate that a sustained contraction of 1 percent of GNP would reduce the Japanese current account by $10.7 billion, and improve the US current account by $41.9 billion, after five years (1987, 60).

Using the Fed numbers, one can perform a counterfactual experiment. What would occur if the United States eliminated the 1987 federal budget deficit of approximately $160 billion through a series of sustained deficit cuts? A simple extrapolation of Loopesko and Johnson's numbers suggests that such a policy would bring the US current account into approximate balance by the mid-1990s, while lowering the Japanese surplus by over $40 billion. Even this, however, would not return Japan to the 1–1.5 percent of GNP current account surplus proposed by Yoshitomi and the group of 33 prominent economists.

Moreover, the two policies (Japanese expansion and US contraction) differ importantly in their effects on growth, with the US fiscal consolidation slowing growth in both countries. (In the United States, the Fed model estimates that a fiscal contraction equal to 1 percent of GNP would initially reduce real income by almost 2 percent.) While a US fiscal contraction would be the single most important policy measure that could be undertaken to reduce global and bilateral imbalances, a fiscal expansion in Japan would thus be desirable to offset the reduction in aggregate demand.[15] Indeed, these estimates suggest that, taken together, currency realignment, achievement of the balanced budget targets in the United States, and further fiscal stimulus in Japan could be sufficient to reduce the Japanese current account to 1–1.5 percent of GNP.

One caveat should be mentioned with regard to fiscal policy actions. A recent line of economic research suggests that changes in private behavior may in part offset changes in fiscal policy. The reason is that private agents realize that current bond-financed deficits carry with them future tax

---

15. This is particularly important for the developing countries because, as Loopesko and Johnson note, the income elasticity of Japanese demand for their exports is relatively high. A slowdown of growth in Japan (in response to a US fiscal contraction) could have serious repercussions in the LDCs, especially in light of their need to repay debt.

obligations. Anticipating higher future taxes, private agents change current spending behavior to smooth consumption intertemporally. A typical result of this kind of analysis is that fiscal stimulus reduces current consumption, as people save to offset the future increase in taxes necessitated by the current deficit. Although the econometric study of this issue is still in its infancy, some recent research indicates that private Japanese behavior has partially offset recent changes in fiscal policy (see, for example, Homma et al. 1986 and Ihori 1987).

Since one would expect the fiscal policy changes under consideration to have an impact on the path of the exchange rate, the issue of the proper role of monetary policy naturally arises. If Japan initiated a fiscal stimulus and monetary policy remained unchanged, it would presumably contribute to a strengthening of the yen. In the absence of compensatory reductions in private expenditures, real interest rates would rise, slowing the outflow of capital. The exchange rate would appreciate, the non-tradables sector would expand relative to the tradables sector, and the trade surplus would decline— thus reducing net exports—as the counterpart to the decline in excess saving.[16] A more contractionary monetary policy would tend to intensify these effects, while a more expansionary monetary policy would tend to offset them.

We would recommend flexibly using fiscal policy to reduce large cyclical movements in the current account. Yoshio Suzuki, Director of the Institute of Monetary and Economic Studies of the BOJ, has observed that the emergence of large current account imbalances may generate "rampant protectionism that can threaten the very existence of the free trade system. It is, therefore, absolutely essential that there be international policy coordination on the fiscal front to prevent extreme imbalances in the current account" (Suzuki 1987, 61).

To this end, a greater degree of consultation among international macroeconomic policymakers would be desirable, as would coordination of policies where feasible.[17] Monetary policy coordination could be considered in this

---

16. Alternatively, if the United States contracted and monetary policy loosened to maintain full employment, the dollar would weaken or, conversely, the yen would rise.

17. It has been argued by some that Japan should finance US trade and fiscal deficits as part of a burden-sharing arrangement. While we do recommend changes in burden-sharing, we do not believe that an implicit macroeconomic bargain is the way to proceed. Such a policy would oblige Japan to react without changes in US macroeconomic policy, which is solely under American control. Instead, we recommend that the United States and Japan assume reciprocal obligations in the provision of international public goods, in particular, defense and aid. These recommendations are outlined in Chapter 7.

context. However, the inherent difficulty of using monetary policy to achieve exchange rate targets cautions against too much emphasis on trying to maintain exchange rates within narrow ranges. Likewise, we are skeptical of the desirability of undertaking policies to encourage the exchange rate to overshoot, which is implicit in some of the more extreme medium-run yen/dollar rates cited earlier.

Altogether, a desirable policy package would include significant deficit reductions in the United States and continued fiscal expansion in Japan through the supplementary budget process and tax reform. It should be recognized, though, that fiscal policy changes of the magnitude needed to take Japan back to the 1.0–1.5 percent of GNP current account surplus advocated by Yoshitomi and the group of 33 economists are unlikely to be realized. This underscores the need to adopt structural reform policies like those outlined in the Maekawa Reports and Chapters 4 and 5, aimed at reducing the excess of private savings over private investment, and to pursue trade liberalization policies aimed at rationalizing production and encouraging expenditure-switching.

Conclusion

In this chapter we have examined the interactions between domestic and external macroeconomic forces. Strong interrelationships were identified among domestic saving and investment, the exchange rate, the current account, and foreign economic activity. In particular, the current account was found to respond most rapidly to changes in domestic activity, with changes in foreign activity taking longer to be felt, and exchange rate effects having the longest lags of all.

The long lag between movements in the exchange rate and changes in trade volumes gives rise to the J-curve effect, in which the trade surplus initially increases in response to a currency appreciation. In the case of Japan, econometric estimates indicate that this "perverse" period lasts around eight quarters, and obscures the effect of the recent yen appreciation. We estimate that the exchange rate changes that occurred through mid-1987 will ultimately reduce the Japanese trade surplus by around 35 percent of its level at that time, or by around 2 percentage points of GNP, through a slowing of exports and a rapid increase in imports. The exchange rate appreciation will reduce profitability in the traded goods sector and encourage expansion in non-traded goods sectors, such as housing construction and services. This increase in domestic absorption will be the counterpart to the reduction in net exports.

However, the pronounced uncertainty concerning the appropriate exchange rate target over the medium run, and the relatively long lags associated with the impact of exchange rate changes, caution against both excessive reliance on the exchange rate as a short-run mechanism for adjustment and an overemphasis on currency market intervention as a policy tool. Instead, given the necessity of a major restructuring of the Japanese economy and the more rapid impact of domestic activity on the trade balance, it is important that a stimulative fiscal stance be sustained. This would directly reduce excess saving and encourage appreciation of the exchange rate, thereby reducing net exports. Such a fiscal expansion could be accomplished through additional supplementary budgets and reform of the tax system. These measures would be especially important in the event of significant fiscal deficit cuts in the United States.

It is important to recognize, however, that even with a substantial fiscal contraction in the United States and expansion in Japan, the Japanese current account may well remain above the 1.0–1.5 percent of GNP high-employment surplus identified by Yoshitomi and the group of 33 economists, thus contributing to protectionist tendencies abroad. This reinforces the desirability of the kinds of structural reforms proposed in the Maekawa Reports and in Chapters 4 and 5, which seek to reduce the excess of private savings over investment, thereby relieving the pressure on fiscal policy to absorb surplus savings.

7

International Leadership

With the second-largest economy, one of the highest per capita incomes, the second-largest exports of manufactured goods, and the greatest net international financial assets, Japan is a major world economic power, but its international influence in other areas has been limited. In accordance with its increasing importance in the world economy, it is appropriate that Japan assume a greater share of the burden for maintaining a peaceful and open world system. As Prime Minister Takeshita put it in his first speech to the Diet as Prime Minister, "It is important that Japan be aware of its position as a mainstay of the international order, and actively play a larger role and accept larger responsibilities from the global perspective" (Takeshita 1988, 3).

The specific forms that these greater responsibilities take will reflect the unique characteristics of Japan's historical experience, and ultimately will be determined by Japan's self-conception of its role in the world. The process will be complicated by economic frictions with the United States and the sensitivity of Japan's neighbors to its potential military power. Nevertheless, Japan's growing economic strength necessitates that it assume greater prominence in world affairs.

The meaning of this expanded role was expressed well in the conclusion of a roundtable discussion among Japanese and foreign experts in *Japan in the Global Community:* "The first step Japan must take is to become a principal supporter of the collective management system, actively assuming its share in the burden of providing international public goods, as well as working for the maintenance and stability of the international system" (Murakami and Kosai 1986, 34).

In this chapter we examine Japan's strategic role and explore two areas of enhanced future responsibilities—military defense and economic assistance to developing countries. These spheres do not exhaust the universe of potential areas of greater Japanese leadership. Neither should they be

157

viewed as separate compartments, but rather as two components of what former Prime Minister Ohira described as a "comprehensive security plan," or what James Robinson, the chief executive officer of American Express, called a "global security initiative."[1] Indeed, the Japanese situation requires that defense and aid be considered together since Japan's reduced military capability forces it to rely more on other foreign policy tools. We will analyze Japan's needs and capabilities in these areas, as well as those of other countries, and suggest some policy initiatives to facilitate the transition to a world of greater Japanese leadership and responsibility.

Defense Issues

After the disaster of the Second World War, Japan adopted, under US pressure, a Constitution that renounces war and narrowly circumscribes the role of the military in Japanese society.[2] The Japanese Supreme Court ruled that Article 9 of the Constitution "in no way denies the inherent right of self-defense . . . and the pacifism of our Constitution has never provided for either defenselessness or nonresistance. . . ." Furthermore, the court held, "Article 9 of the Constitution in no way prohibits a request to another country for security guarantees for maintenance of peace and safety of our country" (Reed 1983, 18). Japanese governments have interpreted the court rulings as affirming the constitutionality of maintaining standing armed forces to deter aggression, but strictly limiting their role to the defense of the home islands. The constitutional prohibition against collective self-defense effectively prevents Japan from joining military alliances such as NATO or ANZUS, and as a matter of policy, the Japanese government has declined to participate in UN peacekeeping activities (Reed 1983, 20–21).

Given the circumscribed role of the military, Japan has been forced to rely heavily on the United States for military protection and for the defense of its vital strategic interests abroad. The centerpiece of this relationship is the 1960 Treaty of Mutual Cooperation and Security, which lays out a set of mutual obligations. Under the treaty the United States promised to defend Japan in case of attack. In turn, Japan agreed to consult with the United States about regional security problems, maintain forces to deter aggression (subject to the constitutional limitation), and come to the assistance of US

---

1. *Financial Times*, 1 October 1987.

2. Article 9 of the Constitution states that ". . . the Japanese people forever renounce war as a sovereign right of the nation and the threat or use of force as a means of settling international disputes . . . land, sea, and air forces, as well as other war potential, will never be maintained."

forces if attacked in Japan. The treaty does not obligate Japan to participate in regional security schemes, nor to come to the aid of the United States if American forces are attacked outside Japan (Reed 1983, 8–9).

Another document signed at the same time as the treaty established the modus operandi of the security cooperation. The Status of Forces Agreement (SOFA) sets forth Japan's obligation to furnish, without cost, areas and facilities for US forces in Japan. The United States agreed in turn to bear, "without cost to Japan," the remaining expenses associated with maintaining the troops (Reed 1983, 9). Pursuant to these agreements the United States provides a conventional and nuclear security umbrella over Japan, and maintains a presence of around 50,000 troops.[3]

The commitment to Japanese security is regarded as an important component of US strategy. Japan straddles the only three straits through which the Soviet Pacific Fleet can reach the ocean from its home ports, leading one Defense Department official to describe Japan in congressional testimony as "the cornerstone of US forward defense strategy in the Asian–Pacific region" (Arkin and Chappell 1985, 486). This sentiment was echoed by former National Security Advisor Zbigniew Brzezinski, when he called for the United States to "maintain and enhance its strategic cooperation with Japan. This relationship must be at the cornerstone of U.S. security policy in the Far East" (Brzezinski 1986, 212).

This view appears to be widely held in the United States. A recent public opinion poll found that 82 percent of the public and 97 percent of political leaders polled believe that the United States has a vital interest in Japan, the highest overall scores for any country (Nishihara 1985, table IV–2a). A recent Gallup poll reported that 72 percent of the respondents felt the commitment of US forces in Japan should either be maintained at current levels or increased (Watts 1985, 34).[4]

There has been growing friction in the diplomatic sphere, however. A case in point is the Middle East. Japan imports roughly 70 percent of its

---

3. Japan, however, contributes to the cost of maintaining these troops as discussed further below.

4. These poll results make very interesting reading in light of the often acrimonious relationship between Japan and the United States in the economic sphere. The number of Americans that regard Japan positively is seven times larger than the number regarding Japan negatively. When asked to choose among a list of attributes, 96 percent indicated that they believed the Japanese were "hardworking"; 92 percent "competitive"; 71 percent "creative" and "peaceful"; 69 percent "group oriented"; and 66 percent "straightforward." Watts concluded that "Japan stands in a category by itself. It is the sole non-Occidental nation that has moved into the forefront of popularity among Americans, between 1980 and 1985 climbing up the "highly favorable" scale by five percentage points—the only upward movement large enough to be called statistically significant" (1985, 5).

oil from Middle East sources, and this oil dependency has encouraged a diplomatically solicitous posture vis-à-vis the producing nations. In the cases of the boycott of Iranian oil after the seizure of the US embassy and sanctions against alleged state-sponsored terrorism, Japan acceded to the US position only after substantial prodding. Likewise, Japan made considerable efforts to placate Iran during the 1987 hostilities in the Persian Gulf and refused to support the proposed trade embargo.[5]

Although Japanese defense expenditures have increased in recent years, they appear low by international standards (table 7.1). Japan devoted 1.0 percent of its GDP to defense in 1986, compared with 3.9 percent in France, 3.1 in Germany, 2.2 percent in Italy, and 5.1 percent in the United Kingdom. The difference was the largest vis-à-vis the United States, where defense expenditures equaled 6.8 percent of GDP. Japan is also behind neutral Sweden (2.8 percent) and other small countries, such as the Netherlands (3.1 percent) and Norway (3.1 percent). In absolute terms, however, Japan ranks fifth behind the United States, the United Kingdom, France, and West Germany. Moreover, these figures understate true Japanese expenditures, which are minimized for domestic political reasons. Using a broader NATO accounting convention, Japanese expenditures are expected to increase to 1.5 percent of GNP in 1988, which, though still low in percentage terms, place it third (behind the United States and the Soviet Union) in absolute terms.[6] The major reason for the increase is that the NATO definition includes pension costs, and 40 percent of all Self-Defense Force (SDF) personnel are officers with sizable pensions (MacIntosh 1987, 50).[7] Wages, in fact, make up around half the budget, and personnel costs are approximately double those of the Warsaw Pact nations (Reed 1983, 39).

In terms of hardware, Japan ranks eighth in the world in submarines and fifteenth in aircraft, although in surface vessels Japan would come in fifth in the NATO ranking, with more combat ships than the United Kingdom. With the development of antiship and ship-to-ship missiles arguably

---

5. *Financial Times*, 9 October 1987. After months of deliberations on the constitutionality of support for the Gulf shipping effort, Japan agreed to provide about $10 million worth of electronic navigation equipment to the navies involved (*Economist*, 7 November 1987). The Japanese could counter that, unlike some NATO allies, Japan did eventually support US-initiated sanctions after the Iranian seizure of the US embassy and the Soviet invasion of Afghanistan. In the latter case, Japan participated in the US-led Olympic boycott and economic sanctions, "while less principled Western allies rushed in to accept Soviet contracts that would have otherwise gone to Japan" (Reed 1983, 57).

6. *Economist*, 23 January 1988.

7. The ratio rises to 1.7 to 1.8 percent of GNP if pre-Self Defense Force (i.e., Imperial Army) pensions are included in the calculation (MacIntosh 1987, 42).

Table 7.1 Burden-sharing among the major industrial nations, 1986
(1986 dollars)

	Millions of Dollars:			As a Percentage of GDP:			Per Capita:		
	Defense Spending	ODA	Total	Defense Spending	ODA	Total	Defense Spending	ODA	Total
Japan	19,577.8	5,481.8	25,059.6	1.0	0.3	1.3	161.1	45.1	206.3
Sweden[a]	3,306.0	1,153.4	4,459.4	2.8	0.9	3.6	395.0	137.8	532.8
Netherlands	5,435.4	1,753.3	7,188.7	3.1	1.0	4.1	373.3	120.4	493.7
Norway	2,157.2	835.1	2,992.3	3.1	1.2	4.3	517.3	200.3	717.6
France[b]	28,260.2	5,217.3	33,477.5	3.9	0.7	4.6	510.2	94.2	604.4
Germany	27,652.3	3,835.6	31,488.0	3.1	0.4	3.5	452.9	62.8	515.8
Italy	13,198.3	2,399.7	15,597.9	2.2	0.4	2.6	231.0	42.0	273.0
United Kingdom	28,048.9	1,814.9	29,863.8	5.1	0.3	5.4	494.2	32.0	526.1
United States	285,226.0	9,647.4	294,873.4	6.8	0.2	7.0	1,180.6	39.9	1,220.5

Sources: Defense expenditure figures from Department of Defense, *Report on Allied Contributions to the Common Defense, A Report to the U.S. Congress by the Secretary of Defense,* April 1988, 90. ODA data from OECD, *Development Cooperation,* various issues. Defense expenditures for Sweden from International Institute for Strategic Studies, *The Military Balance 1986–87,* 1986.
a. The Swedish defense expenditure figure is for the fiscal year 1986–87.
b. Official Development Assistance (ODA) includes flows to Overseas Departments and Territories.

superior to the US Tomahawk cruise missile, and "what are reputed to be the world's best antisubmarine sonars," the Japanese are in the forefront of certain defensive weapons systems (MacIntosh 1987, 44).

Japan's actual military capabilities are far lower than its level of expenditures would suggest, because SDF personnel may not be able either to fulfill their expected mission, or effectively utilize their equipment. For one thing, the Ground Self-Defense Force is far larger than the combined Maritime and Air Self-Defense Forces, though most battle scenarios emphasize the Air SDF's role in naval interdiction in the strategic straits and efforts to control air space around Japan (Reed 1983, 51; MacIntosh 1987, 46–48). Furthermore, the forces that are available appear to be in a poor state of combat readiness. A number of analysts have noted low stocks of ammunition, spare parts, and fuel, and deficiencies in command and control systems, the intelligence apparatus, air defense and antisubmarine weapon systems, training, and mobilization (Japanese Center for Strategic Studies 1981, 13–14; Reed 1983, 52–54; MacIntosh 1987, 50; Kimura 1986, 119–120). These problems are so severe that a US Defense Department official testifying before Congress stated that, "Owing to these shortcomings, the SDF does not constitute an effective deterrence" (Reed 1983, 52), and a Japanese study concluded that "it is conceivable a major proportion of Japan could be devastated during the early stages of a war" (Japanese Center for Strategic Studies 1981, 13).

Consequently, Japan relies heavily on the United States for conventional defense and, in view of its low defense expenditures, it has been singled out by the US Department of Defense as a country making "financial contributions below their fair share" (US Department of Defense 1986, 14). This perceived "free riding," in conjunction with Japan's large trade surpluses, have led to calls by some US military officials and members of Congress for a "security tax" of 2 percent of GNP to be paid by Japan in compensation for defense services (Reed 1983, 2; MacIntosh 1987, 114). One former Defense Department official went so far as to argue that "Japan's failure to accept its regional security responsibilities should be sufficient reason to deny its free access to Western markets" (Sullivan 1981, 56).

Yet Japan now faces what the 1984 *Defense White Paper* described as an "unrelenting buildup" of Soviet forces in the region (Tow 1986, 128). Former US Defense Secretary Harold Brown has observed:

Soviet nuclear missiles or medium-range bombers could obliterate Japan, but Soviet forces in the Far East also pose a massive conventional threat to Japan. The Soviet Pacific Fleet as well as its East Asian ground and air forces have approximately doubled in size since the mid-1960s. Its arrangements for overflight of North Korea by military reconnaissance aircraft and its large naval base at Can Ranh Bay in Vietnam enhance Soviet power projection capability throughout East Asia. During the past two years, the Soviets added SS-20s and Backfire bombers in Siberia, deployed MiG-29s in the Far East, and increased their Pacific Fleet (the USSR's largest) by a VTOL (vertical take-off and landing) aircraft carrier, a cruiser and two guided missile destroyers (Brown 1987, 11).[8]

On Sakhalin Island, the Soviets maintain two motorized rifle divisions (consisting of 300 tanks and 250 armored personnel carriers), MI-24 Hind assault helicopters, radar installations, and airfields—three minutes flying time from Japan—where Backfire bombers are based. On the Northern Islands, which are occupied by the Soviet Union but still claimed by Japan, the Soviets have built a new submarine base and stationed 16,000 troops, long-range 130 millimeter cannons, 40 MiG-23 Floggers capable of hitting not only Hokkaido, but Honshu, MI-24 Hind attack helicopters, and possibly MiG-31 Foxhounds (Nishihara 1985, 39; Tow 1986, 128–129; MacIntosh 1987, 84–85). The preponderance of Soviet forces is so great that the former secretary-general of the Japanese Defense council concluded that Japan's air defenses could be eliminated by the Soviets in two to three days (Tow 1986, 128–129). A Soviet diplomat was less modest, remarking that an invasion of Hokkaido would "take only several tens of minutes if we did it in earnest" (MacIntosh 1987, 85).

The military buildup, and perceived acts of hostility such as the downing of Korean Airlines Flight 007, have contributed to a gradual shift in Japanese public opinion. As one analyst noted, "Moscow's crude use of military power for purposes of regional intimidation seems to have a large counterbalancing effect. The Japanese public seems increasingly willing to modify postwar war-avoidance sentiments in favor of greater resistance to accommodation with the Soviet Union" (Tow 1986, 133). Sixty percent of those questioned in a 1984 Japan Defense Agency poll felt in danger of attack by the Soviet Union. A similar survey by the *Yomuri Shimbun* found that 53.5 percent of those polled felt threatened by the Soviets. No other country received more than an 8 percent positive response (Tow 1986, 141). Domestic political support is growing for a more activist defense posture, although opposition to increased defense expenditure is still high (Nishihara 1985, 42; MacIntosh 1987, 140–141).

Few observers, though, expect the Soviet Union to invade Hokkaido. Rather, the strategic purpose of the military buildup has been described by US and Japanese officials as a Soviet attempt to "divide and rule"—an effort to split the United States from Japan and other pro-Western states in East Asia through intimidation. In fact, the 1984 Japanese Foreign Ministry

---

8. The SS-20s would be removed under the proposed INF treaty.

Diplomatic Bluebook describes the Soviet military buildup as "the cause of the harsh climate (*kibishii kuki*) around Japan" (Tow 1986, 128).

As a result of the perception of greater Soviet hostility, tensions with the United States, and shifts in public opinion at home, the Japanese government has made a greater effort in the defense area. Former Prime Minister Nakasone articulated the goals of improving Japan's air defense; developing capabilities to prevent Soviet naval passage through the three straits; and making the commitment to a 1,000 mile sea-lane defense concrete by defending "the sealanes between Guam and Tokyo and between the Straits of Taiwan and Osaka" (Kimura 1986, 110). As then US Defense Secretary Caspar Weinberger noted, this would be consistent with US strategy, which does not "expect or desire Japan to assume a regional military role to contribute to regional defense. To the extent Japan achieves the capability to provide an effective defense of her own territory, our forces can be deployed against more distant threats not only to the United States and Japan, but to the entire region and the world beyond" (Arkin and Chappell 1985, 493).

A medium-run procurement program (1986–1990) is associated with this new defense posture. The program includes the purchase of surface-to-air missiles from the United States and 56 six-barrel rocket launchers. For the ground forces, planned acquisitions include 72 antitank helicopters and 35 heavy-lift helicopters to improve defensive capabilities on Hokkaido. A new battle tank is also in the works. The air force will receive a new fighter plane based on an American design, and is considering the purchase of refueling aircraft and AWACS airborne early warning aircraft. The navy's plans include improved missile-carrying capabilities and joint research with the United States on improved submarine detection systems (MacIntosh 1987, 44–49). Finally, the latest budget includes funds for over-the-horizon radar research, which can be used to track missiles launched from the Soviet Union and "is especially suggestive of a sharper edge to Japan's defenses."[9]

Procurement targets have not always been met in the past, however (MacIntosh 1987, 49–50). Moreover, the problems of inadequate personnel, the SDF's inappropriate skill mix, and the generally low level of combat readiness all remain. As a consequence, Japan will continue to rely on the United States for conventional defense for the foreseeable future (Reed 1983, 49–50). The issue then becomes how to work out an equitable burden-sharing arrangement. From the US standpoint, while the defense of Japan remains a vital strategic interest, recent exchange rate movements have driven the budgetary costs to the US government sharply upward, and the

---

9. *Economist*, 23 January 1988.

issue could become a serious political controversy in the United States. From the Japanese standpoint, the continued reliance on US conventional forces means that the United States must be placated, but increases in defense expenditures are politically unpopular.

In this light, the recent willingness of Japan to bear a larger share of the costs of maintaining the US troop presence in Japan represents an understandable and politically expedient short-run response. Japan now pays about one-third of the local costs of the American military presence. It is the only US ally to make offset payments of this kind. The Takeshita offer to finance the wage costs of the 21,000 local civilians employed on the US bases (36 billion yen this year) would raise this share to around half.[10] Japan is in no way obligated to do this under the Status of Forces Agreement, and the arrangement, if made permanent, would represent "a significant burden-sharing initiative" (Reed 1983, 42). Further Japanese burden-sharing initiatives consistent with current treaty obligations could include the provision of upgraded or new facilities, the provision of housekeeping services for US military personnel, and the stockpiling of ammunition or other strategic materials (Reed 1983, 43–44).

In the longer run, however, it would be desirable for Japan to improve its own self-defense capabilities. This would permit Japan to "avoid dependence on American nuclear weapons other than to deter Soviet nuclear weapons" (Kosaka 1986, 137). The place to begin would be to achieve stated defense goals. As a tactical matter, one Japanese analyst has argued that "it would be more realistic and more productive for the United States to press the Japanese government first to reach on schedule the targets set by the Mid-term Defense Program Estimate (1983–1987). There is little point in trying to revise this program, inadequate though it is, until it has been achieved" (Kimura 1986, 120).

Eventually, though, the inadequacies of Japan's conventional defense must be addressed, and the resource costs may be large. Harold Brown concluded that "a growth of Japanese defense expenditures by a further 0.3 percent of GNP over the next decade is probably justified. Assuming a 3 percent annual real GNP growth, the combined effect would be to increase the Japanese defense budget over ten years by 60 percent. . . ." (Brown 1987, 31). Some Japanese analyses advocate even larger buildups. A controversial study by former Japanese Defense Minister Shin Kanemaru recommended defense improvements that would have entailed, at a minimum, a doubling of the Japanese defense budget. Two other analysts concluded that simply meeting current commitments to defend the sea-lanes

---

10. *Economist*, 28 November 1987.

and airspace around Japan would involve tripling the budget from its 1981 level (Kase and Scalera 1981, 2). It is widely assumed that these proposed increases in military capability would maintain the Japanese government's current emphasis on reconnaissance, detection, and defense capabilities, and both Japan and the United States would be expected to communicate clearly the purely defensive orientation of the buildup to Japan's neighbors.

Even with large increases in Japanese conventional defense capabilities, Japan will continue to rely heavily on the United States for its nuclear defense and the defense of its strategic interests beyond its immediate territorial vicinity. In this sense Japan will continue to be a "free rider" in security affairs. Some have suggested that Japan should pay a "security tax" or underwrite the cost of Western Alliance defense programs (such as the protection of Persian Gulf shipping) in which Japan has a strategic interest. These proposals are impractical. It is difficult to imagine how such payments would be negotiated and distributed, and they would be politically unacceptable in Japan.

However, reduced participation by Japan in one strategic sphere could be compensated for by increased participation in others. Harold Brown enunciated just such a vision, proposing that "a new division of responsibilities should include a modestly greater Japanese military capability, more Japanese contributions to military technology (including joint development and production programs), a major increase in untied Japanese economic assistance to Third World countries and to handling of Third World debt, and the establishment of the yen as a reserve currency" (Brown 1987, 28). We will now turn to the issue of development assistance.

Financial Assistance to Developing Countries

For purposes of comparison, financial assistance to developing countries is usually expressed in the donor's currency as a percentage GNP. According to this criterion, Japan's official development assistance (ODA) outlays have traditionally been low, as can be seen in table 7.2, which includes data for the 1970–1986 period. In 1986 the Japanese figure of 0.28 placed it fourteenth out of eighteen OECD countries, ahead of only Ireland, New Zealand, the United States, and Austria. Nor has Japan's ODA commitment strengthened over time: The 0.28 percent figure is well below the peak values of 0.33 percent in 1983 and 0.35 percent in 1984. By comparison, large increases were made by Italy (from 0.16 to 0.40 percent) and Germany (from 0.32 to 0.43 percent) over the 1970–1986 period. Even France, the largest aid donor among the major industrial countries, boosted its contribution from 0.66 to

Table 7.2 Official development assistance, 1970 and 1975–1986 (percentage of GNP)

	1970	1975	1976	1977	1978	1979	1980	1981	1982	1983	1984	1985	1986
Japan	0.23	0.23	0.20	0.21	0.23	0.26	0.32	0.28	0.28	0.33	0.35	0.29	0.28
France [a]	0.66	0.62	0.62	0.60	0.57	0.59	0.62	0.73	0.75	0.74	0.77	0.78	0.72
France [b]	0.42	0.38	n.a.	n.a.	n.a.	0.35	0.38	0.45	0.49	0.48	n.a.	n.a.	n.a.
Sweden	0.35	0.78	0.78	0.95	0.86	0.92	0.78	0.83	1.02	0.84	0.8	0.86	0.88
Netherlands	0.62	0.74	0.8	0.81	0.78	0.94	0.97	1.07	1.07	0.91	1.02	0.91	1.00
Norway	0.33	0.65	0.71	0.84	0.90	0.95	0.87	0.85	1.03	1.10	1.03	1.03	1.20
Germany	0.32	0.40	0.36	0.33	0.36	0.44	0.43	0.47	0.48	0.49	0.45	0.47	0.43
Italy	0.16	0.11	0.13	0.10	0.14	0.08	0.17	0.19	0.24	0.24	0.33	0.31	0.40
United Kingdom	0.39	0.39	0.39	0.45	0.47	0.51	0.34	0.44	0.37	0.35	0.33	0.34	0.33
United States	0.32	0.27	0.26	0.25	0.27	0.20	0.27	0.20	0.27	0.24	0.24	0.24	0.23

Source: OECD, *Development Cooperation*, various issues.
a. Includes flows to Overseas Departments and Territories.
b. Excludes flows to Overseas Departments and Territories.

0.72 over this period. Among the smaller industrial countries the increases were even more impressive, with ODA more than tripling in Norway (0.33 to 1.20 percent), and rising substantially in the Netherlands (from 0.61 to 1.00) and Sweden (0.38 to 0.88). Among the OECD countries, Japanese performance compared favorably only with that of the United States, whose ODA fell over this period (from 0.32 to 0.23 percent).

In dollar terms, however, Japanese aid has risen sharply. The dollar value of Japanese ODA more than quadrupled between 1977 and 1986, placing Japan second only to the United States in terms of total assistance. Yet because of the appreciation of the yen, these rapid increases in dollar terms have been achieved with only moderate increases in the ODA budget; ODA disbursements rose by 4.8 percent in yen terms in FY 1986, 5.8 percent in FY 1987, and 6.5 percent in FY 1988. Indeed, the appreciation of the yen has pushed up the dollar value of Japanese ODA so much that the completion date of the government's ambitious Third Medium-Run Target of doubling the 1985 ODA level (in dollars) has been brought forward from 1992 to 1990.

Moreover, the government announced in June 1988 a new medium-run target (1988–1992) of $50 billion, which would make Japan the world's largest aid donor. The government also pledged to increase the share of grants in the ODA program—in the past a large share of Japanese aid was in the form of loans—and reduce formally or informally tied aid. Again, the target was specified in dollars rather than yen, and the Ministry of Finance successfully blocked a Foreign Ministry proposal to specify the target in terms of a percentage of GNP. Given the appreciation of the yen against the dollar, it is unclear what the cost of this program will amount to in yen.

Apart from its ODA allocation, the government has recently announced several additional packages. In May 1987 a three-year $30 billion package was announced. It is not known, however, how much additional financing the package contains and what the concessional element will be. Around $10 billion appears to be money that had already been pledged to multilateral development banks (MDBs), including replenishment of the World Bank's soft loan subsidiary, the International Development Association, and to the Asian Development Bank (ADB); loans to the International Monetary Fund; and $2 billion to the "Japan Special Fund" in the World Bank. The latter would permit the World Bank to raise additional funds in the Tokyo market. Of the $20 billion in new financing, $8 billion consists of subscriptions for bond issues by the MDBs, including the establishment of "Japan Funds" in the ADB and the Inter-American Development Bank (IDB). Another $9 billion consists of cofinancing with the World Bank or other MDBs by the Overseas Economic Cooperation Fund (OECF), the Export–Import Bank of

Japan, and Japanese commercial banks. Finally, $3 billion is to consist of direct untied loans by the Export–Import Bank of Japan.[11]

In addition to this package, the government announced a special fund for sub-Saharan Africa that will provide about $500 million, mostly in non-project grants. A new initiative announced by Prime Minister Takeshita at the December 1987 summit of the Association of Southeast Asian Nations (ASEAN) will provide about $2 billion in development finance to four ASEAN countries (Indonesia, Malaysia, the Philippines, and Thailand). This new ASEAN package could be interpreted as the kind of program that Japan might be expected to pursue in its role as a regional power. The program also illustrates the potential difficulties in matching donor and recipient needs.

Most of the money will be loaned by the OECF to the private industrial sector via the ASEAN countries' national development banks. All the OECF money, which comes from the Japanese postal saving system, is in yen; ASEAN firms' export receipts are largely in dollars. With the yen continuing to appreciate against the dollar, observers anticipate potential repayment difficulties without a concessional element. A possible solution would be to liberalize Japanese markets to absorb greater imports from the ASEAN countries. This was proposed by the ASEAN leaders at the Manila summit.[12]

A more comprehensive plan to expand Japan's financial assistance to developing countries is contained in a set of recommendations by former Foreign Minister Saburo Okita. The most recent "Okita Plan" calls for a $125 billion package, to be spread over 5 years (Okita, Jayawardena, and Sengupta 1987). Of the $25 billion annual expenditure, $10 billion would be disbursed through a new institution, the Japanese Trust Fund, which would offer soft loans to developing countries, with interest rate subsidies financed through the Japanese official development assistance (ODA) budget. Another $10 billion would be lent by an expanded Export–Import Bank. The last $5 billion would underwrite IMF borrowing at concessional rates in Japanese capital markets, with the interest rate subsidy financed through

---

11. The issue of tied loans is a sensitive one, because Japan has been criticized in the Development Assistance Committee of the OECD for, in effect, tying loans by concentrating ODA on capital-intensive projects. More than 45 percent of Japanese aid in 1986 was earmarked for public utility, industrial, mining, and construction projects, with public utilities accounting for nearly 35 percent alone. Completing the projects often involves purchases of sophisticated equipment from the donor country, especially in the areas of telecommunications, power generation, and transportation (*JEI Report*, No. 46B, 1987).

12. *Washington Post*, 16 December 1987.

the Fiscal Investment and Loan Program (FILP) budget. In addition to these recommendations, the plan calls for a tripling of the ODA budget over the 1985–1990 period.

In our judgment the Okita Plan sets the proper course for Japanese policy, though we would place greater emphasis on the concessional element and on lending through the MDBs. In any event, implementation has not been forthcoming. Four obstacles are sometimes cited to the implementation of this kind of expanded program of Japanese financial transfers to the developing countries. With proper policy adjustments, each of these objections can be overcome.

First, the absorptive capacity of recipient countries is questioned. Some argue that there is a dearth of efficient investment opportunities in the developing countries. However, a World Bank analyst recently estimated that over the medium run additional capital flows of $4–7 billion annually would be needed simply to maintain productive capacity in sub-Saharan Africa (Agarwala 1987). In addition, net resource transfers have been negative in Latin America for years, and totaled nearly $16 billion in 1987 (Economic Commission on Latin America and the Caribbean 1987, table 15). One study of LDC financing needs concluded that "there would be substantial advantages in extra lending of $15 to $20 billion a year" for the remainder of the decade (Lessard and Williamson 1985, 89). These countries do not face an absorptive capacity constraint; instead, they need additional capital inflows to reverse recent declines in investment and to sustain growth.

The financing issue is key, because the second objection to expanded Japanese financial transfers is that the Japanese surplus is in private hands and the government is largely incapable of affecting its allocation. Until recently, much of the Japanese capital outflow financed government budget deficits in the United States. The real rate of return on capital is presumably higher in capital-scarce developing countries than it is in the United States. To Japanese private investors, however, US government Treasury bills have a higher *risk-adjusted* rate of return, which makes them relatively more attractive than riskier investments in the Third World.[13] The task, then, is to devise ways of reducing the risks associated with investment in developing capital-scarce economies, and thus encourage the market to allocate capital to its socially most productive uses.

---

13. The recent sharp appreciation of the yen against the dollar may have temporarily sated Japanese private investors' appetites for dollar denominated assets, but this is not really relevant to the point at hand: Among a class of similarly denominated assets, risk-averse investors will prefer assets they regard as relatively safe (such as OECD government bonds) to assets they regard as relatively more risky.

As Lessard and Williamson point out, there is substantial potential for increased lending to the developing countries, but financial instruments and markets necessary to affect the resource transfer do not exist. They analyze how the development of a variety of financial instruments (equities, quasi-equities, stand-alone project loans, index-linked bonds, commodity-linked bonds) and markets (swap markets, options markets) would promote greater financial flows to the developing countries. The establishment and successful operation of these new markets and instruments would involve policy initiatives by both developing- and developed-country governments in close cooperation with the MDBs, which would play a central facilitating role.

Japan could take the lead in this process in a number of ways. First, it could increase its contributions to the MDBs and more forcefully promote the banks' financial market development programs. One possible place to start would be the Asian Development Bank, where Japanese financial contributions are large and the head of the bank is a Japanese national.

Second, within Japan the government could adopt policies to encourage the recycling of capital to the developing countries. The provision of more attractive financial instruments in developing economies would presumably encourage greater capital inflows. For a variety of reasons, however (unfamiliarity, potential political instability, etc.), private investors may still regard investment in these economies as a relatively high risk. The emphasis here could be on risk-pooling to reduce the risk premium associated with any particular investment. The Japanese government could encourage the development of institutions and markets to facilitate risk-sharing among domestic investors. One possibility would be to establish a governmental or quasi-governmental agency to provide insurance for overseas lending and investment. Beyond pooling risk to encourage investment in developing economies, the government could use such an agency to offer insurance at better than actuarial rates and thus, in effect, subsidize private capital flows to Third World countries.

The government could also change relative rates of return on investments in developed and developing countries by differentiating between the two in the tax code. For instance, the government could offer a tax holiday on all profits earned on investments in the poorest countries, an investment analogue to the trade system's Generalized System of Preference scheme (GSP). Finally, the government could adopt guidelines suggesting that a certain share (perhaps 25 percent) of foreign institutional investments be in developing-country liabilities, as recommended by Lessard and Williamson.

One strength of these proposals is that they preserve and enhance the efficiency of market allocation of resources. By developing incomplete markets and addressing market failures, capital will be encouraged to flow into its socially most productive uses. With the tax system or investment guidelines proposals, in which the government intervenes directly to alter the allocation between developed- and developing-country liabilities, allocation according to market criteria is preserved within each class of investment.

The third obstacle to an enlarged Japanese foreign assistance program is the alleged lack of manpower resources within the Japanese government. This problem could be handled in several ways. First, enhanced cooperation with the MDBs would draw upon the existing bank staffs without requiring large personnel increases in the Japanese bureaucracies. This would be particularly true for MDB-administered structural adjustment loans. Second, initiatives could be designed to conserve scarce government staff. The proposal to offer tax preferences for investment in LDCs, for example, shifts the burden of identifying and developing potential projects from the government to the interested firms. The additional staff needed for auditing would be minuscule. Finally, staff constraints could be relaxed by expanding the bureaucracy and upgrading personnel.

These domestic human resource issues point to a fourth objection, however. Increased Japanese funding of MDBs is sometimes opposed on the grounds that Japan lacks influence in these organizations. There is an unease among some Japanese about putting large amounts of funds into institutions over which they may have little control.

In the IBRD (World Bank) and its soft loan window, the International Development Agency (IDA), Japanese contributions have increased relative to the US contribution, although the United States remains the largest contributor. Influence within these organizations is largely determined by the extent of financial contributions, and the United States has maintained blocking power over major policy issues. Furthermore, by custom the president of the World Bank is an American, and the managing director of the IMF, its sister institution, a European. No high ranking positions in either organization are traditionally reserved for a Japanese citizen.

At the Asian Development Bank (ADB), the United States and Japan hold equal capital shares, though the president of the ADB is customarily a Japanese national. Japan is already the largest contributor to the African Development Fund. Only in the Inter-American Development Bank is Japanese participation relatively modest.

We would urge Japan to increase its support for the MDBs. Japan should also assume a greater leadership role within the MDBs in accordance with its increased financial support. Two concrete steps could be undertaken to accommodate a larger Japanese presence. First, where increases in Japanese contributions would threaten US blocking power through dilution of its voting strength, possibly imperiling continued US financial support, the voting percentage needed for blocking could be reduced (as has been done in the past) and Japan could be encouraged to raise its contribution to parity with the United States. Second, leadership positions at the World Bank and the IMF could be opened up to Japan. An obvious possibility would be to select a Japanese national as the managing director of the IMF. Another alternative would be informally to designate a senior position, possibly the vice president of finance at the World Bank, as a Japanese post. All of this would be contingent on increased Japanese contributions to the MDBs.

It is sometimes argued that arrangements of this sort will not work because there is a shortage of qualified Japanese willing to enter the international civil service. While this may have been true in the past, there is no reason to believe it will be true in the future. In the short run, the relatively early retirement age in the Japanese civil service means that there is a pool of former senior government officials who could undoubtedly be induced to enter into international service with the proper incentives. In the longer run, a support system of incentives and rewards for service in international organizations could be more fully integrated into career advancement ladders. International leadership requires the development and support of such a capacity.

Conclusion

The responsibilities of world leadership require Japan to take a more active role in the collective management system and in the provision of international public goods. In this chapter we have examined two potential areas for action—military security and assistance to developing countries.

At the end of the Second World War Japan adopted, at the behest of the United States, a constitution that narrowly circumscribed the use of military force in Japanese foreign policy. As a consequence, Japan relies heavily on the United States both for conventional and nuclear defense. The rising cost to the United States of its commitment to defend Japan has the potential to become a major political conflict if it becomes entangled in other economic disputes between the two countries.

Due to its low expenditures on the military, Japan has been singled out as a "free rider" in the defense area. This has led some to call for a "security tax" of 2 percent of GNP. Leaving aside the arbitrariness of the 2 percent figure and the practical difficulties in allocating the revenue from such a tax among the United States and other countries, this is not a good idea. It would almost certainly trigger a backlash in Japan, and quite possibly a reemergence of the chauvinistic nationalism of the 1930s and 1940s.

A "security tax" is not what is needed. We believe a mixed strategy of burden-sharing with the United States and an increase in conventional defense capabilities would be preferable. This would involve the continuation of the Japanese government policy of footing a larger share of the costs of the US military presence in Japan, while expanding and upgrading its armed forces so that they can fulfill the self-defense responsibilities that the government has outlined. Former US Secretary of Defense Harold Brown has estimated that such a program might ultimately require a 0.3 percent of GNP increase in Japanese defense expenditures. Some Japanese analysts put the figure much higher. The United States could most effectively support such efforts by reaffirming its commitment to the defense of Japan, encouraging the Japanese government to meet its own stated strategic targets and goals, and reassuring other Asian states about the defensive nature of the Japanese program.

Such an arrangement would still leave Japan dependent on the United States for nuclear protection and for the defense of its vital strategic interests abroad. Circumscribed expenditures in the military sphere should be offset by increased expenditures on development assistance as part of a "comprehensive security plan." In the past, however, action along these lines has not always been forthcoming. As one Japanese observer put it:

There is no excuse. Japan's present-day security efforts are in lamentable condition, to say the least. First, take a brief look at the efforts to achieve a comprehensive security capability. Though excellent in theory, it has actually been an excuse, even a lie, to avoid greater defense efforts. The argument for it smacks strongly of a rebuttal to demands that Japan increase its self-defense capabilities. The unstated thrust of the argument is not an increase in economic assistance, but for the prevention of an increase in military expenditure (Kosaka 1986, 136–137).

Japan now needs to make a political commitment to substantial efforts to increase the share of foreign aid in Japanese GNP. Largely as a result of exchange rate changes, Japanese ODA has risen rapidly in dollar terms in the last several years; it is now the second largest in the world, behind the United States, and is expected to exceed the US contribution within a few years. The increase has been much smaller in yen terms, a fact that is important because much of Japanese ODA takes the form of yen-denominated loans. Moreover, Japan ranks near the bottom of the OECD (though still ahead of the United States) in ODA as a share of GNP. Given Japan's relatively small expenditures on military security, we believe that consideration should be given to a much larger development assistance program as part of a comprehensive security strategy. We suggest that a tripling of the ODA budget in yen terms be established as a normative target, with the emphasis placed on concessional aid administered through the MDBs.

Previous proposals for Japanese recycling, such as the Okita Plan, have been criticized on the grounds that developing countries lack the absorptive capacity to use efficiently large capital inflows, that the surplus is in private, not government hands, and that the government lacks sufficient human resources to mount such a program. We believe that by and large these objections are either overstated or can be overcome with appropriate policy action. Our own recommendation would be to emphasize closer cooperation with existing MDBs. This would reduce Japanese staffing requirements and avoid the charges of formal or informal aid-tying that have been leveled against Japan in the past.

Moreover, Japan's influence should rise within these organizations, in parallel with increases in its financial commitments. This would be facilitated by a government commitment to increase the staff resources available for participation in development assistance programs. It could involve expanding the relevant government bureaucracies, upgrading personnel skill levels, and further integrating international service into career advancement ladders.

Taken together, the increased defense and aid efforts would probably require a commitment to a long-run increase in expenditures on the order of 1 to 2 percent of GNP. This would move Japanese expenditures on these international public goods much closer to the OECD average. Selling such a program to the Japanese public (especially the increases in defense expenditures) would require a major effort on the part of the Japanese political leadership, and the political obstacles should not be minimized. But we believe that the case for such an initiative can be made by clearly articulating Japan's long-run interests and educating the public about the long-run costs of not pursuing a more active role in the collective management system.

8

Conclusions and Policy Recommendations

Japan faces a fundamental policy dilemma in its external economic relationships today. While it continues to run large current account surpluses, incurring the wrath of its trading partners, net exports (exports minus imports) are now declining in volume terms, and thus the impact of trade on Japan's economic growth has turned negative.

Policy Dilemmas for Japan

Between 1980 and 1985, increases in the volume of net exports provided nearly one-half of the increment of Japan's real GDP growth. The contribution of net exports to economic growth turned negative in 1986 and in 1987. In 1987, however, this was in large part offset by the expansion of domestic demand, raising the rate of growth of GDP from 2.4 percent in 1986 to 4.2 percent in 1987, compared with the growth rates of 5.1 percent in 1984 and 4.7 percent in 1985. From a postwar peak of $49 billion in 1985, Japan's current account surplus increased further in dollar terms to $86 billion in 1986 and $87 billion in 1987. These increases were caused by the delayed effects of the yen appreciation on current account balances expressed in dollars. While this appreciation has the immediate positive impact of increasing the dollar prices of Japanese exports, its effects on the volume of trade are slower in coming.

Over time, the appreciation of the yen will lead to a decline in the dollar value of the Japanese current account surplus. There are several factors acting in the opposite direction, however, including the relatively low rate of inflation in Japan, rapid productivity growth in tradable goods, and earnings on Japan's growing foreign assets. The importance of these factors will increase over time. Consequently, either the current account surplus will continue to grow, or the yen will have to appreciate continually. There is a need, therefore, for Japan to take measures to resolve its policy dilemma

177

by reducing the current account surplus while providing for rapid economic growth. This can be done through domestic-based expansion.

Japan made great strides in domestic-based expansion in 1987, which have been maintained in 1988, but it has to ensure the continuation of this process. Apart from reducing the current account surplus, domestic-based expansion will permit Japan to exploit the growth potential of its economy. There is a happy coincidence here between the requirements of international equilibrium and Japan's domestic needs. Thus, as explained in detail in Chapter 1, Japan needs to improve the quality of life, which is far from commensurate with its level of per capita income. Indeed, the second Maekawa Report speaks of the need for a "revolutionary improvement in the quality of life in Japan." This will require, in particular, improvements in the housing stock and in physical and social infrastructure. Reducing working hours will also improve the quality of life. At the same time, Japan has to provide for the increasing needs of the aged, as the share of the over-65 age group rises from 11 percent in 1980 to 21 percent in 2000.

Policy Recommendations

The policy dilemma of Japan's external economic relationships can be resolved by a continuation of the shift from export-based to domestic-based expansion. This will simultaneously provide growth momentum for Japan while reducing its current account surpluses. It will require measures to maintain the momentum of domestic-based expansion in the medium term.

A central issue is housing. While high prices have raised the share of residential structures and land to 65 percent of household portfolios, the housing stock is of insufficient quantity and low quality in Japan. Housing is also important because of potential complementary spending on consumer durables and the effects of high prices on the generation of excess savings in Japan. Larger houses and apartments increase demand for household appliances, refrigerators, dishwashers, washing machines, and dryers. Multilevel dwellings can include garages, thereby increasing the ownership of automobiles, which is considerably lower in Japan than in the other major industrial countries.

Improvements in the housing stock also create pressure for better roads and sewer facilities and generate demand for social amenities in the form of parks, playgrounds, and sport facilities. These social investments should be part of a housing policy that encompasses measures affecting the supply of, as well as the demand for, housing.

Adding to the land available for housing is the first consideration. Apart from reforming agricultural policies, the necessary measures include landfilling public waters, promoting the efficient use of government-owned sites, transferring public facilities away from the principal cities, building high-speed transport links between outlying areas and existing cities, and establishing new cities as part of the process of decentralization. Proposals have also been made for transferring the capital outside of Tokyo.

Better utilization of existing land areas would be facilitated by eliminating the preferential tax treatment of agricultural land in urban areas, increasing the tax on holding land (as against selling it), and modifying existing zoning regulations. One may also consider replacing the present system of sunshine rights by compensating owners for the value of the dwelling (but not that of land) overshadowed by a high rise or requiring builders to provide a park area around high rises. These measures would reduce the price of land, thereby increasing the demand for housing. Raising the ratio of mortgage loans to down payments and lengthening loan maturities would have similar effects. Building costs could also be reduced by increasing competition in housing construction.

Lowering the cost of land would affect saving behavior in Japan. At present, 65 percent of household wealth is tied up in largely illiquid housing; the comparable figure for the United States is 31 percent. This contributes to the intergenerational merging of households, with the bequest of houses exchanged by the elderly for care by their children. This "strategic bequest motive" discourages dissaving by the elderly, which is the normal pattern in other developed countries. The Japanese pattern will change if the elderly are not locked into holding a high-priced and illiquid asset, but have alternatives.

Improving the quality of life also calls for reductions in working hours, as proposed in the Maekawa Reports. This would require accelerating the application of recent legislation providing for the adoption of the 40-hour workweek, increasing paid vacation days, and lengthening public holidays. These measures would have beneficial indirect effects on the economy. A shorter workweek would increase the demand for luxuries and semi-luxuries as well as for short-distance travel, while longer vacations would increase the demand for long-distance travel and vacation resorts. As a result, investment demand as well as spending on goods and services, would rise, thereby affecting the savings–investment balance. Greater demand for travel abroad would also reduce the excess of domestic savings over investment. Foreign travel has been rising rapidly, but the potential for future increases is still great.

The measures described above would provide for the continuation of domestic-based economic growth in Japan. They would also tend to reduce the excess of savings over investment that has contributed to the large

Japanese current account surplus. At the same time, Japan can continue to rely for the short term on an expansionary fiscal policy, accompanied by an accommodating monetary policy, in pursuit of the objective of reducing the current account surplus while supporting domestic based growth. In view of the very slow recent rise in consumer prices, Japan has little reason to fear inflation.

In the first half of the 1980s, fiscal policy became increasingly restrictive. Real government spending grew by less than one percent per year and public sector borrowing declined from 7 percent of GDP in 1978 to 3 percent in 1986, as the government pursued the objective of eliminating the issuance of deficit financing bonds by 1990. In May 1987 the government announced a financial package designed to increase domestic demand by 1–2 percent of GDP over a period of several years. A supplementary budget was used to increase government expenditures in FY 1987. The FY 1988 budget calls for lower expenditures than the revised FY 1987 budget, however, and a supplementary appropriation would again be needed to increase expenditures.

A larger and more sustained fiscal package will be desirable in order durably to affect the size and composition of output. Such a package should emphasize the promotion of housing and social infrastructure. As an illustration, we have estimated the impact of a three-year fiscal stimulus program about 50 percent larger than the government's 1987 supplementary budget. The public sector deficit would rise from 3–4 percent of GNP to around 5 percent, with revenues from the privatization sales of NTT and JAL providing an offsetting effect. The current account surplus would fall to around 2 percent of GNP by the beginning of the 1990s, which is the apparent target of the government's 1987–92 plan. The implementation of the described fiscal policy package, in conjunction with other policy reforms, would facilitate the reorientation of manufacturing to production for the domestic market in the medium term. It would also partially compensate for the impact on the world economy of the essential fiscal retrenchment in the United States.

Monetary policy has been accommodating in Japan. The discount rate was cut in February 1987 to its lowest level ever in nominal terms (2.5 percent). The money supply grew rapidly in 1986, reached double-digit levels in 1987, and is expected to continue to rise rapidly, albeit at a somewhat slower pace, in 1988. Monetary policy has thus made room for the increase in domestic demand and has dampened the appreciation of the yen. It should continue to accommodate fiscal expansion.

Japan's International Leadership Role

We have noted that the quality of life is not commensurate with Japan's economic achievements. The same could be said of Japan's role in the international arena. With the second-largest industrial economy, one of the highest per capita incomes, the second-largest exports of manufactured goods, and the greatest net international financial assets, Japan is a major world economic power, but its influence in international economic decision making has been limited.

The policy measures proposed above would conform to the requirements of world economic balance, for they would reduce the Japanese current account deficit while creating an expansionary force in the world economy. They would thus significantly raise Japan's international standing. Japan could enhance its position further by taking on additional responsibilities in defense and in financial assistance to developing countries and by further liberalizing its trade.

While Japan is the world's second-largest exporter of manufactured goods, it remains behind Germany, the United Kingdom, France, and Italy in terms of manufactured imports. The disparity is even larger with the United States, whose manufactured imports were six times those of Japan in 1987. But Japan is also well behind other major industrial countries as far as total imports per capita are concerned. In 1987 it imported barely more than $1,000 per capita, compared with Germany, whose imports approached $4,000; France and the United Kingdom, where they were just below $3,000; and the United States and Italy, where they were close to $2,000. (The data for the EC countries include intra-EC trade.)

Defense spending in Japan has also been much lower than in other major industrial countries. Japan devoted 1.0 percent of its gross domestic national product to defense (1.5 percent using the NATO definition) in 1986, compared with 3.9 percent in France, 3.1 percent in Germany, 2.2 percent in Italy, and 5.1 percent in the United Kingdom. Again, the difference is the largest vis-à-vis the United States, where defense expenditures equaled 6.8 percent of GNP. But Japan was also well behind neutral Sweden (2.8 percent) and other small countries, such as the Netherlands (3.1 percent) and Norway (3.1 percent).

With official development assistance of 0.3 percent of GNP, Japan is near the lower end of the scale as far as foreign aid is concerned. It is above only the United States (0.2 percent), and is exceeded by France (0.7 percent), Germany (0.4 percent) and, by a much larger margin, by several smaller European countries that are at or near the 1 percent mark.

Combining defense spending and overseas development assistance puts Japan in an even lower position. Among the major industrial countries, the

United States leads with combined expenditures equal to 7.0 percent of the gross national product. It is followed by the United Kingdom (5.4 percent), France (4.6 percent), Germany (3.5 percent), and Italy (2.6 percent), with several smaller European countries in intermediate positions (Norway, 4.3 percent; the Netherlands, 4.1 percent; and Sweden, 3.6 percent) and Japan well behind (1.3 percent, or 1.8 percent using the NATO definition of defense spending).

Increased expenditures in these areas will be necessary for Japan to assume a leadership role in the international arena. This objective was expressed well in the conclusions of a roundtable discussion among Japanese and foreign experts in *Japan in the Global Community:* "The first step Japan must take is to become a principal supporter of the collective management system, actively assuming its share in the burden of providing international public goods, as well as working for the maintenance and stability of the international system" (Murakami and Kosai 1986, 34).

Trade Policy

Japan's present current account surplus does not stem from import protection. The Japanese surplus increased to a considerable extent in the space of a few years when several trade liberalizing measures were implemented. Japan has lowered its tariffs to a considerable extent in the postwar period, and its duties on non-agricultural products now approximate those of the European Community and the United States. However, tariffs remain high for fresh and preserved fruits and for wood products. Japan also has the highest duties on alcoholic beverages, whose prices are further raised by indirect taxes that discriminate against imports, thereby favoring domestic producers.

Most other agricultural products are subject to import restrictions in Japan. The level of agricultural protection, measured as the average difference between domestic and world market prices, rose from 41 percent in 1960 to 84 percent in 1980; the increase was only from 33 to 36 percent in the EC and declined slightly, from 1 to 0 percent, in the United States. By 1980 Japanese prices exceeded world market prices three to four times for wheat, coarse grains, rice, beef, and sugar. These differentials have increased further in subsequent years as a result of the appreciation of the yen. The cost of protection for these commodities has been estimated at 1 percent of Japan's GNP. Several other agricultural commodities, as well as fishery products, are subject to quotas. Among manufactured goods, quotas apply to silk and silk products, cotton yarn and wool yarn, leather, and footwear. These measures especially burden developing countries and several of them are directed specifically against such countries.

Informal barriers to trade include administrative guidance; customs procedures; standards, testing, and certification requirements; public procurement practices; the defense of depressed industries; the promotion of high-technology industries; regulations on intellectual property; and distribution channels. While these measures need not have protective effects, they have been used for such purposes in Japan.

Long and arduous bilateral negotiations between the United States and Japan, as well as between the European Community and Japan, have brought import liberalization in certain areas, including improvements in import procedures, the involvement of foreign firms in setting up standards, reductions in the number of products subject to standards, participation in the GATT procurement code, and the purchase of supercomputers. Nevertheless, informal barriers remain in other areas. In particular, Japan promotes high-technology industries, in which the United States has a competitive advantage, through the use of procurement regulations, administrative guidance, and R&D schemes.

Import-penetration ratios (the ratio of imports to domestic consumption) in the manufacturing sector provide evidence for the existence of informal barriers. Between 1975 and 1986, these ratios increased from 7.0 to 13.8 percent in the United States, from 17.9 to 26.7 percent in France, from 24.3 to 37.2 percent in Germany, from 21.9 to 28.8 percent in Italy, and from 22.0 to 31.2 percent in the United Kingdom, while declining from 4.9 to 4.4 percent in Japan. (The ratio was 4.6 percent in 1987.)

It has been suggested that Japan's poor natural resource endowment requires lower imports of manufactured goods. Japan participates little in the process of intraindustry specialization, however, and, taking account of international differences in income levels, population, size, natural resource endowments, and transportation costs, Japan's imports–GNP ratio appears to make it an outlier among industrial countries. According to an estimate cited in Chapter 3, Japanese imports were 25–45 percent lower than would be expected on the basis of international comparisons of national attributes. While these figures lie at the upper end of existing estimates, there is some support for the view that eliminating barriers to trade would generate substantial increases of imports in Japan.

Among the economy's major sectors, it has been estimated that freeing agricultural trade will cause imports to rise twelvefold for beef and lamb, elevenfold for dairy products, tenfold for pork and chicken, fourfold for rice, and by one-fourth for sugar. In conjunction with the decline in the livestock industry, decreases of one-eighth and one-fourth would likely occur, however, in the imports of wheat and coarse grains, respectively. Eliminating trade barriers would also increase imports of fish, fruits and vegetables, beverages, and tobacco, which have an import volume slightly exceeding that of the commodities mentioned above.

Domestic political constraints will not allow the Japanese government to adopt a free trade stance in agriculture any more than in other industrial countries, but liberalizing agricultural imports would simultaneously reduce tensions on the trade front, lower food prices for Japanese consumers, and improve the housing situation in Japan, thereby raising the standard of living of the population. At the same time, the livelihood of farmers could be assured through income maintenance schemes rather than through protection. Furthermore, food security should not be confused with self-sufficiency. Available estimates indicate that Japanese agriculture would survive with varying decreases in output, even under free trade. With free trade, it is estimated that domestic production would decline by one-fifth for rice, one-fourth for pork and poultry, three-tenths for wheat and coarse grains, four-tenths for sugar, and one-half for beef. In the cases of these staples, the beneficiaries of trade liberalization would include industrial as well as developing countries. The industrial countries would gain from trade liberalization in forest products while developing nations would be the principal gainers from liberalized trade in minor agricultural commodities and fishery products.

Developing countries also have considerable potential for increasing their manufactured exports to Japan, which account for less than 2 percent of Japanese consumption, compared with 3 percent of EC and 4 percent of US consumption. Furthermore, industrial countries would benefit from trade liberalization in high-technology products, in chemicals and pharmaceuticals, and in consumer goods. Altogether, each one percentage point increase in Japan's import-penetration ratio would add nearly ten billion dollars to its manufactured imports.

Although political obstacles limit the potential extent of trade liberalization, it should be emphasized that it would be in Japan's own interest to open its economy. Liberalizing imports would lower consumer prices and would also contribute to the acceleration of economic growth through more efficient resource allocation.

Finally, trade policy affects the exchange rate through its impact on saving and investment. In this connection, one should note the apparent reluctance of the government to liberalize imports at a time when Japanese industry has already been adversely affected by *endaka*.

This reluctance is based upon a fallacy. The more Japan protects its industries, the more the exchange rate will have to appreciate and the more its export industries will suffer. There is a danger, then, that continued protection will benefit high-cost industries at the expense of efficient industries. Furthermore, it may be a particularly propitious time for Japan to reduce trade barriers, because the recent strong growth in domestic demand provides a favorable environment for adjustment.

Japan should also take a leading role in the Uruguay Round. It should abandon its basically defensive position by adopting far-reaching import liberalization measures and should pursue the objective of multilateral trade liberalization in agriculture, manufacturing, and services.

Defense Issues

After the Second World War Japan adopted under US pressure a constitution that renounced war and narrowly circumscribed the role of the military in Japanese society. As a result, Japanese military capabilities have been limited to relatively small "defense forces." While Japanese defense spending amounted to as much as 1.7 percent of GNP and 14 percent of government expenditure in 1954, it was subsequently limited to 1.0 percent of GNP and declined to 6 percent of government expenditures.

With per capita defense expenditures roughly one-tenth the level of the United States, Japan has been singled out by the US Department of Defense as a country making "financial contributions below its fair share." Japan is said to be a "free rider" in defense, in the sense that its expenditures are not commensurate with the benefits it receives as a result of the US strategic commitment in the Northern Pacific. Yet there has been a large Soviet military build-up in recent years in East Asia.

As a result of this build-up, tensions with the United States, and shifts in public opinion at home, the Japanese government took some additional steps in the defense area. Former Prime Minister Nakasone articulated the goals of improving Japan's air defense, developing its capabilities to prevent Soviet naval passage through the three straits that separate Japan from Asia, and defending the sea-lanes up to 1,000 miles from Japan. This new defense posture includes a medium-term procurement program.

Japan will nevertheless continue to rely on the United States for nuclear and conventional defense for the foreseeable future. The issue thus becomes how to work out an equitable burden-sharing arrangement. The recent willingness of the Japanese government to finance a larger share of the costs of maintaining the US troop presence in Japan can be regarded as a first step. It would be further desirable for Japan to improve its own self-defense capabilities. The place to start would be actually to achieve stated defense goals. Eventually, though, the shortcomings of Japan's conventional defense must be addressed, and the resource cost of remedying these deficiencies may be large: Estimates range from an increase of 0.3 percent of GNP to a tripling of the present defense effort.

Even with large increases in conventional defense capabilities, Japan will continue to rely heavily on the United States for nuclear deterrence and the defense of its strategic interests beyond its immediate territorial vicinity, such as in the Middle East. In this sense Japan will remain a "free rider" in security affairs. Free riding in one area, however, could be compensated for by increased participation in other areas. It has been suggested by one writer that "a new division of responsibilities should include a modestly greater Japanese military capability, more Japanese contributions to military technology (including joint development and production programs), a major increase in untied Japanese economic assistance to Third World countries and the handling of Third World debt, and the establishment of the yen as a reserve currency" (Brown 1987, 28).

Financial Assistance to Developing Countries

In recent years Japan has significantly increased its assistance to developing countries in dollar terms. The medium-run target (1988–1992) announced in June 1988 is $50 billion, which, if achieved, would make Japan the world's largest aid donor. Little change has occurred in terms of GNP, however. In fact, as a proportion of GNP, Japanese official development assistance was lower in 1986 (0.28 percent) than in 1983 (0.33 percent) or 1984 (0.35 percent).

In May 1987 the government announced a three-year $30 billion package. It is unclear, though, how much additional financing the package contains and what constitutes the concessional element. A special fund for sub-Saharan Africa will provide about $500 million, mostly in non-project grants. Japan will also provide around $2 billion in loans to the ASEAN countries. Some additional ODA increases were announced at the Toronto Summit in June 1988.

A more comprehensive program to expand Japan's financial assistance to developing countries has been proposed by a group led by Saburo Okita, a former foreign minister of Japan. The group calls for a $125 billion package, to be spread over five years. Although much of the financing would consist of loans, the plan calls for a tripling of the ODA budget over a five-year period.

These proposals have been criticized on the grounds that developing countries lack the absorptive capacity efficiently to use large capital inflows, that the Japanese current account surplus is in private, not government, hands, and that the government lacks sufficient human resources to implement such a program. These problems are either exaggerated or can be overcome with appropriate policy action. In particular, closer cooperation with multilateral development banks would reduce staffing requirements for Japan and bring an end to the charges of formal or informal aid-tying which have been leveled against Japan in the past. At the same time, the

Japanese should be given high-level managerial responsibilities in these organizations, as is the case today in the Asian Development Bank.

Japan could also adopt policies to encourage the recycling of capital to the developing countries through risk pooling. One possibility would be to establish a governmental or quasi-governmental agency to provide insurance for overseas loans and investments at better than actuarial rates and thus in effect to subsidize private capital flows to Third World countries. The government could also change relative rates of return on investment in developed and developing countries by differentiating between them in the tax code. For example, it could offer a tax holiday on all profits earned on investments in the poorest countries and in highly indebted countries. Finally, the government could support guidelines suggesting that a certain share (perhaps 25 percent) of foreign institutional investment be in developing country liabilities.

Conclusion

Following the appreciation of the yen, Japan continues to accumulate current account surpluses while the contribution of net exports to its economic growth has turned negative. This has created a policy dilemma whose solution lies in domestic-based economic growth. Japan has made great strides in this direction, but it needs to ensure the continuation of the process.

Aside from reducing the current account surplus and offsetting the adverse impact of US fiscal adjustment on the world economy, domestic-based expansion will also improve the quality of life in Japan, which is not commensurate with its per capita income.

A central issue of public policy is housing. This is not only because of the insufficient quantity and low quality of the housing stock, but also because improved housing is associated with complementary spending on consumer durables and because high prices for housing generate excess savings. A variety of recommendations have been made for increasing the land available for housing, to improve the use of existing land, and to ease the financial burden of house purchases. There is also a need to develop complementary physical and social infrastructure.

The government should also encourage reductions in working hours. This can be accomplished by accelerating the adoption of the 40-hour workweek, increasing paid vacations, and lengthening public holidays.

All of these measures would promote domestic-based growth and reduce the excess of savings over investment. They would need to be supplemented by appropriate short-term measures, in particular fiscal policies. But there is also a need for a sustained fiscal effort to provide for continued expansion and durably improve the savings–investment balance. Such an effort should emphasize the promotion of housing and social infrastructure.

At the same time, Japan should not forgo liberalizing its imports on the grounds that this would reinforce the adverse effects of the high yen on its manufacturing sector. The more Japan protects its high-cost industries, the more the exchange rate will have to appreciate and the more its efficient export industries will suffer. Strong growth in domestic demand provides a favorable climate for liberalization and adjustment.

These policies would conform to the requirements of international economic balance because they would reduce the Japanese current account surplus and create an expansionary force in the world economy. In so doing, they would significantly improve Japan's international standing. Japan could enhance its position further by taking on additional responsibilities in other areas, including defense and assistance to developing countries.

Imports to Japan are limited by high tariffs on selected primary commodities, high levels of agricultural protection, the use of import quotas, and the application of a variety of non-tariff measures. The liberalization of imports is in Japan's interest because it would contribute to improved resource allocation and to higher living standards. It would also benefit industrial and developing countries alike. But Japan should go even further, assuming a leadership role in promoting multilateral trade liberalization in agriculture, manufacturing, and services in the Uruguay Round.

Japan relies heavily on the United States for military protection and the defense of its strategic interests abroad. It spends 1 percent of its gross national product on defense, compared with 7 percent in the United States, 3 to 5 percent in the other major industrial countries, and 3 percent in neutral Sweden. Japan could increase its defense capabilities by building up its conventional forces, naval strength, and air defenses. Japan would still rely on the United States for nuclear protection and for the defense of distant interests, and would thus remain a significant free rider in defense matters. The government could partially offset that, however, by increasing its financial assistance to developing countries.

Japan's official development assistance is less than 0.3 percent of its GNP. Among the major industrial countries, this ratio exceeds only that of the United States, and it is well surpassed by a number of smaller European countries, which spend 0.8–1.0 percent of their gross national product on ODA. ODA near 1.0 percent of GDP can be considered an appropriate objective for Japan. In addition, an increasing portion of this assistance should be channeled through multilateral institutions, both to strengthen these institutions and to avoid tied aid, which may be considered a subsidy to exports. It would also be desirable to provide inducements for the flow of private capital to developing countries.

The recent appreciation of the yen is ultimately expected to reduce the surplus in Japan's trade balance considerably. However, there are several factors acting in the opposite direction, including the relatively low rate of inflation in Japan and rapid productivity growth for tradable goods. The importance of these will increase over time.

Fiscal stimulus measures would reduce the current account surplus further. Additional reductions could be attained through import liberalization as well as through changes in laws and regulations relating to housing, although the effects of these structural adjustments may only be felt with long time lags.

The proposed measures would go a long way toward reducing Japan's large current account surplus, which would otherwise continue to increase as a result of growing earnings on investments abroad. Equally important, these measures would contribute to an improvement in the quality of life in Japan. These considerations put a premium on early action.

Appendices

Appendix A   The Estimation of Comparative Advantage

In this study, two indices of trade specialization have been employed. The export index of revealed comparative advantage (XRCA) has been defined as the ratio of a country's share in the exports of a particular commodity category to its share in total merchandise exports:

$$(A.1) \quad XRCA = \frac{X_{ij}}{\sum_j X_{ij}} \bigg/ \frac{\sum_i X_{ij}}{\sum_i \sum_j X_{ij}}$$

where X stands for exports, and the subscripts i and j refer to industry (product category) and country, respectively. The net export (NX) index has been defined as net exports divided by the sum of exports and imports for a particular industry.

$$(A.2) \quad NX_{ij} = \frac{X_{ij} - M_{ij}}{X_{ij} + M_{ij}},$$

where M refers to imports.[1]

The use of the net export index is superior to the export index of revealed comparative advantage on trade-theoretical grounds. This is because the former indicates the effects of comparative advantage on the relationship between exports and imports rather than on exports alone.

The net export index has the practical disadvantage of being affected by the idiosyncracies of national import protection, however; in the extreme, prohibitive protection will give rise to a net export index of 100 for a differentiated product, some of which is exported. In addition, the results are affected by changes in a country's overall trade balance.

---

1. In the tables that follow, each index has been multiplied by 100 for purposes of presentation.

Revealed comparative advantage indices have been calculated for 57 primary and for 167 manufactured product categories. The results have been aggregated into 20 commodity groups, of which 3 represent primary products and 17 manufactured goods. These results are presented in table A.1 for the export index and table A.2 for the net export index. The average physical and human capital-intensities of the 17 manufactured commodities are given in table A.3.

Estimates have been made for the years 1967, 1971, 1975, 1979, and 1983, so as to permit examining changes in revealed comparative advantage in four-year intervals. The "comparator" countries chosen for the estimation include 18 industrial countries[2] and 19 developing countries in whose exports manufactured goods accounted for at least 18 percent of total exports and exceeded $300 million in 1979.[3]

The Revealed Comparative Advantages of Japan and the United States

A more disaggregated commodity breakdown has been utilized to analyze econometrically the factors determining the structure of comparative advantage in the two countries. Due to complete specialization in some natural resource products (hence an absence of production data for the nonproducing country), the empirical investigation has been limited to 167 manufactured goods. Correspondingly, the econometric results are not fully comparable with those shown in tables A.2 and A.3, which include primary products.

The net export index is used as the dependent variable in the regression results presented in tables A.4 to A.7. Since this index is defined over the range $[-1, 1]$, ordinary least squares (OLS) estimation will not be appropriate, as it could lead to fitted values of the dependent variable outside its defined range. In fact, since the residuals are truncated at the values -1 and 1, they are heteroscedastic.

One way of addressing this problem is to redefine the dependent variable so that it takes values between $-\infty$ to ∞. A customary way of doing so is to use a logistic transformation of the variable:

---

2. Australia, Austria, Belgium, Canada, Denmark, Finland, France, Germany, Ireland, Israel, Italy, Japan, the Netherlands, Norway, Sweden, Switzerland, the United Kingdom, and the United States.

3. Argentina, Brazil, Egypt, Greece, Hong Kong, Indonesia, Korea, Malaysia, Mexico, Morocco, the Philippines, Portugal, Singapore, Spain, Taiwan, Thailand, Tunisia, Turkey, and Yugoslavia (India and Pakistan meet the criteria but have not been included for lack of data. Indonesia has been included even though it meets the second criterion but not the first).

Table A.1 Export indices of revealed comparative advantage, Japan and the United States, selected years

	Japan					United States				
	1967	1971	1975	1979	1983	1967	1971	1975	1979	1983
Industry										
Food, Beverages, and Tobacco	50	48	23	22	18	211	195	262	260	264
Agricultural Raw Materials	15	11	9	7	5	237	332	331	406	396
Non-Oil Mineral Products	15	18	17	26	20	221	244	284	301	286
Textile Mill Products	486	337	258	196	198	63	55	65	94	72
Apparel & Other Finished Textile Products	372	190	64	31	42	68	54	55	57	40
Lumber & Wood Products	96	50	20	11	7	105	110	143	130	122
Furniture & Fixtures	94	64	30	28	37	85	49	57	57	79
Paper & Allied Products	70	73	80	74	63	125	149	133	110	130
Printing & Publishing	57	59	44	56	82	225	218	198	204	232
Chemical & Allied Products	168	158	163	122	100	209	207	180	200	206
Rubber & Plastic Products	307	272	274	254	291	141	118	116	112	119
Leather & Leather Products	280	164	68	44	40	42	28	40	37	42
Stone, Clay, & Glass Products	333	211	183	192	196	128	120	101	105	104
Primary Metal, & Allied Products	354	393	429	390	318	98	94	92	81	76
Fabricated Metal Products	262	240	226	209	210	187	147	156	149	142
Nonelectrical Machinery	115	135	157	215	247	263	263	260	272	289
Electrical Machinery	421	392	334	404	433	210	193	187	210	210
Transportation Equipment	273	300	365	368	370	258	266	242	230	213
Instruments & Related Products	323	286	314	439	432	238	242	212	186	193
Misc. Manufacturing Products	355	238	164	145	206	95	111	111	103	103

Source: GATT tapes

Table A.2 Net export indices of revealed comparative advantage, Japan and the United States, selected years

	Japan					United States				
	1967	1971	1975	1979	1983	1967	1971	1975	1979	1983
Food, Beverages, & Tobacco	-65.3	-61.8	-84.0	-84.3	-82.7	0.4	-11.6	26.4	13.1	14.5
Agricultural Raw Materials	-96.5	-96.2	-96.6	-97.6	-97.1	29.2	48.2	51.1	57.2	59.3
Non-Oil Mineral Products	86.0	75.3	55.9	26.5	49.0	-32.4	-49.0	17.0	-4.4	-35.8
Textile Mill Products	-97.0	-9.6	-95.6	-92.3	-93.0	4.1	15.1	34.8	30.0	42.0
Apparel & Other Finished Textile Products	91.5	76.5	-12.4	-62.5	-28.1	-49.5	-64.8	-54.3	-66.5	-83.2
Lumber & Wood Products	-32.7	-52.8	-87.6	-92.2	-92.7	-42.3	-53.0	-19.7	-44.4	-47.4
Furniture & Fixtures	82.3	68.3	-16.0	-33.9	-12.8	-24.8	-64.4	-38.8	-50.4	-55.5
Paper & Allied Products	66.6	71.0	59.4	42.4	22.2	-39.0	-28.8	-13.8	-35.1	-32.5
Printing & Publishing	-17.7	0.7	-28.3	-13.4	26.2	41.7	33.9	38.3	29.5	17.4
Chemical & Allied Products	13.1	27.5	36.5	12.6	4.0	46.6	37.4	37.7	32.5	22.1
Rubber & Plastic Products	91.5	91.4	86.4	75.4	80.7	27.7	-10.6	-2.4	-31.7	-34.8
Leather & Leather Products	82.0	67.7	6.2	-36.2	-15.0	-70.9	-85.6	74.5	-79.8	-82.4
Stone, Clay, & Glass Products	84.3	79.7	71.8	66.0	72.2	3.7	-8.1	-0.3	-17.9	-27.0
Primary Metal & Allied Products	52.0	84.2	86.0	77.0	71.9	-21.8	35.0	-18.5	-40.7	-47.7
Fabricated Metal Products	75.5	72.4	80.8	81.9	79.8	51.4	25.0	48.3	29.3	13.2
Nonelectrical Machinery	20.5	33.0	55.8	66.5	76.2	52.0	42.4	50.2	35.4	24.8
Electrical Machinery	75.2	77.6	73.9	75.1	80.3	22.4	-1.0	12.8	2.2	-14.4
Transportation Equipment	78.9	79.7	88.1	85.8	86.3	27.0	2.7	18.7	-1.4	-16.8
Instruments & Related Products	60.2	58.8	56.9	64.7	70.7	32.7	27.9	31.2	4.1	-4.6
Misc. Manufacturing Products	52.7	27.1	9.4	10.4	39.1	-36.8	-35.9	-21.8	-34.8	-48.2
Total Trade	-5.5	9.8	-1.8	-3.7	8.1	7.5	-1.6	5.2	-8.9	-14.4

Source: GATT tapes.

Table A.3 Average factor intensities of 17 aggregated product categories (dollars)

	P/L	H/L	K/L	P/H
Industry				
Textile Mill Products	9,404.	17,814.	27,219.	.528
Apparel & Other Textile Products	2,024.	11,967.	13,991.	.169
Lumber & Wood Products	11,266.	12,184.	23,449.	.925
Furniture & Fixtures	4,520.	21,678.	26,198.	.209
Paper & Allied Products	57,609.	40,126.	97,735.	1.436
Printing & Publishing	8,417.	36,191.	44,607.	.233
Chemical & Allied Products	41,417.	33,031.	74,448.	1.254
Rubber & Plastic Products	10,188.	18,579.	28,766.	.549
Leather & Leather Products	5,860.	17,281.	23,142.	.339
Stone, Clay & Glass Products	11,843.	10,003.	21,846.	1.184
Primary Metal & Allied Products	32,937.	30,130.	63,066.	1.093
Fabricated Metal Products	9,073.	27,860.	36,933.	.326
Nonelectrical Machinery	10,045.	29,011.	39,056.	.346
Electrical Machinery	7,122.	30,836.	37,958.	.231
Transportation Equipment	11,602.	27,067.	38,669.	.429
Instruments & Related Products	11,147.	41,230.	52,376.	.270
Misc. Manufacturing Products	5,667.	17,761.	23,428.	.319
All Categories	20,518.	28,278.	48,796.	.701

Note: The table shows average capital–labor ratios in a two-digit industry breakdown. The average capital–labor ratios for the individual commodity groups have been derived by weighting by the share of exports of individual product categories in the total exports for each commodity group aggregated over the countries under study. Physical capital (P) has been defined as the value of fixed investment; human capital (H) as the present value of the difference between the average wage and the unskilled wage. Labor (L) has been measured in terms of margins.

(A.3) $\hat{NX}_{ij} = (NX_{ij} + 1)/2$

(A.4) $NXADJ_{ij} = \ln(\hat{NX}_{ij}/1 - \hat{NX}_{ij})$.

The regressions have been estimated using both the unadjusted (NX) and adjusted (NXADJ) measures as dependent variables. The results were virtually identical. The estimates reported in tables A.4 to A.7 have been obtained using the theoretically preferable adjusted index. The data used to construct these variables originate from the GATT trade tapes.

In the construction of the explanatory variables, factor intensity has been defined as a given factor's share of value-added. The share specification has been adopted since it yields an unambiguous ranking of industries by factor intensity in the multifactor model and has a straightforward interpretation in terms of the multifactor Heckscher–Ohlin model. For both countries, the relative shares of unskilled labor, physical capital, and human capital in value-added, and the share of R&D expenditures in output have been derived from the country's own industrial statistics. This allows production techniques to differ across countries in response to differences in relative factor prices, and avoids the econometric misspecification (errors in variables) caused by incorrectly imposing one country's pattern of factor usage on the other.

The unskilled labor share has been defined as

(A.5) $LABOR_{ij} = (W^u_{ij} \cdot L_{ij})/VA_{ij}$

where W^u_{ij} is the industry unskilled wage, L_{ij} is full-time employment in the industry, and VA_{ij} is value-added. The unskilled wage is defined on an industry-by-industry basis since differences in market structure, union power, and so forth, will cause the renumeration of unskilled workers to vary across industries. In turn, the human capital share is defined as wage payments in excess of those attributed as returns to unskilled labor:

(A.6) $HCAP_{ij} = (W_{ij} - W^u_{ij}) \cdot L_{ij}/VA_{ij}$

In a previous study of Japan (Urata 1983), two measures of human capital intensity were used. One was the wage differential measure described above, and the other was the share of technical and administrative workers. In this study, the wage differential approach has been adopted for a variety of reasons. First, this is an economically more appealing measure based on market information rather than an arbitrary classification of occupations. Second, the wage differential approach coincides with the share of value-added specification, while the skill index does not. Finally, the estimated coefficients Urata obtained using the skill index were generally insignificant. Balassa (1979, 1986) achieved highly significant results in an international investigation of comparative advantage with the use of the wage differential variable.

Physical capital intensity has been defined in both stock and flow terms. The flow measure is the nonwage share of value added, while the stock measure is defined as the ratio of the physical capital stock to value added. While under certain conditions (perfectly competitive markets, no uncertainty) the two measures will yield identical rankings of the industries, in practice they will not. The flow measure contains a risk premium which varies across industries. In turn, the valuation of capital stocks at historical rather than replacement cost makes this measure susceptible to distortion, especially during periods of prolonged inflation. Since neither approach is clearly superior a priori, both have been used.

Research and development intensity has been defined as the share of R&D expenditures in output value. This definition is not exactly comparable with the share-of-value-added definition used for the other factor-intensity variables, but data are only available in this form.

One objection to the specification of the explanatory variables is that the components of value added may fluctuate over the the business cycle and lead to shifts in the factor-intensity rankings. This problem arises, however, only if the cyclical effects have differential impact across industries. If factor shares fluctuate equiproportionately across industries, the parameter estimates will be unaffected. At any rate, in the case of the United States, where some of the variables did exhibit substantial changes from year to year, averages across several periods have been used to eliminate the business cycle effects.[4]

Estimation has been done by regressing net export indices of comparative advantage for the 167 manufactured product categories on the explanatory variables just described. Estimates have been made for the years 1967, 1971, 1975, 1979, and 1983. They are shown in tables A.4 and A.5 for Japan and in tables A.6 and A.7 for the United States.

The regressions have been specified with the R&D variable both included and excluded. The latter is more consistent with the factor-based Heckscher–Ohlin theory and avoids double counting because R&D expenditures are already included in the renumeration of physical and human capital. This may explain the collinearity between the R&D variables, on one hand, and the physical and human capital variables, on the other, which reduce the statistical significance of the latter variables in several of the regressions. This is particularly true for the correlation between the human capital variable and the R&D variable, which in large part represents investment in human capital in the form of scientists and engineers.

---

4. The data sources are described below.

Table A.4 The determinants of comparative advantage: Japan
(explanatory variables in natural units)

	YEAR	N	CONSTANT	LABOR
(3.1)	1967	161		6.308 (5.168)[a]
(3.2)	1967	161	136.372 (2.161)[b]	4.989 (2.991)[a]
(3.3)	1971	159		2.691 (2.527)[b]
(3.4)	1971	159	188.778 (3.131)[a]	0.873 (0.609)
(3.5)	1975	160		−1.626 (1.275)
(3.6)	1975	160	173.491 (2.835)[a]	−3.274 (−2.009)[b]
(3.7)	1979	161		−2.246 (−1.680)[c]
(3.8)	1979	161	105.667 (1.725)[c]	−3.212 (−1.925)[c]
(3.9)	1983	161		−0.845 (−0.604)
(3.10)	1983	161	132.935 (1.984)[b]	−2.109 (−1.192)
(3.11)	1967	161		6.309 (5.261)[a]
(3.12)	1967	161	171.817 (2.719)[a]	4.632 (2.895)[a]
(3.13)	1971	159		2.691 (2.547)[b]
(3.14)	1971	159	206.459 (3.369)[a]	0.695 (0.497)
(3.15)	1975	160		−1.705 (−1.351)
(3.16)	1975	160	124.388 (2.054)[b]	−2.858 (−1.793)[c]
(3.17)	1979	161		−2.334 (−1.796)[c]
(3.18)	1979	161	28.823 (0.448)	−2.520 (−1.535)
(3.19)	1983	161		−1.079 (−0.821)
(3.20)	1983	161	23.464 (0.352)	−1.241 (−0.750)

Note: T-statistics in parentheses.
Explanation of symbols:
LABOR = unskilled labor share of value added
PFLOW = physical capital flow share of value added
PSTOCK = physical capital stock share of value added

PFLOW	PSTOCK	HCAP	RD	$\overline{R}^2$
1.374		−7.077		.097
$(2.173)^b$		$(−2.714)^a$		
	0.024	−8.690		.093
	$(2.008)^b$	$(−2.857)^a$		
1.902		−2.971		.009
$(3.142)^a$		$(−1.041)$		
	0.038	−5.271		.008
	$(3.003)^a$	$(−1.611)$		
1.753		4.154		.021
$(2.851)^a$		(1.282)		
	0.048	1.913		.024
	$(3.083)^a$	(0.523)		
1.077		8.396		.053
$(1.746)^c$		$(2.425)^b$		
	0.048	6.829		.056
	$(3.545)^a$	$(1.754)^c$		
1.344		6.864		.019
$(2.001)^b$		$(1.905)^c$		
	0.034	5.171		.017
	$(2.562)^b$	(1.261)		
1.731		−6.169	−17.963	.103
$(2.733)^a$		$(−2.341)^b$	$(−1.565)$	
	0.022	−8.129	−17.765	.100
	$(1.840)^c$	$(−2.677)^a$	$(−1.552)$	
2.085		−2.509	−9.200	.006
$(3.389)^a$		$(−0.849)$	$(−0.807)$	
	0.037	−4.993	−8.890	.005
	$(2.759)^a$	$(−1.500)$	$(−0.782)$	
1.274		2.844	23.946	.042
$(2.090)^b$		(0.872)	$(2.139)^b$	
	0.050	1.030	24.488	.046
	$(3.953)^a$	(0.284)	$(2.199)^b$	
0.329		6.060	38.680	.111
$(−0.505)$		$(1.780)^c$	$(3.452)^a$	
	0.055	5.130	39.569	.116
	$(4.900)^a$	(1.339)	$(3.562)^a$	
0.257		3.495	45.651	.136
(0.382)		(1.008)	$(5.404)^a$	
	0.039	2.832	45.881	.135
	$(2.531)^b$	(0.709)	$(5.449)^a$	

HCAP = human capital share of value added
RD = research and development expenditures as a percentage of the value of output
a. Coefficient estimate significantly different from zero at the 1 percent level in a two-tailed test.
b. Significant at the 5 percent level.
c. Significant at the 10 percent level.

Table A.5 The determinants of comparative advantage: Japan
(explanatory variables in logs)

	YEAR	N	CONSTANT	LABOR
(4.1)	1967	161	−1486.182 (−3.040)[a]	234.737 (4.237)[a]
(4.2)	1967	161	−27.079 (−0.163)	124.787 (3.037)[a]
(4.3)	1971	159	−1036.440 (−1.802)[c]	110.421 (1.805)[c]
(4.4)	1971	159	169.263 (1.009)	18.873 (0.481)
(4.5)	1975	160	−1135.301 (−1.404)	36.310 (0.504)
(4.6)	1975	160	198.991 (1.204)	−68.158 (−1.638)
(4.7)	1979	161	−1352.347 (−2.316)[b]	51.824 (0.925)
(4.8)	1979	161	53.838 (0.348)	−58.425 (−1.419)
(4.9)	1983	161	−1202.154 (−1.680)[c]	67.100 (1.028)
(4.10)	1983	161	96.876 (0.580)	−30.763 (−0.704)
(4.11)	1967	161	−1447.907 (−3.018)[a]	228.891 (−4.216)[a]
(4.12)	1967	161	−16.524 (−0.102)	120.860 (3.010)[a]
(4.13)	1971	159	−1022.114 (−1.777)[c]	108.272 (1.784)[c]
(4.14)	1971	159	172.787 (1.044)	17.344 (0.448)
(4.15)	1975	160	−1233.125 (−1.636)	51.627 (0.733)
(4.16)	1975	160	173.068 (0.999)	−59.214 (−1.400)
(4.17)	1979	161	−1464.959 (−2.690)[a]	68.437 (1.262)
(4.18)	1979	161	30.888 (0.189)	−49.858 (−1.211)
(4.19)	1983	161	−1337.820 (−2.190)[b]	85.309 (1.455)
(4.20)	1983	161	41.449 (0.244)	−19.953 (−0.480)

Note: T-statistics in parentheses.
Explanation of symbols: See table A.4.
a. Coefficient estimate significantly different from zero at the 1 percent level in a two-tailed test.
b. Significant at the 5 percent level.
c. Significant at the 10 percent level.

PFLOW	PSTOCK	HCAP	RD	$\overline{R}^2$
234.089		−26.570		.089
(3.014)[a]		(−0.943)		
	−16.613	−60.132		.079
	(−1.202)	(−2.054)[b]		
196.315		11.913		.000
(2.131)[b]		(0.406)		
	−9.210	−17.064		−.012
	(−0.627)	(−0.563)		
224.067		89.251		.039
(1.627)		(2.789)[a]		
	3.182	51.402		.022
	(0.251)	(1.707)[c]		
234.951		137.342		.085
(2.328)[b]		(4.172)[a]		
	2.145	97.510		.067
	(0.180)	(2.949)[a]		
208.604		113.874		.043
(1.677)[c]		(3.295)[a]		
	−14.747	84.349		.034
	(−1.032)	(2.417)[b]		
228.833		−22.670	−18.367	.088
(2.989)[a]		(−0.804)	(−1.006)	
	−17.519	−54.301	−21.308	.079
	(−1.256)	(−1.843)[c]	(−1.151)	
194.348		13.251	−6.540	−.006
(2.098)[b]		(0.445)	(−0.364)	
	−9.336	−14.957	−8.121	−.018
	(−0.639)	(−0.484)	(−0.445)	
237.511		75.403	56.513	.082
(1.895)[c]		(2.301)[b]	(2.799)[a]	
	6.106	34.554	55.759	.063
	(0.475)	(1.116)	(2.724)[a]	
251.919		118.593	74.700	.168
(2.737)[a]		(3.697)[a]	(4.941)[a]	
	6.250	74.692	74.029	.148
	(0.492)	(2.322)[b]	(4.768)[a]	
223.995		89.783	100.711	.176
(2.145)[b]		(2.712)[a]	(6.287)[a]	
	−10.470	56.614	99.137	.162
	(−0.772)	(1.659)[c]	(6.084)[a]	

Table A.6 The determinants of comparative advantage: United States
(explanatory variables in natural units)

	YEAR	N	CONSTANT	LABOR
(5.1)	1967	158		−5.542 (−4.590)[a]
(5.2)	1967	158	173.926 (3.638)[a]	−7.143 (−5.306)[a]
(5.3)	1971	162		−6.329 (−4.979)[a]
(5.4)	1971	162	135.729 (2.596)[a]	−7.869 (−5.402)[a]
(5.5)	1975	162		−5.263 (−4.304)[a]
(5.6)	1975	162	126.542 (2.993)[a]	−6.857 (−5.158)[a]
(5.7)	1979	162		−4.521 (−3.836)[a]
(5.8)	1979	162	84.707 (2.293)[b]	−5.791 (−4.638)[a]
(5.9)	1983	163		−4.950 (−4.243)[a]
(5.10)	1983	163	4.556 (0.113)	−5.566 (−4.604)[a]
(5.11)	1967	158		−5.098 (−4.196)[a]
(5.12)	1967	158	146.051 (3.051)[a]	−6.418 (−4.694)[a]
(5.13)	1971	162		−5.891 (−4.590)[a]
(5.14)	1971	162	108.917 (2.040)[c]	−7.162 (−4.775)[a]
(5.15)	1975	162		−4.858 (−4.665)[a]
(5.16)	1975	162	101.846 (1.644)	−6.206 (−4.572)[a]
(5.17)	1979	162		−3.938 (−3.312)[a]
(5.18)	1979	162	49.833 (1.303)	−4.859 (−3.812)[a]
(5.19)	1983	163		−4.406 (−3.678)[a]
(5.20)	1983	163	−28.457 (−0.663)	−4.691 (−3.729)[a]

Note: T-statistics in parentheses.
Explanation of symbols: See table A.4.
a. Coefficient estimate significantly different from zero at the 1 percent level in a two-tailed test.
b. Significant at the 5 percent level.
c. Significant at the 10 percent level.

PFLOW	PSTOCK	HCAP	RD	$\bar{R}^2$
1.598 (3.876)[a]		5.868 (3.067)[a]		.140
	−0.158 (−0.673)	4.098 (1.861)[c]		.136
1.549 (3.263)[a]		5.719 (3.002)[a]		.154
	0.212 (0.824)	4.404 (2.000)[b]		.152
1.611 (4.176)[a]		5.252 (2.905)[a]		.156
	0.323 (1.645)[c]	4.063 (1.998)[b]		.161
1.284 (3.996)[a]		3.432 (2.115)[b]		.125
	0.495 (1.851)[c]	2.639 (1.515)		.145
0.635 (1.862)[c]		4.442 (2.624)[a]		.112
	0.667 (2.327)[b]	4.469 (2.518)[b]		.146
1.318 (3.010)[a]		5.153 (2.666)[a]	9.642 (2.032)[b]	.147
	−0.160 (−0.683)	3.660 (1.663)[c]	9.657 (2.040)[b]	.143
1.279 (2.540)[b]		5.009 (2.623)[a]	9.496 (1.679)[c]	.160
	0.210 (0.836)	3.963 (1.803)[c]	9.481 (1.671)[c]	.157
1.363 (2.372)[b]		4.597 (2.494)[b]	8.750 (1.515)	.162
	0.381 (1.454)	3.657 (1.672)[c]	8.732 (1.515)	.168
0.937 (2.758)[a]		2.517 (1.531)	11.940 (2.727)[a]	.149
	0.496 (2.050)[b]	2.071 (1.187)	11.971 (2.856)[a]	.169
0.307 (0.816)		3.592 (2.076)[b]	11.306 (2.174)[b]	.129
	0.668 (2.564)[b]	3.946 (2.233)[b]	11.350 (2.318)[b]	.164

Table A.7 The determinants of comparative advantage: United States
(explanatory variables in logs)

	YEAR	N	CONSTANT	LABOR
(6.1)	1969	158	−1192.164	−64.090
			(−1.368)	(−1.067)
(6.2)	1967	1958	248.782	−164.044
			(2.626)[a]	(−5.217)[a]
(6.3)	1971	162	−1714.959	−43.886
			(−1.897)[c]	(−0.722)
(6.4)	1971	162	170.701	−181.284
			(1.088)	(−5.164)[a]
(6.5)	1975	162	−1516.748	−32.166
			(−1.743)[c]	(−0.561)
(6.6)	1975	162	143.519	−156.823
			(1.458)	(−4.985)[a]
(6.7)	1979	162	−904.118	−55.323
			(−1.233)[b]	(−1.233)
(6.8)	1979	162	100.786	−134.701
			(1.189)	(−4.999)[a]
(6.9)	1983	163	−951.984	−56.950
			(−1.317)	(−1.229)
(6.10)	1983	163	−56.935	−133.881
			(−0.693)	(−5.179)[a]
(6.11)	1967	158	−605.701	−68.220
			(−0.661)	(−1.110)
(6.12)	1967	158	163.007	−119.857
			(1.770)[c]	(−3.642)[a]
(6.13)	1971	162	−1137.143	−46.011
			(−1.222)	(−0.741)
(6.14)	1971	162	81.299	−135.150
			(0.808)	(−3.871)[a]
(6.15)	1975	162	−1096.443	−33.712
			(−0.568)	(−0.568)
(6.16)	1975	162	78.291	−123.164
			(0.772)	(−3.761)[a]
(6.17)	1979	162	−478.261	−58.074
			(−0.618)	(−1.259)
(6.18)	1979	162	43.258	−105.970
			(0.497)	(−3.740)[a]
(6.19)	1983	163	−467.741	−60.086
			(−0.599)	(−1.254)
(6.20)	1983	163	−120.969	−102.056
			(−1.336)	(−3.756)[a]

Note: *T*-statistics in parentheses
Explanation of symbols: See Appendix Table A.4.
a. Coefficient estimate significantly different from zero at the 1 percent level in a two-tailed test.
b. Significant at the 5 percent level.
c. Significant at the 10 percent level.

PFLOW	PSTOCK	HCAP	RD	$\bar{R}^2$
267.092		132.871		.130
(1.655)[c]		(3.507)[a]		
	15.313	92.560		.122
	(0.822)	(2.740)[a]		
361.012		152.445		.150
(2.134)[b]		(3.938)[a]		
	40.007	94.799		.148
	(1.769)[c]	(2.498)[b]		
324.302		129.308		.145
(2.008)[b]		(3.255)[a]		
	46.281	75.916		.155
	(2.704)[a]	(2.181)[b]		
209.485		90.584		.117
(1.536)		(2.423)[b]		
	51.110	48.129		.157
	(2.836)[a]	(1.655)[c]		
198.315		114.684		.106
(1.484)		(3.126)[a]		
	65.812	71.346		.169
	(3.627)[a]	(2.478)[b]		
145.079		39.095	9.800	.162
(0.851)		(2.654)[a]	(3.018)[a]	
	10.184	81.050	30.879	.160
	(0.538)	(2.403)[b]	(3.141)[a]	
239.993		122.855	30.622	.182
(1.376)		(3.120)[a]	(3.319)[a]	
	34.733	82.696	32.092	.186
	(1.751)[c]	(2.429)[b]	(3.391)[a]	
236.272		107.784	22.275	.167
(1.377)		(2.608)[a]	(2.550)[b]	
	42.432	67.087	23.414	.180
	(2.431)[b]	(1.906)[c]	(2.706)[a]	
121.212		68.658	21.302	.143
(0.837)		(1.791)[c]	(2.514)[b]	
	47.947	40.997	20.688	.183
	(2.748)[a]	(1.380)[b]	(2.613)[a]	
97.868		89.949	24.345	.136
(0.669)		(2.404)[b]	(2.573)[b]	
	62.311	63.575	23.004	.198
	(3.673)[a]	(2.165)[b]	(2.750)[a]	

The regressions have been estimated with the explanatory variable expressed in levels and logs, since trade theory does not provide an indication of the functional form of the relationship between factor intensities and net exports. For the specifications in levels, the constant term has been omitted to avoid a linear dependency in the matrix of explanatory variables. The regressions have been estimated using White's heteroscedastic-consistent covariance matrix estimator which yields a consistent estimate of the covariance matrix (permitting proper inferences to be drawn) even in the presence of heteroscedastic disturbances (White 1980).

The coefficients of determination of the regression equations are very low. This may be explained in part by the existence of large variations in the index of revealed comparative advantage, due to the error possibilities noted earlier, and in part by the difficulties involved in relating trade statistics to the industrial classification scheme. The difficulties are especially pronounced in the case of Japan, whose industrial data were more highly aggregated than its trade data. This may explain that the results for Japan are generally weaker in a statistical sense than those for the United States. Nevertheless, the estimates offer considerable interest since a substantial number of the regression coefficients are significant statistically and, even when they are not, the pattern of changes over time conforms to changes in relative resource endowments.[5]

The results in tables A.4 and A.5 show that at the beginning of the period Japan had a strong comparative advantage in unskilled labor-intensive manufactured goods, but it had a strong comparative disadvantage in human capital-intensive products. In most specifications Japan also appears to have had a comparative advantage in physical capital-intensive products. Regression equations estimated for later years indicate the transformation of the structure of Japan's comparative advantage in manufactured goods from unskilled labor-intensive to human capital-intensive products. At the same time, Japan's position in regard to physical capital-intensive products was approximately maintained over time.[6] The pattern of the regression coefficients is not affected, but their statistical significance is reduced, by adding

---

5. Leamer and Bowen (1981) and Aw (1983) have demonstrated that regressions of trade on factor-intensity variables may yield misleading inferences in the absence of data on factor endowments in the multifactor model. In this paper, however, reference will be made to data on factor endowments below.

6. These results are broadly similar to those obtained by Urata (1983) for unskilled labor and physical capital. However, Urata was unable to obtain significant coefficient estimates for his human capital-intensity variable in the net export regressions. It may be added that Urata did not have a research and development variable, but he did include an energy variable that was significant statistically for 1975, although not for 1967, the two years for which estimates were made.

the R&D variable, owing to the existence of collinearity among the explanatory variables, as noted above. The R&D variable itself goes from negative to positive and it is highly significant statistically in later years.

The United States in turn appears to have had a comparative advantage in human capital-intensive and physical capital-intensive manufactured goods in 1967 while it had a strong disadvantage in unskilled labor-intensive products. The situation changed little in subsequent years. The coefficients obtained for unskilled labor and human capital accord with previous results reported by Branson and Monoyios (1977), Stern and Maskus (1981), and Maskus (1983), although these previous studies obtained negative coefficients on physical capital, in contrast to the more plausible positive coefficients reported in tables A.6 and A.7. Adding the R&D variable does not change these conclusions and, with the partial exception of the results for the last two years, the regression coefficients of the factor-intensity variables remain highly significant. The regression coefficient of the research and development variable, too, is highly significant statistically, and it shows the continued comparative advantage of the United States in R&D-intensive products.

These results are consistent with the calculations presented in Noland (1985) which indicate that, during the period under consideration, both the United States and Japan were relatively abundant in both physical and human capital. Japan increased its endowments of physical and human capital relative to the rest of the world. In contrast, while the United States remained a physical and human capital-abundant country, it accumulated these factors more slowly than the rest of the world; consequently, its relative abundance in both of these factors declined.

Japanese and US Revealed Comparative Advantages in High-Technology Products

The changing pattern of comparative advantage in high-technology products has attracted considerable attention in recent years. For purposes of analysis, high-technology products have been defined as products where the ratio of research and development expenditures to the value of output exceeded 3.5 percent in the mid-1970s in the United States.

There are altogether 19 such product categories. US and Japanese export and net export indices of revealed comparative advantage for these products are shown in tables A.8 and A.9, in the order of the share of R&D expenditures. The overall rankings, of the indices among the 167 manufacturing product categories are reported in parentheses.

Table A.8 Export indices of revealed comparative advantage, high-technology products: Japan and the United States, selected years (indices in column 1; rankings in column 2)

	Japan									
	1967		1971		1975		1979		1983	
	(1)	(2)	(1)	(2)	(1)	(2)	(1)	(2)	(1)	(2)
Industry										
Telephone & Telegraphic Equipment	101	120	190	71	199	54	249	41	335	37
Aircraft Engines	10	161	4	163	7	161	9	159	15	155
Aircraft	38	155	17	159	4	164	6	162	5	161
Computers	84	132	42	149	68	125	96	109	297	41
Photographic Equipment & Supplies	465	33	343	32	403	20	573	11	620	7
Drugs	67	140	62	137	43	137	52	130	44	136
Electronic Components	208	74	168	76	207	50	316	33	345	33
Optical Instruments	1145	2	882	3	808	3	910	3	700	5
Agricultural Chemicals	137	98	91	122	82	113	74	125	106	108
Scientific Instruments	138	96	110	111	119	92	195	60	165	81
Calculating & Accounting Machines	99	123	433	24	718	4	1076	2	1098	2
Synthetic Fibres	473	31	361	27	517	14	327	32	286	42
Cellulosic Fibres	550	21	451	20	501	16	420	20	383	28
Platework & Boilers	206	75	262	49	253	36	233	48	227	57
Steam Engines & Turbines	188	84	212	62	204	51	250	40	132	92
Internal Combustion Engines	102	119	148	87	177	66	248	42	269	45
Office Machinery	89	127	73	135	75	119	137	88	139	77
Typewriters	194	80	211	64	170	69	261	38	558	11
Medical Instruments	128	104	144	90	142	82	157	76	151	82
Average		89		79		69		61		60

Source: GATT tapes.

	United States								
1967		1971		1975		1979		1983	
(1)	(2)	(1)	(2)	(1)	(2)	(1)	(2)	(1)	(2)
85	124	61	129	84	118	127	94	147	82
452	7	559	5	504	6	545	3	597	2
648	1	976	1	924	1	724	1	661	1
87	121	126	90	300	14	518	4	433	8
284	27	283	23	257	24	257	26	239	33
175	72	161	70	152	70	189	50	244	31
278	29	283	22	244	29	255	28	278	21
97	116	123	93	114	100	118	100	149	77
202	52	225	37	223	35	360	11	382	11
373	12	381	9	288	16	203	41	226	35
455	6	424	7	68	178	57	141	86	118
138	94	184	59	121	92	284	22	167	59
33	153	58	133	62	135	191	49	385	10
287	25	203	46	260	22	216	40	244	32
147	87	196	52	264	21	326	14	594	4
317	22	322	16	288	15	322	15	304	18
420	9	576	4	534	4	497	6	544	3
101	108	47	140	54	142	113	105	149	76
365	13	340	10	312	13	286	21	316	17
	54		47		49		39		32

Net export indices of revealed comparative advantage, high-technology products: Japan and the United States, selected years (indices in column 1; rankings in column 2)

Industry	Japan									
	1967		1971		1975		1979		1983	
	(1)	(2)	(1)	(2)	(1)	(2)	(1)	(2)	(1)	(2)
Telephone & Telegraphic Equipment	68.6	77	94.1	17	88.2	22	89.1	15	90.2	27
Aircraft Engines	−85.0	161	−93.3	159	−83.7	155	−77.0	154	−70.8	156
Aircraft	−88.0	144	−83.3	156	−93.7	157	−89.2	158	−93.0	158
Computers	−30.9	149	−43.1	151	−55.8	150	17.9	133	61.3	81
Photographic Equipment & Supplies	70.9	76	63.6	77	66.8	62	73.7	50	79.3	55
Drugs	−47.0	155	−49.0	154	−57.1	151	−56.0	145	−56.3	150
Electronic Components	46.2	107	30.5	117	43.7	89	56.1	79	64.1	78
Optical Instruments	92.5	28	89.6	34	84.3	32	84.5	29	82.2	46
Agricultural Chemicals	34.9	113	10.7	133	23.2	110	24.5	109	55.8	81
Scientific Instruments	13.0	128	8.3	136	26.3	107	30.4	104	28.8	117
Calculating & Accounting Machines	−26.2	148	51.9	89	87.6	24	94.9	7	97.8	6
Synthetic Fibres	99.2	7	97.6	8	97.4	5	62.3	70	85.6	39
Cellulosic Fibres	99.6	3	99.9	1	99.6	1	98.9	3	99.7	2
Platework & Boilers	48.3	100	34.9	112	69.7	55	84.1	31	72.1	69
Steam Engines & Turbines	17.3	124	41.5	102	42.2	92	72.1	52	55.9	86
Internal Combustion Engines	65.2	92	80.8	52	84.1	35	85.9	25	91.9	21
Office Machinery	−60.9	160	−48.8	153	0.2	126	31.8	101	51.5	94
Typewriters	27.9	117	36.4	110	57.2	81	78.8	37	94.4	14
Medical Instruments	28.2	116	38.1	107	13.3	115	13.6	115	23.6	118
Average		100		94		79		71		70

Source: GATT tapes.

	United States								
1967		1971		1975		1979		1983	
(1)	(2)	(1)	(2)	(1)	(2)	(1)	(2)	(1)	(2)
19.8	86	−14.8	100	34.8	73	15.1	82	−23.0	100
55.3	44	63.7	29	65.7	29	56.9	27	46.6	27
89.5	7	93.9	5	91.7	3	85.2	4	77.4	8
36.8	68	9.8	98	71.5	25	73.4	8	47.7	25
44.5	59	34.9	60	44.7	62	19.6	77	0.1	76
58.9	41	51.1	41	53.6	50	37.1	55	34.3	35
50.8	51	36.8	57	24.7	86	6.8	90	3.4	82
−45.8	131	−36.9	121	−30.1	127	−31.1	124	−30.6	108
79.5	17	70.4	23	55.6	46	66.0	14	62.4	14
72.4	29	71.7	20	70.4	26	28.4	68	23.6	47
61.9	38		54		141		143		138
16.8	89	40.2	49	−55.7	31	−63.8	3	−64.3	31
−41.8	127	47.3	96	64.0	90	85.5	6	40.6	3
94.0	3	8.0	15	23.3	9	81.6	5	92.4	5
39.9	63	74.4	74	85.0	35	83.6	37	84.8	7
26.5	80	22.4	93	60.2	95	47.0	83	83.1	78
65.4	35	1.4	22	14.5	38	14.8	39	−1.7	48
−47.1	133	70.6	142	58.8	144	46.9	138	22.5	124
67.1	33	−69.7	27	−63.8	33	−55.1	37	−45.7	26
	57	64.6	56	61.2	54	47.0	52	46.8	49

Data Sources

The industrial data for Japan have been taken from *1973 Census of Manufactures, Report by Industry* (May 1976), published by MITI's Research and Statistics Department. The Japanese unskilled wage has been defined as the average wage of workers 17 years old and under, and those 24 years old and under. As Urata observed, "Japanese workers usually gain their professional skills through on-the-job training so that close relation exists between workers' skill level and their duration of employment at a particular company. While data on duration of employment are not available, the immobility of Japanese labor markets means that the workers' age may be a good proxy for employment and hence skill level" (1983, 679). The data are derived from the Ministry of Labor's *1973 Industrial Wage Structure* (1974). They have been collected by Dr. Anne Loup-Richards of the OECD. Data on research and development expenditures have been kindly provided by Mr. H. Katayama of MITI's Agency of Industrial Science and Technology. Since the R&D data cover the 1971–1982 period, the 1971 values were used in the 1967 regressions, and 1982 values in the 1983 regressions.

For the United States, data on value added, employment, and wages have been obtained from the Census Bureau's *Census of Manufactures* (various issues). The unskilled wage data (annual earnings of full-time workers aged 18–19) come from the Bureau of Labor Statistics' Bulletin 2031, *Annual Earnings and Employment Patterns of Private Non-Agricultural Employees, 1973–1975* (1979), tables A-3, B-3, and C-3.

The R&D data have been taken from the Federal Trade Commission (FTC) statistical report, *Annual Line of Business 1974; 1975;* and *1976* (September 1981, September 1981, and May 1982, respectively). These data are preferable to the widely used National Science Foundation (NSF) data on two counts. They are far more disaggregated (employing a four-digit SIC as opposed to the two-digit SIC of the NSF data) and, in contrast to the NSF figures which are calculated using raw data classified by firm, the FTC figures are constructed using raw data classified by plant. Hence these figures yield a more accurate indication of R&D expenditures in different product classes for multiproduct firms.

The data for value added, wages, and employment have been averaged for the 1973–1975 period. The data on R&D expenditures have been averaged over the midsample 1974–1976 period, the only years available.

Appendix B   Informal Barriers to Imports

Information on informal barriers to imports in Japan reported in this appendix has been derived from statements by the US administration and the EC Commission; official communications of the governments of the East Asian NICs; surveys in the ASEAN countries (Sanchez 1987); and newspaper reports. The use of newspaper reports has been criticized on the grounds that they represent a collection of "anecdotes." Following a discussion of Japanese protection among academic economists, a knowledgeable observer of Japan addressed this issue:

> A major question was . . . what to make of all these anecdotes (horror stories). . . . In entry cases, whether imports or investment, the practice seemed to differ from the law and policy. How seriously do we take these anecdotes? To this lawyer sitting there mostly listening, it was somewhat disconcerting to have everyday businessmen's problems of the past thirty years treated as aberrational oddities. These horror stories have been too common and important to handle simply by shrinking them down to the status of anecdotal trash to be swept under the rug. Rather, I should have thought that cumulatively they state in a more meaningful way the operative Japanese policy towards foreigners in Japan. The anecdotes *are* Japanese policy; Japan is restrictive; it is a difficult place for foreigners to do business . . . to recognize the cultural problem does not change a fact that Japan is not "open" (Henderson 1986, 135).[1]

While some speak of "Japan bashing" whenever Japanese protectionist measures are criticized, a well-known columnist half facetiously, half seriously, put forward "a modest proposal for Japan: create a new ministry.

---

1. The same author suggests that "the anecdotes explain the awkward gap between Japanese enunciations of liberalization and the continued practice of restricting competitive foreigners, especially where they have the technological edge" (Henderson 1986, 135).

Call it the Ministry of Japan Bashing. Its job would be to criticize the sacred cows and pet projects of Japanese interest groups and other Japanese ministries. These are the policies that hamper Japan in reducing its massive trade surplus and assuming greater international responsibility."[2]

Administrative Guidance

According to one definition, "administrative guidance is a process that consists of a government ministry's giving suggestions or advice to private business or public organizations over which the ministry has regulatory jurisdiction" (USTR 1982, 58–59). Administrative guidance does not carry a legal sanction; rather, its impact is said to derive from the fact that it originates with government officials "who may have the power to provide— or withhold—loans, grants, subsidies, licenses, tax concessions, government contracts, permissions to import, foreign exchange, approval of cartel arrangements" (Ackley and Ishi 1976, 237).

The Petroleum Industry Law requires that all prospective importers of petroleum products notify MITI of their plans, and MITI may issue formal administrative guidance to modify these plans.[3] Administrative guidance on the imports of petroleum products has aimed at protecting the domestic refinery industry. In fact, the share of crude oil in the total imports of petroleum has traditionally been much higher in Japan (80–85 percent) than in the United States (65–70 percent), and Germany (55–60 percent).

The Korean government requested that Japan eliminate administrative guidance, which was said to limit the imports of monosodium glutamate, cotton yarn and mixed yarn, baseball gloves, soluble phosphate fertilizers, and steel pipes.[4] In its reply, the Japanese government denied that any form

---

2. Robert S. Samuelson, "A Modest Proposal for Japan," *Washington Post,* 5 August 1987.

3. In the well-known Lions case, an attempt to import gasoline from Singapore came to naught as bank credit was withdrawn from the firm at the insistence of MITI (*Economist*, 19 January 1985). Mr. Matsumura Hiroshi, a spokesman for MITI's Petroleum Planning Division, was reported to have said that "a fierce price war would probably ensue, hurting small, financially weak petrol stations" if gasoline was freely imported into Japan. He added that, "if such imports are allowed, it would set a precedent which would have undermined Japan's policy of refining crude oil at home and disrupted the supply and price structure of other petroleum products here" (Lim 1987, 23). It has also been reported that pressure was exercised to block gasoline imports from the Philippines (Lim 1987, 28).

4. All references to Korean observations on Japanese protection, and the official replies of the Japanese government, are taken from the English translation of the official report (in Korean) of the First Investment Office, Overseas Cooperation Council of the Republic of Korea, entitled "Korean Demand for Removal of Nontariff Barriers and Official Japanese Response," September 1984. See Balassa 1986c for a more detailed discussion.

of administrative guidance is applied to these imports. It has been reported, however, that the importation of steel from Korea has been subjected to limitations. These limitations do not permit the exploitation of Korea's cost advantage over Japan.

Customs Procedures

It has been claimed that "Japanese customs regulations appear to many exporters as Japan's first line of defense against imports. Japan's customs regulations are not designed per se to restrict trade. The fastidious inter- pretation of these regulations by customs officials, however, can be very restrictive" (Weil and Glick 1979, 863).

Note has been taken of the difficulty encountered in bringing demonstra- tion samples to Japan, in which the restrictive interpretation of customs regulations greatly increases costs and delays the presentation of samples. Complaints have also been raised about delays in clearing customs and about customs authorities increasing the valuation of intercorporate trans- actions for duty purposes. In addition, products subject to import license receive a permit for a period of three to seven years and the application process has to be started again following a license's expiration. The permits are given to the Japanese importer rather than the foreign exporter. This creates problems in the event that the exporter wishes to change importers, use more than one importer, or undertake production in Japan.

The Korean government objected both to article-by-article inspections when the number of articles shipped differed from the number shown on the invoice and to extensive audits of Korean trading firms by Japanese customs, because the inspection of all confidential papers was said to have led to leakages of trade secrets. The Japanese government replied, "Efforts are being made to implement customs inspection in an efficient manner and highly selective 'need to inspect' basis." The query concerning the inspection of Korean trading firms remained unanswered.

Similar complaints were raised by Singapore exporters of PVC hoses, canned pineapple, and beer. In the first case, a shipment was not cleared on the grounds that sufficient information on the origin of the products was not provided; in the second case, substantial delays in customs clearing were experienced and information was requested that the producers con- sidered confidential; and, in the third case, difficulties were encountered at customs when the date of the certificate was later than the shipping date or when the crest stamp or the endorsement seal were not clear (Lim 1985, 38–40).

The Korean government requested the removal of all customs controls on imports of cosmetics and entered a complaint about the Japanese government's failure to permit a Korean firm to export cosmetics to Japan. In its reply, the Japanese government confirmed that cosmetics can be imported only by holders of import permits. It was added that complaints by would-be foreign exporters cannot be investigated until a competent Japanese importer is identified.

Import procedures for foodstuffs and pharmaceuticals have been improved. In the case of continual imports of foods, which are stable in quality and have few sanitation problems, notification is not needed for each shipment. Customs procedures for several pharmaceuticals and cosmetics have also been simplified.[5]

However, there continue to be complaints about difficulties in clearing individual shipments through customs. This has especially been the case for exports from East Asian countries, Indonesia in particular (Sanchez 1987, 5). Customs regulations are also said to be responsible for the fact that there are hardly any Korean cars in Japan.

Standards, Testing, and Certification Requirements

According to a source cited earlier:

Unlike the customs procedures discussed above, Japanese product approval procedures are import-restrictive in theory as well as in practice. The applicable product approval standards, the methods by which such standards are promulgated and the procedures established to test and certify imported products for compliance with these standards all provide significant impediments to the importation into Japan of many U.S. goods (Weil and Glick 1979, 865–66).

Complaints about the standard-setting process concerned the exclusion of foreign firms from this process, which permits Japanese producers to influence the standards to their benefit. Further complaints were voiced about changes in standards to the detriment of foreign producers and the lack of sufficient notice of these changes. Finally, objections were raised to the setting of standards based on design rather than performance.[6]

---

5. On this point we are indebted to Shunichiro Ushijima, Chief Coordinator of the Office of Trade and Investment Ombudsman, an agency established in 1982 to deal with complaints about import procedures. Ushijima also provided information on the changes under way in the standard setting process.

6. As to the first point, standards set for the permissible tilt of vaporizers excluded the US-made product. As to the second, the allowable heat for the electric control of griddles was reduced slightly below the capability of appliances imported from the

In response to repeated US complaints, under the July 1985 Action Program the government of Japan declared that foreigners will be provided with opportunities to give their opinion on proposed standards. However, "it is still difficult for foreigners to have meaningful input into the Japanese standard-drafting process [as the] program is neither sufficiently transparent nor does it permit effective foreign participation" (USTR 1986, 149–151). Nevertheless, foreign pressure appears to have been effective in revising standards in some cases.[7]

With regard to product testing and certification, it has been noted that imported products could not use the factory-registration and model-approach system, which allowed for the self-certification of Japanese producers, but were subject to lot testing at the time of importation. It has further been suggested that the "lot inspection system is an excellent nontariff barrier. It is time-consuming and costly, placing imported goods at a substantial disadvantage in competing with Japanese goods using the factory-registration and model-approval system" (Rapp 1986, 33).

As the United States started formal proceedings in GATT in June 1982, the Japanese government agreed to bring its laws and procedures into line with internationally accepted standards and practices for certifying imported products. But, as noted in the May 1984 trade package, the passing of 16 laws on establishing product standards and certification failed to end the problem.

Questions of standards, testing, and certification again came to the fore at the Market-Oriented Sector-Selective (MOSS) negotiations between Japan and the United States in 1985.[8] In the course of these negotiations, the

---

United States that had made considerable inroads in the Japanese market. As to the third, physical characteristics for small boats were determined in a way that excluded US boats, even though they met the stringent flotation standards established by the US Coast Guard (Weil and Glick 1979, 866–71). One may further refer to the case of soft drink dispensers. After 10 years of sales by a US company, the Ministry of Health and Welfare changed health standards so that only one Japanese manufacturer could meet the new requirements. Following complaints by the US company, an official of the ministry threatened that all its installed dispensers would have to be taken out (Interview with Clyde V. Prestowitz, *Japan Economic Survey*, December 1982, 9).

7. Standards set for ski equipment, allegedly to fit the wetter Japanese snow, excluded foreign-made equipment and foreign manufacturers who were not apprised of the standard-setting process, although they supplied about one-half of skis sold in Japan (*Financial Times*, 4 September 1986). Bowing to foreign opposition, the standards were modified as of the beginning of the next season. MITI also withdrew its proposed standard for computer software that would have discriminated against imported software (American Chamber of Commerce 1986, 47). It is feared, however, that the creation of a special division on information in MITI's Japanese Industrial Standards system would discriminate against foreign suppliers (USTR 1986, 151).

8. Measures accepted in 1985 to liberalize standards and testing requirements are listed by Christelow (1985–86, Appendix).

Japanese Ministry of Post and Telecommunications established a plan, under the Approvals Institute for Telecommunications Equipment, based upon accepting manufacturer-generated data to meet standards limited to ensuring that the equipment does not harm the Japanese telecommunications network. MITI also undertook to reduce the number of products subject to standards, to grant foreigners greater access to the standard-setting process, and to permit US testing firms to conduct initial inspections of US factories.

Furthermore, the Ministry of Health and Welfare declared its willingness to accept foreign clinical test data for a number of pharmaceuticals; it accepted the import of a human growth hormone drug on the basis of foreign testing; and it approved four new food additives. But between 1972 and 1982 Japan approved only 7 new food additives while 146 recommendations were made by the International Food Additive Code of the UN Food and Agriculture Organization (among which the United States accepted 92). Japan adopted 11 new food additives in 1983 (Joint Economic Committee 1986, 21). In addition, regulations effective since 1 March 1988 require synthetic additives to be labeled, but exempt so-called natural additives, thereby discriminating against foreign products that tend to use synthetic additives much more frequently than Japanese products.[9]

In 1984, the private US Underwriters Laboratory (UL), which had long certified Japanese factories for exporting to the United States, was approved under both Japan's Electrical Products Safety Law and its Consumer Products Safety Law to carry out factory inspections and product testing in the United States for exporting to Japan. Although UL has approved 5,000 Japanese factories to export to the United States, very few US factories have been approved. US industrial products subject to standards thus continue to be at a disadvantage in Japan since they require lot inspection, a time-consuming process (Rapp 1986, 35).

The Korean government requested exemption from the requirement that the importation of medical instruments be made contingent on approval by a Japanese pharmacist or physician and suggested using the certification provided by the Korean Export Inspection Center instead. This request was refused on the grounds that "the inspection is necessary from the point of view of public health and sanitation." The Korean government entered further complaints concerning the application of what it considered excessively rigorous standards and duplicate inspections in Japan. With respect to furniture and electronic products, it claimed that "pursuant to guidelines provided by the MITI, private sector associations are conducting excessively stringent safety tests [and] Korean products are subjected to tests that are

---

9. *Financial Times*, 16 February 1988.

more stringent than that applied to Japanese products." According to the official Japanese response, the "standards are minimum standards deemed necessary to protect the life and health of the consumer, and the standards are enforced by the private sector on a voluntary basis. . . . Besides, all safety tests are performed without discrimination."

Taiwan's government has complained that the system of import permissions, "on the excuse of quarantine problems," limits Taiwanese exports of fruits and vegetables to Japan. It also claimed that Japanese customs often delay the inspection of flowers and eel, resulting in the deterioration of the merchandise. Philippine and Thai exporters also cited problems encountered in the application of standards in Japan (Sanchez 1987, 5).

Singapore's exporters reported that "Japan has on occasion confiscated and destroyed considerable consignments of orchids from Singapore simply because an insect or insects have been found in one of the orchids" (Lim 1985, 41). In addition, Japanese authorities stopped the importation of Australian frozen beef through the Singapore airport on the grounds that some beef consumed in Singapore originates in Argentina, where it may be subject to foot-and-mouth disease (Lim 1985, 34). According to the Chilean Agricultural Federation, Japan used the existence of fruit flies in a remote region of Chile as an excuse for prohibiting fruit and vegetable imports from the entire country (Balassa et al. 1986, 257). Finally, complaints have been raised concerning the allegedly excessive health restrictions in Japan on fruits and vegetables imported from the United States (Joint Economic Committee 1986, 22–3).

The Hong Kong Industry Department collected information on Japanese standards, testing, and certification requirements on electrical products, toys, food, cosmetics, and textile products—Hong Kong's principal exports. The compilation shows that the products in question are often subject to several laws, each of which sets up particular requirements. Electrical products thus are affected by the Electrical Appliance and Material Control Law, the Consumer Product Safety Law, and the Industrial Standardization Law; toys are subject to the Food Sanitation Law, the Explosive Control Law, the Electrical Appliance and Material Control Law, and the Safety Toys and Safety Goods standards; food products are subject to the Food Sanitation Law and the Law Concerning Standardization and Proper Labeling of Agricultural and Forestry Products; cosmetics products are affected by the Pharmaceutical Affairs Law; and textile products are subject to the Industrial Standardization Law.

Singaporean producers also complained about the stringent and complicated testing system in Japan. According to the Hong Kong Trade Department, "the Japanese testing and certification procedures are generally considered as a non-tariff barrier to exports to Japan." A particular case concerns "tiger balm" oil, which is popular with Japanese tourists because of its alleged restorative properties. Requests by Japanese companies for import permits have been repeatedly refused by government authorities in Japan.

In early 1985, the Japanese government announced the implementation of measures to liberalize the procedures applied. However, according to a communication received from Singapore's Department of Trade, "Our overall assessment is that while it is true that the Japanese have started to introduce measures to facilitate access to their market, in the area of standards and certification we do not seem to enjoy any significant benefits from the proposed measures so far."

Public Procurement Practices

According to a source cited earlier:

One of the most significant barriers to trade with Japan is brought about by the procurement policies of the public corporations of the Japanese government. . . .There are approximately 115 of these agencies—with separate budgets estimated to total about half of Japan's official national budget—including such entities as the Nippon Telegraph and Telephone Corporation (NTT), the Japan National Railways, Japan Electric Power Development Corporation, and the Japan Tobacco and Salt Public Corporation (Weil and Glick 1979, 879).[10]

NTT and JTS have subsequently been privatized by law, but the Japanese government retains substantial ownership in the first, and 100 percent ownership in the second, for the time being.

With Japan's accession to the GATT Government Procurement Code, "buy Japanese" policies are supposed to have ceased. At the same time, a number of Japan's state corporations, including the National Space Development Agency, Electrical Energy Company, Japan Atomic Energy Research Institute, and Japan Broadcasting Company, are exempt from the application of the code. The code has also not been applied in practice by the Ministry of Education, thereby creating difficulties for US computer sales to the national universities.

NTT is Japan's largest buyer of telecommunications equipment. Following a formal undertaking to open procurement to imports, NTT purchases from foreign firms increased nearly eightfold between 1981 and 1984, when

---

10. These barriers are said to be reinforced by *amakudari* (literally, descending from heaven), the practice of government officials who, upon retirement at about age 50, become employed by public corporations and the firms that sell to them.

purchases from US firms were about $160 million.[11] But US sales of telecommunications equipment in Japan amounted to only $186 million in 1985, while Japanese sales in the United States were $1.9 billion.[12]

Japan's purchase of satellites is of particular interest, given US leadership in their production. The importation of satellites was discouraged under Japan's 1983 "Long Range Vision on Space Development," but, under US pressure, this policy has been modified. Private Japanese companies can now purchase communications satellites abroad, and two firms have actually made purchases. Government entities may also do so, provided that the purchase does not conflict with domestic policy objectives, yet to date this has not occurred.

It has been suggested, however, that "because procurement by public organizations including NTT must be 'consistent with the national development policy,' NTT is effectively precluded from purchasing foreign [communications] satellites, probably through 1992" (USTR 1985, 124). Moreover, the importation of other kinds of satellites remains restricted and NTT must continue to fund current space satellite programs (Rapp 1986, 36).

The Japanese government has refused to purchase nuclear reactors made abroad. When a request was made for the purchase of a Canadian reactor that was said to have met the most exacting specifications, the request was turned down on the grounds that the domestic industry should be promoted.

The Japanese government has also required the local production or assembly of military equipment, even though this often costs considerably more than US-made equipment.[13] Although in response to US pressure the Japanese government has abandoned the plan to develop its own jet fighter, a new plane will be built by Mitsubishi Heavy Industries, with US firms

---

11. We are indebted to Tetsuro Yamazoe, Director of the International Procurement Office of NTT, for providing this information.

12. While it is reported that NTT has provided information on its procurement procedures abroad, according to the White Paper of the American Chamber of Commerce in Japan, "the privatization of NTT may have hindered rather than helped US companies. Since NTT issued stock in April, 1985 it has stated that it is now a private firm and hence no longer bound to observe the prior procurement treaties. Its purchasing decisions, it says, will be based on commercial criteria only. But NTT's willingness to give foreign equipment equal consideration has yet to be demonstrated" (1986, 37). This view is disputed by NTT officials, who note that NTT has continued to abide by the US–Japan telecommunications accord, and point to the pressure to purchase from the lowest-cost supplier in the new competitive environment (*Business Week*, 24 November 1986).

13. A Japanese-made F-15 fighter costs almost twice as much as a McDonnell Douglas F-15 costs the US Air Force. The Japan Defense Agency pays the difference as a direct subsidy for the creation of a Japanese aerospace industry ("Survey of Japanese Industry," *Financial Times*, 15 December 1986, 4).

receiving 35 to 45 percent of development and production work.[14] The transfer of technology under the agreement represents an important advance for the Japanese aircraft industry.[15]

Procurement practices are also said to depend on the nationality of the producer abroad. It has thus been reported that "Japanese electronic subsidiaries practically do not have . . . problems and complaints compared to American electronic firms exporting to Japan; [and] Japanese procurement practices are seen as severely penalizing telecoms equipment and semiconductor manufacturers in Singapore" (Lim 1985, 28).

A US Commerce Department official stated that Japan refuses to allow foreign companies to bid on the big construction and engineering projects, but its firms get major jobs in the United States; eighteen Japanese companies won $1.7 billion in construction business in the United States in 1985.[16] In 1986, the value of the contracts won by Japanese firms in the United States was estimated at $2.2 billion compared with $180 million of contracts won by US firms in Japan, whose construction market is about the same size as that of the United States.[17]

US Trade Representative Clayton Yeutter also charged that Japan reneged on its promise to open its markets by denying US firms the opportunity to bid on the construction of the $8 billion Kansai International Airport. In fact, foreign firms could not participate in the large first phase, involving the construction of a 1,265-acre artificial island in Osaka Bay and a bridge to the mainland. In response to a plea from President Reagan, Japanese officials subsequently agreed to permit foreign firms to bid on future phases of the project, but, according to an official Japanese statement, the contracts awarded to foreign firms have amounted to only $17.7 million.[18] Originally, the exclusion of foreign contractors from the construction of the Kansai airport was defended on the grounds that it was built by a private corporation, albeit under public auspices.[19] In November 1987, however, the Japanese government effectively limited foreign contractors to private commissioning entities, excluding them from the public construction market. Yet this is a

---

14. *Wall Street Journal*, 6 June 1988.

15. *Business Week*, 20 June 1988.

16. *Washington Post*, 6 June 1986.

17. *Economist*, 28 November 1987.

18. *Washington Post*, 23 August 1987; *Financial Times*, 18 November 1987.

19. While Japanese representatives argued that the airport was not built by a public corporation, US officials noted that five-sixths of the funding comes from local and national governments and that the airport is being built by a firm in which the Japanese government has a majority interest (*Financial Times*, 4 June 1986; *Washington Post*, 23 August 1986).

very lucrative market, with estimates of public projects for the next decade ranging from $60 to $200 billion.[20]

In response to US complaints, Prime Minister Takeshita indicated that a number of public projects would be opened to American construction firms, provided that they had international construction experience.[21] An agreement has subsequently been reached between US and Japanese officials, but the modalities of its implementation are yet to be determined.[22]

Japanese government procurement practices have been criticized for their reliance on single tenders, short bid times, complex qualification procedures, and their lack of transparency. In fact, in a May 1985 Keidanren poll of foreign businesses in Japan, twice as many respondents considered government and public corporation procurement programs to be poor rather than good (KKC Brief no. 29 1985, 5). Needless to say, firms located abroad encounter greater difficulties than foreign businesses located in Japan.

In the framework of the July 1985 Action Program, the Japanese government undertook the obligation to reduce single tendering through repetitive retendering, greater internal monitoring, and increased public information. In addition, bid time would be extended from 30 to 40 days, and information would be made public about winning bids. While it is too early to evaluate the implementation of these measures, the complexity of procedures, as well as their lack of transparency, would also need to be remedied.

Transparency would be increased under the new guidelines concerning the purchase of supercomputers, issued in August 1987. Supercomputers have long been a contentious issue because US firms have 90 percent of sales worldwide but only 15 percent in Japan. The largest US producer of supercomputers, Cray Research, argues, however, that dumping is a more serious obstacle to sales in Japan than are procurement practices.[23]

The Defense of Depressed Industries

In 1978, 14 sectors were designated "structurally depressed industries" in Japan under the Law on Temporary Measures for the Stabilization of Specific

---

20. *Financial Times*, 18 November 1987; *Economist*, 28 November 1987. The exclusion of foreign contractors was accomplished by setting work experience in Japan as a criterion under the Japanese tender system. However, foreign contractors could not acquire work experience in Japan without a license (*Financial Times*, 19 November 1987).

21. *Wall Street Journal*, 15 January 1988.

22. *Wall Street Journal*, 30 March 1988.

23. *Washington Post*, 8 August 1987. MITI has in turn complained that official statements about the possibility of antidumping action represent pressure to buy US rather than Japanese supercomputers (*New York Times*, 11 November 1987).

Industries. They included electric and open-hearth steel, aluminum smelting, nylon staple, polyester staple, polyesterfilament, polyacrylnitrate filament, ammonium, urea, phosphoric acid (by wet process), cotton and wool spinning, wool yarn, ferro-silicon, corrugates cupboard, and shipbuilding.

The law established a "Basic Stabilization Plan" aimed at reducing existing capacity; created a special credit guarantee fund; and empowered the supervising ministries to order the setting up of cartels, with the participation of firms carrying out the plan. While reductions in capacity were undertaken in the industries covered by the law, aluminum smelting apart, operating rates increased. In fact, the output of the Japanese basic materials industry rose by 6 percent between 1978 and 1984. The production of chemicals, iron and steel, and nonferrous metals also grew more rapidly in Japan than in the United States and the major EC countries in the 1975–84 period. And while increases in textile output in Japan were slightly smaller than in the United States, production declined in absolute terms in the principal EC countries (OECD 1985, tables 20 and A9). Increases in production were attained as import penetration ratios changed little in Japan while rising to a substantial extent in the other major industrial countries (table 3.2). These conclusions apply *a fortiori* to depressed industries, the exception being nonferrous metals, in which substantial increases in aluminum imports occurred (Brodin and Blades 1986).

The question arises of how imports could be restrained when the stabilization law did not introduce protectionist measures. Another question is why aluminum smelting represents an exception as far as import penetration is concerned. We will consider the latter question first. Uekasa notes that "aluminum refining is so extraordinarily energy-intensive that aluminum has been called 'congealed electricity' and Japanese aluminum refineries depended on oil-based thermal power generation for 60 percent of their needs in 1973." He adds that, following the quadrupling of oil prices, domestic production costs reached 170–190 thousand yen per ton compared with an import price of 129 thousand yen. With further increases in oil prices, the per ton domestic cost of aluminum smelting reached 500 thousand yen in Japan in March 1982, compared with an import price of 200 thousand yen (Uekasa 1985, 33).

Since aluminum is the principal input for the aluminum fabrication industry, which competes in foreign markets, low-cost imports benefit the Japanese processing industry. In fact, between 1979 and 1982, imports rose from 37 to 83 percent of domestic aluminum consumption and account for almost the entire Japanese consumption today.[24] Aluminum is imported

---

24. Considerations of input costs also explain the differential pricing of oil refinery products, in which the price of naphtha is maintained at low levels and high prices are set for gasoline.

mostly from fully or partially owned Japanese subsidiaries abroad, which benefited from preferential tariff treatment until early 1987.

Different considerations apply to other industries, where it was considered necessary to restrain imports in conjunction with domestic adjustment measures. In these industries, it was feared that increases in imports would jeopardize the situation of domestic firms.

Administrative guidance has been relied upon to limit imports of cotton yarn and, subsequently, of cotton cloth. In 1975 and again in 1977, MITI's Textiles Product Division sent letters to trading firms requesting them to limit imports. In April 1981, following the establishment of a cartel for cotton textiles, the head of MITI's Basic Consumer Industries Bureau called on trading firms "to exercise utmost restraint" in importing and to report their imports to MITI on a monthly basis (Dore 1986, 24). Since the instructions were not followed by all importers, in 1982 the Japanese government constrained Korea, the principal supplier, to reduce its exports of cotton yarn. In addition, MITI secured a pledge from China and Pakistan to limit their exports of cotton yarn to Japan.[25] There appears to be little inclination in Japan to shift out of textiles. The "New Textile Vision," drafted in October 1983, thus suggests that "it is possible enough for the textile industry in Japan to develop, ahead of other nations, into an advanced nation type industry with international advantages."

In the case of clothing, the industry with the highest labor intensity, MITI is providing funds to develop an automated sewing system over the 1982–90 period. The purpose of this system is reportedly to offset the labor cost advantage of developing countries in clothing production.[26] At the same time, East Asian clothing manufacturers, which had great success in entering foreign markets elsewhere, find the Japanese market so difficult to penetrate that they reportedly consider it futile to undertake the effort.[27]

In addition, Japan does not permit imports of ships from Korea and other low-cost developing country suppliers. It has been reported that "even though Japanese shipbuilders saw new orders fall to $4.7 billion [in 1985]—half the 1983 level—they have remained afloat because Japanese shipowners keep placing orders with them."[28] At the same time, the government provided a guarantee fund of $222 million for the shipbuilding industry.[29]

---

25. *Japan Textile News Weekly,* 15 and 22 March, 1985.

26. *Japan Textile News,* March 1983.

27. "Many Hong Kong clothing manufacturers, who have opened up vast markets in the West and kept up with the sweeping twists and turns of fashion trends there with rare skill and lightning flexibility, are skeptical about spending time trying to break into the Japanese market. Under the apparently smooth waters of a quota-free market, they detect the reefs of non-tariff barriers and a closed marketing system" (*Japan Textile News,* May 1982).

28. *Business Week,* 10 March 1986.

29. *Journal of Commerce,* 19 March 1986.

The guarantee fund was made available under the Temporary Measures Law for Structural Improvement of Specific Industries, enacted in March 1983 for five years in the place of the Law for the Stabilization of Specific Industries, which had expired. The new law, adopted over the opposition of the Japanese Fair Trade Commission (JFTC), covers 22 sectors, with petrochemicals and their derivatives, soda ash, paper, cement, and sugar added to the list.[30]

The law aims at retrenchment as well as revival in these industries, with capacity reductions being accompanied by mergers, joint production, and specialization agreements, which may involve the establishment of cartels. There are legal cartels for petrochemicals, chemical fertilizers, chemical fibers, aluminum, ferroalloys, electric furnace steelmaking, and paper (Van den Panhuyzen 1985, 69). The following discussion covers two products that have not had legal cartels but have been subject to collusion among producers.

Under the new law, the Japanese government issued a plan to reduce capacity in the production of urea. The plan did not envision increases in imports and it assumed the maintenance of exports that would be cross-subsidized by domestic producers. In 1985 imported urea was quoted at $192 per ton, compared with the Japanese factory price of $230–240 that, in part, offset losses on export prices at $195. Nevertheless, imported urea provided less than 3 percent of domestic consumption in 1983. One observer of this situation suggested that "there is apparently a consensus among Japanese government officials, urea manufacturers, and distributors to keep price-competitive imports out of Japan, and several U.S. firms have received suggestions that they not attempt to export more to Japan" (Rapp 1986, 30). In fact, the MAFF intervenes in the process in conjunction with the setting of the rice subsidy and of the terms for reimbursing fertilizer suppliers. Zennoh, which handles 70 percent of the sale of chemical fertilizers in Japan and is also a major producer, does not import urea.

Soda ash, used in glass manufacturing, steel making, and in certain chemical processing, represents a similar case. The United States has a considerable advantage in its production because of the abundance of natural resources unavailable in Japan, where firms have to use higher-cost synthetic processes. This advantage was translated into duty-free prices of US imports of $175–190, and dutiable prices of $180–200 per ton, compared with $250–290 per ton for the domestic product in Japan in 1985. Nevertheless, imports

---

30. Before the new law was enacted, it was reported that "officials of Japan's Fair Trade Commission (JFTC), the country's antitrust watchdog, bitterly oppose MITI on cartels. 'Japan advocates a free economy,' says Shogo Itoda, a JFTC official, 'and it is important for these companies to make the effort to restructure on their own. Government measures that limit competition sap the industry of its vitality' " (*Business Week*, 14 February 1983).

had only 5 percent of the Japanese market in 1981. The five US exporters were each assigned an informal quota of 12,000 tons. Additional exports were excluded by Japanese producers who reportedly threatened users with a cutoff of supplies and regulated imports through the ownership of the only dock where soda ash could be imported (Rapp 1986, 27–29).

When MITI rejected American complaints in this matter on the grounds that they were based on a misunderstanding of the Japanese market structure, the US Embassy in Japan filed a brief with the JFTC. The JFTC ruled that there was unreasonable restraint of imports by an illegal cartel. It issued a "cease and desist" order but did not raise charges against the trading companies; it did not levy fines or other sanctions on soda ash producers; and it did not direct producers to cease pressuring domestic customers to refrain from purchasing imported soda ash through threats of refusing to deal with them (First 1986, 67–69).

By 1984, US soda ash exports to Japan quadrupled, reaching 200 thousand tons, 15 percent of Japanese consumption. However, in September 1984, the US–Japan Trade Study Group commented that "Japanese [soda ash] producers are now reportedly trying to check [the U.S.] import surge by pressuring users and distributors to limit purchases from U.S. suppliers" (1984, 69). MITI's vice minister for international affairs also reportedly told the head of the US soda ash exporters' association that American sales had gone far enough (Prestowitz 1988, 164). In fact, these sales have not surpassed 220,000 tons annually.

A respected US columnist has suggested that the Japanese have developed "a rational way of phasing an industry down and out, [in the absence of which] the tendency in this country and in Western Europe is to protect with quotas and other artificial means."[31] However, the Japanese have cast their net much wider than have the United States or the European Community, protecting 22 industries. Reductions in capacity also involve linear cuts in each firm rather high-cost industrial firms closing down. Finally, a variety of measures are used to limit imports in the case of depressed industries.[32] These measures have been summarized as follows:

Some (including fabricated aluminum, paper, plywood, and lumber) are protected from a large increase in imports by high tariffs. Others such as chemical fertilizers, however, seem import resistant due to various legal arrangements, while apparent industry collusion safeguards soda ash, synthetic rubber, and caustic soda firms. The total Japanese market for such products exceeds $80 billion, yet with the exception of aluminum-ingot and electric-furnace products, import penetration is surprisingly low, usually less than 6 or 7 percent (Rapp 1986, 23–24).

---

31. Hobart Rowen, "A Clue to Japanese Success," *Washington Post*, 25 June 1986.

32. On the issue of protection of depressed industries, see also First 1987, 1331.

The Promotion of High-Technology Industries

As noted in Chapter 2, in 1981 MITI launched a 10-year Next-Generation Industries Basic Technologies Project. In the framework of 12 research projects, this initiative encompasses biotechnology, new materials (such as fine ceramics and electrical conductors), as well as further research on electronics. Other areas supported by the Japanese government include space technology, aircraft, telecommunications, computer software, and medical equipment. The funds made available for these projects have been relatively limited, but MITI and other government agencies play an important organizing function that results in a multiplication of the research effort. MITI selects a relatively small number of firms to participate in joint projects and assumes a major role in the selection of research agendas for the projects. While there have been a few instances in which technologically advanced firms decided not to participate, firms usually vie for membership. For example, the Chuo Koron techno-science team reported that "about 100 firms have expressed their wish to participate in the project and approximately 50 firms are eager to join the bio-technology project" (Yamamura 1983, 34). In addition, 44 firms, including Hitachi, Mitsubishi, NEC, and Sumimoto, joined the research consortium on superconductors organized by MITI, even though participants must pay over $800,000 to join and annual dues of about $110,000.[33]

This is hardly surprising. The projects have a long-term character and greatly reduce the high risk involved. The participating firms obtain legal title to the resulting patents and also benefit through their involvement in the standard-setting process. If past experience is a guide, firms can also expect that they will have assured domestic markets.[34]

According to the White Paper of the American Chamber of Commerce in Japan, "a 'buy from Japanese computer companies' attitude continues to exist today in both Japan's public and private sectors, despite the action plan announced in July 1985 by Prime Minister Nakasone, and other market opening measures resulting from the MOSS negotiations" (1986, 24). The Chamber also claimed that "the Government of Japan, with the close cooperation of the Japanese silicon industry, has kept the Japanese silicon

---

33. *Wall Street Journal*, 28 April 1988.

34. The OECD notes that "the advantages of such cooperation are evident: every firm can learn from each other's mistakes, and the costs of research are much lower. The emergence of consensus between the major companies about further strategy is also important, and uncertainty is thus reduced" (1985, 75). Furthermore, "discriminatory public purchasing policy (for example, the procurement policies of NTT) and administrative guidance about imports also helped firms to reap economies of scale and to move down the 'learning curve' before facing international competition" (75).

market essentially off limits to foreign producers," and that " 'a buy from Japanese semiconductor companies' attitude persists today among Japanese companies" (34, 33).

Evidence on this point is provided by studies of market shares. It has been noted with respect to 16K RAMs that:

U.S. firms dominated both home market and third-country markets, primarily in Europe. Yet they had a small share in Japan, probably again in specialized types of RAMs [Random Access Memory chips] rather than the basic commodity product. Transport costs for RAMs are small; they are . . . commodity-like in their interchangeability. So the disparity in market shares suggests that some form of market closure was in fact happening (Baldwin and Krugman 1986, 11).[35]

At the same time, the security of the domestic market may permit selling below cost abroad.[36]

The existence of dumping by Japanese producers of semiconductors in the US market was alleged by knowledgeable observers, who cited "industry sources [that] anticipate intense trade frictions over such products as the 64K DRAM to flare up by 1985" (Yamamura and Vanderberg 1986, 270). This has, in fact, occurred. According to preliminary rulings of the US Commerce Department, in March 1986 Japanese producers dumped EPROMs as well as 256K DRAMS in the United States. Furthermore, in June 1986 the US International Trade Commission established the existence of dumping of 64K DRAMS. Subsequently, an antidumping complaint was entered concerning Japanese sales of semiconductors in the European Community.[37]

---

35. Reported US market shares were 88 percent for the United States, 13 percent for Japan, and 22 percent for the rest of the world. The comparable Japanese shares were 12, 87, and 28 percent (Baldwin and Krugman 1986, Table 3).

36. Reference has been made to the so-called "10 percent rule" contained in a memorandum sent to Hitachi distributors in the United States concerning the sale of EPROMs (Erasable Programmable Read-Only Memories)—a memorandum that was subsequently said not to reflect Hitachi's marketing strategy. The memorandum, which was published in the *Wall Street Journal* (5 June 1985), included the following:
>Quote 10% Below Competition.
>If they requote . . .
>The bidding stops when Hitachi wins . . .
>Win with the 10% rule . . .
>Find AMD and Intel sockets . . .
>Quote 10% below their price . . .
>If they requote,
>Go to 10% *again*
>Don't quit till you *win* . . .
>25% DISTI profit margin
>Guaranteed.

37. *Financial Times*, 1 July 1986.

The March 1986 ruling of the Commerce Department was not followed up under the subsequent agreement reached by the US and Japanese governments on semiconductors. The agreement signed in July 1986 called for Japanese firms to sell at "fair market value"—that is, the cost of production and a modest profit—in the United States, and to open markets to US exports of semiconductors. However, the US government subsequently charged that, in dumping semiconductor chips in third markets, from which some were then resold in the United States, and in failing to admit imports from the United States, Japan violated the agreement. The United States therefore imposed retaliatory tariffs on Japanese electronics products in April 1987.

Retaliatory tariffs were partially removed in November 1987 as Japanese firms stopped third-country dumping. However, the access of the US semiconductor industry to the Japanese market has reportedly not improved, although there may also be supply problems owing to the rapid increase of demand for semiconductors in the United States.

A high-technology sector of growing importance is that of telecommunications services. Within this sector, pocket pagers represent an interesting case. Motorola wanted to provide this service in Japan but was not allowed to operate on its own. At the end, it was offered a one-seventh share of NTT's purchases of pagers. This one-seventh share raised Motorola's sales of communications equipment to Japan to $20 million, compared with worldwide sales of $2.0 billion (Yoffie 1986, 7a).

Motorola is also a world leader in cellular telephones, which transmit through radio waves rather than wires and can be used in cars. After successfully removing technical barriers that effectively excluded its products from the Japanese market, Motorola sought to find a partner in Daini Denden, a new Japanese telecommunications company formed to compete with NTT, to offer cellular telephone services in Japan. Its efforts have been opposed, however, by another new Japanese company, Teleway, which has been given the large Tokyo market from which Motorola is excluded.[38]

In turn, the British company, Cable and Wireless (C&W), was to have a 20 percent share in International Digital Communications (IDC), a new consortium set up to build a cable as part of its worldwide independent telecommunications network, and to provide a competing international telephone service to Kokusai Denshin Denwa (KDD) in Japan. Pacific Telesis, a US company, was to have a 10 percent share and Merrill Lynch a 3 percent share in the venture. This effort was opposed by a newly established Japanese consortium, International Telecoms Japan (ITJ), which proposed to lease circuits from KDD, rather than build its own cable.

---

38. *New York Times*, 6 April 1987.

While foreign firms can, by law, own up to one-third of Japan's second international telephone service, the Minister of Post and Telecommunications (MPT) expressed opposition to "foreign telecoms companies, including Britain's Cable and Wireless (C&W) having a key role in a new international telecoms venture in Japan." In fact, C&W was offered a 3 percent share and no say in management in a newly established consortium, set up by MPT.[39]

Following sharp protests from the United Kingdom and the United States, an alternative was proposed, with eight core partners, including C&W and Pacific Telesis, having equal ownership stakes and participating in the management of the new company.[40] As this was not acceptable to the British and US interests, the Japanese Prime Minister said before the Venice summit that there was no objection to separate licenses being awarded to each consortium. Frustrated by the subsequent lack of progress, the IDC Consortium proposed to separate the construction and operation of the cable while the members of the two consortia, either individually or collectively, would decide whether to use it.[41] Following repeated interventions by Prime Minister Thatcher and President Reagan, the two consortia have subsequently received separate licenses.

Foreign carriers are excluded from the domestic common carrier market in Japan. While competition between domestic and foreign firms in enhanced communications services like value-added networks is permitted, entry is subject to approval by MPT.

Regulations Concerning Intellectual Property

The US–Japan Trade Study Group defined intellectual property as follows:

Intellectual property includes such intangible but highly valuable assets as the inventions underlying a company's technology, its proprietary information, the styling of its products and the brand names and symbols that ensure recognition of its products by the public. These forms of property can be legally protected in most industrial countries by patents (for inventions), design registrations (for product styling), trademarks and service marks (for product or company identification), copyrights (for works of authorship) and trade secrets laws (for confidential business and technical information) (1984, 57).

---

39. *Economist*, 14 March 1987; *Financial Times*, 28 March 1987.

40. *New York Times*, 6 April 1987.

41. *Financial Times*, 27 July 1987.

The Japanese patent system has been subject to considerable criticism. It takes about six years for the Japan Patent Office (JPO) to register patents, compared with two years in the United States and one year in the United Kingdom. At the same time, once a patent application has been filed and published in Japan, the applicant is said to be vulnerable to unauthorized copying of his invention by competing firms (US–Japan 1984, 57–8). The technical details and drawings that need to be provided in the patent application may help others to apply for patents of their own. The time allowed for opposing such applications is very short for foreign firms; documents have to be submitted in Japanese; and the JPO is said to reject documents for even small translation errors (US–Japan 1984, 60).

Even in the absence of unauthorized copying, the delay experienced in obtaining patents permits Japanese firms to develop products having similar characteristics on their own. This is said to have occurred in the case of fiber optics, where patent protection to US products was delayed by 7 to 10 years.[42] The same fate befell Sohio, which created a process for making high-tech ceramics that was imitated by Japan's Kyocera Corporation following the submission of Sohio's patent application in Japan. Sohio is given little chance to succeed in its patent infringement suit.[43] More generally, it has been suggested that, "if foreign companies apply for crucial patents which may give them an important competitive advantage, MITI may delay awarding the patent until Japanese producers have a chance to catch up or apply for patents to cover similar technology" (Vogel 1987, 12).

In any case, registering patents is a slow process (as is registering trademarks), requiring about four years, compared with one year in the United States. Furthermore, the protection of trademarks in Japan does not extend to service marks, the equivalent to trademarks for service companies (US–Japan 1984, 61–2).

In the United States the rights to a trademark belong to the firm that first used it commercially, but in Japan foreign trademarks may be registered by Japanese companies with a view toward preempting their subsequent introduction by foreign firms that have used them at home or abroad. A case in point is the cigarette industry. The Japanese tobacco monopoly applied for Japanese trademark rights to 50 foreign brands, including names such as Newport, Tareyton, and Century.[44] In another instance, Nippon Shoe Co. registered the 70-year-old American footwear trademark Allen Edmonds and had to be paid "compensation" to desist from using the

---

42. We are indebted to Alan Wolff on this point.

43. *Business Week*, 15 June 1987.

44. *Wall Street Journal*, 7 March 1986.

trademark.[45] Finally, Japanese companies registered Mickey Mouse as a trademark, and the petitions by Walt Disney Productions to invalidate the trademark were rejected. Popeye has suffered a similar fate (Doi 1986, 180).

The EC Commission, in particular, objected to the use of European trademarks in Japan. It also noted that Japanese firms often use European-sounding names and designations, as in the case of wine, to imply the foreign origin of the product. Furthermore, the Commission charged that "the counterfeiting of European products, particularly luxury goods, continues to be a widespread phenomenon, owing to a failure to take proceedings or apply effectively the sanctions laid down by law" (EC Commission 1985, 19).

Japan is the only major industrial country without effective protection of trade secrets (US–Japan 1984, 63). Yet such protection is considered vital, in particular to the US information-processing and pharmaceutical industries.

US pharmaceutical firms have also objected to Japanese regulations that give licensees virtual control over licensed products, making it difficult for inventors to regain the rights for their manufacture and sale.[46] In fact, the agreement of the licensee is said to be necessary to undertake production. Having been given the right to set up plants in Japan, US drug companies would like to begin the manufacture of products they earlier licensed in Japan.[47]

Distribution Channels

Japan's complicated and archaic distribution system is also said to obstruct foreign imports. This is the case even for foreign businesses located in Japan. According to one survey, more than twice as many of those polled who considered the distribution system to be good, thought the system was poor (KKC Brief no. 29 1985, 5). In the present context, however, distribution channels concern us only to the extent that imports are disadvantaged. Such will be the case if the importer is also a producer. Examples are herring, oil refining, and soda ash.

The manufacturers of light industrial products in Singapore complained that "they are unable to set up subsidiaries, marketing network or distribution routes in Japan" (Lim 1985, 31). More generally, it has been said that distribution channels in Japan are excessively complicated and discrim-

---

45. *Washington Post*, 9 April 1987.

46. *Business Week*, 22 April 1985.

47. *Washington Post*, 26 April 1985.

inate against the sale of foreign-made goods. An expression of these complaints was given in a private communication to the authors from the Singapore Department of Trade:

Commercial practices, many unique only to Japan, had severely inhibited the ability of companies wishing to enlarge their share of the market. For example, it is virtually impossible to sell to Japan without having an affiliate company doing the marketing and distribution. . . . The structure of Japan's distribution network is a major impediment to our exporters gaining a bigger share of the market. The distribution network is so complex that the imported product becomes very expensive by the time it reaches the consumer.

The existence of vertical distribution chains in the automobile, consumer electronics, appliance, pharmaceutical, cosmetic, and confectionary industries tends to limit imports. These distribution chains operate on the basis of long-term contracts, with rebates provided by the manufacturer to ensure the loyalty of the wholesaler and the retailer. Moreover, in cases where importers and distributors belong to the same grouping (keiretsu), they will favor within-group sales to imports. It appears that imports are also disadvantaged in cases where the choice is between buying from another group or from abroad.[48]

It has been reported that, in the face of opposition from the National Committee on Agricultural Cooperation and the Japan Table Chicken Association, imports of chickens were kept to 7 percent of domestic consumption in 1984, even though the difference between the price of domestic and imported chickens greatly exceeded the tariff (Torii 1985, 30). In addition, in the case of textiles, representatives of trading companies repeatedly stated that they would accept foreign orders only if this would not adversely affect domestic industry.[49] These actions were said to have

---

48. Clyde V. Prestowitz, former Counselor to Commerce Secretary Malcolm Baldrige, cites a prominent Japanese business executive as having said: "We buy first within our group, then within Japan and only as a last resort from foreigners" (Wall Street Journal, 26 September 1986).

49. A vice president of Chori Co., Ltd., one of Japan's largest textile and apparel importers, commented in 1980: "The fundamental principle of Chori is to import those goods after having accepted orders from domestic sewing industrialists. This is the consideration not to oppress domestic industrialists. Furthermore, as for the imports of fiber, yarn, and fabrics, this company will import such restricted merchandise that do not compete with domestic goods" (Japan Textile News, September 1980). Similarly, the Assistant General Manager of the Textile Trade Department of another trading company, Itoman & Co., Ltd., commented in 1978 that "a drastic import of textile goods will deal a big blow to domestic manufacturers and will cool down domestic market conditions. In consequence, trading companies will import

been in response to demands by MITI to limit imports in order to avoid market disruption (Dore 1986, 24).

This is not to say that individual importers might not buy low-cost imports in competition with domestic production, as has happened in some instances in regard to textiles. But the concentration of the trading companies, with the nine *sogo shosha* accounting for about one-half of Japanese trade, facilitates exerting pressure on importers. The domestic sale of imported goods is also hindered by a 1974 law and by informal administrative directives, which were renewed in 1984, limiting the establishment of supermarkets and department stores (EC Commission 1985, 19). Large retail establishments are especially suited for selling imports, as shown by the experience of several retail chains in the United States.

The so-called "Fair Competition Codes" of the JFTC also limit the possibilities of foreign firms to introduce new marketing techniques in Japan. Products whose imports are adversely affected by these codes reportedly include beverages, pet foods, detergents, and consumer appliances (USTR 1985, 129). Finally, a government survey found that distribution markups on imports of whiskeys, candies, edible oils, men's overcoats, and footwear are over twice as high as on competing domestic products. The differences can be explained only in part by tariffs; their existence suggests the presence of exclusive distribution arrangements (Christelow 1985–86, 14).

---

so as not to cause a big loss to domestic business circles concerned" (*Japan Textile News*, September 1978). *Japan Textile News* commented in September 1980 that, for Japanese trading companies, "it is one of the most important tasks how to import textiles without oppressing the domestic textile industry."

Appendix C Explaining International Differences in Imports

This appendix describes the methodology utilized by Balassa 1986 in estimating a model designed to explain international differences in the relative importance of imports in terms of particular national characteristics. It also presents revised results derived from the model and compares these results with estimates from alternative models by Bergsten and Cline 1987; Saxonhouse 1983 and 1986; Noland 1987a; and Lawrence 1987.

Description of the Methodology

The starting point of the methodology is Chenery's model, first introduced in 1960 and used repeatedly on subsequent occasions and, most recently, in 1986. The model postulates that differences in imports are determined by national variations in the level of economic development and market size.

International differences in imports had originally been expressed in terms of per capita imports; this variable has subsequently been reformulated as the ratio of imports to GDP and it is used here in this form. The level of economic development has been represented by per capita GDP,[1] and market size by population.[2]

As to the former, the hypothesis is tested that the ratio of imports to GDP varies with the level of economic development. This may be due to demand

---

1. In the present study, the authors attempted to replace per capita incomes with variables representing physical and human capital (Balassa 1979). Due to the high intercorrelation between the two variables, however, statistically significant results have not been obtained.

2. In subsequent work, Chenery (1986) introduces these variables in a quadratic form as well. This has not been done in the present study.

as well as to supply factors. The demand for, and the supply of, importables may rise more or less rapidly than GDP, depending on changes in the composition of domestic expenditure and production, respectively.

As to the latter, Chenery (1960) put forward the proposition that, due to the exploitation of economies of scale, the ratio of imports to GDP will decline as population increases. The same result may obtain, however, without introducing economies of scale. In international comparisons, the ratio of internal to external trade will be positively related to the size of the population since, in a larger country, a higher proportion of trade will be internal rather than external.

In the present investigation, it is further hypothesized that the ratio of imports to GDP is negatively correlated with the availability of natural resources. If it is assumed that the elasticity of substitution between natural resources and reproducible factors is lower than among reproducible factors, countries poor in natural resources can be expected to import natural resource-intensive (primary) products in exchange for manufactured goods. The availability of natural resources may be represented by the share of primary imports in total imports. Alternatively, one may introduce natural resource variables—such as arable land, petroleum, and other minerals—directly into the estimation. The two alternatives have their advantages and disadvantages.

William Cline suggested that the ratio of primary imports to total imports is affected by the policies applied. In cases where agricultural protection is high, then, there will be a shortfall of actual, from predicted, imports. This may not be a disadvantage, however, since the purpose of the exercise is to indicate the effects of trade policies on import shares. Using natural resource variables in turn has the advantage of introducing such variables directly. At the same time, it has the disadvantage of not covering the full range of primary activities and neglecting differences in quality (arable land) or essentially utilizing dummy variables (the availability of petroleum and other mineral resources).

In the present investigation, we have made use of both alternatives. Primary imports have been defined to include SITC classes 0–4 and 68 (nonferrous metals). Arable land, petroleum resources, and other mineral resources have been expressed in per capita terms.[3]

It is also hypothesized that the ratio of imports to GDP is negatively correlated with transportation costs which lead to the substitution of

---

3. Data on arable land and petroleum resources have been made available by Gary Saxonhouse; data on other mineral resources, including bauxite, copper, fluor, iron ore, lead, manganese, nickel, phosphate, potash, pyrite, salt, tin, and zinc, have been collected by Marcus Noland.

domestic products for imports. Using distance as a proxy for transportation costs will not be appropriate, since transportation costs are several times lower by sea than by land, and decline greatly with distance.[4] In particular, employing a distance variable as a proxy for transportation costs introduces a bias with respect to Japan, which cannot use land routes in its international trade and which, apart from Australia, is situated the longest average distance from its trading partners among industrial countries.[5]

The use of the distance variable thus gives rise to a problem of identification in the case of Japan—whether the statistical results pertaining to this variable reflect transportation costs or other national characteristics, trade policies in particular. The use of the distance variable also neglects the fact that the cost of transporting petroleum, accounting for one-third of Japanese imports, is lower for Japan than for most major industrial countries.[6]

The point of departure in estimating the cost of transportation in individual countries has been the average ratio of transportation costs to import value. This ratio has been derived from information on c.i.f. and f.o.b. import values, reported in the IMF's *International Financial Statistics*.

The ratio for each country is, however, affected by the relative shares in its total imports of primary and manufactured products that have different transportation costs.[7] Correspondingly, the c.i.f.–f.o.b. ratios have been adjusted for international differences in the commodity structure of imports.[8] This has been done by taking the relative shares of primary and manufactured goods in Switzerland, the industrial country with the lowest average c.i.f.–f.o.b. price difference (3.0 percent in 1973) as the point of departure.

Transportation costs for manufactured goods and primary products for Switzerland have been derived from information provided by Lipsey and Weiss (1974) on individual commodities, which have been averaged using the Swiss import structure as weights. Transportation costs for manufactured goods have been assumed to be invariant among countries and transportation

---

4. In the case of pig iron, the per mile cost of sea transport was estimated to be one-fourth that of land transport (Balassa 1977).

5. These strictures also apply to the recent paper by Saxonhouse (1986), which assumes that there is a fixed transport cost up to 700 miles, since this cost is taken to be invariant irrespective of the means of transportation utilized. The marginal cost of transportation beyond 700 miles is assumed to be constant.

6. We are indebted to Masahiro Sakamoto for this information.

7. Estimates for the early 1960s were published in Balassa 1964. Subsequent estimates on ocean charges are provided by Lipsey and Weiss 1974.

8. Bergsten and Cline (1987) fail to make this adjustment. At the same time, they use a simple average of the c.i.f.–f.o.b. ratio and air cargo rates. This is inappropriate because transportation by air accounts for a small proportion of the total trade of the countries concerned and because it is already included in the c.i.f.–f.o.b. trade figures.

costs for the primary commodities imported by industrial countries other than Switzerland have been derived on the basis of the commodity composition of their imports.[9] An alternative variant involves the assumption that each country's transportation costs for primary as well as for manufactured goods are a constant multiple of the cost for Switzerland, again taking the relative shares of primary and manufactured imports in Switzerland as the standard of comparison.[10] Calculations have further been made by using unadjusted c.i.f.–f.o.b. ratios and a distance variable in the place of transportation costs.

In the case of Japan, the average c.i.f.–f.o.b. price difference was 15.9 percent in 1973, the first year of the estimation, while the adjusted transportation cost was 11.9 percent under the first alternative and 7.3 percent under the second. Among the major industrial countries, the corresponding figures for the United Kingdom were 9.5, 9.3, and 5.3 percent. In turn, the distance variable used by Gary Saxonhouse was 5,870 miles in the first case and 2,282 miles in the second.[11]

Estimated Results

Estimates have been made for total imports, that is, the imports of all commodities taken together, as well as for primary imports and for manufactured imports. Separate estimates have been made for imports from all areas (world imports), from industrial countries, and from developing countries. The statistical analysis has been undertaken for a group of 18 industrial countries, defined as those having per capita incomes of $2,200

---

9. Assuming transportation costs for manufactured goods to be 2.5 percent, transportation costs for primary commodities imported by Switzerland have been estimated at 4.3 percent of f.o.b. value in 1973. (In Balassa 1986, transport costs for manufactured goods have been assumed to be 2 percent of f.o.b. import value.) Next, for individual countries, transportation costs for primary commodities have been derived from data on the c.i.f.–f.o.b. ratio for total imports and the share of primary commodities in these imports, assuming that transportation costs for manufactured goods were uniformly 2.5 percent of c.i.f. value. Finally, for each country, average transportation costs have been calculated by averaging the transportation costs for primary commodities so obtained and the assumed 2.5 percent ratio for manufactured goods, using the Swiss commodity composition of trade as weights, so as to normalize the country data to a standard commodity composition.

10. The constant multiple has been derived by calculating the effects of differences in the commodity composition of imports on the observed differences in average c.i.f.–f.o.b. ratios under the assumption that transportation costs amounted to 2.5 percent of the f.o.b. value of manufactured goods in Switzerland.

11. We are indebted to Gary Saxonhouse for providing this information.

or higher and at least a 20 percent share of manufactured goods in total exports in 1973. The group includes the United States, Canada, Austria, Belgium, Denmark, Finland, France, Germany, Ireland, Israel, Italy, the Netherlands, Norway, Sweden, Switzerland, the United Kingdom, Australia, and Japan.

The inclusion of developing countries in the investigation would not be appropriate. First, lower levels of economic development in these countries may affect their participation in the international division of labor beyond the impact of measurable variables, such as per capita income. Second, protection levels in the developing countries are much higher than in the industrial countries. Japan should be compared with the latter rather than with the former.

The dependent and the independent variables have been expressed in logarithmic terms. However, an alternative estimate has also been made by using the ratio of imports to GDP, rather than its logarithm, as the dependent variable. Dummy variables have also been introduced in the estimation for Japan, the member countries of the European Community, and the member countries of the European Free Trade Association (EFTA). These are to test whether Japan is an "outlier" among the industrial countries as far as import shares are concerned, and whether participation in the European Community and the EFTA affects trade flows.

The equations have been estimated by utilizing data for the years between 1973 and 1983 for each of the 18 industrial countries. When combining cross-section and time-series data, correction has been made for serial correlation (which was not the case in the original Balassa (1986) paper).

Tables C.1 and C.2 report the estimates obtained by using the primary import-share variable and the individual natural resource variables, respectively. The adjusted coefficients of determination of all the estimating equations are very high, ranging from 0.977 to 0.995. In addition, the estimated coefficients exhibit some common characteristics. This will be apparent in the following discussion of the results pertaining to total, manufactured, and primary imports originating from the world, the industrial countries, and the developing countries, respectively.

The first question to be answered is whether the differences between the regression coefficients of the per capita income and population variables are statistically significant, thereby warranting their separate introduction, as opposed to their combination, the approach taken by Bergsten and Cline (1987). In practically all instances, the variables are significant, thus justifying their separate introduction.

The per capita income variable is positive, and it is not significant statistically in one-half of the cases, when it is combined with the primary import-share variable. With few exceptions, it is also positive when com-

Table C.1 Factors affecting international differences in imports, including primary import-share variable, 1973–1983

	Constant	ln(Y/P)	lnP	M_p/M
Total Imports From:				
World	−1.717	0.123	−0.466	1.969
	(−2.64)***	(1.62)	(−19.46)***	(9.82)***
Industrial Countries	−2.606	0.217	−0.486	0.795
	(−4.35)***	(3.13)***	(−22.92)***	(4.29)***
Developing Countries	−7.171	0.382	−0.186	3.691
	(−7.99)***	(3.58)***	(−5.18)***	(12.23)***
Manufactured Imports From:				
World	−1.631	0.127	−0.430	0.114
	(−2.48)**	(1.64)	(−17.80)***	(−0.57)
Industrial Countries	−1.662	0.114	−0.467	−0.057
	(−2.57)**	(1.52)	(−19.88)***	(−0.29)
Developing Countries	−11.079	0.821	−0.228	0.476
	(−11.33)***	(6.81)***	(−4.41)***	(1.50)
Primary Imports From:				
World	−3.822	0.137	−0.439	4.257
	(−5.67)***	(1.70)*	(−17.41)***	(20.88)***
Industrial Countries	−6.587	0.443	−0.507	2.269
	(7.56)***	(4.39)***	(−18.16)***	(10.30)***
Developing Countries	7.813	0.433	−0.407	5.693
	(−6.47)***	(3.21)***	(−8.54)***	(18.04)***

Source: See text.

Note: T-statistics in parentheses. Three asterisks indicate coefficient estimates significantly different from zero in a two-tailed test at the 1 percent level; two asterisks indicate significance at the 5 percent level; one asterisk indicates significance at the 10 percent level.

Explanation of variables: Y/P = per capita income; P = population; M_p/M = share of primary products in total imports; T = transportation costs; Japan, EC, and EFTA = dummies for Japan, the EC, and the EFTA, respectively.

bined with the individual natural resource variables; the exceptions do not reach the 5 percent level of significance.

The population variable has the expected negative sign and it is statistically significant at the 1 percent level in all equations but one, where its level of significance is 5 percent. The coefficient values for the variable are higher

Table C.1—*Continued*

T	Japan	EC	EFTA	$\bar{R}^2$
−0.041	−0.467	0.256	−0.095	0.977
(5.22)***	(4.35)***	(4.140)***	(1.39)	
−0.032	−0.373	0.597	0.136	0.987
(−4.05)***	(−3.04)***	(10.08)***	(2.20)**	
−0.018	−0.621	0.263	−0.173	0.996
(−2.18)**	(−4.62)***	(3.44)***	(−2.09)**	
−0.051	−0.607	0.383	−0.014	0.987
(−6.60)***	(−5.35)***	(6.07)***	(−0.21)	
−0.044	−0.720	0.469	0.08	0.989
(−5.63)***	(−6.29)***	(7.51)***	(1.14)	
0.001	−0.189	0.297	−0.364	0.994
(0.05)	(−0.90)	(2.19)**	(−3.09)***	
−0.055	−0.530	0.372	−0.039	0.99
(−6.97)***	(−4.35)***	(5.73)***	(−0.58)	
−0.014	−0.026	0.902	0.002	0.995
(−1.26)***	(−0.18)	(11.54)***	(0.02)	
−0.019	−1.047	0.141	−0.643	0.995
(−1.99)**	(−6.72)***	(1.49)	(−6.61)***	

for imports from the industrial countries than for imports from the developing countries, indicating the differential effects of market size in the two cases.

The primary import-share variable has the expected positive sign for total imports and for primary imports and it is statistically significant at the 1 percent level in all cases. It is not significant, however, in the equations for manufactured imports.

Among the natural resource variables, the results for arable land correspond to expectations: the coefficients are negative and highly significant statistically. The coefficients are generally negative for petroleum resources, but few of the coefficients are statistically significant. Finally, the coefficients of the non-oil mineral variable are, contrary to expectation, positive in all but one case and highly significant statistically.

Similar results have been obtained for the non-oil mineral variable by

Table C.2 Factors affecting international differences in imports, including natural resource variables, 1973–1983

	Constant	ln(Y/P)	lnP	A/P
Total Imports From:				
World	0.818	−0.133	−0.277	−0.568
	(1.33)	(−1.81)*	(−15.19)***	(−7.90)***
Industrial Countries	−1.585	0.136	−0.372	0.610
	(−2.35)**	(1.67)*	(−1.80)***	(−7.93)***
Developing Countries	3.468	−0.010	−0.094	−0.231
	(−3.27)***	(−0.08)	(2.57)***	(−2.08)**
Manufactured Imports From:				
World	−3.320	0.342	−0.440	−0.369
	(−4.25)***	(3.48)***	(−15.02)***	(−4.891)***
Industrial Countries	−3.371	0.345	−0.472	−0.434
	(−4.19)***	(3.42)***	(−16.64)***	(−5.30)***
Developing Countries	−11.489	0.914	−0.155	−0.393
	(−10.08)***	(6.35)***	(−3.04)***	(−2.62)***
Primary Imports From:				
World	−0.860	−0.085	−0.193	−0.689
	(1.32)	(−0.10)	(−6.95)***	(−7.50)***
Industrial Countries	−3.937	0.220	−0.289	−1.240
	(−4.96)***	(2.43)**	(−8.67)***	(−10.41)***
Developing Countries	0.393	−0.278	−0.091	−0.842
	(0.27)	(−1.68)*	(−2.18)**	(−5.96)***

Source: See text.
Note: For explanation of symbols see table C.1.
Explanation of variables: Y/P = per capita income; P = population; A/P = ratio of arable land area to population; M/P = per capita value of mineral production (see text and fn. 3); O/P = per capita value of oil production; T = transportation costs; Japan, EC, and EFTA = dummy variables for each.

Noland (1987) and for the more narrowly defined iron ore variable by Saxonhouse (1986) and Bergsten and Cline (1987). A conceivable explanation is complementarity with other imports; for example, the importation of coking coal together with iron ore. Nevertheless, this unexpected result, together with the lack of consistency of the estimates for petroleum resources, points to the advantages of the primary import-share variable over the separate introduction of natural resource variables.

With the exception of the equation for manufactured imports from the developing countries, the regression coefficient of the transportation cost

Table C.2—*Continued*

M/P	O/P	T	Japan	EC	EFTA	$\overline{R}^2$
5.567	−0.013	−0.036	−0.239	0.176	−0.235	0.983
(6.28)***	(−0.90)	(−4.62)***	(−2.65)***	(2.59)***	(−3.12)***	
7.078	−0.013	−0.052	−0.430	0.440	−0.222	0.991
(7.93)***	(−0.90)	(−6.29)***	(−3.25)***	(5.33)***	(−2.30)**	
3.159	−0.05	−0.017	0.544	0.475	0.101	0.992
(2.32)***	(−1.68)*	(−1.36)	(3.62)***	(3.52)***	(0.66)	
3.779	−0.001	−0.045	−0.804	0.311	0.300	0.990
(3.93)***	(−0.051)	(−5.63)	(−6.52)***	(3.26)***	(−2.98)***	
4.691	0.002	−0.050	−0.900	0.355	−0.283	0.998
(4.62)***	(0.14)	(−6.13)***	(−7.17)***	(3.85)***	(−2.72)***	
−0.286	0.007	0.010	−0.589	−0.129	−0.665	0.992
(−0.16)	(0.33)	(0.74)	(−3.23)***	(−0.90)	(−5.76)***	
4.776	−0.040	−0.028	0.333	0.282	−0.295	0.988
(4.35)***	(−2.82)***	(−2.61)***	(3.07)***	(3.00)***	(2.86)***	
10.374	−0.007	−0.023	0.044	0.625	−0.400	0.997
(7.38)***	(−0.52)	(−2.34)**	(0.20)	(3.58)***	(−2.20)**	
6.825	−0.177	−0.037	−0.100	−0.366	−1.294	0.986
(4.20)***	(−3.70)***	(−1.96)*	(−0.53)	(−1.90)*	(−5.12)***	

variable is negative, as expected. Moreover, the large majority of the coefficients for this variable are highly significant statistically.

Among the dummy variables, the Japanese dummy is negative and, with two exceptions, highly significant statistically in the equations incorporating the primary import-share variable. This result obtains in the total import and the manufactured import equations incorporating the natural resource variables as well, the only exception being total imports from the developing countries, where it has a positive sign and it is significant statistically. However, in the equations incorporating the natural resource variables, the Japanese dummy is not significant statistically for primary imports from the industrial and the developing countries; it has a positive sign and it is significant statistically for primary imports from all sources.

The latter result may be due to the intercorrelation of the Japanese dummy with natural resource variables. Nevertheless, the overall conclusion remains: Japan is an outlier among the industrial countries. For total, manufactured,

Table C.3   Factors affecting international differences in total imports from the world, 1973–1983: alternative specifications

	Constant	ln(Y/P)	lnP	M_p/M
Alternative Dependent Variable: M/Y	0.484	0.001	−1.01	0.336
	(2.45)	(0.05)	(−13.68)***	(7.27)***
Alternative Transportation Cost Variables				
a) Unadjusted cif/fob	−1.709	0.116	−0.461	2.017
ratio	(−2.51)**	(1.46)*	(−19.14)***	(10.09)***
b) Adjusted cif/fob ratio by the use of alternative	−1.818	0.151	−0.466	2.054
procedure	(−2.55)	(1.85)*	(−19.01)***	(10.14)***
c) Distance Variable	−1.408	0.148	−0.438	1.498
	(−2.68)***	(2.35)*	(−20.70)***	(8.48)***

Source: See text.
Note: For explanation of symbols see table C.1.
Explanation of variables: Y/P = per capita income; P = population; M_p/M = share of primary products in total imports; T = transportation costs; Japan, EC, and EFTA = dummy variables for each.

and primary imports from all sources of supply, the coefficients of the Japanese dummy variables derived from the equations incorporating the import-share variable are −0.47, −0.61, and −0.53. The coefficient of the dummy variable on world imports in each product category lies between those for imports from industrial and from developing countries.[12]

Finally, in most instances, the EC dummy variables are positive and highly significant statistically, indicating the effects of integration in the European Community. In turn, the EFTA dummy variable is generally negative and statistically significant. A possible explanation is the trade-diverting effects of the EFTA, which are due to its location on the periphery of the European Community.

---

12. The corresponding dummy variables are −0.24, −0.80, and 0.33 in equations incorporating the individual natural resource variables for total, manufactured, and primary imports from all sources of supply. However, there is a lack of consistency across equations for imports from the industrial and the developing country sources of supply.

Table C.3—*Continued*

T	Japan	EC	EFTA	$\bar{R}^2$
−0.008	−0.090	0.052	−1.080	0.955
(−4.39)***	(−2.83)***	(2.79)***	(−6.34)***	
−0.042	−0.407	0.271	−0.082	0.942
(−4.72)***	(−3.51)***	(4.40)***	(−1.20)***	
−0.110	−0.432	0.286	−0.075	0.937
(−4.07)***	(3.72)***	(4.57)***	(−1.06)***	
−0.184	−0.054	0.055	−0.408	0.964
(−11.50)***	(−0.53)	(1.11)***	(−8.62)***	

Estimation has also been done by introducing a US dummy in place of the Japanese dummy, simultaneously with the EC and the EFTA dummies, in equations for total, manufactured, and primary imports from all sources of supply. The regression coefficients of the US dummy variable are negative when the import-share variable is used, and positive when the natural resource variables are used; the signs are reversed in the developing country equations. However, they are not significant statistically in any of the cases.

Table C.3 provides estimates under alternative specifications of the dependent variable and the transportation cost variable. This has been done for the case of total imports from all sources of supply, when the primary import-share variable is employed. It is apparent that using the ratio of imports to GDP, rather than its logarithm, hardly affects the results. This is not surprising, since changing the form of the dependent variable does not affect the basic structure of the model. Nor does the use of the c.i.f.–f.o.b. ratio in an unadjusted form, or the use of an alternative adjustment for this ratio, appreciably affect the results. Yet neither the Japanese dummy nor the EC dummy is significant statistically if a distance rather than a transportation cost variable is utilized. For reasons noted earlier, this variable is a poor proxy for transportation costs.

Table C.4 Comparison of results obtained by Bergsten–Cline and Balassa

	Constant	ln(Y/P)	A/P	M/P
Bergsten-Cline	0.773	−0.063	−0.038	0.041
	(28.4)***	(26.2)***	(7.25)***	(3.96)***
Balassa	1.329	−0.231	−0.518	5.431
	(10.7)***	(−23.6)***	(−9.99)***	(8.58)***

Source: See text.
Note: For explanation of symbols see table C.1.
Explanation of variables: Y/P = per capita income; A/P = ratio of arable land area to population; M/P = per capita value of mineral production; O/P = per capita value of oil production; T = transportation costs; Japan = dummy variable for Japan.

Results Obtained in Alternative Models

Bergsten and Cline (1987) also combined cross-section and time-series data for the industrial countries when testing the hypothesis that Japan is an "outlier" among industrial countries. However, they used different specifications of several of the variables. In particular, they combined per capita GDP and population into one variable; they used a single variable for the EC countries; and, as noted above, they utilized a simple average of the unadjusted c.i.f.–f.o.b. ratio and air cargo rates. The results obtained for total imports from all sources of supply show the Japanese dummy to be positive and not significantly different from zero.

Table C.4 shows the Bergsten–Cline results, together with estimates made with a modified version of the Balassa model discussed above. Modification has involved (1) combining the per capita income and population variables; (2) using a single variable for the European Community; and (3) employing the unadjusted c.i.f.–f.o.b. ratio.[13] The results obtained show the dummy variable for Japan to be negative and statistically significant at the 7 percent level.

It appears, then, that adopting the Bergsten–Cline specification reduces but does not eliminate the statistical significance of the Japanese dummy variable. For various reasons, though, the specifications used by these authors are not appropriate for the problem at hand. To begin with, in view of the statistically significant differences between the regression coefficients

---

13. We have not been able to obtain data on air cargo rates, but, at any rate, this would have involved double counting, as noted above. A further difference between the two equations is that Bergsten and Cline's sample included New Zealand, which does not fit the criteria used to identify industrial countries.

Table C.4—*Continued*

O/P	T	Japan	$\overline{R^2}$
0.010	−0.001	0.008	0.895
(7.57)***	(9.70)***	(0.47)	
−0.002	−0.033	−0.120	0.931
(−0.311)	(−4.99)***	(−1.86)*	

of the per capita income and population variables, they should be introduced separately in the estimating equation. Furthermore, in the absence of the complete integration of EC member nations, now planned for 1992, it is not appropriate to consider them as a unit; at any rate, this choice greatly reduces the degrees of freedom in the estimation. Finally, apart from the duplication involved in including air cargo rates in addition to the c.i.f.– f.o.b. ratio in the calculations, Bergsten and Cline considered only transport costs in trade among the industrial countries, although the dependent variable of their model is the ratio for total imports from all sources of supply.

Saxonhouse (1986) estimated a Heckscher–Ohlin model of trade in 109 product categories for a sample of 22 countries for the years 1964, 1971, and 1979. Taking net exports to be a function of factor endowments and distance from trading partners, Saxonhouse compared equations estimated including, as well as excluding, Japan. Having found that actual values fell outside the confidence interval in only 20 percent of the cases, which represent 6 percent of Japan's trade, Saxonhouse concluded that Japan is not an "outlier" among the countries under consideration.

But the method that Saxonhouse uses to estimate the model reduces the likelihood that the model could identify protection. He uses a two-step procedure, in the first step estimating international differences in "factor quality." However, these terms will pick up difference in protection as well as differences in quality. Thus, if protection is correlated with factor intensity, one cannot distinguish between differences in quality (or efficiency) and protection in Saxonhouse's model.[14] For example, Saxonhouse's model does

---

14. If, for example, Japan protects industries that utilize unskilled labor intensively, net exports will be higher than they otherwise would have been. Thus, Japanese unskilled labor will appear to be internationally efficient. In the second stage regression, the protected industries will not appear as outliers because an adjustment has been made for the "superior efficiency" of Japanese unskilled labor, whereas in reality net exports are higher than otherwise predicted because of protection. At the same time, as shown by Staiger, Deardorff, and Stern (1987), Japanese protection affects factor use to a considerable extent.

not identify Japan's rice sector as protected, although there is incontrovertible evidence that it is.

A further problem with Saxonhouse's model is the probable heteroscedasticity of the residuals, which he does not report.[15] If the residuals are heteroscedastic, inferences about the confidence intervals are invalid. This may be particularly problematic, since the country sample includes both developing and developed countries of widely disparate size and economic characteristics.[16]

Noland (1987a) employed an estimating equation derived from the Helpman–Krugman model. The variables of the equation are those in table C.2, although Noland used GDP instead of population as a variable for market size, introduced an indicator of international per capita income differences, and excluded the EFTA dummy variable. The equation was estimated for the years 1980 and 1984 for total imports from all sources of supply, with studentized residuals calculated for each of the industrial countries.

The studentized residuals are of interest, because they are the t-statistics one would obtain if a dummy variable for each observation were added to the original model (Belsley, Kuh, and Welsch 1980, 20). A studentized residual of less than 2.0 in absolute value indicates that the coefficient on a dummy variable for that observation would not be considered significantly different from zero at conventional levels of statistical significance. Sample "outliers" can thus be identified as those observations with studentized residuals greater than 2.0 in absolute value.

Table C.5 reports Noland's results for 1980 and 1984, together with results obtained by the use of the Balassa model for 1980 and 1983.[17] Noland's result for 1980 for Japan was -0.124 and Balassa's was -1.172 (-1.229 if the primary import variable is used in place of natural resource variables). But the year 1980 may not represent an equilibrium situation, because there could not yet have been an adjustment to the tripling of oil prices occurring in that year. It can be assumed, however, that adjustment was accomplished by 1983. In fact, the results of the Balassa model show studentized residuals of -2.111 and -1.428 for Japan, depending on whether the primary import variable or the natural resource variables are used in the estimating equation.

---

15. Leamer (1984) and Noland (1988c) examine the sources of heteroscedasticity in models such as the one Saxonhouse uses.

16. Nor can one assume identical production functions and utility functions, which underlie models of this kind, in the case where developed and developing countries are combined in the sample for which estimates are made.

17. While these results pertain to imports, Noland has also done calculations for exports and for total trade.

Table C.5 Studentized residuals

	Balassa				Noland	
	1980		1983		1980	1984
	Import share variable	Natural resource variables	Import share variable	Natural resource variables	Natural resource variables	
Australia	−0.739	−0.016	−0.170	0.093	0.147	0.015
Austria	−0.837	−1.087	−0.640	−1.031	0.317	1.770
Belgium	2.992	2.969	2.953	3.042	1.854	0.924
Canada	0.171	0.890	0.068	0.582	1.914	0.177
Denmark	−0.585	0.096	−0.417	0.429	−0.010	−0.602
Finland	−0.794	−0.770	−0.885	−0.844	0.221	−0.477
France	−0.221	−0.466	0.214	−0.045	−1.310	−0.322
Germany	0.543	0.093	0.609	0.169	−0.872	−0.244
Ireland	−0.252	−0.406	−0.306	−0.618	−0.374	−0.834
Israel (a)	−0.060	0.309	−0.236	0.197	0.070	−0.271
Italy	0.326	0.291	0.025	0.162	0.128	−0.566
Japan	−1.229	−1.172	−2.111	−1.428	−0.124	−1.580
Netherlands	1.990	1.858	1.623	1.637	1.328	0.966
New Zealand	n.a.	n.a.	n.a.	n.a.	0.070	−0.271
Norway	−1.453	−0.970	−1.470	−0.697	−2.359	−0.287
Spain	n.a.	n.a.	n.a.	n.a.	−0.776	0.790
Sweden	0.484	−1.032	0.793	−0.451	−0.083	0.273
Switzerland	0.111	−0.377	−0.229	−0.936	−0.724	0.873
UK	0.249	0.171	0.636	0.327	−0.267	0.114
US	−0.995	−0.167	−0.916	−0.334	0.328	0.676

Source: See text.

Finally, a studentized residual of −1.580 was obtained by Noland for Japan in 1984.

Lawrence (1987) also used the Helpman–Krugman model in deriving his estimating equations. He employed two tests of out-of-the-ordinary import behavior, relating import shares to production shares and export shares. He also utilized data for 22 industries in 13 industrial countries, thereby greatly increasing the degrees of freedom in the pooled regressions.

The results reported in table C.6 show Japan to be an outlier as far as import shares are concerned. Thus, in all three years for which estimates have been made, the dummy variable for Japan is negative and statistically significant at the 1 percent level. Only France comes close to this result in the share-of-production model; the United Kingdom in the export share

Table C.6 Coefficients of country dummy variables estimated by Lawrence

	Production share model			Export share model		
	1970	1980	1983	1970	1980	1983
Australia	0.74	0.42	0.28	1.30	1.62	1.60
	(3.5)	(1.9)	(1.2)	(5.0)	(6.9)	(6.2)
Belgium	0.15	0.10	0.07	0.46	0.39	0.41
	(0.9)	(0.7)	(0.4)	(2.2)	(2.2)	(2.0)
Canada	0.46	0.33	0.21	0.41	0.19	−0.16
	(2.9)	(2.3)	(1.3)	(2.1)	(1.1)	(0.8)
Finland	−0.54	−0.55	−0.45	−0.25	−0.26	−0.12
	(3.2)	(3.7)	(2.8)	(1.2)	(1.4)	(0.6)
France	−0.17	−0.15	−0.13	−0.41	−0.33	−0.32
	(1.0)	(1.0)	(0.8)	(2.0)	(1.9)	(1.6)
Germany	0.21	0.28	0.33	0.05	0.16	0.21
	(1.3)	(1.9)	(2.1)	(0.3)	(0.9)	(1.0)
Italy	−0.42	−0.20	−0.17	−0.51	−0.05	−0.06
	(2.5)	(1.3)	(1.0)	(2.5)	(0.2)	(0.3)
Japan	−0.67	−0.60	−0.63	−0.72	−0.79	−0.85
	(3.7)	(3.7)	(3.5)	(3.2)	(3.9)	(3.8)
Netherlands	0.24	0.09	0.02	0.42	0.22	0.11
	(1.4)	(0.6)	(0.2)	(2.0)	(1.2)	(0.5)
Norway	−0.32	−0.22	−0.31	0.12	−0.10	−0.09
	(1.8)	(1.4)	(1.8)	(0.6)	(0.5)	(0.4)
Sweden	0.27	0.22	0.25	0.38	0.16	0.37
	(1.7)	(1.5)	(1.6)	(2.0)	(0.9)	(1.9)
United Kingdom	−0.15	−0.12	−0.13	−0.84	−0.37·	−0.42
	(0.7)	(0.8)	(0.8)	(3.7)	(2.1)	(2.2)
United States	0.24	0.58	0.84	−0.33	−0.31	−0.21
	(1.3)	(3.4)	(4.6)	(1.5)	(1.5)	(1.0)

Source: Lawrence (1987, Table 10).

model. Japan is different from other countries in that it imports substantially less than would be expected on the basis of international comparisons of the national attributes of industrial countries.

Appendix D   The Interaction of Macroeconomic Forces

The scientific discussion of causality extends back to Hume (1748), but was first formalized by Granger (1969). There are two central notions to Granger's conceptualization of causality. The first is that y_1 causes y_2 if taking into account past observations of y_1 leads to improved predictions of y_2. The second is that the future cannot predict the past; causality can only run from the past to the present or future, it cannot run in the reverse direction.

Granger developed his idea of causality in the context of unbiased least-squares predictions, and characterized prediction accuracy in terms of the variance of one-step-ahead forecasts. Let U be an information set including all past and present information, and $\hat{U}$ be the same information set excluding present values. Similarly, let Y_1 consist of all past and present observations on the variable y_1, and $\hat{Y}_1$ be the past observations alone. The variable y_1 is said to cause y_2 if the one-step-ahead forecast of y_2, $\hat{y}_2$, based on all information (including Y_1) is more accurate than the forecast using all information (excluding Y_1). Using these definitions, conditions of causality can be precisely stated:

(1) y_1 causes y_2 if $\sigma^2\ (\hat{y}_2|\hat{U}) < \sigma^2(\hat{y}_2|\hat{U} - \hat{Y}_1)$. That is, including past values of y_1 reduces the forecast variance of y_2.

(2) y_1 causes y_2 instantaneously (contemporaneously) if $\sigma^2(\hat{y}_2|U) < \sigma^2(\hat{y}_2|U - Y_1)$. Here, including past and current values of y_1 reduces the forecast variance of y_2. For bivariate relationships, similar conditions can be derived by reversing the roles of y_1 and y_2.

(3) Feedback is said to occur if $\sigma^2(y_2|\hat{U}) < \sigma^2(\hat{y}_2|\hat{U} - \hat{Y}_1)$, and $\sigma^2(\hat{y}_1|\hat{U}) < \sigma^2(\hat{y}_1|\hat{U} - \hat{Y}_2)$. In other words, strict causality runs in both directions between y_1 and y_2. Instantaneous (contemporaneous) feedback can be defined by replacing the strict causality conditions in the definitions with the instantaneous causality conditions in (2).

Table D.1 States of causality

Description	Notation
(1) Instantaneous causality only	$(y_1 - y_2)$
(2) y_1 causes y_2 only and not instantaneously	$(y_1 \rightarrow y_2)$
(3) y_1 causes y_2 only and instantaneously	$(y_1 \Rightarrow y_2)$
(4) y_2 causes y_1 only and not instantaneously	$(y_2 \rightarrow y_1)$
(5) y_2 causes y_1 only and instantaneously	$(y_2 \Rightarrow y_1)$
(6) Feedback, not instantaneously	$(y_1 \leftrightarrow y_2)$
(7) Feedback, instantaneously	$(y_1 \Leftrightarrow y_2)$
(8) Independence	$(y_1 \nleftrightarrow y_2)$

(4) x and y are said to be independent if neither causes the other:
$$\sigma^2(\acute{y}_2|U) = \sigma^2(\acute{y}_2|U - Y_1) \text{ and}$$
$$\sigma^2(\acute{y}_1|U) = \sigma^2(\acute{y}_1|U - Y_2).$$

Taken together, these conditions yield eight possible states of causality, which are summarized in table D.1.

Sims (1972) developed a way of implementing Granger's notion of causality using regressions involving past, current, and future values of Y_1 and Y_2. Sims' insight was that "if and only if causality runs one way from current and past values of some list of exogenous variables to a given endogenous variable, then in a regression of the endogenous variable on past, current, and future values of the exogenous variables, the future values of the exogenous variables should have zero coefficients" (541). Consider the jointly covariance-stationary processes shown in (D.1), where $a(L)$, $b(L)$, $c(L)$, and $d(L)$ are polynomials in the lag operator L, and u_t and v_t are mutually uncorrelated white noise processes:

$$y_{1t} = a(L)u_t + b(L)v_t$$
(D.1)
$$y_{2t} = c(L)u_t + d(L)v_t.$$

Sims shows that under the hypothesis that y_1 does not cause y_2, (D.1) can be rewritten as

$$y_{1t} = a(L)u_t + b(L)v_t$$
(D.2)
$$y_{2t} = c(L)u_t.$$

Solving for u_t and substituting the second equation into the first yields

(D.3) $y_{1t} = a(L)c^{-1}(L)Y_{2t} + b(L)v_t$

Thus, current Y_1 contains information from current and past values of both u_t and v_t; Y_2 contains no information from current or past values of Y_1 that are not already contained in past values of Y_2. This means that current and past values of Y_1 will not improve predictions of future Y_2, once the information in past Y_2 are taken into account. Equivalently, in a regression of Y_1 on past, current, and future values of Y_2, the null hypothesis that Y_1 does not cause Y_2 implies that the coefficients on future values of Y_2 equal zero.

Sims' procedure is to estimate the regression

$$(D.4) \quad y_{1t} = \sum_{i=-n_1}^{n_2} \beta_i y_{2t-i} + w_t$$

and test the hypothesis that all the coefficients on the future values of Y_2 (i.e., negative lags) are jointly equal to zero. The procedure is then reversed to test the hypothesis that Y_2 causes Y_1.

In practice, several difficulties are likely to be encountered when this procedure is used. First, the stochastic processes may not be stationary. Economic time-series commonly exhibit secular trends. Second, the disturbance term in (D.4) will typically exhibit serial correlation. Although OLS parameter estimates will be consistent, estimates of the standard errors will be biased and inconsistent, and hypothesis tests will consequently be invalid. Sims' solution is to filter X and Y before estimating (D.4) to generate stationary series and to eliminate serial correlation.[1] He suggests using the filter $(1 - 0.75L)^2$, arguing that this filter "approximately flattens the spectral density of most economic time series" (545).

In addition, the lengths of leads and lags must be specified. Incorrectly excluding leads and lags may lead to biased coefficients (omitted variable bias), while the inclusion of extraneous leads and lags uses up degrees of freedom. In Sims' regressions of quarterly data on GNP and the money supply, he used leads and lags of four and eight quarters, respectively, a practice followed by many subsequent researchers.

Bivariate Econometric Estimation

Bivariate Granger–Sims causality tests were performed on a set of variables relating to the Japanese current account for the period 1970:1 to 1984:4.

---

1. Transforming the data with a lag polynomial is called filtering the data. If the filter $(1 - 0.75L)$ is used, filtering the data means that the data are subjected to the transformation $z_t = y_t - 0.75y_{t-1}$. The purpose is to transform the data to a white noise process. For this reason, filtering is also referred to as prefiltering, whitening, and prewhitening.

These variables included GNP, gross saving (GS), gross domestic investment (I), the current account (CA), the real interest rate (RREAL), the exchange rate (ER), and partner-country economic activity (GWP). Data on GNP, GS, I, and CA were taken from the Bank of Japan, *Economic Statistics Annual,* various issues. The real interest rate was defined as the interest rate on long-term central government bonds minus the rate of inflation. The interest rate data were from the OECD, *Main Economic Indicators,* various issues. The rate of inflation was calculated as the annualized change in the wholesale price index found in the *Economic Statistics Annual.* The exchange rate was the MERM exchange rate taken from the *IFS, Supplement on Exchange Rates.* Partner-country income was a trade-weighted measure of partner-country GDP.[2] All series were quarterly and deseasonalized at the source.

Each series was measured in logs and prewhitened using the filter $(1-0.75L)^2$.[3] Visual inspection of the plots of the filtered variables indicated that they were indeed stationary. Each regression was estimated with four leading and eight lagged observations of the dependent variable. These results are reported in table D.2. Three summary statistics are shown. The revised Ljung–Box Q statistic is used to test the hypothesis that the regression residuals are serially uncorrelated.[4] Significant values of the Q statistic indicate that the hypothesis of no serial correlation can be rejected and that inferences based on the F statistics may not be valid. Two F statistics are reported. The first, labeled $F1$, is the test of the hypothesis that the coefficients

---

2. This variable was constructed by Shigeru Akiyama using national accounts data on the World Bank–IMF computer data bank. The trade weights are from 1976 to 1978. The partner countries include Australia, Austria, Belgium, Brazil, Canada, Denmark, France, Germany, Hong Kong, Indonesia, Ireland, Italy, Korea, Malaysia, Mexico, the Netherlands, Norway, the Philippines, Singapore, South Africa, Spain, Sweden, Switzerland, Taiwan, Thailand, United Kingdom, United States, and Yugoslavia.

3. As shown in Feige and Pearce (1979), the results may be sensitive to the filter used to prewhiten. As a check, the regressions were also estimated using the filters $(1-L)$ and $(1-L)^2$. For some series, plots of the $(1-L)$ transformed variables did not appear stationary. The results obtained using the $(1-L)^2$ filter appeared preferable. The estimates are similar to the ones reported in this section, with one exception noted below. Further, it should be noted that Geweke, Meese, and Dent (1983) conclude, on the basis of Monte Carlo experiments, that, in the presence of serial correlation (hence prefiltering), the Sims tests tend to reject the null hypothesis X does not cause Y, when it is in fact true.

4. For small samples, the appropriate chi-square statistic to test for white noise residuals is

$$Q = n(n + 2) \sum_{k-1}^{m} r_k^2 \bigg/ (n - k) \sim \chi_m^2$$

where n is the number of observations, m is the number of autocorrelations, and r_k is the sample autocorrelation coefficient for lag k.

on all leading observations of the right-hand side variable are zero. Rejection of this hypothesis indicates that the right-hand side variable (Y_1) does not cause, in the sense of Granger–Sims, the left-hand side variable (Y_2), $(Y_1 \nrightarrow Y_2)$. The second F statistic, $F2$, is the test of the hypothesis that the coefficients on the leading and current observations of the right-hand side variable are zero. Rejection of this hypothesis implies that the right-hand side variable does not cause and does not instantaneously cause the left-hand side variable, that is, $(Y_1 \nRightarrow Y_2)$.

Finally, although it would be tedious to report every estimated coefficient, the individual coefficient values are not completely without interest. If the estimated coefficients on future variables are larger than on past values, this may indicate causality, although the F statistics are insignificant due to multicollinearity. Regressions in which this appears to be the case are noted below.

The causality relationships implied by the estimates reported in table D.2 are summarized in table D.3. Perhaps it is not surprising that the data reveal feedback relationships between saving, investment, and income, and uni-directional causality from real interest rates to investment. Further, changes in partner-country economic activity cause changes in domestic saving and investment.[5]

The results reported in table D.2 indicate that unidirectional causality runs from variations in domestic saving and investment to the current account, although the high value of the Q statistic in the saving regression suggests that caution should be exercised in interpreting this result. However, estimates obtained using the $(I-L)^2$ prefilter imply that this relationship is characterized by simultaneous feedback.[6] In addition, the data indicate that a one-way causality runs from the exchange rate to domestic saving.

As indicated by the estimates in table D.2, instantaneous causality runs from real interest rates and foreign economic activity to the exchange rate. No causal relationship between the real interest rate and the current account was uncovered, although the data indicate that a one-way causality runs from the current account to foreign income. The meaning of this result is not clear.[7] What seemed most surprising however, was the apparent absence

---

5. It should be noted, however, that the regressions estimated to test the reverse relationship exhibited some strange results, namely, very high Q statistics, and strange patterns of coefficients. Some future coefficients were large, as were the values of the seventh and eighth lagged coefficients.

6. When the variables were expressed in level rather than logarithmic form, the regression results indicated that causality ran from the current account to investment.

7. One would typically think of changes in world economic activity inducing charges in the current account. However, it has been suggested that, for a large country such as Japan, changes in the current account may act as a "locomotive" for changes in partner economic activity.

Table D.2 Bivariate regression results

Dependent variable	Independent variable	Q	F1	F2	$\bar{R}^2$
GNP	GS	23.248	7.531***	6.552***	.886
GS	GNP	28.587[c]	3.709**	4.340***	.935
GNP	I	54.249[a]	2.168*	2.269*	.712
I	GNP	18.812	2.668*	3.785***	.881
GNP	CA	29.991[b]	0.770	1.241	.517
CA	GNP	18.968	1.826	1.493	.952
GNP	RREAL	40.991[a]	1.122	0.900	.503
RREAL	GNP	15.549	1.538	1.231	.996
GNP	ER	46.076[a]	0.519	0.432	.311
ER	GNP	22.431	0.656	0.537	.347
GNP	GWP	81.475[a]	1.195	1.537	.507
GWP	GNP	23.432	1.731	1.407	.612
GS	I	19.257	1.139	11.602***	.989
I	GS	24.628	1.139	17.768***	.987
GS	CA	26.741[b]	2.463*	3.427**	.761
CA	GS	19.091	1.319	1.088	.971
GS	RREAL	95.881[a]	0.623	0.643	.470
RREAL	GS	13.345	1.037	1.436	.996
GS	ER	134.809[a]	0.313	0.292	.283
ER	GS	22.150	1.402	2.094*	.440
GS	GWP	146.474[a]	0.203	0.162	.280
GWP	GS	14.628	3.429**	4.577***	.600
I	CA	24.915	2.085	2.227*	.690
CA	I	18.098	1.840	1.473	.970
I	RREAL	96.304[a]	0.485	0.479	.497
RREAL	I	14.321	2.284*	2.207*	.997

of any causal relationship between the exchange rate and the current account, except indirectly though domestic saving.

Finally, it should be noted that several regressions exhibit a combination of very high Q statistics (indicating the presence of serially correlated residuals), and relatively low R^2s. This fact suggests that relevant explanatory variables have been omitted from the regression. It could indicate a misspecification of the bivariate relationship (possibly due to some sort of regime change or shock), or simply the omission of another relevant explanatory variable. Lütkepohl (1982) has demonstrated that spurious results may be obtained in bivariate Granger–Sims causality tests due to the omission of relevant explanatory variables. The obvious solution would

Table D.2—*Continued*

Dependent variable	Independent variable	Q	F1	F2	$\bar{R}^2$
I	ER	141.723[a]	0.357	0.300	.334
ER	I	30.421[b]	0.422	0.541	.357
I	GWP	150.516[a]	0.206	0.180	.310
GWP	I	10.160	2.313*	2.353*	.545
CA	RREAL	38.389[a]	1.824	1.478	.962
RREAL	CA	10.975	0.910	0.774	.996
CA	ER	19.902	0.661	0.864	.953
ER	CA	26.352[c]	1.337	1.073	.462
CA	GWP	17.404	2.718*	2.904**	.965
GWP	CA	16.562	0.236	0.189	.697
RREAL	ER	13.723	1.449	2.147*	.997
ER	RREAL	18.206	0.442	1.318	.430
RREAL	GWP	12.769	2.391*	1.935	.997
GWP	RREAL	24.718	2.153	1.986	.487
ER	GWP	26.625[c]	0.507	1.385	.430
GWP	ER	26.816[c]	2.208*	3.115**	.611

Note: The column Q reports the Ljung–Box statistic.
a. Hypothesis of no serial correlation in the residuals can be rejected at the 1 percent level.
b. Hypothesis can be rejected at the 5 percent level.
c. Hypothesis can be rejected at the 10 percent level.
The column F1 reports the F statistic for the hypothesis that the coefficients on leading variables (negative lags) are zero. The column F2 reports the F statistic for the hypothesis that the coefficients on leading and current variables are zero.
*** indicates that the hypothesis can be rejected at the 1 percent level; ** at the 5 percent level; * at the 10 percent level.
See text for definitions of variables.

be to adopt vector autoregression (VAR) methods developed by Sims. The usefulness of VARs is constrained in small samples, however, by a paucity of degrees of freedom. In this light, the bivariate tests may be useful in informing the specification of the VARs.

Multivariate Analysis

In response to these concerns, the analysis has been recast in a multivariate framework. Sims (1980) demonstrated how the technique of Granger–Sims causality analysis could be extended to the multivariate case through the

Table D.3 Bivariate causality summary

y_1/y_2	GNP	GS	I	CA	RREAL	ER	GWP
GNP	—	$(y_1{\leftrightarrow}y_2)^*$	$(y_1{\leftrightarrow}y_2)^*$	$(y_1{\leftrightarrow}y_2)$	$(y_1{\leftrightarrow}y_2)$	$(y_1{\leftrightarrow}y_2)$	$(y_1{\leftrightarrow}y_2)$
GS		—	$(y_1{\Leftrightarrow}y_2)$	$(y_1{\rightarrow}y_2)^*$	$(y_1{\leftrightarrow}y_2)$	$(y_2{\Rightarrow}y_1)$	$(y_2{\rightarrow}y_1)^*$
I			—	$(y_1{\rightarrow}y_2)$	$(y_2{\rightarrow}y_1)^*$	$(y_1{\leftrightarrow}y_2)$	$(y_2{\rightarrow}y_1)^*$
CA				—	$(y_1{\leftrightarrow}y_2)$	$(y_2{\leftrightarrow}y_1)$	$(y_1{\rightarrow}y_2)^*$
RREAL					—	$(y_1{\rightarrow}y_2)$	$(y_1{\rightarrow}y_2)$
ER						—	$(y_2{\rightarrow}y_1)^*$
GWP							—

* indicates that the relationship also holds simultaneously.

use of vector autoregression (VAR) techniques. The procedure is straight-forward. A set of k regressions of the form

$$(D.5) \quad y_{jt} = x_t + BY_{t-i} + w_{jt} , \ i = 1,\ldots,n$$
$$j = 1,\ldots,k$$

is estimated where x_t is a matrix of deterministic variables, Y is $(k \times n)$ matrix of endogenous variables; y_j is the jth column of Y; B is a $(n \times k)$ matrix of estimated lag coefficients; and w is a $(1 \times t)$ vector of disturbances. In other words, each endogenous variable in the system is regressed on the deterministic variables, its own lagged values, and the lagged values of the other endogenous variables in the system. F tests are then performed to test the null hypothesis that the n elements of each of the k rows of B are jointly equal to zero. Acceptance of the null implies that with $B_k = 0$, the best linear one-step-ahead forecast of y_{jt} does not involve lagged values of Y_k which is precisely the Granger–Sims definition of the variable Y_k not causing the variable Y_j. Again, the procedure is then reversed to test the hypothesis that Y_j causes Y_k.

Implementation of VAR techniques is not free of difficulties. The most obvious difficulty is that the estimation of even relatively simple VARs involves the estimation of a large number of parameters. In practice, VAR systems of more than about six equations become unwieldy. Likewise, the available sample size acts as a bound on the number of parameters that can be estimated. This constraint is particularly significant for the investigation at hand, since the relevant sample period only extends back to the advent of the floating rate system.

Thus it is important to characterize the model as parsimoniously as possible. The results of the previous section suggest some possible avenues. Given the strong simultaneity among GNP, saving, and investment, and their similar responses to the other variables in the system, it seems reasonable to combine them into a single variable, domestic absorption (ABSORB). Second, while the real interest rate was found to cause investment and the exchange rate in the Granger–Sims sense, no causal relationships running to real interest rates were uncovered. This suggests that the real interest might be regarded as causally prior to the other variables and would be a natural candidate for exclusion from the set of endogenous variables.

The potential lack of degrees of freedom also leads to some methodological difficulties. Sims notes that, since the estimated model is autoregressive, the statistical tests are based on asymptotic distribution theory (1980, 17). However, for many of the hypothesis actually tested, the degrees of freedom in the numerator and denominator are similar, and the F tests may not be robust in the presence non-normality. Non-normal errors are most likely to occur when dummy variables are used for specific periods, such as the oil shocks, as is the case here. In particular, if the distributions of the residuals have fat tails, there will be a bias toward rejection of the null hypothesis; that is, there will be a tendency to conclude that a causal relationship exists even if it in fact does not.

In light of these potential problems, Sims suggests calculating the likelihood ratio tests as though the sample size were $t - g$, where t is the sample size, and g the number of estimated coefficients in each equation. This adjustment has the effect of making the tests more "conservative" in rejecting the null. All the statistical tests reported below are calculated using this adjustment.

VAR summary results are reported in table D.4.[8] The reported statistics include the F statistics to test the block exogeneity of each variable, the adjusted coefficient of determination ($\bar{R}^2$), and the adjusted Ljung-Box Q statistic. Due to the high degree of collinearity among the regressors, it is difficult to identify the true specification of the model. Further, the significance levels of individual F tests may be misleading due to the non-normality of the disturbance terms because of kurtosis (as discussed above), or autocorrelation (as evidenced by significant Q statistics). The block exogeneity of the real interest rate was tested. A chi-square statistic of 40.05 (32) with a marginal significance level of 0.155 for the likelihood ratio test was obtained, indicating that the exogeneity of the real interest rate could not be rejected at conventional levels of significance. This result could be interpreted as consistent with the results obtained for the United States by Litterman and Weiss (1985), who found that the *ex ante* real interest rate was causally prior to the universe of money, prices, nominal rates, and

---

8. All regressions included trend terms and dummy variables for the oil shock periods. The variables were not filtered and were expressed in levels.

Table D.4 VAR summary results

Dependent variables	Independent variables						
	CA	ABSORB	GWP	ER	RREAL	$\overline{R}^2$	Q
CA	3.194[c]	1.532	2.676[c]	3.778	2.567	0.904	18.093
ABSORB	4.853[b]	3.034[c]	4.092[b]	3.520[b]	2.153	0.892	27.283
GWP	0.813	1.990	22.639[a]	2.999[c]	1.819	0.999	24.811
ER	8.139[a]	3.463[c]	6.400[b]	9.093[b]	4.592[c]	0.984	25.896
RREAL	4.672[b]	3.906[c]	3.252	3.201	5.118[b]	0.954	33.925[b]
CA	5.095[a]	0.879	1.583	2.238[c]	—	0.829	19.795
ABSORB	5.142[a]	3.191[b]	2.709[c]	2.047	—	0.904	14.857
GWP	0.476	0.847	4.058[b]	1.749	—	0.999	29.843[c]
ER	1.654	1.226	1.096	8.584[a]	—	0.954	17.501
RREAL	—	—	—	—	—	—	—

Note: Numbers under variable headings are the F-statistics for inclusion of that variable and its lagged values in the regression equation. In the upper panel, the real interest rate is included in the set of endogenous variables. In the lower panel, the real interest rate is excluded.
a. Significant at the 1 percent level.
b. Significant at the 5 percent level.
c. Significant at the 10 percent level.

output. It might also be consistent with the results of Noland (1987b) who found that the real interest rate was causally prior to a universe of domestic absorption, trade partner income, the exchange rate, and the current account. However, given the fairly low significance level of the test, results are reported with the real interest rate both included and excluded from the set of endogenous variables. In addition, both specifications were estimated with six- and eight-quarter lags. The null hypothesis that the coefficients on the seventh and eight lags of the endogenous variables were jointly equal to zero could be rejected at the 1 percent level for both specifications. Hence all the reported estimates refer to the eight-lag specifications.

Viewed together, these estimates yield a general picture of the causality relations among the variables. Domestic absorption (ABSORB), partner income (GWP), and the exchange rate (ER) all exert independent causal influence on the level of the current account.

Conversely, the current account partner income, and in one specification, the exchange rate, causes domestic absorption in the sense of Granger–Sims. When real interest rates are included, all the variables in the system cause the exchange rate.

The general impression is that the current account interacts strongly with the other variables, although the apparent statistical significance varies with the precise specification of the regression. An alternative, and perhaps more informative, way of presenting the results of the regressions is through variance decomposition. First, the autoregressive process (D.5) is transformed to obtain its moving average representation (MAV):[9]

$$(D.6) \quad y_t = X_t B + \sum_{i-1}^{n} A_i u_{t-i}$$

where $X_t B$ is the deterministic part of y_t, A_i are moving average parameters, and u_t is a vector white noise process, called an innovation process for Y_t. A matrix G is then chosen to factor the variance–covariance matrix $V = E u_t u_t'$, so that $GG' = V$ and $G^{-1} V G'^{-1} = I$. Choleski factorization yields a G matrix which is lower triangular with positive elements on the diagonal. It has a very useful interpretation, since the ith diagonal element of the matrix is the standard deviation of the residual from a regression of the ith variable on variables 1 to $i-1$. An innovation process v_t is defined as $v_t = G^{-1} u_t$ which satisfies $E v_t v_t' = I$, thus is uncorrelated across time and equations, and is said to be orthogonalized.

The influence of each variable in the system on the other variables can then be represented by the decomposition of the variance of each element of y_t. In this way, the variance of an element of y_t is apportioned to itself and the other elements of y_t. By triangularizing the system (by successively reordering the variables so that each is in turn the first), the response of the system to orthogonal shocks and the influence of the variables in the system on each other can be shown.[10] The variance decomposition for the model is presented in table 6.1 in the text.

Yet another way of representing the information contained in the VARs is to trace out the implied long-run behavior of the figure variables in response to shocks to the system. This is done in figures 5.3 and 5.5 of the

---

9. See Sargent 1979, 271–272.

10. It should be noted the shares attributed to each variable are not invariant to their ordering. In particular, variables early in the ordering (close to the left-hand side of table 6.1) will tend to have larger shares, while those variables toward the end of the ordering (close to the right-hand side of the table) will tend to have smaller shares. The sensitivity of the decomposition to ordering is a function of the degree of orthogonality in the correlations among the variables. Analogous to the case of multicollinearity, if some variables are highly collinear and the orthogonal part of their variance is not highly correlated with the "dependent" variable, then their decomposition shares will be sensitive to their ordering. However, if the orthogonal part of their variance is highly correlated with the "dependent" variable, then the shares will be robust to changes in ordering. The calculated forecast standard errors are of course invariant to the ordering of the variables.

text, in which the response of Japanese investment to shocks in domestic and world demand are plotted.

In addition to this model, another model focusing on bilateral relationship between Japan and the United States was estimated. Income in each country (JGNP, USGNP), the bilateral current account balance (BILATCA), and the bilateral exchange rate (YENDOL) were regarded as endogenous.[11] This implies an intuitively appealing set of relationships between economic activity, excess demands, and the exchange rate, as could be generated by a variety of theoretical models.

The model was estimated with 6, 8, and 10 lags of the endogenous variables included. The likelihood ratio test of hypothesis that the values of the seventh and eighth lag coefficients were jointly equal to zero could be rejected at the 1 percent level; the hypothesis that the values of the ninth and tenth lag coefficients were jointly equal to zero could be rejected at the 10, though not the 5, percent level.[12] Summary results for the 10 lag specification are reported in table D.5. The reported statistics include the F statistics to test the block exogeneity of each variable, the adjusted coefficient of determination ($\bar{R}^2$), and the adjusted Box–Ljung Q statistic for serially correlated errors.

The estimates in table D.5 are appealing in that the adjusted coefficients of determination are high, and the Q statistics are low, indicating an absence of serial correlation in the error terms. (Three of the four reported Qs are insignificant at the 50 percent level.) However, many of the individual F statistics are insignificant, suggesting a high degree of collinearity among the series. Taken at face value, the F statistics imply that the bilateral current account balance, the exchange rate, and Japanese economic activity all cause US economic activity in the sense of Granger–Sims. This is surprising since a priori one might expect USGNP to be the least endogenous, indeed causing the other series, strictly or with feedback.

However, variance decompositions indicate that the bilateral current account balance (BILATCA) is highly endogenous, with its own innovations accounting for only 10 percent of forecast variance at 12 quarters. Both US and Japanese economic activity have strong feedback effects on BILATCA,

---

11. Specifically, real gross national product is used as the measure of the national income. The Japanese data come from the Bank of Japan, *Economic Statistics Annual*, various issues. The US data are from the Department of Commerce, *Survey of Current Business*, various issues. All series were deseasonalized at the source. The yen–dollar rate is the quarterly period average found in the IMF, *International Financial Statistics*.

12. All regressions included a trend term, and dummy variables for the oil-shock period. The chi-square statistic for the exclusion of lags 9 and 10 was 45.72 (32 degrees of freedom), significance level 0.055.

Table D.5　VAR summary results

Dependent Variables	Independent Variables (10 LAGS)					
	BILATCA	YENDOL	JGNP	USGNP	$\bar{R}^2$	Q
BILATCA	0.72	1.74	1.46	0.28	.960	20.20
YENDOL	1.67	8.05[a]	1.90	2.87[b]	.960	19.68
JGNP	1.19	1.16	3.09[b]	1.12	.940	23.34
USGNP	3.60[b]	7.30[a]	4.30[b]	10.39[a]	.998	14.44

Note: Superscripts indicate levels of statistical significance for the null hypothesis that all lagged coefficients of the variable are jointly equal to zero.
a. Null hypothesis can be rejected at the 1 percent level.
b. Null hypothesis can be rejected at the 5 percent level.
c. Null hypothesis can be rejected at the 10 percent level.

with USGNP predominant. Similarly, the exchange rate, YENDOL, is quite endogenous, with own innovations accounting for less than one-third forecast variance at four quarters. Again, both Japanese and US economic activity have a substantial impact on the exchange rate, although USGNP is causally prior, which is consistent with both the regression results in table D.5 and the BILATCA variance decompositions.

Likewise, US economic activity has significant feedback effects on JGNP, although, again, a statistically significant effect was not found in table D.5. And the variance decomposition for USGNP indicates significant feedback effects from JGNP. Overall, the decompositions indicate that each of the four series strongly influences the others, with USGNP playing a prominent role.

Simulation Exercises

For simulation purposes, a set of relatively diffuse Bayesian priors were imposed on the lagged coefficients of the endogenous variables to mitigate the problem of overparameterization and forecast drift. Given the large number of parameters to be estimated, it is generally quite difficult to obtain a precise estimate of each coefficient; this is especially true when the sample period is relatively limited. A typical response to the degrees-of-freedom problem is to limit the number of regressors; in autoregressive models this usually means dropping lags, in effect setting their coefficients equal to zero with certainty. The problem with this approach is that the exclusion of variables with nonzero coefficients (for example, the selection of too short lag lengths in autoregressive systems) will in general lead to biased estimation of the included variables. An alternative strategy is to specify a more inclusive model, and use Bayesian priors to shape the pattern of coefficients.

In the case of autoregressive systems, for instance, the coefficients on long lag terms could be assigned prior distributions with mean zero, and standard deviations an inverse function of lag length (that is, as the lag lengthens, the prior collapses around zero). In this way, the structure of the model is informed by the underlying data. The Bayesian approach is adopted here.[13]

The VAR models were further used to simulate the effects of alternative fiscal policies on the Japanese current account. For the global current account estimates, the endogenous variables, each with eight lagged values, were the current account, domestic absorption, partner income, and the exchange rate. The real interest rate (eight lagged values), and the government budget deficit (ten lagged values), were included as exogenous variables.[14]

For the bilateral current account simulations, the endogenous variables were the bilateral current account balance, US and Japanese GNP, and the exchange rate. The government (both central and local) fiscal deficits were regarded as exogenous policy instruments.

It should be reiterated that the numerical estimates obtained from the simulations are conditional on the specification, and prior used to estimate the model. Nonetheless, the qualitative results are robust.

---

13. Specifically, in this paper, the prior distributions on the lags of the endogenous variables were independent normal; the mean of the first lagged value of the dependent variable was set equal to the coefficient estimated in the VAR reported in the previous section. The means of all other lagged values were set equal to zero. The standard deviation of the prior distribution of the lag of variable y_j in equation y_k is given by

$$S(i,j,k) = [hg(i)f(j,k)] \, s_j/s_k$$

where s_j, s_k are the standard errors of a univariate autoregression of variables j, and k. (This scaling by standard errors adjusts for differences in magnitudes of the variables in the system). The function $g(i)$ was specified as $g(i) = i^{-d}$. A variety of values for h, d, $f(j,k)$ were tried; no configuration changed the qualitative simulation results, although the quantitative outcomes were marginally affected. The results reported herein were obtained with h, d, $f(j,k)$ set equal to 0.2, 1.0, and 0.5, with the exception of the baseline scenario which was estimated with the tighter prior implied by 0.1, 2.0, 0.5. The lag lengths on the exogenous variables were chosen by calculating F tests for different lag intervals, and scanning the individual estimated coefficients for large values. In the case of the government deficit, large and statistically significant coefficients were obtained for some of the later lags, so the lag length was extended to 10 quarters to guard against misspecification bias.

14. The fiscal deficit includes both central and local government deficits. The data come from the Bank of Japan, *Economics Statistics Annual*. The real interest rate was modeled in a number of ways to generate the counterfactual data for simulations; it was found to most closely approximate an AR(1) process, which in turn was used to generate the data for the reported simulations.

References

Ackley, Gardner and Hiromitsu Ishi. 1976. "Fiscal, Monetary, and Related Policies." In *Asia's New Giant*, edited by Hugh Patrick and Henry Rosovsky, 153–247. Washington: The Brookings Institution.

Agarwala, Ramgopal. 1986. "Resource Requirements for Restoring Growth." In *African Debt and Financing*, SPECIAL REPORT 5, edited by Carol Lancaster and John Williamson. Washington: Institute for International Economics.

Amano, Akihiro. 1987. "The Effectiveness of Exchange Rate Adjustments." Paper presented to the United States–Japan Consultative Group on International Monetary Affairs, Washington, 2–3 October.

American Chamber of Commerce in Japan. 1986. *United States–Japan Trade White Paper*. Tokyo.

Anderson, Kym and Rod Tyers. 1987. "Japan's Agricultural Policy in International Perspective." *Journal of the Japanese and International Economies* 1 (June): 131–46.

Ando, Albert and Alan J. Auerbach. 1987. "The Cost of Capital in the U.S. and Japan: A Comparison." *NBER Working Paper* 2286.

Ando, Albert and Arthur Kennickell. 1985. "How Much (or little) Life Cycle is There in Micro Data? The Cases of the U.S. and Japan." Unpublished paper. Photocopy.

Arkin, William M. and David Chappell. 1985. "Raising the Stakes in the Pacific." *World Policy Journal* 2:481–500.

Aw, Bee-Yan. 1983. "The Interpretation of Cross-Section Regression Tests of the Heckscher–Ohlin Theorem with Many Goods and Factors." *Journal of International Economics* 14:166–7.

Balassa, Bela. 1964a. "The Purchasing Power Parity Doctrine: A Reappraisal." *Journal of Political Economy* 72:584–596.

———. 1964b. *Trade Prospects for Developing Countries*. Homewood, IL: Richard D. Irwin.

———. 1965. "Trade Liberalization and 'Revealed' Comparative Advantage." *Manchester School* 33:99–123.

———. 1977a. "Effects of Commercial Policy on International Trade, the Location of Production, and Factor Movements." In *The International Allocation of Economic Activity*, edited by Bertil Ohlin, Per-Ove Hesselborn, and Per Magnus Wijkman, 230–58. London: Macmillan & Co.

———. 1977b. " 'Revealed' Comparative Advantage Revisited: An Analysis of Relative Export Shares of the Industrial Countries, 1953–1971." *Manchester School* 45:327–44.

———. 1979. "The Changing Pattern of Comparative Advantage in Manufactured Goods." *Review of Economics and Statistics* 61 (May): 259–66.

———. 1986a. "Comparative Advantage in Manufactured Goods: A Reappraisal." *Review of Economics and Statistics* 68 (May): 315–319.

———. 1986b. "Intra-Industry Specialization: A Cross-Country Analysis." *European Economic Review* 30:27–42.

———. 1986c. "Japanese Trade Policies Towards Developing Countries." *Journal of International Economic Integration* 1 (Spring): 1–15.

———. 1986d. "Japan's Trade Policies." *Weltwirtschaftliches Archiv* 122:745–90.

Balassa, Bela, Gerardo M. Bueno, Pedro-Pablo Kuczynski, and Mario Henrique Simonsen. 1986. *Toward Renewed Economic Growth in Latin America*. Mexico City: El Colegio de Mexico; Rio de Janeiro: Fundaçao Getúlio Vargas; Washington: Institute for International Economics.

Balassa, Bela and Constantine Michalopoulos. 1986. "The Extent and the Cost of

Protection in Developed-Developing Country Trade." In *The New Protectionist Threat to World Welfare,* edited by Dominick Salvatore. Amsterdam: North–Holland.

Baldwin, Richard and Paul R. Krugman. 1986. "Market Access and International Competition: A Simulation Study of 16K Random Access Memories." *NBER Working Paper* 1936.

Baumol, William J. 1986. "Productivity Growth, Convergence, and Welfare: What the Long-Run Data Show." *American Economic Review* 76 (December): 1072–1085.

Belsley, David A., Edwin Kuh, and Roy E. Welsch. 1980. *Regression Diagnostics.* New York: Wiley.

Bergsten, C. Fred and William R. Cline. 1987. *The United States–Japan Economic Problem,* POLICY ANALYSES IN INTERNATIONAL ECONOMICS 13. Washington: Institute for International Economics.

Bergsten, C. Fred, Shafiqul Islam, and C. Randall Henning. 1987. *The United States as a Net Debtor,* POLICY ANALYSES IN INTERNATIONAL ECONOMICS. Washington: Institute for International Economics. Forthcoming.

Blades, Derek. 1983. "Alternative Measures of Saving." *OECD Occasional Studies.* Paris: Organization for Economic Cooperation and Development.

Blades, Derek and John M. Sturm. 1982. "The Concept of Measurement of Savings: The United States and Other Industrialized Countries." In *Saving and Government Policy,* Federal Reserve Bank of Boston Conference Series, No. 25.

Borrus, Michael, James E. Millstein, and John Zysman. 1983. "Trade and Development in the Semi-Conductor Industry: Japanese Challenge and American Response." In *American Industry in International Competition: Government Policies and Corporate Strategies,* edited by John Zysman and Laura Tyson, 142–248. Ithaca, NY: Cornell University Press.

Boskin, Michael J. and John M. Roberts. 1986. "A Closer Look at Saving Rates in the United States and Japan." Paper prepared for Japan Ministry of Finance–American Enterprise Institute Conference, Washington, 9–10 April.

Branson, William H. and Nicolaos Monoyios. 1977. "Factor Inputs in U.S. Trade." *Journal of International Economics* 7:111–131.

Brodin, Anders and Derek Blades. 1986. "The OECD Compatible Trade and Production Data Base, 1970–1983." *Working Paper* 31 (May), OECD Department of Economics and Statistics. Paris: Organization for Economic Cooperation and Development.

Bronfenbrenner, Martin and Yasukichi Yasuba. 1987. "Economic Welfare." In *The Political Economy of Japan.* Vol. 1, *The Domestic Transformation,* edited by Kozo Yamamura and Yasukichi Yasuba, 93–136. Stanford, CA: Stanford University Press.

Brown, Harold. 1987. *U.S.–Japan Relations: Technology, Economics and Security.* New York: Carnegie Council on Ethics and International Affairs.

Brzezinski, Zbigniew. 1986. *Game Plan,* Boston: Atlantic Monthly Press.

Calder, Kent F. 1982. "Opening Japan." *Foreign Policy Review* (Summer): 82–97.

Chenery, Hollis B. 1960. "Patterns of Industrial Growth." *American Economic Review* 50 (September): 624–54.

Chenery, Hollis B., Sherman Robinson, and Moshe Syrquin. 1986. *Industrialization and Growth: A Comparative Analysis.* New York: Academic Press.

Christelow, Dorothy. 1985–1986. "Japan's Intangible Barriers to Trade in Manufactures." *Federal Reserve Bank of New York, Quarterly Review* (Winter): 11–18.

Cohen, Stephen D. 1985. *Uneasy Partnership: Competition and Conflicts in U.S.–Japanese Trade Relations.* Cambridge, MA: Ballinger.

Collis, David J. 1987. "The Machine Tool Industry and Industrial Policy 1955–82." Harvard University Graduate School of Business Administration, February. Photocopy.

Corden, W. Max. 1987. "Protection and Liberalization: A Review of Analytical Issues." IMF, *Occasional Paper* 54 (August), Washington.

Dixit, Avinash. 1987. "Hysteresis, Import Penetration, and Exchange Rate Pass-through." Princeton University, September. Photocopy.

Doi, Teruo. 1986. "The Role of Intellectual Property Law in Bilateral Licensing Transactions between Japan and the United States." In *Law and Trade Issues of the Japanese Economy: American and Japanese Perspectives,* edited by Gary R. Saxonhouse and Kozo Yamamura, 157–87. Seattle: University of Washington Press.

Dore, Ronald. 1986. "Protection in Japan: The Role of Domestic Institutions." Paper prepared for the Kiel Conference on Free Trade in the World Economy: Towards an Opening of Markets, 24–26 June.

Dreyfuss, Joel. 1987. "How Japan Picks America's Brains." *Fortune,* 21 December.

Drucker, Peter F. 1987. "Japan's Choice." *Foreign Affairs* 65 (Summer): 973–1041.

Eads, George C. and Kozo Yamamura. 1987. "The Future of Japanese Industrial Policy." In *The Political Economy of Japan.* Vol. 1, *The Domestic Transformation,* edited by Kozo Yamamura and Yasukichi Yasuba, 423–68. Stanford, CA: Stanford University Press.

Economic Commission on Latin America and the Caribbean. 1987. "Preliminary Overview on the Latin American Economy 1987." December.

European Communities Commission. 1985a. *Study on EC Wines and Liquor Exports to Japan.* Prepared for the Commission by PA International Consulting Services, Ltd., Tokyo.

————. 1985b. *Analysis of the Relations between the Community and Japan.* Communication to the Council, COM (85) 574 final, Brussels, 15 October.

Feige, Edgar L. and Douglas K. Pearce. 1979. "The Casual Causal Relationship Between Money and Income: Some Caveats for Time Series Analysis," *The Review of Economics and Statistics* 61:521–533.

First Maekawa Report. See *Report of the Advisory Group on Economic Structural Adjustment.*

First, Harry. 1986. "Japan's Antitrust Policy: Impact on Import Competition." In *Fragile Interdependence: Economic Issues in U.S.–Japanese Trade and Investment,* edited by Thomas A. Pugel and Robert G. Hawkins, Chapter 3. Lexington, MA: Lexington Books.

————. 1987. "Structural Antitrust Rules and International Competition: The Case of Depressed Industries." *New York University Law Review* (November): 1301–57.

Fitchett, Delbert A. 1988. "A Sunset Industry in the Land of the Rising Sun? Agriculture and Agricultural Protectionism in Japan—A Survey Paper." World Bank, Washington. Photocopy.

Frankel, Jeffrey A. 1984. *The Yen–Dollar Agreement: Liberalizing Japanese Capital Markets,* POLICY ANALYSES IN INTERNATIONAL ECONOMICS 9. Washington: Institute for International Economics.

Fukukawa, Shinji. 1987. "A New Industrial Structure: MITI's Policies Toward the 21st Century." *Speaking of Japan* 7 (January): 1–10.

Gerschenkron, Alexander. 1952. "Economic Backwardness in Historical Perspective." In *The Progress of Underdeveloped Areas,* edited by Bert F. Hoselitz. Chicago: University of Chicago Press.

Geweke, John, Richard Meese, and Warren Dent. 1983. "Comparing Alternative Tests of Causality in Temporal Systems." *Journal of Econometrics* 21:161–194.

Government of Japan. 1986. "On the Outline of Procedures for the Promotion of Economic Structural Adjustment." Tokyo, 1 May.

Granger, Clive W. J. 1969. "Investigating Causal Relations by Econometric Models and Cross Spectral Methods." *Econometrica* 37:424–438.

Greenberg, Edward and Charles E. Webster, Jr. 1983. *Advanced Econometrics: A Bridge to the Literature.* New York: Wiley.

Hamada, Koichi, and Kazumasa Iwata. 1985. "The Significance of Different Saving Ratios for the Current Account." Unpublished paper, October. Photocopy.

Harvey, A. C. 1981. *The Econometric Analysis of Time Series.* Deddington, Oxford: Philip Allan.

Hayashi, Fumio. 1985. "Taxes and Corporate Investment in Japanese Manufacturing." *NBER Working Paper* 1753.

———. 1986. "Why is Japan's Saving Rate Apparently So High?" In *NBER Macroeconomics Annual 1986*, 147–210. Cambridge, MA: National Bureau of Economic Research.

Hayashi, Fumio, Takatoshi Ito, and Joel Slemrod. 1988. "Housing Finance Imperfections and National Saving: A Comparative Simulations Analysis of the U.S. and Japan." *Journal of the Japanese and International Economies.* Forthcoming.

Henderson, Dan F. 1986. "Access to the Japanese Market: Some Aspects of Foreign Exchange Controls and Banking Law." In *Law and Trade Issues of the Japanese Economy: American and Japanese Perspectives,* edited by Gary R. Saxonhouse and Kozo Yamamura, 131–56. Seattle: University of Washington Press.

Hill, Hal and Brian Johns. 1985. "The Role of Direct Foreign Investment in Developing East Asian Countries." *ASEAN–Australian Working Papers* 18.

Hillman, Jimmye S. and Robert A. Rothenberg. 1985. "Wider Implications of Protecting Japan's Rice Farmers." *The World Economy* (March): 43–62.

Homma, M. et al. 1986. "The Debt Neutrality Hypothesis." Economic Planning Agency.

Honma, Masayashi and Yujiro Hayami. 1986. "Structure of Agricultural Protection in Industrial Countries." *Journal of International Economics* (February): 115–30.

Horioka, Charles Yuji. 1984. "The Applicability of the Life-Cycle Hypothesis of Saving to Japan." *Kyoto University Economic Review* 54:31–56.

———. 1985a. "The Importance of Saving for Education in Japan." *Kyoto University Economic Review* 55:41–78.

———. 1985b. "Household Saving in Japan: The Importance of Target Saving for Education and Housing." Paper prepared for Japan Economic Seminar. Washington, 21 September.

———. 1986. "Tenure Choice and Housing Demand in Japan." Unpublished paper. Photocopy.

———. 1987. "The Cost of Marriages and Marriage-Related Saving in Japan." *Kyoto University Economic Review* 57:47–58.

———. 1988. "Housing Demand and Saving for Housing in Japan." Paper presented at joint TCER–NBER Conference, "Saving: Its Determinants and Macroeconomic Implications." Tokyo, 9–10 January.

Horiye, Yasuhiro. 1987. "Export Behavior of Japanese Firms." *Monetary and Economic Studies, Bank of Japan* 5:33–104.

Horiye, Yasuhiro, Sadao Naniwa, and Suzu Ishihara. 1987. "The Changes of Japanese Business Cycles." *Monetary and Economic Studies, Bank of Japan* 5:49–100.

Hume, David. 1955. *An Inquiry Concerning Human Understanding.* Indianapolis: Bobbs–Merrill.

Ihori, Toshihiro. 1987. "The Size of Government Spending and the Private Sector's Evaluation." *Journal of the Japanese and International Economies* 1:82–96.

Inoguchi, Kuniko. 1987. "Prosperity Without the Amenities." In *The Trade Crisis: How Will Japan Respond,* edited by Kenneth B. Pyle, 61–70. Seattle: Society for Japanese Studies.

Ishikawa, Tsuneo and Kazuo Ueda. 1984. "The Bonus Payment System and Japanese

Personal Savings." In *The Economic Analysis of the Japanese Firm,* edited by M. Aoki. Amsterdam: Elsevier Science Publishers.

Jaikumar, Ramchandran. 1986. "Post Industrial Manufacturing." *Harvard Business Review* (November–December): 69–76.

Japan Economic Institute. 1987. *Japan's Expanding U.S. Manufacturing Presence.* Washington, December.

Johnson, Chalmers. 1982. *MITI and the Japanese Miracle: The Growth of Industrial Policy, 1925–1975.* Stanford: Stanford University Press.

Joint Economic Committee, US Congress. 1986. "Japanese Import Barriers to U.S. Agricultural Products"; "The Common Agricultural Policy of the European Community and its Implications for U.S. Agricultural Trade." "Studies Prepared for the Use of the Republican Members of the Joint Economic Committee, Congress of the United States by the Congressional Research Service, Library of Congress." Washington: US Government Printing Office.

————. 1987. "Cracking the Japanese Market: Hearing before the Subcommittee on Trade, Productivity, and Economic Growth of the Joint Economic Committee, Congress of the United States." Washington: US Government Printing Office.

Kase, Hideaki and Garrett Scalera. 1981. "The Defense of Japan: An Alternative View from Tokyo." *International Briefing* 9. Washington: The Heritage Foundation.

Kawai, Masahiro. 1987. "The Japanese Demand for Long-Term Assets in the 1980s." Paper presented to the United States–Japan Consultative Group on International Monetary Affairs, Washington, 2–3 October.

Kawai, Masahiro and Hirohiko Okumura. 1987. "Japan's Portfolio Investment in Foreign Securities." Paper presented to the United States–Japan Consultative Group on International Monetary Affairs, Washington, 2–3 October.

Kimura, Hiroshi. 1986. "The Soviet Military Buildup: Its Impact on Japan and Its Aims." In *The Soviet Far East Military Buildup,* edited by Richard H. Solomon and Masataka Kosaka. Dover, MA: Auburn House.

Kiuchi, Takashi. 1987. "The Responses of Japanese Industries to Recent Currency Realignments." Paper presented to the United States–Japan Consultative Group on International Monetary Affairs, Washington, 2–3 October.

KKC Brief No. 29. 1985. "Manufactured Import Markets: Open or Closed?" Keizai Koho Center, Japan Institute for Social and Economic Affairs. Tokyo, July.

Kodama, Fumio. 1986. "Technological Diversification of Japanese Industry." *Science* 233:291–96.

Kojima, Kiyoshi. 1985. "The Allocation of Japanese Direct Foreign Investment and its Evolution in Asia." *Hitotsubashi Journal of Economics* 26 (December): 99–116.

Kosaka, Masataka. 1986. "Theater Nuclear Weapons and Japan's Defense Policy." In *The Soviet Far East Military Buildup,* edited by Richard H. Solomon and Masataka Kosaka. Dover, MA: Auburn House.

Krafcik, John. 1986. "Learning from NUMMI." Internal working paper, International Motor Vehicle Program, Massachusetts Institute of Technology. Photocopy.

Krause, Lawrence B. 1986. "Does a Yen Valued at 100 per Dollar Make Any Sense." Unpublished paper. Washington: The Brookings Institution. Photocopy.

Kravis, Irving B., Alan Heston, and Robert Summers. 1982. *World Product and Income.* Baltimore and London: The Statistical Office of the United Nations and the World Bank.

Krugman, Paul R. 1984. "The U.S. Response to Foreign Industrial Targeting." *Brookings Papers on Economic Activity, 1984,* 77–131.

————. 1986. "Is the Japan Problem Over?" Paper presented at the Conference on Trade Frictions, New York University Center for Japan–U.S. Business and Economic Studies, New York.

————. 1988. "Sustainability and the Decline of the Dollar." In *External Deficits and the Dollar,* edited by Ralph Bryant et al. Washington: The Brookings Institution.

Krugman, Paul R. and Richard E. Baldwin. 1987. "The Persistence of the U.S. Trade Deficit." *Brookings Papers on Economic Activity, 1987* 1:1–56.

Kuznets, Simon. 1952. "Long Term Changes in the National Income of the United States of America since 1870." In *Income and Wealth of the United States: Trends and Structure,* edited by Simon Kuznets. *Income and Wealth Series II,* International Association for Research in Income and Wealth. Cambridge: Bowes and Bowes.

Landau, Ralph and Nathan Rosenberg, eds. 1986. *The Positive Sum Strategy: Harnessing Technology for Economic Growth.* Washington: National Academy Press.

Lawrence, Robert Z. 1987. "Imports in Japan: Closed Markets or Minds?" *Brookings Papers on Economic Activity, 1987* 2:517–54.

Leamer, Edward E. 1984. *The Sources of International Comparative Advantage.* Cambridge: Massachusetts Institute of Technology Press.

————. 1987. "Measures of Openness." *UCLA Working Paper* 447. University of California, Los Angeles.

Leamer, Edward E. and Harry P. Bowen. 1981. "Cross-Section Tests of the Heckscher–Ohlin Theorem: Comment." *American Economic Review* 71:1040–43.

Lessard, Donald R. and John Williamson. 1985. *Financial Intermediation Beyond the Debt Crisis,* POLICY ANALYSES IN INTERNATIONAL ECONOMICS 12. Washington: Institute for International Economics.

Lim, Hua Sing. 1985. "Singapore–Japan Trade Frictions: A Study of Japanese Non-Tariff Barriers." University of Singapore, Department of Japanese Studies, September.

————. 1987. "Singapore–Japan Trade Friction." *ASEAN Economic Bulletin* 4 (July): 9–29.

Lincoln, Edward J. 1988. *Japan Facing Economic Maturity.* Washington: The Brookings Institution.

Lipsey, Robert E. and Irving B. Kravis. 1987. "Is the U.S. a Spendthrift Nation?" *NBER Working Paper* 2274.

Lipsey, Robert E. and Merle Yahr Weiss. 1974. "The Structure of Ocean Transport Changes." In *Explorations in Economic Research,* 162–193. Cambridge, MA: National Bureau of Economic Research.

Litterman, Robert B. and Laurence Weiss. 1985. "Money, Real Interest Rates, and Output: A Reinterpretation of Post-War U.S. Data." *Econometrica* 53:129–156.

Loopesko, Bonnie E. and Robert A. Johnson. 1987. "Realignment of the Yen–Dollar Exchange Rate: Aspects of the Adjustment Process in Japan." *International Finance Discussion Paper* 311. International Finance Division, Board of Governors of the Federal Reserve System, Washington.

Lütkepohl, Helmut. 1982. "Non-Causality Due to Omitted Variables," *Journal of Econometrics* 19:367–378.

MacIntosh, Malcolm. 1987. *Japan Re-Armed.* New York: St. Martin's.

Maizels, Alfred. 1963. *Industrial Growth and World Trade.* London: National Institute of Economic and Social Research.

Makin, John H. 1985. "Saving Rates in Japan and the United States: The Roles of Tax Policy and Other Factors." Paper prepared for the Savings Forum, Philadelphia, 2–3 May.

Marris, Stephen. 1987. *Deficits and the Dollar,* POLICY ANALYSES IN INTERNATIONAL ECONOMICS 14 (revised). Washington: Institute for International Economics.

Marston, Richard C. 1986. "Real Exchange Rates and Productivity Growth in the United States and Japan." *NBER Working Paper* 1922.

Maskus, Keith E. 1983. "Evidence on Shifts in the Determinants of the Structure of U.S. Manufacturing Foreign Trade, 1958–1976." *Review of Economics and Statistics* 65:415–422.

McKinnon, Ronald I. and Kenichi Ohno. 1986. "Getting the Exchange Rate Right: Insular vs. Open Economies." Paper presented at the American Economic Association annual meeting, New Orleans, 28–30 December.

———. 1987. "Purchasing Power Parity as a Monetary Standard." Unpublished paper, Stanford University. Photocopy.

Ministry of International Trade and Industry, Japan. 1986. *White Paper on International Trade, 1986.* Tokyo, September.

———. 1987. *White Paper on International Trade, 1987.* Tokyo, June.

Morishima, Michio. 1982. *Why has Japan "Succeeded"? Western Technology and the Japanese Ethos.* Cambridge: Cambridge University Press.

Mundell, Robert A. 1987. "A New Deal on Exchange Rates." Paper presented at the Japan–U.S. Symposium, Tokyo, 29–30 January.

Murakami, Yasusuke and Yutaka Kosai, eds. 1986. *Japan in the Global Community: Its Role and Contribution on the Eve of the 21st Century.* Tokyo: University of Tokyo Press.

Mutoh, Hiromichi. 1988. "The Automotive Industry." In *Industrial Policy of Japan,* edited by Ryutaro Komiya, Masahiro Okuno, and Kotaro Suzumura, 307–31. San Diego: Academic Press.

Nakao, Eiichi. 1988. "Policy Speech by Minister of State for Economic Planning Eiichi Nakao to the 112th Session of the National Diet." Tokyo, 25 January. Photocopy.

Nishihara, Masashi. 1985. "East Asian Security and the Trilateral Countries." *Triangle Paper* 30. New York: New York University Press.

Noguchi, Yukio. 1983. "The Failure of the Government to Perform its Proper Task: A Case Study of Japan." *ORDO* 34:59–70.

Noland, Marcus. 1985. "The Determinants of Comparative Advantage: Empirical Analysis in a Multicountry Time-Series Cross-Section Framework." Ph.D. diss., The Johns Hopkins University.

———. 1987a. "A Cross-Country Model of International Trade Protection." Unpublished paper. Institute for International Economics, Washington. Photocopy.

———. 1987b. "Determinants of the U.S. Current Account." Unpublished paper. Institute for International Economics, Washington. Photocopy.

———. 1988a. "Japanese Household Portfolio Allocation Behavior." *Review of Economics and Statistics* 70 (February): 135–39.

———. 1988b. "Japanese Trade Elasticities and the J-curve." *Review of Economics and Statistics.* Forthcoming.

———. 1988c. "A Note on Comparative Advantage in Services." Unpublished Paper. Institute for International Economics, Washington. Photocopy.

Nomura Research Institute. 1986. *The World Economy and Financial Markets in 1995: Japan's Role and Challenges.* Tokyo: Nomura Research Institute.

Office of Technology Assessment, US Congress. 1988. *Paying the Bill: Manufacturing and America's Trade Deficit.*

Ogura, Seiretsu and Naoyuki Yoshino. 1988. "The Tax System and the Fiscal Investment and Loan System." In *Industrial Policy of Japan,* edited by Ryutaro Komiya, Masahiro Okuno, and Kotaro Suzumura. San Diego: Academic Press.

Ohkawa, Kazushi and Miyohei Shinohara, with Larry Meissner. 1979. "Basic Statistical Tables." In *Patterns of Japanese Economic Development: A Quantitative Appraisal,* edited by Kazushi Ohkawa, Miyohei Shinohara, and Larry Meissner. New Haven: Yale University Press.

Okimoto, Daniel L. 1986. "The Japanese Challenge in High Technology." In *The Positive Sum Strategy: Harnessing Technology for Economic Growth,* edited by Ralph Landau and Nathan Rosenberg, 541–67. Washington: National Academy Press.

———. "Outsider Trading: Coping with Japanese Industrial Organization." In *The Trade Crisis: How Will Japan Respond?,* edited by Kenneth B. Pyle, 85–116. Seattle: Society for Japanese Studies.

Okimoto, Daniel L. and Gary R. Saxonhouse. 1987. "Technology and the Future of the Economy." In *The Political Economy of Japan.* Vol. 1, *The Domestic Transformation,* edited by Kozo Yamamura and Yasukichi Yasuba, 385–419. Stanford, CA: Stanford University Press.

Okita, Saburo, Lal Jayawardena, and Arjun K. Sengupta. 1987. "The Potential for the Japanese Surplus for World Economic Development." Helsinki: World Institute for Development Economics Research.

Okumura, Hirohiko. 1987. "Recent Developments in Japanese Portfolio Investments in Foreign Securities." Paper presented to the United States–Japan Consultative Group on International Monetary Affairs, San Diego, 21–22 February.

Organisation for Economic Cooperation and Development. 1985. *OECD Economic Surveys 1984/1985, Japan.* Paris.

———. 1986a. *OECD Economic Surveys 1986/1987, Japan.* Paris.

———. 1986b. *Urban Policy in Japan.* Paris.

———. 1987. *National Policies and Agricultural Trade: Japan.* Paris.

Ozaki, Robert J. 1984. "How Japanese Industrial Policy Works." In *The Industrial Policy Debate,* edited by Chalmers Johnson, 47–70. San Francisco: Institute for Contemporary Studies.

Ozawa, Teretomo. 1986. "Japanese Policy Toward Foreign Multinationals: Implications for Trade and Competitiveness." In *Fragile Interdependence: Economic Issues in U.S.–Japanese Trade and Investment,* edited by Thomas A. Pugel, 141–62. Lexington, MA: Lexington Books.

Pangetsu, Mari. 1980. "Japanese and Other Foreign Investment in the ASEAN Countries." *Research Paper* 73. Australia–Japan Research Centre.

Planning Subcommittee of the Coordination Committee, Industrial Structure Council of Japan. 1986. "An Outlook for Japan's Industrial Society Toward the Twenty-First Century." Tokyo.

Policy Recommendations of the Economic Council—Action for Economic Restructuring ("second Maekawa Report"). 1987. Economic Council, Tokyo, 14 May.

Porter, Michael E. 1987. "De-industrialization: Problem or Opportunity?" Harvard University Business School. Photocopy.

Press, Frank. 1987. "Technological Competition and the Western Alliance." In *A High Technology Gap? Europe, America and Japan,* edited by Andrew J. Pierre, 11–43. New York: Council on Foreign Relations.

Prestowitz, Clyde V. Jr. 1988. *Trading Places.* New York: Basic Books.

Pyle, Kenneth P. 1987. "In Pursuit of a Grand Design: Nakasone Betwixt the Past and the Future." In *The Trade Crisis: How Will Japan Respond?,* edited by Kenneth P. Pyle, 5–32. Seattle: Society for Japanese Studies.

Rapp, William V. 1986. "Japan's Invisible Barriers to Trade." In *Fragile Interdependence: Economic Issues in U.S.–Japanese Trade and Investment,* edited by Thomas A. Pugel and Robert G. Hawkins, Chap. 2. Lexington, MA: Lexington Books.

Ray, G. F. 1987. "Labour Costs in Manufacturing." *National Institute Economic Review* (June): 71–74.

Reed, Robert F. 1983. *The U.S.–Japan Alliance: Sharing the Burden of Defense.* Washington: National Defense University Press.

Reich, Michael R., Yasuo Endo, and C. Peter Timmer. 1986. "Agriculture: The Political Economy of Structural Change." In *America versus Japan,* edited by Thomas K. McCraw, Chap. 5. Boston: Harvard Business School Press.

Report of the Advisory Group on Economic Structural Adjustment for International Harmony ("first Maekawa Report"). 1986. Tokyo, 7 April.

Resolving the Global Economic Crisis: After Wall Street. 1987. A Statement by Thirty-three Economists from Thirteen Countries. SPECIAL REPORT 6. Washington: Institute for International Economics.

Sanchez, Aurora. 1987. "Non-Tariff Barriers and Trade in ASEAN." *ASEAN Economic Bulletin* 4 (July): 1–8.

Sargent, Thomas J. 1979. *Macroeconomic Theory.* Orlando, FL: Academic Press.

Sato, Kazuo. 1985. "Japan's Saving and Investment." In *Japan's Contemporary Political Economy and Future Prospects,* edited by Kozo Yamamura and Yasukichi Yasuba. Forthcoming.

Sato, Kazuo. 1987. "The Wealth Target and Saving: Theory and Japanese Evidence." Unpublished paper. Photocopy.

Saxonhouse, Gary R. 1983a. "The Micro- and Macro-Economics of Foreign Sales to Japan." In *Trade Policies in the 1980s,* edited by William R. Cline, 259–304. Washington: Institute for International Economics.

————. 1983b. "What is All this About 'Industrial Targeting' in Japan?" *World Economy* (September): 253–74.

————. 1985. "What's Wrong with Japanese Trade Structure." *Seminar Discussion Paper* 166. Research Seminar in International Economics, University of Michigan.

————. 1986. "What is Wrong with the Japanese Trade Structure?" *Pacific Economic Papers* (July).

Saxonhouse, Gary R., and Robert M. Stern. 1988. "An Analytical Survey of Formal and Informal Barriers to International Trade and Investment in the United States, Canada, and Japan." *Seminar Discussion Paper* 215. Research Seminar in International Economics, University of Michigan.

Schultze, Charles L. 1983. "Industrial Policy: A Dissent." *The Brookings Review* (Fall): 3–12.

Scott, Bruce R. 1985. "National Strategies: Key to International Competition." In *U.S. Competitiveness in the World Economy,* edited by Bruce R. Scott and George C. Lodge. Boston: Harvard Business School Press.

————. 1987. "U.S. Competitiveness in the World Economy: An Update." Paper presented at the Workshop on Competitiveness, Harvard Business School, 12–18 July.

Second Maekawa Report. See *Policy Recommendations of the Economic Council.*

Shibuya, Hiroshi. 1988. "Japan's Household Savings: A Life-Cycle Model with Implicit Annuity Contract and Rational Expectations." Unpublished paper. IMF, Washington. February.

Shinjo, Koji. 1988. "The Computer Industry." In *Industrial Policy of Japan,* edited by Ryutaro Komiya, Masahiro Okuno, and Kotaro Suzumura, 333–65. San Diego: Academic Press.

Shinohara, Miyohei. 1982. *Industrial Growth, Trade and Dynamic Patterns in the Japanese Economy.* Tokyo: University of Tokyo Press.

Shoven, John B. 1985. "A Comparison of the Taxation of Capital Income in the United States and Japan." Unpublished paper. Stanford University. Photocopy.

Shoven, John B. and Toshiaki Tachibanaki. 1985. "The Taxation of Income from Capital in Japan." Paper presented at the Center for Economic Policy Research Conference on Government Policy Towards Industry in the United States and Japan. Stanford, California, 2–3 May.

Sims, Christopher A. 1972. "Money, Income & Causality." *American Economic Review* 62:540–552.

————. 1980. "Macroeconomics and Reality." *Econometrica* 48:1–48.

Staiger, Robert W., Alan V. Deardorff, and Robert M. Stern. 1987. "The Effects of Protection on the Factor Content of Japanese and American Foreign Trade." Paper presented at the annual meeting of the American Economic Association, Chicago, 27–29 December.

Stern, Robert M. and Keith E. Maskus. 1981. "Determinants of the Structure of U.S. Foreign Trade, 1958–1976." *Journal of International Economics* 11:207–224.

Sullivan, Leonard Jr. 1981. "The Real Long-Range Defense Dilemma: Burden Sharing." *Armed Forces Journal International* (October): 56–90.

Summers, Robert and Alan Heston. 1984. "Improved International Comparisons of Real Product and Its Composition." *Review of Income and Wealth,* Series 30 (June): 207–60.

Suzuki, Yoshio. 1987. "An International Monetary System for Restoring World Economic Order." *NIRA* (June): 55–61.

Symposium. See Landau and Rosenberg.

Tachi, Ryuichiro, et al. 1985. "The 'Softization' of the Japanese Economy." *Japanese Economic Studies* (Spring): 67–104.

Takenaka, Heizo. 1986. "Economic Incentives for Industrial Investment: Japanese Experience." Institute of Fiscal and Monetary Policy, Ministry of Finance, Government of Japan. February.

Takeshita, Noboru. 1988. "Policy Speech by Prime Minister Noboru Takeshita to the 112th Session of the National Diet." Tokyo, 25 January. Photocopy.

Timmer, C. Peter and Michael R. Reich. 1983. "Japan and the U.S. Trading Shots over Beef and Oranges." *Challenge* (September–October): 18–24.

Torii, Yasuhiko. 1985. "The Real Causes of Economic Friction: Industrial Structures, Industrial Policy, Distrust of Japan." *Boeko to Kanzei* (August): 30–33.

Tow, William T. 1986. "Japan: Security Role and Continuing Policy Debates." In *Asian Pacific Security,* edited by Young Whan Kihl and Lawrence E. Grinter. Boulder, CO: Lynn Rienner.

Tyson, Laura and John Zysman. 1983. "American Industry in International Competition." In *American Industry in International Competition: Government Policies and Corporate Strategies,* edited by John Zysman and Laura Tyson, 15–59. Ithaca, NY: Cornell University Press.

Ueda, Kazuo. 1985. "The Japanese Current Account Surplus and Fiscal Policy in Japan and the U.S." Paper prepared for the International Symposium on "Current Policy Issues in the United States and Japan" (NBER-MOF). Tokyo, 21–22 October.

————. 1987. "Japanese Capital Outflows: 1970 to 1986." Unpublished paper. Osaka University, August.

Uekusa, Masu. 1985. "Industrial Organization: The 1970s to the Present." Unpublished paper. Photocopy.

UN Conference on Trade and Development. 1982. *Protectionism and Structural Adjustment in the Agricultural and Other Commodity Sectors.* Geneva, 18 February.

United States Department of Defense. 1987. *Report on Allied Contributions to the Common Defense: A Report to the U.S. Congress by the Secretary of Defense,* April.

United States Department of Education. 1987. *Japanese Education Today.* Washington: US Government Printing Office.

United States Trade Representative. 1982. *Japanese Barriers to U.S. Trade and Recent Japanese Government Trade Initiatives.* Washington: U.S. Government Printing Office.

——. 1985. *Annual Report on National Trade Estimates, 1985.* Washington: U.S. Government Printing Office.

——. 1986. *1986 Report on Foreign Trade Barriers.* Washington: U.S. Government Printing Office.

——. 1987. *1987 National Trade Estimate Report on Foreign Trade Barriers.* Washington: U.S. Government Printing Office.

Urata, Shujiro. 1983. "Factor Inputs and Japanese Manufacturing Trade Structure." *Review of Economics and Statistics,* 65:678–84.

US–Japan Trade Study Group. 1984. *Progress Report: 1984.* Tokyo, September.

Van den Panhuysen, W. 1985. "Japan's Industrial Policy: From Promotion to Protection." *Tijdschrift voor Economie en Management* 1:45–74.

Vincent, D. P. 1988. "Effects of Agricultural Protection in Japan: An Economy-wide Analysis." Paper prepared for the Global Agricultural Trade Study organized by the Centre for International Economics, Canberra, Australia.

Vogel, Ezra F. 1987. "Japanese Science Policy." Unpublished paper. Harvard University. Photocopy.

Watts, William. 1985. "The United States and Asia: Changing American Expectations." Unpublished paper. Potomac Associates, Washington. Photocopy.

Weil, Frank A. and Norman D. Glick. 1979. "Japan—Is the Market Open? A View of the Japanese Market Drawn From U.S. Corporate Experience." *Law & Policy in International Business* 3:815–907.

White, Halbert. 1980. "A Heteroscedastic Consistent Covariance Matrix Estimator and a Direct Test for Heteroscedaticity." *Econometrica* 47:817–838.

Williamson, John. 1983. *The Exchange Rate System,* POLICY ANALYSES IN INTERNATIONAL ECONOMICS 3. Washington: Institute for International Economics.

World Bank. 1987. *World Development Report, 1987.* Washington: International Bank for Reconstruction and Development.

Woronoff, Jon. 1985. *Inside Japan Inc.* Tokyo: Lotus Press.

Yamamura, Kozo. 1983. "Joint Research in High Technology Industries: A Comparative Study of Japanese and American Antitrust Structure." Paper presented to the Law and Economics Conference, Hawaii, August.

——. 1987. "Shedding the Shackles of Success: Saving Less for Japan's Future." In *The Trade Crisis: How Will Japan Respond?,* edited by Kenneth B. Pyle, 33–60. Seattle: Society for Japanese Studies.

Yamamura, Kozo and Jean Vandenberg. 1986. "Japan's Rapid-Growth Policy on Trial: The Television Case." In *Law and Trade Issues of the Japanese Economy: American and Japanese Perspectives,* edited by Gary R. Saxonhouse and Kozo Yamamura, 238–87. Seattle: University of Washington Press.

Yamawaki, Hideki. 1986. "Exports, Foreign Market Structure, and Profitability in Japanese and U.S. Manufacturing." *Review of Economics and Statistics* 68:618–627.

——. 1988. "The Steel Industry." In *Industrial Policy of Japan,* edited by Ryutaro Komiya, Masahiro Okuno, and Kotaro Suzumura, 281–305. San Diego: Academic Press.

Yoffie, David B. 1986. "Protecting World Markets." In *America versus Japan,* edited by Thomas K. McCraw, 35–76. Boston: Harvard Business School Press.

Yoshikawa, Hiroshi and Fumio Ohtake. 1987. "Postwar Business Cycles in Japan: A Quest for the Right Explanation." *Journal of the Japanese and International Economies* 1: 373–407.

Yoshitomi, Masaru. 1985. "Japan as Capital Exporter and the World Economy." *Group of Thirty Occasional Papers* 18. New York: Group of Thirty.

Zietz, Joachim and Alberto Valdes. 1985. "The Costs of Protectionism to Less-Developed Countries: An Analysis of Selected Agricultural Products." World Bank, Washington. Photocopy.

Index

Brzezinski, Zbigniew, 159
Business cycle
changes in activity of, 136–37

Calder, Kent F., 72, 72 n26
Canada
effect of yen appreciation on, 42–43
Capital formation, 4
Capital investment
human, 209
physical, 209
See also Cost of capital; Replacement
investment
Capital outflow
policy change affecting, 124
Cartels
in depressed industries, 59, 227, 228
Causality, 255–56
tests using Granger-Sims techniques
for, 257–63, 266
See also Macroeconomic variables
Chappell, David, 159
Chenery, Hollis, 239, 239 n2, 240
Christelow, Dorothy, 219 n8, 237
Cline, William R., 69, 70, 146, 239,
240, 241 n8, 243, 246, 250–51
Cohen, Stephen D., 75 n31
Collis, David J., 39 n10
Collusion
among producers, 228–29
Comparative advantage
analysis of high technology products
and, 209–14
estimates of, 193–94
for Japan and United States, 209
regression analysis for manufactured
goods to show, 31–33
revealed, 27–28, 194–209
shifts in, 27–34
Comparative disadvantage, 30–31
Computer industry
financing by MITI for, 39–40
Corden, W. Max, 71
Corporations, public
procurement policies of, 222
Cost of capital, 112–14
Cotton textiles
cartel formed for, 227

Council on Education Reform. See
Education
Credit. See Borrowing, business
Current account
definitions of, 135–36
effect of yen appreciation on, 177–78
factors creating changes in level of,
149–54
Customs
as informal import barrier, 57,
217–18

Data sources
for causality tests, 258
for high technology analysis, 210–14
Deardorff, Alan V., 70, 251 n14
Defense policy
and build-up of Soviet forces, 162–64
and "free-rider" status, 166, 173–74
procurement program under, 164–65
recommendations for changing, 181–
82, 185–86
reliance on United States, 158, 161,
164, 166
spending and equipment under, 160,
165–66
Demand, domestic
as factor in economic growth, 16–21
recommendation to increase, 19
Dent, Warren, 258 n3
Depressed industries, 225–29
changes of output capacity in, 226
collusion among producers in,
228–29
establishment of cartels in, 59,
226, 228
guarantee fund for, 228
import barriers for, 59–60
See also Temporary Measures Law
Development assistance
contributions for official, 166–67
direct grants to specific countries, 169
increase in amounts of, 167–68, 170
obstacles to implementation of,
170–73
pledges and loans to supranational
and regional development
banks, 168

recommendations for program of,
186–89
untied loans to Export-Import Bank
of Japan, 169
See also Japanese Trust Fund; Okita
Plan
Direct foreign investment
changes in volume of, 14
Distribution system
function as import barrier, 61–62,
235–37
Dixit, Avinash, 145
Doi, Teruo, 235
Dollar depreciation
effect on Japanese economy of, 7, 12
Dore, Ronald, 227, 237
Dornbusch, Rudiger, 146
Dreyfuss, Joel, 45 n19
Drucker, Peter F., 75 n31
Dumping
trade actions related to, 60, 231–32

Eads, George C., 40, 41, 42
Education
recommendations for improvement
of, 46–47
See also Research
Elderly population, 20–21, 107
Endaka. See Yen appreciation
Endo, Yasuo, 54, 73
EPA (Economic Planning Agency), 149
Exchange rate
effect of changes in, 136
effect of changes on per capita
income of, 12
effect of trade liberalization on, 184–
85
effect on trade balance, 141–45
factors influencing effect of changes
in, 144–45
theories to calculate targets for, 145–
47
Excise tax
to supplement tariffs, 50
Expectations of future. *See* Life cycle
hypothesis
Export growth
changes in, 13–14, 15, 27
markets and products for, 25
Export-Import Bank of Japan, 169

Export index
and net export index, 193–94
Extraordinary Measures Law for the
Promotion of the Machine Industry,
1956, 39

Feige, Edgar L., 258 n3
Feldstein, Martin, 146
Firm
expected changes in structure of, 47
First, Harry, 229
Fiscal policy, 148–49
differences for individual and
business, 96–98
effect of stimulation by, 150–54
as factor influencing personal saving,
96, 100
recommendations for changes in, 180
reform to adjust degree of saving,
106–07
See also Taxation
Fitchett, Delbert A., 72, 72 n27, 101
Foreign Capital Law of 1950
effect of, 37–38, 40
See also Licensing regulation
Foreign direct investment
acquisition of existing firms, 122–23
differences for developing and
developed countries, 119–22
increase in volume and targets of,
118–19
limitation in Japan of, 37–38
presumed effects of, 123
volume of financial investment, 123–
24
Foreign Exchange Law of 1980
liberalization of controls on capital,
124
Foreign sourcing
level of, 15
Frankel, Jeffrey A., 124 n14

GATT (General Agreement on Tariffs
and Trade)
Government Procurement Code of,
222
recommendations of, 47, 50, 55, 56
Gerschenkron, Alexander, 114
Geweke, John, 258 n3

Income, per capita, 3, 12
Income, retirement
  expectation and effect on saving of,
    88–93
  See also Bequests
Income, untaxed, 93
Industrial capacity
  changes in, 15
  in steel and auto industries, 36–38
Industrial policy
  effect on favored industries under,
    41–42
  role of MITI in, 35–42
Infrastructure development
  recommendations for, 19–20
  See also Quality of life
Inoguchi, Kuniko, 17
Intellectual property
  regulations to protect, 233–35
  See also Patent system; Trademark
    registration
Investment
  in automated equipment, 116–18
  cyclicality in, 125–26, 136
  effect of subsidies on, 114
  measures to provide stability for,
    129–32
  See also Cost of capital; Direct foreign
    investment
Investment, financial, 123–24
Investment rate, 111, 112
  application of Q-theory for, 113
  model estimating factors influen-
    cing, 112
Ishi, Hiromitsu, 216
Ishikawa, Tsuneo, 85, 86
Ito, Takatoshi, 88, 93, 107
Iwata, Kazumasa, 81

Jaikumar, Ramchandran, 117
JAL (Japan Air Lines)
  revenues from sale of, 16
Japan
  changes in composition of output
    in, 118
  comparative advantage for, 209
  effect of yen appreciation on, 42–43
  influence in international community
    of, 166–75, 181
  influence in multilateral development
    banks of, 172–73

See also Leadership, world
Japanese Trust Fund
  soft loans to developing countries,
    169–70
Jayawardena, Lal, 169
Johns, Brian, 121
Johnson, Chalmers, 36
Johnson, Robert A., 143–44, 145, 150,
    152, 153 n15

Kasami, Nobumitsu, 74
Kase, Hideaki, 166
Kawai, Masahiro, 124
Kennickell, Arthur, 86, 87 n4, 90, 92,
    92 n9
Kimura, Hiroshi, 162, 164, 165
Kiuchi, Takashi, 123
Kodama, Fumio, 33
Kojima, Kiyoshi, 119
Kosai, Yutaka, 17, 157, 182
Kosaka, Masataka, 165, 174
Kraftcik, John, 118
Krause, Lawrence B., 146
Kravis, Irving B., 105
Krugman, Paul R., 41, 41 n14, 135,
    146, 231, 231 n35
Kuznets, Simon, 81

Labor costs
  comparison among industrialized
    countries of, 43
Labor-intensive industry, skilled and
    unskilled
  changes in comparative advantage in,
    31
Land prices
  effect of high price on retirement
    planning, 91–93
  factors influencing increase in, 54
Land use policy, 92, 104
  public policy recommendations for,
    178–79
  recommendations for change in,
    100–06
  See also Housing
Lawrence, Robert Z., 69, 70, 239, 253
LDP (Liberal Democratic Party)
  agricultural constituency of, 72,
    101–02

Leadership, world, 157–175
  defense issues and, 158–66
  recommendations to expand, 181–82
Leamer, Edward E., 70, 70 n21,
    208 n5, 253 n15
Leather products
  specialization in, 31
  tariff and nontariff barriers for, 55
Leisure
  factors to increase, 20
Lessard, Donald R., 170, 171
Licensing regulation
  in high technology industries, 38, 40
Life cycle hypothesis
  bequest motive in, 90–93
  as factor influencing saving, 86–88
Lim, Hua Sing, 221, 224, 235
Lincoln, Edward J., 130
Lipsey, Robert E., 241, 241 n7
Litterman, Robert B., 137 n2, 263
Loopesko, Bonnie E., 143–44, 145, 150,
    152, 153 n15
LPD (Liberal Democratic Party)
  agricultural constituency of, 72
Lütkepohl, Helmut, 260

Machine tool industry, 39
  See also High technology industries
MacIntosh, Malcolm, 160, 160 n7, 162,
    163, 164
Macroeconomic variables
  analysis of behavior of, 137–52
  causality in, 255–56
Maekawa Reports
  on imports of agricultural products,
    72, 74
  origin of, 17 n14
  proposals for public works projects
    by, 100
  proposals for structural reform noted
    in, 155
  recommendation for infrastructure
    development, 19–20
  recommendations for import
    liberalization, 74–75
  recommendations for manufactured
    products, 73
  recommendations for reduction in
    working hours, 20, 178, 179

recommendations to improve quality
    of life, 17, 19–21
  See also Hours of work; Quality of life
MAFF (Ministry of Agriculture,
    Fisheries and Forestry)
  as import regulatory agency, 56
Maizels, Alfred, 3 n1
Makin, John, 94
Manufactured products
  effect of informal import barriers on
    trade in, 56–61
Marris, Stephen, 146
Marston, Richard C., 145
Maruyu system. See Tax exemptions
Maskus, Keith, 209
McKinnon, Ronald I., 135, 145
Meese, Richard, 258 n3
Michalopoulos, Constantine, 50
Military protection
  by United States, 158
Millstein, James E., 40
Ministry of Health and Welfare
  role in setting standards for imports,
    220
Ministry of Post and
    Telecommunications
  as regulatory agency, 58, 60, 61
  role in standard setting for imports,
    220
MITI (Ministry of International Trade
    and Industry)
  advanced technology projects of, 38–
    39, 60, 230–33
  and nontariff barriers, 55
  role in industrial policy of, 35–42
  role in patent protection, 234
  role in raising informal import
    barriers, 227
  role in standard setting for imports,
    219 n7, 220
  use of administrative guidance by,
    216
  See also Depressed industries; High
    technology; Import barriers
Miyauchi, Atsushi, 76 n35
Model
  to analyze relative country openness,
    69–70
Monetary policy
  effect of easing of, 147–48
  recommendations for changes in, 180

Monoyios, Nicolaos, 209
Morishima, Michio, 36, 37
Mortgages, reverse
  proposals for implementation of,
    105–06
Mundell, Robert A., 135
Murakami, Yasusuke, 17, 157, 182
Mutoh, Hiromichi, 37

Nakao, Eiichi, 21
Nakasone, Yasuhiro, 46, 53 n11, 164,
  185, 230
Next-Generation Industries Basic
  Technologies Project. See MITI
  (Ministry of International Trade
  and Industry)
NICs (newly industrialized countries)
  effect of yen appreciation on, 42–43,
    144
  increase in imports from, 75
Nishihara, Masashi, 159, 164
Noguchi, Yukio, 92 n8, 92 n10
Noland, Marcus, n17, 18, 70, 104,
  137 n2, 141 n5, 143 n6, 209, 239,
  240 n3, 246, 249, 252 n15,
  252–53, 264
Nontariff barriers, 51–56
  for agricultural products in EC
    (European Community), 51
  definition of, 51
  silk products and, 54–55
NTT (Nippon Telephone and Telegraph)
  privatization of, 16, 148 n11, 151,
    180, 222, 223 n12
  procurement policy of, 222–23

ODA (Official development assistance).
  See Development assistance
OECD (Organization of Economic
  Cooperation and Development), 62,
  86, 87, 101 n15
Ogura, Seiretsu, 97, 114 n3
Ohmae, Kenichi, 75
Ohno, Kenichi, 135, 145
Ohtake, Fumio, 125, 132, 136
Oil prices
  effect of changes in, 25–26

effect on investment of, 128–29
Okimoto, Daniel L., 41, 44, 45
Okita, Saburo, 169
Okita Plan, 169–70, 175
Okumura, Hirohiko, 118, 124
Old age. See Elderly population;
  Retirement
Openness, relative
  empirical investigation to identify,
    69–71
"Outlier" status
  in trade, 70–72
Output
  changes in composition of, 116–18
Ozaki, Robert J., 36
Ozawa, Teretomo, 14, 46 n22

Pangetsu, Mari, 119, 120, 121
Patent system
  function as import barrier of, 61, 234
Pearce, Douglas K., 258 n3
Pension funds
  reason for increase in contributions
    to, 107
  See also Retirement
Petroleum Industry Law
  role of MITI in enforcement of, 216
  See also Administrative guidance
Porter, Michael, 15
Press, Frank, 46 n21
Prestowitz, Clyde V., 219 n6, 229,
  236 n48
Privatization sales
  of NTT and JAL, 148 n11, 151, 180
  retention of public ownership
    after, 222
  as source of revenue, 16
  See also Corporations, public; Fiscal
    policy
Procurement practices, public
  as informal import barriers, 58–59,
    222–25
Productivity
  comparison of United States and
    Japan in, 43
Public policy
  as factor influencing personal saving,
    95–96
  recommendations for, 178–82

recommendations related to
investment for, 129–33
See also Fiscal policy
Purchasing power parity
comparison among industrialized
countries of, 12
Pyle, Kenneth P., 46

Quality of life
in Japan, 17–18, 178
public policy recommendations for
improving, 18–21
See also Hours of work; Housing;
Land use policy
Quotas
comparison among industrialized
countries and, 53
effect of removal of, 71

Rapp, William V., 59, 60, 219, 220,
228, 229
Reed, Robert F., 158, 159, 160,
162, 165
Regression analysis
for comparative advantage, 31–33
Reich, Michael R., 54, 73, 75 n31
Replacement investment, 115–16
Research, 44–46, 60
Retirement
age at, 108
cost of, 108, 109
proposal for housing equity
conversion at, 105–06
See also Bequests; Income, retirement
Roberts, John M., 100
Rosovsky, Henry, 41 n13
Rothenberg, Robert A., 53

Sanchez, Aurora, 75, 215, 221
Sargent, Thomas, 265
Sato, Kazuo, 87, 93, 97
Saving
accounting standards to analyze,
78–81
bonus payment system and, 85–86
business, 96–97
definitions of, 77–78

effect of lower housing costs on
personal, 105
effect of low rate of return on
personal, 93
effect of national, 77, 100
factors influencing changes in rate of
national, 81–84
factors influencing high rate of
personal, 84–96, 108–10
government, 99–100
interaction among sectors of economy
for, 78
life cycle hypothesis and personal,
86–88
motives for personal, 100
recommendations for change in
national, 100–08
retirement income and personal,
88–93
Saxonhouse, Gary R., 38, 39, 45, 70,
70 n22, 74 n30, 135, 239,
240 n3, 241 n5, 242, 246, 251–52
Scalera, Garrett, 166
Schultze, Charles L., 35–36
Scott, Bruce R., 29 n6, 64
Security tax
as offset to defense "free-rider" status,
166, 173–74
Semi-conductor industry
MITI promotion of, 40–41
Sengupta, Arjun K., 169
Service industry
changes in concentration of, 15–16
Shibuya, Hiroshi, 86, 87 n4, 95
Shinohara, Miyohei, 36–37
Shoven, John B., 93–94, 97, 98
Silk products
nontariff barriers applied to, 54–55
Sims, Christopher A., 125 n16, 136 n1,
139 n3, 256–57, 261–63
Simulation, 266–67
Slemrod, Joel, 88, 93, 94, 107
Social security. *See* Pension funds;
Retirement
Soda ash industry
as example of collusion to limit
imports, 228–29
protection by informal barriers to
trade, 59, 60
Special interest groups
as factor influencing policy, 101–02

Trade policy, 49–75
  recommendations for, 181–85
Treaty of Mutual Cooperation and
  Security of 1960, 158–59
Tyers, Rod, 51, 53 n10, 70–71, 73,
  76 n36

Ueda, Kazuo, 85, 86, 124
Uekusa, Masu, 226
United States
  comparative advantage for, 209
  effect of yen appreciation on, 42–43
Urata, Shujiro, 195, 208 n6
Urea industry
  as example of collusion to limit
    imports, 228
  protection by informal barriers to
    trade, 59
Ushijima, Shunichiro, 218 n5

Valdes, Alberto, 52 n6
Vandenberg, Jean, 39, 231
Van den Panhuyzen, W., 228
Very Large-Scale Integration Project. *See*
  MITI (Ministry of International
  Trade and Industry)
Vincent, D. P., 54
Vogel, Ezra F., 234

Watts, William, 159, 159 n4
Weil, Frank A., 57, 217, 218, 219 n6,
  222
Weiss, Laurence, 137 n2, 263
Weiss, Merle Yahr, 241, 241 n7
White, Halbert, 208
Williamson, John, 146, 170, 171
Woronoff, Jon, 19 n26

Yamamura, Kozo, 39, 40, 41, 42,
  74 n29, 230, 231
Yamawaki, Hideki, 37, 144
Yasuba, Yasukichi, 17
Yen appreciation
  effect of, 42, 71
  effect on current account, 177–78
  effect on investment of, 126–27
  effect on trade balance of, 141–42
  factors tending to increase, 48
  fiscal policy response to, 148
  pass-through effect of, 143–45
Yoffie, David B., 232
Yoshikawa, Hiroshi, 125, 132, 136
Yoshino, Naoyuki, 97, 114 n3
Yoshitomi, Masaru, 149, 154, 155

Zietz, Joachim, 52 n6
Zoning laws. *See* Housing
Zysman, John, 40

Other Publications from the Institute

POLICY ANALYSES IN INTERNATIONAL ECONOMICS

American Trade Politics: System Under Stress
I. M. Destler/*1986*
$30.00 (cloth)	0–88132–058–7	380 pp
$18.00 (paper)	0–88132–057–9	380 pp

The Future of World Trade in Textiles and Apparel
William R. Cline/*1987*
$20.00   0–88132–025–0   344 pp

Capital Flight and Third World Debt
Donald R. Lessard and John Williamson, editors/*1987*
$16.00   0–88132–053–6   270 pp

The Canada–United States Free Trade Agreement: The Global Impact
Jeffrey J. Schott and Murray G. Smith, editors/*1988*
$13.95   0–88132–073–0   211 pp

Managing the Dollar: From the Plaza to the Louvre
Yoichi Funabashi/*1988, 2nd ed. rev. 1989*
$19.95   0–88132–097–8   307 pp

Reforming World Agricultural Trade
Twenty-nine Professionals from Seventeen Countries/*1988*
$3.95   0–88132–088–9   42 pp

World Agricultural Trade: Building a Consensus
William M. Miner and Dale E. Hathaway, editors/*1988*
$16.95   0–88132–071–3   226 pp

Japan in the World Economy
Bela Balassa and Marcus Noland/*1988*
$19.95   0–88132–097–8   306 pp

America in the World Economy: A Strategy for the 1990s
C. Fred Bergsten/*1988*
$29.95 (cloth)	0–88132–089–7	235 pp
$13.95 (paper)	0–88132–082–X	235 pp

United States External Adjustment and the World Economy
William R. Cline/*1989*
$25.00   0–88132–048–X   392 pp

Free Trade Areas and U.S. Trade Policy
Jeffrey J. Schott, editor/*1989*
$19.95   0–88132–094–3   400 pp

Dollar Politics: Exchange Rate Policymaking in the United States
I. M. Destler and C. Randall Henning/*1989*
$11.95   0–88132–079–X   192 pp

SPECIAL REPORTS

FORTHCOMING

International Aspects of United States Tax Policy: An Overview
Daniel J. Frisch

Oil Crisis Intervention: A Blueprint for International Cooperation
Philip K. Verleger, Jr.

The Debt of Low-Income Africa: Issues and Options for the United States
Carol Lancaster

Reciprocity and Retaliation: An Evaluation of Aggressive Trade Policies
Thomas O. Bayard

Third World Debt: A Reappraisal
William R. Cline

Energy Policy for the 1990s: A Global Perspective
Philip K. Verleger, Jr.

The Politics of International Monetary Cooperation
C. Fred Bergsten, I. M. Destler, C. Randall Henning, and John Williamson

The Taxation of Income From International Financial Investment
Daniel J. Frisch

The Outlook for World Commodity Prices
Philip K. Verleger, Jr.

The Managed Trade Option
Laura Tyson

The Future of the World Trading System
John Whalley

TO ORDER PUBLICATIONS PLEASE WRITE OR CALL US AT:

Institute for International Economics
Publications Department
11 Dupont Circle, NW
Washington, DC 20036
202-328-9000